Eighteenth-Century Keyboard Music

Eighteenth-Century Keyboard Music

SECOND EDITION

ROUTLEDGE STUDIES
IN MUSICAL GENRES

EDITED BY

Robert L. Marshall

Routledge

New York and London

Published in 2003 by
Routledge
29 West 35th Street
New York, NY 10001
www.routledge-ny.com

Published in Great Britain by
Routledge
11 New Fetter Lane
London EC4P 4EE
www.routledge.co.uk

Routledge is an imprint of the Taylor & Francis Group.
Printed in the United States of America on acid-free paper.

10 9 8 7 6 5 4 3 2 1

Library of Congress Cataloging-in-Publication Data

Eighteenth-century keyboard music / edited by Robert L. Marshall.— 2nd ed.
        p.   cm.–(Routledge studies in musical genre)
    Includes bibliographical references and indexes.
    ISBN 0-415-96642-6 (alk. paper)
        1. Keyboard instrument music–18th century–History and criticism.
    2. Performance practice (Music)–18th century. 3. Keyboard instruments.
    I. Title: 18th-century keyboard music. II. Marshall, Robert Lewis. III. Series.
ML705.E37 2003
786'.09'033–dc21   2003046791

Contents

Preface

The eighteenth century, the century of revolution, abundantly deserves its reputation with respect to the history of music. When it began,
the human voice still reigned, unchallenged after millennia, as the principal and most respected agent of musical expression. If anything, by
1700 its prestige was greater than ever before, thanks to its glorification
in the most prestigious musical form of the time: Italian opera seria.
Instrumental music, for its part, clearly less lofty in status, was dominated by the violin, and, once again, a largely Italian repertoire of chamber music and concertos. Among keyboard instruments the organ and
its repertoire, rooted in and nourished by the needs and traditions of
the church, continued to thrive, and in the music of J. S. Bach, were
about to reach their artistic zenith. The stringed keyboard instruments,
on the other hand, by and large had a far more modest role to play in
European musical life. The principal, if not sole, task of the harpsichord,
after all, was to accompany; that of the clavichord was even more
humble—being mostly relegated to private, domestic music making or
serving as a practice instrument.

By century's end, the unlikely but popular opera buffa had risen to
a position of artistic, if not social, parity with opera seria; instrumental
music, similarly, had developed a repertoire as significant as its vocal
counterpart—a repertoire whose source of vitality, embodied in innumerable manifestations, was a principle of musical organization that effectively had not existed in the year 1700 but by 1800 had become
ubiquitous: the sonata, or sonata-allegro, form. One of the greatest beneficiaries of this development was a keyboard instrument with a hammer
mechanism that effectively had not existed in the year 1700 either. By
century's end this new instrument, known by a host of names, most commonly "pianoforte" or "fortepiano," had become ubiquitous, too, while
both the harpsichord and clavichord had fallen into oblivion and the
organ, artistically speaking, into irrelevance.

Given such enormous transformations, can the structure of this
book—beginning around 1700 and ending around 1800—be justified?
Can such a volume have any compelling coherence? The best-known

musical "fact" about the eighteenth century, after all, is that it was split almost precisely in half into two distinct, and virtually antithetical, stylistic periods. Yet despite the prima facie appearance of a fundamental shift at some point (ca. 1720? ca. 1730? ca. 1750?) from a well-established and long-standing "Baroque" style to something quite different, the century need not be viewed as an altogether artificial and arbitrary division: beginning before the end of one stylistic period (the Baroque) and breaking off before the end of another (the Classical). In fact, a strong case can be made for regarding the hundred years from 1700 to 1800 as constituting a meaningful historical unit—one capable, we trust, of validating the conception of this volume.

The case begins with an argument of a distinctly technical character. The generation of composers who came to maturity circa 1700 was the first born into the fully established system of functional tonality—to inherit it, so to speak, as a native language—after it was first consolidated in the music of the Italian concerto composers of the preceding generation. Tonality, of course, was to prevail as the supreme system of musical syntax in Western civilization for the next two hundred years. But its gradual dissolution had begun, significantly, by the beginning of the nineteenth century. And by the end of Beethoven's life almost all the "self-evident" principles of organization and coherence that underlay the tonal system had suffered at the least their first significant challenges.

For our purposes, it is important to recognize, too, that the first and the principal benefits of the tonal system were to be derived in the realm of instrumental music. Instrumental music had been a distinctly limited channel for the cultivation of ambitious musical invention until the last two decades of the seventeenth century; but then—for the first time in the history of Western music—the establishment of functional tonality enabled the construction of autonomous, closed, instrumental compositions on a large scale. The consequence was the rapid evolution and perfection of two impressive instrumental forms: the concerto and, about a generation later, the sonata. While the violin and other melody instruments were the first important protagonists of the modern concerto, the modern sonata was first nurtured and cultivated on keyboard instruments. Before long, however—still in the early decades of the new century—sonata form had engendered the early prototypes of the symphony and the string quartet.

By the late 1690s the solo concerto had begun to supplant the concerto grosso as the concerto genre of choice. There was, at just the same time, a notable shift of emphasis (signaled by Corelli's sonatas op. 5, published in 1700) from the trio to the solo sonata. The new-found fascination with the persona of the instrumental soloist was to have a profound effect on the nature of musical form. It led, for example, to the introduction of a new and potentially dramatic principle of solo-tutti thematic differentiation. But the enhanced stature of the soloist—more properly, the individual instrumentalist—also led to a reappraisal of the nature and status of keyboard instruments. Keyboard instruments—and their players—were, after all, uniquely autonomous. But if the secular keyboard repertoire was to expand its expressive and stylistic range (and its audience appeal) significantly beyond the limits represented by toccatas, variations, stylized dances, and learned contrapuntal inquiries, then the instrument itself would have to become more responsive, sensitive, touch-sensitive. Enter, at the threshold of the new century, Bartolomeo Cristofori, with his "arpicembalo che fà il piano e il forte."

The turn of the century was a watershed in other ways as well. It may or may not have more than nominal significance that the first use of the term "sonata" with reference to works for solo keyboard seems to appear in Johann Kuhnau's *Biblische Historien,* published in 1700; but it is certainly significant that in this collection Kuhnau not only transferred the Italian church sonata to the solo harpsichord but combined it with the largely French idea of programmatic instrumental music. The program, however, was something typically German and Lutheran owing to its religious theme. At just the same time—the 1690s—the Frenchman Couperin began to adopt the Italian sonata as well, composing trios that he would later publish under the title *Les Nations.* That is, both the coming of age of instrumental music and the interest in exploring and exploiting the distinctions between the national styles of music—what Couperin himself in another collection would call *Les goûts-réunis*—had begun in earnest just about the year 1700.

The phenomenon of national styles, and the compulsion to confront the challenge posed by their existence, constitutes one of the characteristic hallmarks of eighteenth-century music. The entire century—the celebrated style shift notwithstanding—was occupied first with their definition and description; then with attempts at their combination, coordination, and fusion; and finally with their transcendance and transformation into something perceived as ideologically and aesthetically far more desirable: a universal musical style. The duration of this process, incidentally, was approximately coterminous with the actual calendrical century.

The crystallization of discrete and powerful national musical styles was complete by—and recognized by—the beginning of the eighteenth century.[1] During the first part of the century theorists and commentators were accustomed to discussing music in terms of national styles. Contemporaries perceived a bipolar hegemony shared by Italy and France. As for other nations, it was their mission—quite explicit in the case of the Germans—to effect some sort of reconciliation, or union, of the principal national styles with their own traditions. The early fruits of this effort to create the *vermischter Geschmack*—the mixed style—propagated by Quantz and others are evident in J. S. Bach's "fusion of national styles" (to borrow the apt description of Manfred Bukofzer).[2]

By the second half of the century, the notion of a union or synthesis of national styles had matured into the idea of a universal musical style—of music as a universal language. The ultimate form of this universal musical language was rooted in formal conventions and procedures developed first in Italy—basically those manifested in the Italian sonata—but colored by folk music idioms imported from many national and ethnic traditions and enriched, finally, with sophisticated harmonic and contrapuntal techniques inherited from the Germans. This is a description, of course, of the music of the Viennese Classical Masters. The telling point, however, is that the "heroes" of this development—Bach, Gluck, Mozart, Haydn, Beethoven—all but Gluck profoundly important in the development and cultivation of both instrumental music in general and keyboard music in particular—were consciously aware of their historical and cultural missions. Joseph Haydn once remarked, "My language is understood in the whole world."[3]

The present volume is most decidedly a "history of heroes." After two historically conceived chapters tracing the development of keyboard instruments and performance practices throughout the course of the century, entire chapters are devoted in turn to the keyboard music of Johann Sebastian Bach, Domenico Scarlatti, Carl Philipp Emanuel Bach, Joseph Haydn, Wolfgang Amadeus Mozart, and Ludwig van Beethoven. Even the chapters on French and Early Italian Classical Masters have major figures—Couperin, Rameau, Johann Christian Bach—as their primary focus. But the approach throughout consists in equal measure of critical and historical analysis. That is, the objective is not only to understand the accomplishments of the protagonists, but also to evaluate the historical context to which they belonged, and to assess their contributions to the stylistic development of keyboard music and the keyboard idiom.

It is currently fashionable, however, to disparage the writing of history in terms of its "heroes" in favor of its institutions. This position has been argued most eloquently by the late Carl Dahlhaus.[4] Since the leading musical institution during the eighteenth century was "opera, and indeed mainly opera seria," it is not surprising that J. S. Bach, for example, is dismissed by Dahlhaus as a historically irrelevant "outsider," an "esoteric who knowingly withdrew from the world and drew the compositional consequences from that." But even Bach, the outsider and esoteric, was capable of observing from his historical vantage point in the century's evolution—namely at the moment of *vermischter Geschmack* on the road to the universal style—that "German musicians are expected to be capable of performing . . . all kinds of music, whether it comes from Italy or France, England or Poland." As the pertinent chapter in this volume will argue, J. S. Bach certainly "drew the compositional consequences" from *that*!

One final word on heroes: it is symptomatic that the eighteenth century did not just produce an inordinate number of musical geniuses: it created the very idea of the musical genius—defined, that is, as a human personality rather than as a gift or talent one possessed. The conceit was evidently the inspiration of Diderot, who, in offering Jean-Philippe Rameau as the symbol of this "genius" in his novel *Le Neveu de Rameau*, even introduced the necessary linguistic adjustment, replacing the hitherto normal usage *avoir de génie* with the new formulation *être un génie*.[5]

With respect to the institutions, theorists and commentators of the time emphasized that art music was cultivated not just in the opera house but in three domains: the church, the chamber, and the theater, each with its own appropriate conventions, styles, and genres. Despite their passion for Italian opera, the courts were by no means oblivous to the importance and attractions of the new instrumental music. Frederick the Great, after all, did not only engage Hasse to write operas but also C. P. E. Bach to write keyboard and other instrumental works for his chamber. Domenico Scarlatti certainly composed and performed his keyboard sonatas for the delectation of a monarch. It would be hard, though, to determine the relative importance of the courts and the bourgeoisie in cultivating the development of instrumental music in the eighteenth century. Commercial concert life was just beginning at this time. Moreover, music publishing was an emphatically middle-class business whose growth in importance during the course of the century had an overwhelming impact not only on the circulation of particular works and the making of individual reputations but also in transmitting and disseminating new styles and genres—among them the sonata and other new keyboard genres aimed at the delectation and edification of *Kenner und Liebhaber*.

We must return to the fundamental problem of eighteenth-century music raised at the outset of these remarks, namely, the "fact" that the century was split into two antithetical periods. The question can be framed as a paradox: "How could Mozart be possible so soon after Bach?"—or, in terms of the subject matter of this volume: How could Mozart's piano sonatas be possible so soon after Bach's fugues for the clavier? The traditional answer only aggravates the question by positing a style shift around mid-century: the end of the "Baroque" era marked by the deaths of Bach and Handel followed at once by a radically simpler, preparatory "Pre–Classical" style until, after a mere thirty years of evolution, the mature masterpieces of Mozart and Haydn in the early 1780s heralded the advent of the "High Classical" or "Viennese Classical" style.

The answer to the paradox lies in the recognition that it is not really a question of chronology but of geography, that is, once again, of national culture and tradition. The historical process in fact did not go directly "from Bach to Mozart" at all. Rather (to oversimplify), both masters essentially belonged to, and indeed represented in each instance the historical culmination of two long and distinct lines of development: in the case of Bach the Protestant tradition of central and northern Germany, for Mozart the Catholic—really the secular—tradition that had its roots in the south, that is, in Italy.[6] Of course, Bach would not have been possible without Italy (and France), and Mozart (and Haydn) would not have been possible without Bach.

There remains one last question. Granted that the history of eighteenth-century music in fact began around 1700, when did it end? This is more difficult to say. Plausible suggestions would be 1798, the year of Haydn's *Creation,* or 1803, the year of the "Eroica": both are landmark works that confirm the arrival not only of new harmonic, tonal, and formal procedures but of a new musical aesthetic—indeed of a new musical ethos—as well. But the keyboard clearly had a pivotal historical role to play at the end of the century, too. We shall learn in the closing pages of this volume that the seeds of something new, including the seeds of dissolution, can be found in Beethoven's piano sonatas of 1800–1801: in particular, the sonatas of op. 27 and 31—not least, the "Moonlight" and "Tempest" sonatas, works whose familiar nicknames, though of questionable authenticity, are, in light of what was to come, nothing less than prophetic.

Robert L. Marshall

Notes

1. See, in particular, François Raguenet's *Parallèle des Italiens et des Francais,* published in 1702, and the response by Le Cerf de La Viéville, *Comparaison de la musique italienne et de la musique française,* published in 1705. Pertinent excerpts are printed in translation in Oliver Strunk, *Source Readings in Music History,* revised edition, ed. Leo Treitler (New York, 1998), 670–82.

2. Manfred F. Bukofzer, *Music in the Baroque Era* (New York, 1947).

3. Cited in Friedrich Blume, *Classic and Romantic Music* (New York, 1970), 28.

4. Carl Dahlhaus, *Die Musik des 18. Jahrhunderts,* Das neue Handbuch der Musikwissenschaft, vol. 5 (Laaber, 1985). The introductory chapter, translated by Ernest Harriss, appears in *College Music Symposium* 26 (1986): 1–6. Citations from that chapter in the following are taken from the Harriss translation.

5. Herbert Dieckmann, "Diderot's Conception of Genius," cited in Edward E. Lewinsky, "Musical Genius: Evolution and Origins of a Concept," *The Musical Quarterly* 50 (1964): 335.

6. See Hans Heinrich Eggebrecht, "Über Bachs geschichtlichen Ort," reprinted in Walter Blankenburg, ed., *Johann Sebastian Bach,* Wege der Forschung, vol. 170 (Darmstadt, 1970), 247–89.

Acknowledgments

This volume, part of the series *Studies in Musical Genres and Repertories*, owes its existence to the initiative of Maribeth Anderson Payne, former editor-in-chief of Schirmer Books, who recognized the promise and value of such an enterprise to musical scholars and performers alike, or, as the eighteenth century would have it, to all musical *Kenner und Liebhaber*. This volume was to be written during the same period that witnessed the commemoration of the bicentennial of Mozart's death— an event that consumed the time and energies of many of us and led to a number of difficulties and delays. A special word of appreciation is due therefore to Ms. Payne and Schirmer Books—and to all the contributors—for their patience and continued commitment.

The following institutions and libraries have kindly granted permission to reproduce illustrations of material in their collections or under their copyright: Staatliches Institut für Musikforschung, Berlin; Staatsbibliothek zu Berlin—Preußischer Kulturbesitz, Musikabteilung; Verwaltung der Staatlichen Schlösser and Gärten, Berlin; Civico Museo Bibliografico Musicale, Bologna; Music Library, Stadt- und Universitätsbibliothek, Frankfurt am Main; Royal College of Music, London; Biblioteca Real, Palacio de Oriente, Madrid; Alpiarça, Portugal; the Yale Music Library, New Haven; Metropolitan Museum of Art, New York; Huntington Library, San Marino, California; University of Illinois at Urbana-Champaign; Library of Congress, Washington, DC; Sheridan Germann, Boston; Rafael Puyana, Paris; Doblinger Verlag, Vienna; Wiener Urtext Edition Musikverlag, Ges.m.b.H. & Co. K. G., Vienna; G. Henle Verlag, Munich.

Second Edition

This volume offers a corrected and updated version of the original edition. While the substantive content remains essentially unaltered, the contributors have taken the opportunity of the new printing to eliminate obvious errors and misprints, to clarify potential ambiguities, and to include in the selected bibliographies at the end of the individual chapters some of the more significant scholarly literature on eighteenth-century keyboard music to have appeared since the volume's original publication in 1994.

The editor wishes to express his appreciation to R. Larry Todd, general editor of the series, Routledge Studies in Musical Genres, originally published by Schirmer Books, and to Richard Carlin, Executive Editor of Music and Dance at Routledge, for providing the initiative and impetus for this re-publication.

Contributors

EVA BADURA-SKODA has been Professor of Music at the University of Wisconsin and a guest professor at universities in Canada, the United States, and Europe. She is the author of numerous studies and editions of works by Haydn, Mozart, and Schubert. She recently wrote the script for three documentary films on the history of the pianoforte and supervised their production. Professor Badura-Skoda has been decorated with the Austrian *Ehrenfreuz für Kunst und Wissenschaft*.

WILLIAM DRABKIN, Reader in Music at the University of Southampton, has published studies of Classical chamber music, Beethoven, Italian opera, and Schenkerian analysis. He is the author of books on Beethoven's *Missa solemnis* and Haydn's early string quartets and is general editor of a translation of Heinrich Schenker's *Das Meisterwerk in der Musik* (3 vols., 1994–97) and *Der Tonwille* (two vols., forthcoming).

DANIEL E. FREEMAN, an authority on the musical culture of eighteenth-century Bohemia, is the author of *The Opera Theater of Count Franz Anton von Sporck in Prague* and articles on early Classical keyboard concertos, baroque opera, and the music of Josquin, Vivaldi, J.S. Bach, and Mozart. He has completed a biography of the Czech composer Josef Mysliveček and is preparing a study of Mozart in Prague.

FREDERICK HAMMOND, Irma Brandeis Professor of Romance Studies at Bard College, is a distinguished harpsichordist. In addition to numerous articles, his publications include two books on Girolamo Frescobaldi and the forthcoming *Music and Spectacle in Baroque Rome: Barberini Patronage under Urban VIII*.

MARK KROLL, Professor emeritus at Boston University, is an accomplished harpsichordist, fortepianist, and authority on baroque and early nineteenth-century performance practice. His publications include scholarly editions of arrangements by J.N. Hummel and a study of Beethoven's piano performance. He is co-editor of a book on Beethoven's violin sonatas (forthcoming) and is currently preparing the first English-language biography of Hummel.

ROBERT D. LEVIN, Dwight P. Robinson, Jr. Professor of the Humanities at Harvard University, has performed throughout the world. Renowned for his improvised cadenzas, he has recorded a Mozart concerto cycle and the Beethoven concertos. His recordings also include J.S. Bach's complete keyboard concertos and the *Well-Tempered Clavier*. A noted Mozart scholar, Levin's completions of the *Requiem* and other unfinished works have been recorded and performed extensively. He is a member of the American Academy of Arts and Sciences.

LAURENCE LIBIN is Research Curator at The Metropolitan Museum of Art and author of *American Musical Instruments in The Metropolitan Museum of Art* and *Keyboard Instruments*. He has taught at Columbia and New York Universities and writes extensively about the history and construction of European and American instruments.

ROBERT L. MARSHALL, Louis, Frances and Jeffrey Sachar Professor emeritus of Music at Brandeis University, is the author of *The Compositional Process of J.S. Bach*, *The Music of Johann Sebastian Bach: The Sources, the Style, the Significance*, and *Mozart Speaks: Views on Music, Musicians and the World*. His publications have received the Otto Kinkeldey Award of the American Musicological Society as well as the ASCAP–Deems Taylor Award.

DAVID SCHULENBERG, Professor of Music at Wagner College (Staten Island, New York), is the author of *Music of the Baroque*, *The Keyboard Music of J.S. Bach*, and *The Instrumental Music of C.P.E. Bach*. A contributing editor to *Carl Philipp Emanuel Bach: The Complete Works*, he was a visiting fellow of the Japan Society for the Promotion of Science and is a recipient of the Scheide Research Grant of the American Bach Society. A harpsichordist, he has recorded *Johann Joachim Quantz: Flute Sonatas*.

ELAINE SISMAN is Professor of Music at Columbia University. The author of *Haydn and the Classical Variation*, *Mozart: The "Jupiter" Symphony*, and editor of *Haydn and His World*, she specializes in music and aesthetics of the 18th and 19th centuries, and has written on such topics as memory and inventions in late Beethoven, ideas of pathétique and fantasia around 1800, Haydn's theater symphonies, and the sublime in Mozart's music. She was recently elected to the board of the Joseph-Haydn Institut in Cologne.

CHAPTER ONE

The Instruments

Laurence Libin

Eighteenth-century keyboard instruments comprise three main families differentiated by their means of tone production. Stringed keyboards include those wherein stretched strings are sounded by plucking (as in the harpsichord and spinet), striking (clavichord and piano), or, rarely, bowing (*Bogenclavier*). Organs constitute a second family, involving whistle-like flue pipes and pipes that incorporate vibrating reeds. Large church organs commonly have both flue and reed pipes; portable chamber organs often have only flues, but one variety, called the regal, is limited to a single rank of reeds. The third category, in which hammers hit resonant solid bodies such as bells, includes tower carillons and keyed glockenspiels.

Aside from the types named above, the eighteenth century knew many other keyboard instruments, now mostly forgotten. Some of these merit description even though they engendered no lasting repertoire; their importance lies in revealing the fascination musical mechanisms of all kinds held among the intelligentsia, and in illustrating the central role of keyboards in musical culture. Why musicians preferred some types of keyboard instruments and ignored others can be understood only against this background.

Idioms and Instruments

Before 1800, much music was played interchangeably on different keyboard instruments without concern for modern precepts of authenticity or faithfulness to a composer's intentions. Often, composers seem to have had no particular instrument in mind for their works but were content to have them played, with appropriate adjustments, on any available kind. Publishers appealed to a broad market by indicating on title pages that pieces could be played, for example, on either harpsi-chord or piano, or simply skirted the issue by specifying "for clavier," a generic designation for keyboards, though commonly confined to stringed types after the mid-eighteenth century.[1]

Despite this apparently casual attitude, composer-performers who were intimately familiar with their instruments' expressive and technical possibilities developed distinctive idioms for various keyboards. François Couperin's *pièces croisées* (pieces requiring crossed hands) and many of J. S. Bach's "Goldberg" variations, for example, were conceived for two-manual harpsichords and suffer when played on other instruments. Emergence of idiomatic writing was tied to larger stylistic developments as well as to increasing availability and functional divergence of key-boards during the century. Thus, while the first music published for the nascent piano, Lodovico Giustini's twelve sonatas *"da cimbalo di piano e forte"* ("for harpsichord with soft and loud [gradations]"), printed in Florence in 1732,[2] is nearly indistinguishable from contemporary Italian harpsichord music, by the 1790s an unmistakably pianistic style had emerged, notably in slow movements of Mozart's late keyboard concer-tos, where texture, articulation, phrasing, and dynamics are treated with great sensitivity to the piano's unique properties.

Some of Haydn's clavier sonatas of the mid-1770s and 1780s ad-umbrate the full-fledged piano idiom, which arose in the wake of an intellectual movement, *Empfindsamkeit,* that rejuvenated the clavichord in German-speaking lands. C. P. E. Bach's highly influential *Versuch über die wahre Art das Clavier zu spielen* (Berlin, 1753 and 1762), among other treatises, identifies idiomatic effects for the clavichord, among them *Bebung,* a vibrato inimitable on organ, harpsichord, or piano. Bach's im-passioned compositions, aimed at connoisseurs, as well as his astonishing style of playing, fully realized the clavichord's potential to stir emotion. The instrument's capacity for intense affects, quite out of proportion to its tiny sound, undoubtedly appealed to Haydn, whose *empfindsamer* so-los from the late 1760s and early 1770s sound to perfection on a good clavichord.

Not all keyboard instruments fared so well in the face of stylis-tic ferment. When the intricate, colorful style of the early eighteenth-century *clavecinistes* was overshadowed by Italian and Central European developments, the French Baroque harpsichord, to which François Couperin's *ordres* were subtly but inseparably tailored, lost its central rea-son for existence. Other nations' harpsichords suffered the same fate, as limpid textures premised on dynamic expressiveness overwhelmed counterpoint and florid embellishment, to which the harpsichord's clear but rigid sound was exquisitely suited. Mozart sometimes played the harpsichord in public as late as 1787, but by that time it was no longer the instrument of choice for concerts.[3] The latest known Italian harpsichord, by Vincenzo Sodi, was constructed in 1792; harpsichord building ceased in England about 1809.[4]

No inherent structural or mechanical defects led to the harpsichord's desuetude; in terms of design it was at least as refined as the piano that replaced it, and its tone at the fullest was no less loud or sustained than the early piano's. Only dynamic flexibility was conspicuously lacking; otherwise, the harpsichord's demise was by no means inevitable.

The survival or decline of different instruments can hardly be separated from the viability—not necessarily the quality—of their respective repertoires. Church organs continued to be erected despite the waning vitality of organ design and liturgical composition after mid-century. Likewise, despite a paucity of adventurous music, carillons filled their niche in Dutch and Flemish civic life so well that, like certain archaic reptiles, they seemed immune both to evolution and extinction. Although the Louvain carillonneur Matthias van den Gheyn (1721–1785) wrote eleven noteworthy preludes,[5] most carillon music consisted of sacred and (especially in Catholic cities) secular tunes arranged for individual carillons by their own players, as had long been customary. These arrangements were usually improvised; little carillon music was notated, much less published, except as a guide for programming automatic carillons.

In an age when polite society for the most part fervently pursued novelty, those instruments thrived that best accommodated evolving needs for increased power, range of notes, and above all, dynamic nuance. As popular musical fashion, led after about 1760 by operatic reforms, moved toward more vocally oriented modes of expression, progressive critics complained increasingly of the harpsichord's (and to a lesser extent the organ's) dynamic inflexibility.[6] While the harpsichord gradually became outmoded as listeners tired of its intrinsic limitations, the piano adapted successfully to the new musical challenges.

Whether musicians drove or followed instrument makers in the direction of enhanced expressive possibilities and greater range is controversial. Certain composer-performers, such as J. S. Bach and Jan Ladislav Dussek, actively collaborated with keyboard builders in advancing their designs; others, including Mozart, contented themselves with the best available new instruments but made no excessive demands on them that might have inspired further innovation.

Some craftsmen, among them the renowned piano and organ builder Johann Andreas Stein (1728–1792) and his children and successors Nannette (1769–1833) and Matthäus Andreas (1776–1842), were themselves serious performers who kept in close touch with new music; Mozart, who praised Stein's pianos, in 1777 played his three-clavier concerto, K.242, with Stein as another of the soloists. Stein's own perception of the shortcomings of conventional keyboard instruments led him to invent the *Melodica,* an organ of three-and-one-half-octave range, with loudness, pitch, and vibrato all governed by finger pressure. The short-lived *Melodica* (no example survives), which Stein intended only for playing melodies, is one example among many where eighteenth-century builders, carried away by technological prowess, mistook musical needs; practical composers, in contrast, never wrote for instruments that did not yet exist.[7]

Social Contexts

Fashions such as rococo and neoclassical taste in furniture design shaped eighteenth-century keyboard instruments no less than did strictly compositional demands and performers' preferences. Other forces that affected production and usage of these instruments include the growth of commerce and spread of wealth; development of new audiences and concert venues; changing patterns of artistic patronage; wartime disruption of manufacture and migration of craftsmen; and manufacturing and marketing innovations. In order to comprehend the effects of these factors on the development of different keyboard instruments, it will be necessary to define their essential structural and musical characteristics. First, however, some preliminary remarks should help clarify general issues of construction and distribution.

Because of their complexity and cost, throughout the eighteenth century keyboard instruments remained products of basically urban technology, destined for a limited clientele of individuals and institutions that also formed the core market for cultivated music. Evidently most stringed keyboards were purchased to be played by female amateurs and children in genteel domestic circumstances; this situation held true through the Victorian era and determined the nature of much keyboard repertoire intended for salon or private performance. The majority of professional keyboard players and virtually all church organists and carilloneurs before 1800 were male, though toward the end of the century a growing number of women such as Nannette Stein (who also built pianos) and Mozart's pupil Josepha von Auernhammer gained recognition as concert pianists.

The prevalent stereotype of stringed keyboards being particularly appropriate for women to play owes much to old iconographic and literary conventions wherein female keyboard players, including St. Cecilia, metaphorically express social concord by virtue of their ability to play chords and polyphony and thus to reconcile differences harmoniously.[8] Eighteenth-century aesthetes perceived that a continuo player binds an ensemble much as a mother regulates her family. More to the point, stringed keyboards do not cause calluses or distort posture as many other instruments do, and they provide for entertainment and instruction in the home, where music was cultivated as an innocent pastime that enhanced a woman's attractiveness.

Keyboard instruments flaunted their owners' status even on colonial frontiers, but the most elegant examples came from cultural centers where musical life flourished. In the 1790s, Vienna alone counted scores of citizen (*bürgerlicher*) organ and piano builders, and many others worked without civic sanction in nearby suburbs. Dozens more were active in London and other northern cities, and innumerable individual builders inhabited towns all over western Europe and Britain. Despite cataclysms such as the Seven Years' War (1756–1763) and the French Revolution, as well as periods of economic depression, the ranks of these specialized craftsmen burgeoned during the century. A rough parallel can be drawn with the contemporaneous growth of music publishing.

The Industry

Workshops varied in size from small dynastic operations where one master employed several apprentices and journeymen who turned out a few instruments a year, to John Broadwood's pioneering London manufactory, which in 1784 alone sold thirty-eight harpsichords and 133 pianos, most of standardized design and some second-hand.[9] In 1790, Vienna's leading piano builder, Anton Walter (1752–1826), employed fourteen workers and claimed to have sold more than 350 instruments in the previous ten years. Studies of manufacturing methods suggest that while many makers, especially those with little schooling, worked empirically and intuitively, others who may have had some mathematical facility—chiefly organ builders and bell founders, who could not easily alter specifications once work began—calculated and planned on paper in advance of construction. For example, by 1758 Georg Andreas Sorge (1703–1778) had applied logarithms to the scaling of organ pipes.[10]

While tone quality was of course a major consideration for all instrument makers, mechanical reliability and efficiency particularly concerned makers and players of keyboards. That keyboard artisans regarded themselves on a par with mechanics, who enjoyed higher status than carpenters and joiners, is shown by their adopting the mechanic's practice of prominently displaying their names on their products. Probably as much imagination and effort went into perfecting key mechanisms as into tonal design; after all, tonal preferences are subjective whereas judging reliability of moving parts is not. At least at the beginning of the century an old belief persisted that in theory, an instrument's geometrically neat proportions should automatically ensure appealing tone; but as the Enlightenment grappled with irrational aspects of beauty, abstract proportional schemes based on local units of measurement gave way to scientific elucidation of timbre. This growing preoccupation with musical acoustics involved intellectuals such as Abbé Georg Joseph Vogler (1749–1814, teacher of Carl Maria von Weber and Giacomo Meyerbeer) and Ernst Florens Friedrich Chladni (1756–1827), both of whom designed novel keyboard instruments.[11]

Carillon construction had few points of contact with other kinds of keyboard manufacture; bell-founding differed considerably from casting organ pipe metal, and carillon key mechanisms had little in common with other types. Organs and stringed keyboards, however, could be made in a single establishment, and many German-speaking builders signed themselves *Orgel- und Instrumentmacher* (*Instrument* was a generic German term for stringed keyboards). Bach's friend Gottfried Silbermann (1683–1753), for one, built church organs alongside clavichords, pianos, and other instruments. Such versatile builders sometimes combined pipes with strings in hybrid models that gave unusual tonal effects. Handel used a combined organ-harpsichord in *Saul* and for at least one concerto of 1739; in the same year his acquaintance in Hamburg, Johann Mattheson, recommended such an instrument for accompanying church sonatas. In 1770 Johann Andreas Stein built a two-manual instrument consisting of a grand piano atop an organ, and in 1784 Michael Arne performed a concerto on a piano with organ attachment. A later tangent piano combined with a three-stop organ, attributed to the Regensburg firm of Späth and Schmahl, shows that builders and buyers took such hybrids seriously throughout the century, though no music known today specifically requires their resources.

Keyboard-making requires mechanical ingenuity that is applicable to nonmusical devices as well. Jean Marius, a member of France's Académie Royale des Sciences, whose inventions include a water pump, seeder, tent, and umbrella, patented in 1700 a folding harpsichord (*clavecin brisé*) and devised a portable organ as well as bowing, hammer, and pedal mechanisms for stringed keyboards. Around mid-century, members of the Kintzing family of Neuwied, Germany, constructed fine clocks as well as pianos and clavichords, some in conjunction with the noted furniture maker David Roentgen. Joseph Merlin, who received a British patent in 1774 for a combined harpsichord-piano, invented roller skates, and in 1792, Tobias Schmidt, a piano builder in Paris, constructed a prototype guillotine.

Most keyboard craftsmen specialized in producing instruments of only a few types—though some builders listed more than a dozen models they could make to order. In 1802, Friedrich Carl Wilhelm Lemme of Brunswick (1747–1808) advertised eight models of pianos and fourteen of clavichords. Some peculiar designs were the exclusive products of individual workshops; for example, a portable piano resembling a harp lying on its side seems to have been a speciality of the Späth and Schmahl families, who were related by marriage.

Considering difficulties of travel and communication, a surprising amount of technical cross-fertilization occurred among geographically separated craftsmen. Technical treatises found their way even as far as America, where Georg Andreas Sorge's instructions for making pipes and bellows (1764) apparently influenced Moravian organ builders in Pennsylvania. The Benedictine monk François Bédos de Celles's exhaustive *L'Art du facteur d'orgues*, which appeared between 1766 and 1778 as part of the *Descriptions des arts et métiers* published by the Académie Royale des Sciences, circulated widely.[12] (Characteristically, Dom Bédos also wrote a treatise on sundials.)

Journalists also spread useful information; for example, Scipione Maffei's important account in the *Giornale dei letterati d'Italia* (Venice, 1711) of Bartolomeo Cristofori's recently invented piano was translated in Mattheson's *Critica musica* (Hamburg, 1722) and reprinted several times.[13] Meanwhile, Italian musicians probably introduced grand pianos into Germany, where in the 1730s Cristofori's model was being copied by Gottfried Silbermann; his nephew Jean-Henri Silbermann took the model thence into Alsace. Other musicians carried Florentine pianos to Portugal and Spain; there they were copied by builders such as Henrique van Casteel, who may have brought Cristofori's design from Lisbon to Brussels.[14]

As apprentices and journeymen, many youthful builders traveled extensively. The journal of J. A. Stein, a native of Heidelsheim, records visits or periods of work in Strasbourg (where he was briefly employed by the organ builder Johann Daniel Silbermann), Regensburg (where he worked for Franz Jacob Späth), Augsburg, Gochsheim, Paris, and elsewhere; he settled finally in Augsburg, but his son and daughter carried on work in Vienna.[15] Organ builders sometimes relocated their households to follow commissions; a big job might take months to complete, and permanent emigration opened new opportunities. Johann Clemm (1690–1762), a pioneer in transmitting German organ-building practices to America, brought his family to Philadelphia in 1733; about 1745 he moved to New York to care for a large organ he had constructed, and in 1757 he resettled in Pennsylvania where he trained younger craftsmen. Through such movements, instrument development kept pace with dissemination of music.

Until the abolition of craft guilds, which took place in France only in 1791, many harpsichord makers throughout Europe still belonged to ancient cooperative brotherhoods such as the Guild of St. Luke. This guild also embraced painters whose collaboration was responsible for the gorgeous decoration of many baroque harpsichords. Some builders, among them Cristofori, worked under powerful patronage that might exempt them from strict guild regulation, which could inhibit innovation. Keyboard craftsmen in Britain, long free from guild control, and beneficiaries of industrialization, early applied factory methods to keep up with burgeoning demand for pianos. A concentration in London after 1756 of shrewd, competitive Saxon refugees from the Seven Years' War spurred production on a scale never seen before. About 1783, their leader, Johannes Zumpe, retired to Germany a rich man, having founded a major industry that was boosted in 1786 by a commercial treaty that bolstered piano exports to France.

Construction, Mechanisms, Ranges

The common operating feature of all three keyboard families is the keyboard itself, the row of levers upon which a player exerts direct effort. Keyboards, also called claviers, had achieved considerable mechanical sophistication since the Middle Ages. Keys were designed for feet, and fists on the carillon, as well as for fingers. The basic arrangement of naturals and interspersed, raised accidentals (the modern piano's white and black keys) was standardized long before 1700, though even until 1800 key colors varied according to regional custom and availability of suitable materials. In northern Europe, naturals were often black and accidentals white, but this reversal of modern coloration has no musical significance.

Carillon keys, being very large and widely spaced, require no coloring to help differentiate accidentals from naturals, but on smaller claviers such as the harpsichord's or piano's, ivory, less costly bone, or, in Italy, honey-colored boxwood usually covers the light-colored keys and ebony or stained hardwood caps the dark ones. Except on the carillon and church organ, where the playing desk (console) is normally out of view, claviers rivet visual attention during performance; hence further decoration of keys and their surroundings is customary. Before 1800, carved arcades, molding, or embossing adorned the naturals' vertical fronts. Some luxurious keyboards sported geometric inlays or mother-of-pearl or tortoiseshell veneers.

Keys control intermediate devices such as valves, hammers, or jacks that activate more or less distant sonorous elements, sounding them individually or severally. Keys of instruments made before 1800 tend to be slightly narrower than modern piano keys, and hand stretches beyond an octave were rare; for the most part, then, hand size was not a limiting technical factor, as it was to become in some Romantic piano music. The relatively light "touch" of eighteenth-century keyboard instruments, excepting some large organs, fostered a relaxed, fleet, well-articulated technique that depended less on weight and strength than does modern piano technique. Indeed, proper performance practice—for example, correct fingering for crisp ornaments and audible inner voices—was premised on a delicate, responsive touch; a sluggish "action," as the whole clavier mechanism is called, would have been incompatible with textural clarity.

Fully chromatic manual keyboards of sixty-one notes (five octaves) were normal for large harpsichords and pianos of Mozart's day, and by the end of the century this compass was sometimes exceeded. About 1700, however, many keyboards covered only four octaves, and a range of four and one-half octaves was adequate for most music at least up to 1750 (carillons rarely exceeded two and one-half octaves). As late as the 1770s, many claviers were made with so-called short octaves, in which some little-used accidental notes in the extreme bass are omitted; instead, the normal order of pitches is rearranged so that those same keys sound still lower natural notes. For example, the keys that appear to sound BB, C, C♯, D, D♯ actually sound GG, C, AA, D, BB, requiring some zigzag fingering. This economy of notes saved money and space and increased overall range at the cost of complete chromaticism.

Expansion of range from four to five octaves and beyond proceeded irregularly, and keyboard tessitura (average overall range) was never uniform all over Europe. The gamut might begin on C, F, or G, occasionally E (or an octave lower or higher); the top note, too, varied even among instruments built at the same time by a single maker. Because many instruments were made to order, customers' preferences could determine a particular instrument's complement of keys and ancillary devices.

Widening and exploitation of extremes of range involved builders and musicians in a race that neither consistently led, but that created a vigorous market for the latest instruments. Furthermore, during the century pitch levels and tuning systems were in flux. (Carillons and organs, however, were difficult to retune. A factor usually overlooked in explaining Classical composers' lack of interest in organ composition is that most existing organs were tuned in unequal temperaments that made certain intervals excruciating. The Brunswick organ and clavier maker Barthold Fritz advocated equal temperament as early as 1756; his advice was reiterated in treatises by Georg Joseph Vogler [1776], Johann Samuel Petri [1782], Daniel Gottlob Türk [1789], and others.) The net effect, in up-to-date musical circles at least, was that older instruments soon became obsolete. Although many existing harpsichords were modernized or even rebuilt as pianos, more often they were consigned to the woodpile as pianos with stylish cases became all the rage. For this reason as well as through attrition due to wear and accidental loss, the surviving sample of unaltered eighteenth-century keyboard instruments is pitifully small and not fully representative.

The Harpsichord

Harpsichords typically have one or two keyboards, also called manuals, governing two or three sets of strings tuned either at unison pitch (designated "8-foot" pitch after the nominal length of the CC string) or an octave higher ("4-foot" pitch, with strings half as long). The strings press upon a bridge that conveys their vibration to the amplifying soundboard. Each string is plucked by a short plectrum of crow quill protruding from a tongue pivoted in a jack, a wooden strip that rests vertically atop the back end of the key lever. As a finger depresses the head of a key, its tail ascends, lifting the jack and causing its quill to pluck; upon descent, the tongue tilts back to prevent a second pluck and a cloth damper silences the string.

An important characteristic of the typical harpsichord is its inability to produce gradual dynamic change; instead, loud and soft contrasts, if they occur, are abrupt, or "terraced." This inflexibility is due to the invariable force of the plucking action regardless of how forcefully or quickly a key is depressed. Though a percussive attack can overwhelm tonal beauty with noisy clatter, a fast or slow, hard or soft touch negligibly affects the instrument's loudness. Harpsichord music is therefore not premised on dynamic shading the way piano music is, but depends on other means, such as manipulation of texture and dissonance, to create an illusion of swelling and fading.

Often, in order to permit dynamic and tonal change, the row of jacks corresponding to each set, or choir, of strings can be disengaged so that choirs can sound alone or in combination. In two-manual harpsichords, upper-manual jacks can be mechanically coupled to the lower manual so that all choirs can be plucked at once. The material of the string, usually iron or brass, the point along its length where it is plucked, the stiffness of the quill, and acoustical characteristics of the soundboard chiefly determine tone quality, which can be artificially modified by devices such as mutes. In certain instruments, when one set of jacks is disengaged its dampers do not touch their strings, which vibrate sympathetically to enrich and prolong the sound of another choir. The artful selection of tonal effects, called registration, is usually left to a performer's discretion, though treatises discuss the subject. While French composers were more generous than others in indicating registral preferences, C. P. E. Bach's *Sonta per cembalo a due tastature* (Wq. 69, H. 53, 1747) may be unique in specifying registration throughout the piece.[16]

A harpsichord's strings run approximately parallel to the long straight side, or spine, of the case and perpendicular to the keyboard end, giving rise to a wing-shape case (hence the designation *Flügel*). In the compact form known as the bentside spinet, which was particularly popular in England, the keyboard lies at an acute angle to the spine.

Having only one manual and one set of strings, the spinet offers no tonal variety (Ill. 1.1).

The standard French two-manual harpsichord of the period has 8-foot and 4-foot choirs on the lower manual, a single brighter-sounding 8-foot on the upper, a coupler connecting the manuals, and, often after mid-century, a stop controlling a row of soft pads that partially mute the strings by pressing against them. For quiet solo effects a fourth set of jacks with soft leather plectra (*peau de buffle*) was employed occasionally after about 1768. Although with rare exceptions French harpsichord pieces fit within the compass GG–d^3, as early as 1707 the range FF–e^3 appears in a harpsichord by Nicholas Dumont, and one by Pierre Donzelague, dated 1711, has the oldest known FF–f^3 compass of any French harpsichord. Owing chiefly to their string scaling and plucking points, Parisian instruments by members of the illustrious Blanchet and Taskin families possess lush, colorful tones perfect for the genre pieces of Rameau and his followers, many of whose solos are in fact transcriptions of ensemble works. This characteristic rich sound harkens back to seventeenth-century Flemish harpsichords, which were enlarged and enjoyed great favor in France after 1700.

English harpsichords, like French, owe much to older Flemish models, although their styles diverged. The basic equipment of an En-

ILLUSTRATION 1.1. Bentside spinet, John Crang, London, 1753; 1976.77a,b. The Metropolitan Museum of Art, New York.

glish double-manual harpsichord, defined by Hermann Tabel (fl. 1715–1738) early in the eighteenth century, resembles the French, but some English instruments have a further register known as the "lute," consisting of jacks that pluck quite near the ends of the strings to produce a nasal quality. Unlike French instruments, in which the tonally contrasting upper-manual and lower-manual unisons are of approximately equal loudness and therefore suitable for *pièces croisées,* English harpsichords have a quieter upper-manual 8-foot choir effective mainly for echoes. The range FF–f^3, omitting FF $\sharp$, was standard from the 1720s; Tabel's former apprentice Jacob Kirckman (1710–1792) expanded this to FF–c^4 in one known instrument, and after 1765 Burkat Shudi made numerous harpsichords encompassing CC–f^3. The FF $\sharp$ key was normally included after 1780. In that year John Joseph Merlin built the only extant English harpsichord with a 16-foot choir.

Eighteenth-century Italian harpsichords normally have one manual, typically with 50 to 56 notes beginning on C or GG (short octaves) but unusually up to FF–g^3, and two (rarely three) 8-foot choirs. Cristofori made one strange instrument with 8-foot, 4-foot, and 2-foot registers. These resonant instruments, commonly strung with brass wire, tend to be delicately constructed, with thin sides that need the protection of a separate outer case to which the lid is attached. Inner and outer cases are sometimes fused in a type known as the false inner-outer case. Italian harpsichords, while tonally less versatile than French and English, have a crisp, assertive quality well suited to contrapuntal clarity and to continuo-playing in orchestras. Often, these instruments were fitted with pedalboards of one to two octaves to facilitate performance of organ music or doubling of bass notes.

Spanish harpsichords resemble Italian ones, but too few survive to define many peculiarly Iberian qualities except for details of decoration. Three Spanish harpsichords owned by Queen Maria Barbara possessed five-octave compasses, either FF–f^3 or GG–g^3; Domenico Scarlatti and Antonio Soler both call for the top g, a note rare on Italian harpsichords. Another of Maria Barbara's harpsichords had an extraordinary complement of four choirs and five registers; its exact disposition and origin are unknown.[17]

Extant German harpsichords are scarce and only instruments of the Hamburg school are well known; extant examples by the Hass and Fleischer families have varied dispositions, sometimes including 2-foot and 16-foot choirs and three manuals. Recently, modern builders have attempted to replicate more modest Saxon types known to J. S. Bach. Modern copies of instruments by Michael Mietke (from whom, in Berlin, Bach bought a two-manual harpsichord in 1719) possess an aural warmth quite unlike the thick, hard brilliance of Hamburg instruments. (See chapter 3.) Bach's harpsichord music seldom requires a range greater than C–d^3, but several of Bach's late works descend to GG, a note more often called for by Handel. A fully chromatic five-octave compass, FF–f³, is found in a Saxon harpsichord dated 1722, but became common only in the second half of the century.

Little if any music requires the resources of the largest Hamburg harpsichords; on the contrary, most keyboard music from before 1750 can be effectively performed on a simple Italian instrument. Changes of registration within a work are seldom needed to sustain interest, which is more effectively generated internally by manipulation of texture and tessitura and by imaginative embellishment. Indeed, one feature that helps distinguish harpsichord music from organ music is that while the latter, due partly to the organ's prolonged duration of notes, tends to maintain a fixed number of lines so as not to confuse voice-leading, harpsichord music more freely adds and omits voices and implies voice-leading in the manner of lute style.

Various mechanical "improvements" to the harpsichord were intended to provide greater expressive possibilities. Doubtless the piano's dramatically rising popularity after about 1770 motivated some of these efforts, but their origins predate the invention of the piano. It seems as though delight in gadgetry rather than musical necessity prompted some inventors, and many patents were granted for devices that serious composers ignored despite their appeal among novelty-seeking amateurs.[18]

To facilitate changing registration, hand stops were generally arranged over the keyboard rather than at the side of the case as in many seventeenth-century instruments, but some harpsichords retained inconvenient side-drawn stops as late as about 1770. As early as the seventeenth century builders employed pedals to change registers while playing, but the system was not frequently adopted before the mid-eighteenth century. C. P. E. Bach credits Johann Hohlfeld (1711–1771), a former lace maker, with inventing a pedal mechanism that ". . . has made the harpsichord, particularly the single-manual kind, a much-improved instrument, and, fortunately, eliminated all the difficulties connected with the performance of a *piano*. If only all harpsichords were similarly constructed as a tribute to good taste!"[19] The "machine stop" found on some English harpsichords after about 1765 can provide a crescendo or diminuendo effect when its pedal, which controlled the 4-foot and one or two 8-foot choirs, is moved slowly; Haydn's harpsichord made by Burkat Shudi (now in the Kunsthistorisches Museum, Vienna) has this device. Knee levers, supposedly introduced by Pascal Taskin in 1768, likewise move plectra into play gradually, allowing limited dynamic gradation; this feature is required for the *Simphonie de clavecins* composed about 1773 by Armand-Louis Couperin.[20]

To broaden the harpsichordist's palette of timbres, jacks were sometimes fitted with plectra of material other than quill and soft leather.[21] String material, too, was subject to variation, and harpsichords strung with gut rather than metal wire were known all over Europe; they are particularly well documented in Germany, where they were known variously as *Lauten-clavessin, Lautenclavicymbel, Lautenwerck,* or *Theorbenflügel.* No example survives. At his death, J. S. Bach owned two gut-strung harpsichords, one of which reportedly had been made according to his own design by the Silesian organ builder Zacharias Hildebrandt; it was smaller than a normal harpsichord and had two gut 8-foot choirs and a brass-strung 4-foot.[22] Jakob Adlung says that "The *Lautenwerck* is the most beautiful of keyboard instruments after the organ. . . ."[23] To allow tonal and dynamic contrast, Johann Nikolaus Bach (a second cousin of J. S. Bach) made lute-harpsichords with two and three manuals; the jacks probably lacked dampers, leaving the strings free to vibrate sympathetically. A number of works of J. S. Bach, including the suite in E minor BWV 996, his arrangement of the violin partita in E major BWV 1006a, and even continuo parts in the St. John Passion, have been proposed as meant for the gut-strung harpsichord, but the composer never specifies its use in any extant manuscript.[24]

The *Bogenclavier,* a distinct kind of keyboard instrument with strings activated by bowing, is also recorded chiefly in German sources. The type existed since the sixteenth century, but like the *Lautenwerck,* no unquestionably authentic example survives from before 1800. It typically involved a moving loop of horsehair against which gut strings were drawn individually by hooks connected to the keys. Other versions utilized treadle-operated rotating wheels like the hurdy-gurdy's. The *Bogenclavier*'s advantages over the harpsichord include its ability to sustain notes as long as the bow kept moving, and like the clavichord, to shade dynamics and yield a vibrato as well as a portato (*Tragen der Töne*) in response to finger pressure. Despite these useful qualities, bowed claviers attracted little attention from composers, perhaps because too few of these instruments were available to enable music composed specifically for them to become popular. Nevertheless, C. P. E. Bach composed a sonata (Wq. 65/48, H. 280, 1783) for one. Such instruments must have been expensive to build, strenuous to play, and hard to maintain, judging from the specifications of Roger Plenius's lyrichord (patented in 1741), which used lead weights on levers to maintain string tension and involved fifteen wheels rotated by clockwork at different speeds.[25] Along with the *anémocorde* invented in 1789 by Johann Jacob Schnell, an isolated effort to sound strings with jets of wind from bellows, such experiments of the late eighteenth century exemplify a confidence in technology that was boundless, if often misplaced.

The Clavichord

Clavichords are mechanically the simplest but technically the most demanding of keyboard instruments. They are built in the shape of a rectangular box with the keyboard on one long side and strings stretched diagonally from the tuning pins at the player's right, over the sound-board and key levers to hitchpins along the back, opposite the player. From each key lever a thin brass wedge, the tangent, protrudes vertically beneath the strings and strikes them when the key is pressed. Remaining in contact with its strings—normally two per note—while a key is held, the tangent forms a temporary bridge that, together with the permanent bridge affixed to the soundboard, defines the strings' vibrating length and therefore the note's pitch. Volume drops off rapidly after impact, and on release of the key, cloth strips woven among the strings to the left of the tangents stop any remaining vibration. The distance a tangent travels is only a few millimeters, so its key needs to be only shallowly depressed.

Among all keyboards the clavichord is most responsive to touch and is therefore highly expressive under the hands of a skilled performer. By varying finger pressure while a note is held, the player can impart a subtle vibrato. Too strong a blow will distort pitch or even dislodge strings; therefore, a clavichord cannot sound very loud, though a good one can effectively accompany a voice or another single instrument. On the other hand, no other instrument can play more quietly than a clav-ichord, so its dynamic range, from virtual inaudibility to *mezzoforte,* is extensive. The clavichord's quiet, rapidly decaying notes can impose considerable strain on listeners especially in a noisy setting, hence the instrument is not suitable for long concerts.

Because of its simplicity and small size, the clavichord can be con-structed inexpensively. During the eighteenth century countless ones were made, and many survive, usually looking rather plain and lacking legs, though some had their own stands. Some lavishly decorated ex-amples are known, notably from Hamburg, where in the 1740s and later makers such as Johann Adolph Hass occasionally included additional strings at 4-foot pitch for the bottom octave or more to reinforce the sound. In such instruments each tangent might govern its own strings, but normally two or three tangents will strike one bichord at different points along its length, giving several successive pitches from the same strings. Clavichords with shared strings are called "fretted" while those with exclusively independent strings are called "unfretted." Many eigh-teenth-century clavichords are fretted in the bass and unfretted over the rest of their range.

Fretted clavichords are musically somewhat limited in that certain harmonic intervals cannot be sounded because a pair of strings can emit only one note at a time regardless of how many tangents strike those strings at once. In case two tangents should strike their shared strings simultaneously, the tangent closest to the soundboard bridge will deter-mine the sounding pitch. To minimize this limitation, only notes a half-step apart and rarely sounded at once are fretted together. J. S. Bach's entire *Well-Tempered Clavier* presents very few intervals that cannot be played on a standard four-and-one-half-octave (C–f³ or C–g³) fretted clavichord.²⁶ The oldest known clavichord with a fully chromatic five-octave range (FF–f³), by Hieronymus Albrecht Hass, is dated 1742; a lowest note of C, coinciding with the usual bottom note of German organ manuals, was more common before 1750, as befit the clavichord's important role as a practice instrument for organists. For this purpose, some clavichords were made with pedalboards.

The fretted (*gebunden*) clavichord is unsurpassed for refining a player's articulation and digital dexterity. Novices may experience difficulty playing two notes fretted on the same strings in quick succession, as in a trill, if one key is not released before the other is depressed. An offsetting advantage of fretted stringing is that the narrow width of the string band allows more uniform key lengths and more even touch from bass to treble than in unfretted (*bundfrei*) clavichords. Fewer strings simplify tuning and reduce stress on the case.

In German-speaking lands including German-settled North America, and in Iberia and Scandinavia, clavichords served as instructional instruments into the nineteenth century. Curiously, their presence is seldom documented after 1700 in Britain and France, but in Germany they inspired an important repertoire of household music in the *empfindsamer Stil*.²⁷ As a vehicle for sentiment the clavichord had no peer.

Jakob Adlung's *Anleitung zur musikalischen Gelahrtheit* (Erfurt, 1758) describes mechanical ways to alter the clavichord's timbre.²⁸ These methods include sliding the keyboard slightly forward, causing the tangents to strike only one of each pair of strings or engaging a leather-covered portion of the tangents in contrast to their bare brass surface. A particularly effective device was the so-called pantalon register, consisting of a separate set of tangents mounted on a hinged strip beneath the keyboard and passing between the keys. In operation, the pantalon's tan-

ILLUSTRATION 1.2. Clavichord with pantaleon stops, Christian Kintzing, Neuwied, Germany, 1763; 1986.239. The Metropolitan Museum of Art.

gents remain in contact with the strings and prolong their vibration after the keys are released; the resulting resonance is like that of a hammer dulcimer. The pantalon register (named for Pantaleon Hebenstreit's dulcimer; see below), which can be applied only to *bundfrei* clavichords, can be divided to affect bass and treble separately; it occurs only in Germany (Ill. 1.2).

The Piano

It is not always possible to ascertain just when the words *cembalo* and *clavecin,* which normally mean a harpsichord, refer instead to a clavichord or to a piano in eighteenth-century writings. Cristofori's piano was initially called by various names including *gravicembalo col piano e forte* ("harpsichord with soft and loud") or *cembalo con martelli* ("harpsichord with hammers"); it is still termed "A newly invented harpsichord called a *piano et forte*" in the earliest known French advertisement for a piano (1759).[29] Mozart's autographs of the piano concerti K.488 and K.491, both completed in 1786, specify *cembalo* for the solo, but here too the word is used generically; only in the concerti K.537 (1788) and K.595 (1791) does Mozart finally indicate *Fortepiano* or *Pianoforte* (the terms are synonymous). Compounding uncertainty, the German term *Flügel,* used in the nineteenth century to mean a grand (wing-shaped) piano, in Mozart's era commonly meant a harpsichord.

One essential mechanical feature distinguishes pianos from clavichords: while a clavichord tangent remains in contact with the strings so long as the key in which it is imbedded is depressed, a piano hammer is separate from its key and rebounds immediately upon striking. Therefore, unlike a clavichordist, a pianist cannot inflect pitch by varying finger pressure; but the piano mechanism's greater leverage multiplies hammer velocity, vastly increasing maximum loudness. After the hammer rebounds, the strings continue to sound until silenced by a damper that comes into play when the key is released. Material, mass, and striking point of the hammer greatly affect tone.

Mechanically, the simplest means to cause the hammer to rebound occurs in the confusingly named tangent piano, wherein the hammer (not a fixed tangent in the clavichord's sense) is simply a vertical shaft of wood or metal that rests on the end of the key and is held loosely in a rack beneath the strings. As the key is depressed, its motion is abruptly arrested by a stationary rail; momentum carries the hammer shaft onward to the strings. After impact, the hammer returns to rest on the key. This system, already applied in the seventeenth century and developed by Jean Marius in 1716, requires a certain minimum force of attack to throw the shaft clear of the key; insufficient speed will result in no impact, and therefore a tangent piano can be hard to play at low dynamic levels. At the other extreme, a violent attack can cause the shaft to jangle against the strings. Despite these difficulties, tangent pianos were built in small numbers throughout the eighteenth century, and some surviving examples are noteworthy for their tonal beauty.

Still better control over touch arises when a shorter, lighter hammerhead is attached to a hinged lever, or shank, that rises quite close to the strings before key descent is arrested and momentum takes over; this arrangement, in which the hammer moves in a small arc, is the basis of the fully developed piano action. An intermediate lever can be interposed between key and hammer shank to cause greater acceleration. The hammerhead can be captured by a "back check" upon rebounding, to avoid extraneous motion.

Documentary evidence strongly indicates that Bartolomeo Cristofori (1655–1731) was the first builder to develop a mechanism along these lines, which he initiated about 1698 (Ill. 1.3).[30] Cristofori's four

ILLUSTRATION 1.3. Grand piano, Bartolomeo Cristofori, Florence, 1720; 89.4.1219. The Metropolitan Museum of Art, Crosby Brown Collection.

extant piano mechanisms date from the 1720s (one mechanism survives without the rest of its instrument). All incorporate intermediate levers, and "escapements" that allow the hollow, cylindrical parchment hammerheads to drop far enough away from the strings to prevent jangling after impact. Because of the number and arrangement of moving parts (five per key, including the damper affixed to a vertical slip like a harpsichord jack), the touch is heavier than that of an Italian harpsichord and the mechanism is costly to construct. Cost and complexity may have inhibited the spread of Cristofori's idea outside circles of courtly patronage; in Germany, where pianos first reached a bourgeois market, simpler actions having only two or three moving parts per key were more widely adopted.

The tone of the oldest extant Cristofori piano (1720), which originally had the fifty-four-note compass GG–c^3, is clear and colorful though not especially incisive. Probably in the eighteenth century its lightweight, hollow hammerheads (like those later used by Silbermann and even Stein) were replaced with solid wood-core heads to strengthen the sound. Timbre-altering stops are absent, as they are from most Italian harpsichords. Early Florentine "harpsichords with hammers" are suitable for accompanying a singer or several other instruments, but are less apt for playing in a large ensemble where the conventional harpsichord's louder, brighter tone proves more effective. Cristofori's piano was, however, principally intended for solo playing, according to Maffei.[31] Some of Scarlatti's sonatas were undoubtedly played on Florentine pianos in Iberia, where Scarlatti's student Queen Maria Barbara owned five, kept at several palaces.[32] Significantly, Giustini's seminal piano sonatas were dedicated to Scarlatti's patron, Don Antonio of Portugal. Elsewhere, also in a courtly context, J. S. Bach intended the keyboard part in the trio sonata of his *Musical Offering* for one of the Cristoforian pianos Gottfried Silbermann made for Frederick the Great.[33]

Cristofori's principles were embodied initially in harpsichord-like horizontal and upright forms—the latter derived from the clavicytherium and employed in a piano dated 1739, by Cristofori's follower Domenico del Mela—though Cristofori may also have experimented with rectangular or polygonal shapes. Cristofori's innovations were not limited to his hammer mechanism; he also employed a special double-wall case to isolate the soundboard from the pull of the strings. To withstand hammer blows with minimal deflection and to produce optimum sound, piano strings are normally thicker and tauter than harpsichord strings. Heavier stringing under greater tension, and consequently stronger cases, were quickly recognized as central to the piano's development; more heavily constructed and louder pianos, such as Anton Walter's, were increasingly favored for concert use in the late eighteenth century. However, Cristofori's complicated structural solution was not generally adopted; later builders preferred instead to thicken and reinforce the simpler single-wall case. Builders, especially in England, even employed iron reinforcing elements toward the end of the century, as the desire for greater power, rising pitch, and expanding keyboard range imposed more stress on piano cases.

Unlike modern pianos, which ideally maintain tonal consistency from bottom to top note, eighteenth-century pianos typically vary in timbre from bass to treble; the top notes are dry and short-sustaining, the middle register more vocal, and basses reedy. Further, tone color changes according to the dynamic level. Whether or not built-in timbre gradation was intentional, it tickles the ear, infusing music with color even in the absence of muting and other artificial effects. Tone-altering devices may first have been applied to pianos in Germany, where builders of ubiquitous "square" (actually clavichord-shaped) pianos sought to imitate the spectrum of sounds that the virtuoso Pantaleon Hebenstreit (1667–1750) coaxed from his extraordinary dulcimers (themselves called by his name as early as 1705) by using hard and soft beaters on their metal and gut strings. In the 1790s German squares were still sometimes called *pantalon* in tribute to Hebenstreit's dulcimers, several of which were built by Gottfried Silbermann.

The dulcimer's characteristic prolonged resonance was mimicked in pianos by temporarily disengaging the dampers by means of a hand stop or, in the cheapest types, omitting dampers altogether. The oldest dated square piano (1742), by Johann Socher of Sonthofen in Bavaria, already has a damper stop, as do Silbermann grands. C. P. E. Bach refers to the piano's undamped resonance as particularly suited to free improvisation.[34] This dramatic effect is particularly appropriate in slow-moving, arpeggiated, homophonic pieces. Lifting dampers intermittently by means of pedals or knee levers, which superseded less convenient hand stops, was to become an important expressive means, although it was not indicated in published scores before about 1793, when Daniel Steibelt included pedal markings for both dampers ("*les étouffoirs*") and mute ("*la sourdine*") in his *6me Pot Pourri* (Paris: Naderman).[35]

Most Cristofori and Silbermann grand piano actions can be shifted sideways so their hammers strike only one of each pair of strings, a procedure that corresponds to inactivating one register of a typical Italian harpsichord. Silencing half the strings simplifies tuning and also alters timbre and reduces overall loudness. The *una corda* (one string) shift came to be used for expressive purposes in English grand pianos, which evolved from the Cristofori-Silbermann model. It does not occur in eighteenth-century Viennese-type grands, where a mute or "moderator" stop has a similar tonal function, nor is it readily applicable to square pianos because of their diagonal alignment of hammers with respect to the strings.

A few pianos reportedly reached England from Italy and Germany before 1760, and Frederic Neubauer advertised pianos for sale in London in 1763. The decade of the 1760s saw the piano finally emerge identifiably in public concerts. Johann Baptist Schmid played the piano in concerts in Vienna on March 6 and May 13, 1763; what works he performed is unknown.[36] Charles Dibdin accompanied a singer on a piano at the Theatre Royal, Covent Garden, London, in 1767. Henry Walsh played a piano solo in Dublin on May 19, 1768, and Queen Christina's music master, J. C. Bach, who purchased a square by Johann Zumpe, played a solo in a public benefit concert in London on June 2, 1768; in the same year, on September 8, one Mme. Lechantre introduced the piano, perhaps an imported Zumpe-model square, at the *Concert Spirituel* in Paris.[37]

Responding to a mild craze for *pianos anglais,* in 1777 Sébastian Erard (1752–1831) began building square pianos in Paris under the patronage of the Duchesse de Villeroy. Perhaps fearing deadly consequences of his association with the nobility, Erard went to London during the Revolution; there in 1792 he opened a branch of his Parisian firm, which also manufactured harps. Learning from competitors, Erard improved standard English piano actions and brought his designs back to Paris in 1794; two years later he built his first grand piano, using a developed form of English grand action.

John Broadwood (1732–1812), a former apprentice of the harpsichord builder Burkat Shudi, began making square pianos about 1773 (the year Muzio Clementi's Opus 2 sonatas, often called the first "real" piano music, were published), producing his first grand piano about 1781. One of the first builders to employ scientific methods in piano design, Broadwood sought to equalize string tension in order to stabilize the piano case and generate a more uniform tone quality. He attempted to rationalize the piano's geometry and introduced important innovations; these included extending the range to five and one-half octaves, FF–c^4, supposedly at the suggestion of Dussek in 1789 (Dussek briefly lent his Broadwood grand to Haydn in 1791). The optional additional notes had become common on grands by 1793 and were also applied to squares (Ill. 1.4). The next step in enlargement, taken by Broadwood in 1794, was downward to CC, giving a six-octave range increasingly demanded by virtuosi and in popular arrangements and duets.

In Brunswick by 1802, F. C. W. Lemme was prepared to build five-and-one-half-octave grands "in the style of the great English masters," and English-action pianos were also being constructed in Vienna. However, typical Austrian and German grand pianos of the late eighteenth century, exemplified by products of Stein and Walter, differ mechanically, structurally, and tonally from English and derivative French instruments. The typical Viennese-style piano familiar to Mozart, Haydn, and the young Beethoven has a lighter, shallower touch, quieter but clearer sound, especially in the bass, and more efficient damping than contemporary English grands, which often have three strings per note

ILLUSTRATION 1.4. Square piano, John Broadwood and Son, London, 1797; 1982.76. The Metropolitan Museum of Art.

over most of the compass while Viennese counterparts typically retain double-stringing except for the highest octave or two. Austrian and German builders usually employ dampers throughout the compass to guarantee clarity; English pianos often omit dampers in the top octave or so to promote a lingering resonance. English grands also have somewhat more massive hammers than, say, Stein's pianos, which sometimes still have hollow hammers like Cristofori's and Silbermann's. The loudness of Viennese-style pianos diminishes rapidly after a strong attack, giving an effect of sudden diminuendo impossible to achieve on modern instruments having a less marked decay.

The normal Viennese compass of five octaves, FF–f³, was sometimes extended up to g³ after about 1790. Certain Viennese-style grands, notably several built in Salzburg by Johann Schmidt about 1785, incorporate extra bass strings and a short-octave pedalboard that allows performance of notes below FF (Ill. 1.5). Separate pedal pianos could also be placed beneath standard grands. In 1785 Mozart purchased a pedal piano that he used principally for improvisation, though a passage in his D-minor Concerto K.466 requires pedals for notes out of reach of the left hand.[38]

ILLUSTRATION 1.5. Grand piano with pedalboard, attributed to Johann Schmidt, Salzburg, about 1785; 89.4.3182. The Metropolitan Museum of Art, Crosby Brown Collection.

Tonal devices on typical Viennese pianos are usually limited to a damper lifter (often divided for separate bass and treble control), moderator (sometimes offering two stages of muting), and "bassoon" stop (a roll of parchment that buzzed against the bass strings when lowered onto them); the vogue for Turkish music led to addition of percussion devices after 1800. These effects were operated by a combination of hand stops and knee levers until about 1810, when pedals were adopted. English grands, which usually have only damper and *una corda* controls, already had pedals (taken over from the harpsichord) by 1772. At first, pedals were attached to the front legs; later they were centered under the keyboard as expansion of range and consequent widening of the case made use of leg-mounted pedals inelegant.[39]

Certain stylistic developments in Viennese Classical piano music, such as extended range and greater sonority, have been posited to the influence of distinctive pianos. Alec Cobbe states, "The markedly different and more massive style of writing in Mozart's sonata in A minor (K.310), composed after his arrival in Paris in 1778, could be ascribed to what must have been his first experience of English instruments. . . ."[40] (In fact, the child Mozart might already have heard pianos in London in 1764–1765.) Mozart grew increasingly devoted to the piano after he moved to Vienna in 1781, where piano manufacture advanced markedly after the death of Empress Maria Theresa, a musical conservative who reportedly disliked the instrument.[41] Joseph II, on the other hand, promoted the piano; he sits at one in a painting by Joseph Hauzinger (Vienna, Kunsthistorisches Museum), a rare eighteenth-century view of a male amateur pianist. Once settled in Vienna, Mozart acquired a grand piano by Walter that has both hand stops and knee levers (the latter seemingly added after the piano's construction) and embarked upon writing his most characteristic keyboard concertos.

Haydn encountered English pianos, including Broadwoods, in London and took back to Vienna a FF–c^4 grand by Longman & Broderip, a firm that also published his music; Haydn composed his last three piano sonatas mindful of the imposing capabilities of that piano. At various times Haydn owned pianos by other prominent makers including Wenzel Schanz in Vienna (purchased in 1788) and Erard. Haydn's sensitivity to the qualities of different pianos is evident from his correspondence with Maria Anna von Genzinger, to whom he recommended purchasing a new Schanz piano and disparaged Walter's.[42]

The Organ

Organ pipes stand in ranks, each of a different timbre, on a windchest to which pressurized air is supplied by bellows, in the eighteenth century usually pumped by hand or foot (Ill. 1.6). In all but the smallest organs, a weighted reservoir connected to the bellows maintains constant air pressure. Pumping required a usually reluctant assistant, so organists often practiced at home on more convenient stringed claviers. Day-to-day upkeep such as touching up tuning was an organist's responsibility; the builder came for major overhauls, perhaps annually or less often.

The shape and, to a lesser extent, material of a pipe chiefly affect its tone, while length and presence or absence of a stopper at the top end determine pitch (stopped cylindrical and rectangular pipes sound an octave lower than unstopped pipes of the same length). Wind enters a pipe through a hole in its toe. Typically, a slider controlled by a knob at the console admits or cuts off wind to each rank, and individual notes

ILLUSTRATION 1.6. Chamber organ, German, 1700; 89.4.3516. The Metropolitan Museum of Art, Crosby Brown Collection.

sound when keys open their respective valves in the windchest; mechanical linkages that can span long distances connect keys and valves.

In organs having more than one manual, ranks are grouped into divisions, each controlled by a separate keyboard (including the pedalboard) and having its own windchest. Divisions complement one another tonally but may have distinct functions: one for reinforcing hymns, one to accompany the choir, another for echoes or solo effects, and so on. Different manuals can be played simultaneously or in alternation for contrast, or coupled together for greater power.

The most characteristic organ tone is produced by so-called principal ranks, which are supplemented by colorful flute- and string-toned ranks; all these pipes are flues of different designs, flute pipes being wider and string pipes more slender than principals. Reed ranks may also be present but less numerous; they are more expensive and harder to maintain than flues and tend to yield more pungent tone. North German organs known to Bach might employ reeds for one-quarter or slightly more of their ranks. A higher proportion of reeds is often encountered in Spanish organs; the French Baroque organ registration, too, depends on a goodly number of characteristic reed ranks.

In addition to fundamental ranks at 8-foot pitch and one or more octaves higher or lower, eighteenth-century organs ordinarily have "mutation" ranks at 2-2/3-foot, 1-3/5-foot, and other pitches that color the fundamental. Further, "mixtures" of very high-pitched mutation and super-octave ranks operating together as a unit add brilliance. Each division is commonly based upon a chorus of principal ranks at various pitches including mutations and mixtures, plus other ranks of contrasting timbre. A secondary flute chorus is not unusual, and even reeds may be present at several octaves though not as mutations or mixtures. In large organs, manual choruses may be based on 16-foot ranks and the pedal division may descend to 32-foot pitch; ranks of such size are very costly and require considerable space and volume of wind.

Up to the mid-eighteenth century, a normal manual compass was C–c³, though Italian organs, which usually have one manual, might have more notes, and certain divisions of French organs might have fewer. Range increased gradually during the century, but fully chromatic five-octave manuals remained exceptional. Rarely did pedalboards exceed twenty-nine notes; Gottfried Silbermann normally kept to a C–c¹ pedalboard, omitting C-sharp. In Germany and the Lowlands, where contrapuntal music was highly cultivated, pedal divisions equaled manuals in scope and tonal variety. French pedal divisions were small—being used mainly for holding long notes—and English organs seldom had pedals at all; the earliest known independent pedal division in England dates from 1778.

While most organs had one or two manuals and fewer than twenty ranks, organs having four or even five manuals and more than eighty ranks might be found in great churches; some edifices had two organs that could be played antiphonally. Church organists led congregational singing, provided continuo in concerted works, supplied interludes during the liturgy, and sometimes gave public recitals in which all the resources of the organ might be tested; much of the great Baroque organ repertoire was intended for such recitals, not for liturgical use. As their stately cases indicate, organs symbolized civic pride; their construction involved close scrutiny and much debate, and selection of a builder and organist was highly politicized.

Because organs were custom-built, specifications varied greatly, and textbook rules for registration were of questionable value except in regions where some standardization occurred. English organ-building, much injured by Cromwell and thereafter not very adventurous, tended toward uniformity by 1800. English organs generally eschewed reeds and mixtures and left players a limited choice of colors; on the other hand, as early as 1712 Abraham Jordan achieved dynamic control by enclosing several ranks in a box with adjustable louvres, and this so-called Swell division was a common feature of London's organs after 1730. Parisian organs about 1700 were sufficiently standardized that composers such as François Couperin could give quite specific directions for registration; Bach gave virtually no such indications.[43]

Fine eighteenth-century organs of whatever nationality and size are characterized by tonal clarity and interest. Separate voices stand out distinctly in counterpoint, and even in full chords the tone is not turgid. Individual ranks have sharply delineated personalities that nevertheless blend into a cohesive ensemble. Both grandeur and intimacy arise from these instruments.

It may be a striking commentary on the organ's diminishing role in secular musical life after the death of Bach that although Mozart considered it "the king of instruments," a sentiment widely voiced in his day, he composed no significant solo works for the instrument, nor did Haydn or Beethoven. Much if not most organ music was still improvised; but that composers of great stature who were familiar with fine organs should no longer have cared to notate organ works indicates that they perceived limited interest in the medium. No doubt this lack arose both from the organ's indelible association with a church in decline (for example, due to liturgical reforms of Joseph II, or French anticlericalism), and from its inability to convey satisfactorily a chief element of Classical style—its dynamic flexibility.

Carillons and Other Keyboard Instruments

Like the organ, the carillon was both a reassuring civic symbol and an object of some mystery, being huge, remote, and mostly invisible. In the eighteenth century the name "carillon" was not applied exclusively to immense sets of tower bells; other meanings were common outside the Lowlands, though all embraced the sense of struck metallic components. In England "carillon" also meant a portable keyboard instrument having two or more octaves of chromatically tuned metal bars or, less likely, small bells. Handel employed this carillon's magical aura in *Saul* and other staged works. The *stromento d'acciaio* (steel instrument) that simulates Papageno's bells in Mozart's *Die Zauberflöte* (1791) evokes the same charming effect, though whether that instrument was keyed is uncertain.

A hammer-action instrument having three octaves of thin glass bars was confusingly called *fortepiano à cordes de verre,* or "glass-cord" in Benjamin Franklin's terminology, when presented by its Parisian inventor, Beyer, to the Académie des Sciences in 1785; it was judged suitable to accompany a singer. A related type incorporating musical glasses rubbed by a keyed mechanism dates from about the same time; Dussek toured Germany in 1784–1785 with such a "keyed armonica," to use yet another current name. A few years later, in 1788, the English musician and mechanic Charles Claggett introduced an instrument in which keyed hammers struck tuning forks or tuned metal rods fixed to a soundboard or box. More extraordinary was the *clavecin électrique* (1759) designed in Rouen by the Jesuit scientist Jean-Baptiste de La Borde; in it, a clapper, hung between two electrically charged, unison-pitched bells, repeatedly struck both bells so long as their key, which cut off current to one bell, was depressed. An engraving of the instrument published in 1761 shows it as having a two-octave compass.[44]

Instruments like this, or like Louis-Bertrand Castel's synesthetic *clavecin oculaire* (1734), indicate intense effort that stemmed not so much from musical necessity as from acoustical experiments by scientists such as La Borde and Chladni; the latter developed various friction idiophones including one with keys ("clavicylinder"). Such activity was fostered by the many academies and Masonic lodges where musicians and natural philosophers met.

In conclusion, it is clear that eighteenth-century keyboard instruments fulfilled many vital social functions. As articles of commerce, vehicles for scientific inquiry and technological innovation, and status symbols, as well as by making music, they kept pace with trends that shaped the century and embody the spirit of the Enlightenment.

Notes

1. See under "Clavier" in Don Michael Randel, *The New Harvard Dictionary of Music* (Cambridge, MA, 1986), and note 11, below.

2. Facsimile edited by Rosamond E. M. Harding (Cambridge, 1933). Sonatas of Guistini have been recorded on the 1720 Bartolomeo Cristofori piano at the Metropolitan Museum of Art by James Bonn (Pleiades Records, P105, 1977) and by Mieczyslaw Horszowski (Titanic Records, Ti-79, vols. 1 and 2, 1980).

3. Georg Kinsky, "*Mozart-Instrumente*" in *Acta Musicologica* 12 (1940): 15; Mary Sue Morrow, *Concert Life in Haydn's Vienna: Aspects of a Developing Musical and Social Institution* (Stuyvesant, NY, 1989), 166.

4. See under "Kirkman" in Boalch 1974; for Sodi see *"Clavicembali e spinette dal XVI al XIX secolo,"* catalogue of an exhibition at the Chiesa di San Georgio in Poggiale, Bologna, 1 November–21 December 1986, 121.

5. Modern edition by X. V. Elewick (Brussels, 1877).

6. François Couperin earlier admitted that the harpsichord was perceived as dynamically inflexible (*L'art de toucher le clavecin,* Paris, 2nd ed. 1717, 15–16; facsimile ed., New York, 1969). C. P. E. Bach, in his *Versuch . . .,* remarks that ". . . the clavichord and pianoforte enjoy great advantages over the harpsichord and organ because of the many ways in which their volume can be gradually changed." (English translation by William J. Mitchell, *Essay on the True Art of Playing Keyboard Instruments* [New York, 1949], 369.)

7. Mozart's rare use of notes outside the normal keyboard compass or out of reach of the player's hands can be explained by his access to exceptional instruments such as the pedal piano; see note 37, below. The apparently impossible crescendo-decrescendo marking <> over a held note in piano works of Beethoven, Schubert, and Brahms is not meant literally but indicates that the note should be played *as though* the effect could be achieved—a typically Romantic idea. See Konrad Wolff, "Accent? Decrescendo?" in *American Music Teacher* (1989): 14–17, 63. Pianos with a pedal-operated lid flap can, of course, produce this effect, as can the *Bogenclavier,* but performance on these instruments was not intended.

8. See Laurence Libin, "An Eighteenth-Century View of the Harpsichord" in *Early Music* 4 (1976): 16–18.

9. See David Wainwright, *Broadwood by Appointment; A History* (London, 1982), 60.

10. *Georg A. Sorgens . . . zuverlaessig Anweisung Claviere und Orgeln behoerig zu temperiren und zu stimmen* (Leipzig and Lobenstein, 1758); see Carl O. Bleyle, "Georg Andreas Sorge: an 18th-century Proponent of logarithmic Scaling for Organ-pipes" in *Organ Yearbook* 6 (1975): 53–63.

11. For descriptions and references, see under "Chladni, Ernst" and "Vogler, Georg Joseph" in Stanley Sadie, ed., *The New Grove Dictionary of Music and Musicians* (London, 1980).

12. Trans. Charles Ferguson (Raleigh, NC, 1977).

13. Maffei's account is reprinted and translated in Edward F. Rimbault, *The Pianoforte, Its Origin, Progress, and Construction* (London, 1860), 95–102.

14. Stewart Pollens, "The early Portuguese piano" in *Early Music* 13 (1985): 18–27.

15. Stein's diary is privately owned by a Streicher descendant in Austria.

16. Modern edition for organ by Jean Langlais (Chicago, 1957).

17. For more detailed descriptions of Spanish harpsichords see chapter 5, pp. 168–170.

18. One device that permits limited dynamic nuance in the harpsichord is the so-called nag's head swell, a hinged lid flap lifted by a pedal; it was employed by Jacob Kirckman in London as early as 1754. Fifteen years later Kirckman's competitor Shudi patented the "Venetian swell," a panel of pedal-operated louvers like Venetian blinds above the soundboard.

19. Mitchell, *op. cit.,* 368–369.

20. Modern edition in David Fuller, ed., *Armand-Louis Couperin. Selected Works for Keyboard, Part I: Music for Two Keyboard Instruments,* in *Recent Researches in the*

Music of the Pre-classical, Classical, and Early Romantic Eras, vol. I (Madison, WI, 1975), 1–37.

21. The Philadelphia statesman, mechanic, and musician Francis Hopkinson (1737–1791), fed up with unreliable crow quills, experimented with hard leather, leather-covered cork, and wood plectra; his methods, communicated to the American Philosophical Society between 1783 and 1787, interested Thomas Jefferson and illustrate the serious attraction keyboard technology held for cultured gentlemen even in distant colonies.

22. Hildebrandt's *Lautenclavicymbel* was described by Johann Friedrich Agricola; see Hans T. David and Arthur Mendel, eds., *The Bach Reader* (New York, 1966), 259.

23. Adlung 1768, 133.

24. See Nicholas Goluses, "J. S. Bach and the Transcription Process" in *Guitar Review* 77 (1989): 16–17; and Uta Henning, "The Most Beautiful among the Claviers" in *Early Music* 10 (1982): 477–86.

25. See Eric Halfpenny, "The Lyrichord" in *Galpin Society Journal* 3 (1950): 46–49.

26. Edwin M. Ripin, "A Reassessment of the Fretted Clavichord" in *Galpin Society Journal* 23 (1970): 43.

27. Because of terminological ambiguities noted elsewhere it is impossible to identify the earliest music specifically intended for clavichord, but C. P. E. Bach "was almost certainly the earliest important composer to conceive his music in terms of the clavichord" (Edwin M. Ripin, "Clavichord" in *The New Grove Dictionary of Music and Musicians* 4:466). His rondo entitled *Abschied von meinem Silbermann'schen Clavier* (Wq. 66, H. 272, 1781) exemplifies the clavichord's full-blown *Strum und Drang* idiom.

28. Jakob Adlung, *Anleitung zur musikalischen Gelahrtheit* (Erfurt, 1758), 568–72.

29. The original language is quoted in Eugène de Bricqueville, *Les ventes d'instruments de musique au XVIIIe siècle* (Paris, 1908), 11. According to Eva Badura-Skoda (see chapter 2, p. 59), the noun "pianofort(e)" was coined by Gottfried Silbermann.

30. Mario Fabbri, "*Il primo 'pianoforte' di Bartolomeo Cristofori*" in *Chigiana* n.s. 21 (1964): 162–72 (the authenticity of Fabbri's evidence is questionable); Stewart Pollens, "The Pianos of Bartolomeo Cristofori" in *Journal of the American Musical Instrument Society* 10 (1984): 32–68.

31. Cited in Rimbault, *op. cit.*, 96–97.

32. Ralph Kirkpatrick, *Domenico Scarlatti* (New York, 1968), 175–78, 183–84. See also chapter 5.

33. Christoph Wolff, "New Research on Bach's *Musical Offering*" in *The Musical Quarterly* 57 (1971): 403; Stewart Pollens, "Gottfried Silbermann's Pianos" in *The Organ Yearbook* 17 (1986): 103–21. Bach's *Sonata sopr'il Soggetto Reale* from BWV 1079 has been recorded using the 1746 Silbermann piano preserved in Potsdam (VEB Deutsche Schallplatten Berlin, Eterna Edition 8-27-844, 1983).

34. Mitchell, *op. cit.*, 431.

35. For further discussion and musical examples see David E. Rowland, "Pianoforte Pedalling in the Eighteenth and Nineteenth Centuries" (Ph.D. dissertation, University of Cambridge, 1985).

36. Vienna, Hofkammerarchiv, Hofzahlamtsbücher 367, 368; information courtesy of Dexter Edge.

37. For references see Howard Schott, "From Harpsichord to Pianoforte: A Chronology and Commentary" in *Early Music* 13 (February, 1985): 28–38; Virginia Pleasants, "The early Piano in Britain (c1760–1800)" in *Early Music* 13 (1985): 39–44.

38. Mozart's use of f$\sharp^3$ (which implies the presence of g^3) in the two-clavier sonata, K.375a, written in 1781 for Josepha von Auernhammer, suggests a remarkably early instance of upward extension of the piano's range. Mozart's autograph of the pedal passage from K.466 (first movement, mm. 88–90) is reproduced in facsimile in the *Neue Mozart-Ausgabe* V/15, Bd. 6 (1961), xiv.

39. One amusing device encountered in some English squares is a pedal-operated lever that allows a separately hinged section of the lid to slam closed, a startlingly effective way to punctuate battle pieces. The same lever can gradually open the flap to create a crescendo and a subtle change of timbre, or even a crescendo and decrescendo (or the reverse) on a held note or chord. The device was inspired by Kirckman's nag's head swell (see note 18 above).

40. Alec Cobbe, *A Century of Keyboard Instruments 1760–1860;* catalogue of an exhibition at the Fitzwilliam Museum, Cambridge, 5 July–31 August 1983, 10.

41. Few Viennese pianos predate 1780, but the Kunsthistorisches Museum owns a square piano believed to be Viennese that could have been made as early as the 1760s. Eva Badura-Skoda (personal communication, 17 June 1992), citing research by Helga Michelitsch-Scholz, states that "Empress Maria Theresa must have played a piano in her 'student days' under the supervision of her teacher Wagenseil. . . ."

42. Haydn's letters to Maria Anna von Genzinger, 20 June and 4 July 1790, translated in H. C. Robbins Landon, *Haydn: Chronicle and Works*, vol. 2, *Haydn at Eszterháza 1766–1790* (London, 1978), 743–46. On Haydn's keyboard instruments and the piano's role in Viennese music, see A. Peter Brown, *Joseph Haydn's Keyboard Music: Sources and Style* (Bloomington, IN, 1986), 136–44. See also Eva Badura-Skoda's remarks on this subject, chapter 2 (p. 60).

43. Peter Williams, *A New History of the Organ From the Greeks to the Present Day* (Bloomington, IN, 1980), 106–17.

44. The engraving, from La Borde's *Le clavessin électrique, avec une nouvelle théorie du méchanisme et des phénomènes de l'électricité* (Paris, 1761), is reproduced in the article "Clavecin électrique" in *The New Grove Dictionary of Musical Instruments* 1: 415.

Selected Bibliography

Adlung, Jakob. *Musica mechanica organoedi*. Berlin, 1768. Facsimile with afterword by Christhard Mahrenholz, Kassel, 1931.

Blanchard, Homer D. *The Bach Organ Book*. Delaware, OH, 1985.

Boalch, Donald H. *Makers of the Harpsichord and Clavichord, 1440–1840*. 3rd ed., ed. Charles Mould. Oxford, 1996.

Cole, Michael. *The Pianoforte in the Classical Era*. Oxford, 1998.

Douglass, Fenner. *The Language of the French Classical Organ*. New Haven, 1969.

Harding, Rosamond E. M. *The Piano-Forte: Its History Traced to The Great Exhibition of 1851.* 2nd edition. Surrey, 1978.

Henkel, Hubert. *Beiträge zum historischen Cembalobau.* Leipzig, 1979.

Hubbard, Frank. *Three Centuries of Harpsichord Making.* Cambridge, MA, 1967.

Koster, John. "Pianos and other 'Expressive' *Claviere* in J.S. Bach's Circle." *Early Keyboard Studies Newsletter* 7, 1993.

Libin, Laurence. *Keyboard Instruments.* New York, 1989.

Maunder, Richard. *Keyboard Instruments in Eighteenth-Century Vienna.* Oxford, 1998.

Müller, Werner. *Gottfried Silbermann: Persönlichkeit und Werk.* Frankfurt-am-Main, 1982.

Place, Adélaide de. *Le Piano-forte à Paris entre 1760 et 1822.* Paris, 1986.

Ripin, Edwin M. "Expressive devices applied to the eighteenth-century harpsichord." *The Organ Yearbook* 1 (1970): 65–80.

Rosenblum, Sandra P. *Performance Practices in Classic Piano Music; Their Principles and Applications.* Bloomington, IN, 1988.

Sadie, Stanley, ed. *The New Grove Dictionary of Musical Instruments.* London, 1984.

———, ed. *The New Grove Dictionary of Music and Musicians.* London, 1980.

van der Meer, John Henry. "The Dating of German Clavichords." *The Organ Yearbook* 6 (1975): 100–13.

Williams, Peter. *The European Organ 1450–1850.* London, 1966.

CHAPTER TWO

Aspects of Performance Practice

Eva Badura-Skoda

The quest for a performance that is as authentic as it can possibly be has come to be a genuine concern for many instrumentalists in our century. Indeed, a work impresses us most deeply when it is rendered in a manner that comes closest to what the composer envisaged. At present only opera directors, it seems, feel free to pay no attention whatever to the notion of original intent—much to the dismay of connoisseurs and lovers of operas of the past. Fortunately, however, nearly all keyboard players nowadays sense a need to ferret out the composer's intentions residing behind the notation of works they want to perform.

The notion that a masterwork of the past should be played "in style" and with the musical means its composer had in mind did not originate in our century. In 1739 Johann Mattheson concluded his celebrated book *Der Vollkommene Capellmeister* with these words: "The greatest difficulty associated with the performance of someone else's work is probably the fact that keen discernment is necessary in order to understand the real sense and meaning of unfamiliar thoughts. For those who have never discovered how the composer himself wished to have the work performed will hardly be able to play it well. Indeed, he will often rob the thing of its true vigor and grace, so much so, in fact, that the composer, should he himself be among the listeners, would find it difficult to recognize his own work."[1]

Problems of Text and Notation

At some point every serious musician feels uneasy about a previously trusted edition. He is disturbed, perhaps, by an incongruous ornament or an articulation mark, or by a *forte* sign in a passage that he thinks should be played softly. In consulting other editions he soon makes a depressing discovery: printed editions of the same work often contradict each other not only with respect to details but even the most fundamental matters. Carl Czerny's famous edition of Bach's *Well-Tempered Clavier* prints an extra bar at the end of the B-flat-major prelude from the first book; and in Hans von Bülow's equally well-known edition of the *Chromatic Fantasy and Fugue* the editor arbitrarily changed Bach's tonal answer (starting on d) to a real answer (starting on e). But we find such distortions not only in old editions prepared by famous pianists of the past. Many modern editions, too, although proudly labelled "Urtext," unfortunately do not measure up to the demands made on them by the earnest musician. In the recent past music publishers, for purely commercial purposes, have frequently made improper use of such fashionable terms and concepts as "Urtext," "authenticity," and "historical performance." In fact, the term "Urtext," if we take it literally, is a misnomer.[2] In only a handful of cases does a musical artwork exist in a single autograph version that is notated so faultlessly that the composer found it unnecessary to make any subsequent changes either in later manuscript copies or in a printed edition. In such rare instances a facsimile edition of the autograph may be properly called an "Urtext" edition. In all other cases, however, a printed edition is inevitably a transcription and represents the interpretative reading of an editor who cannot possibly follow the handwritten copy in every detail.

If we take the term "Ur-text" even more literally ("ur" = original, first), then we confront additional problems. Audiences in the concert hall do not normally wish to hear the "Ur"-text, or first version, of a work—for example, Bach's French Suites in their very first autograph version—but rather the revised and more beautiful later versions prepared by Bach and transmitted in copies written out by his pupils. Similarly, few would prefer to listen to Beethoven's "Ur"-text of a sonata played with all the missing flats and sharps of the autograph version, instead of the corrected, emended version Beethoven took care to have published in the first printed edition. First versions of famous works are unquestionably of scholarly interest, but they include, by definition, readings that were rejected and invalidated by the composer himself. They should be replaced in the concert halls by final versions, wherever such versions exist.[3]

The music editor faces a threefold task. First he must try to determine: What did the composer *actually* write? This involves the collection and investigation of sources—the task of "source criticism." He must then ask: What did the composer *intend* to write? Not infrequently a composer's notation is unclear, incorrect, or incomplete. Moreover, a slip of the pen may actually obscure his intentions. The editor's second task—the task of "text criticism"—is to correct such errors. Finally, the editor must consider: How ought the composer to have notated his composition, in order to be correctly *understood* today? This is the task of text "elucidation." The answer here, though sometimes difficult, is usually easier to find than for the two previous questions. Modern editors agree that elucidations are welcome, provided they do not obscure the appearance of the original text and are clearly identified as editorial interpolations. A good "Urtext," or "critical," edition will always indicate which markings are the composer's and which are editorial additions. They are usually printed in italics or parentheses; further explanations normally appear as footnotes. A preface should inform the musician about the editor's procedure.

Editors differ, however, about the extent to which performance hints are necessary in a modern edition; nor do they always agree about the details of a stylistically proper performance. How should or could a particular ornament be interpreted? Did not nearly every composer entertain different notions in this respect? Should the editor help the performer find the proper solution—assuming there is indeed only one (in his opinion); and should he indicate the existence of an option wherever there was more than one "correct" solution? Are there not various ways to interpret an arpeggio or an appoggiatura? Short or long, accented or unaccented, anticipated or on the beat? Which one sounds best? A good edition should certainly point out alternative solutions.

To return to text problems: In the second movement of his last piano sonata, the sonata in E-flat major Hob. XVI/52 Joseph Haydn wrote the following in mm. 40 and 48 (Ill. 2.1). Something is clearly wrong in m. 40: Haydn wrote one eighth-note more in the upper staff than in the lower. And there is a surplus of eight thirty-second-notes (i.e., one quarter-note) in m. 48. That is, there is a change of meter from 3/4 to 4/4.

What did Haydn intend in these passages? Various solutions have been offered. In his edition (*Diletto musicale* 168, *Doblinger*) Paul Badura-Skoda changes the eighth-note in the bass of m. 40 to a quarter and leaves all note values in m. 48 as Haydn wrote them.[4] The meter thus changes twice from 3/4 into 4/4 for one measure each time. Although this looks odd to modern eyes, it is something that had been done quite often in older times and could easily have occurred to a composer with

ILLUSTRATION 2.1. Joseph Haydn: Autograph Score of the Piano Sonata in E-flat Major Hob. XVI/52. Movement 2, mm. 40 and 48. Courtesy of the Library of Congress.

the imagination of Joseph Haydn, who often broke rules in favor of sounds pleasing to the ears. In the 1790s, however, it was certainly an unusual idea (Ex. 2.1).

EXAMPLE 2.1. Haydn: Piano Sonata Hob. XVI/52. Movement 2, mm. 33–54, as edited by Paul Badura-Skoda. By permission of Doblinger Verlag, Vienna

Christa Landon (*Universal-Edition*) concurs in principle with Paul Badura-Skoda's solution but chooses a different notation. She changes Haydn's normal-sized notes in both measures to small notes (Ex. 2.2).[5]

EXAMPLE 2.2. Haydn: Piano Sonata Hob. XVI/52. Movement 2, mm. 38–40, 48–49, as edited by Christa Landon. By permission of Wiener Urtext Edition Musikverlag, Ges.m.b. H. & Co. K. G. Vienna

A far less convincing solution has been offered by Georg Feder.[6] In order to avoid a change of meter, Feder alters some of the thirty-second-notes in both measures to sixty-fourth-notes, with the result that the two passages sound oddly rushed (Ex. 2.3).

EXAMPLE 2.3. Haydn: Piano Sonata Hob. XVI/52. Movement 2, mm. 38–48, as edited by Georg Feder. By permission of G. Henle Verlag, Munich

This example suffices to demonstrate the difficulties a composer's writing error may cause the modern editor who cannot believe that Haydn actually meant an audacious meter change; and it demonstrates

the different solutions to which various editors may come in grappling with such a problem.

Tempo

Everyone will agree that *uniquely* correct tempi do not exist: the interpreter clearly enjoys a certain degree of freedom in choosing a tempo. But he must be careful to select a tempo that falls within the boundaries of the artistically and stylistically valid. Some may claim that the choice of a tempo is not only a matter of temperament but also one of taste. This cannot be denied; but it is important to remember that taste— though ultimately an inborn gift, comparable to other natural talents— can be influenced not only by education, but also by trends and fashions, and fashions have changed quite often in the past. Musicians of the eighteenth century constantly spoke of *taste, Geschmack, gusto, goût,* terms we also find discussed in most eighteenth-century dictionaries.[7] Unfortunately, the individual writers often leave us in the dark as to what, specifically, they considered "tasteful." But from their statements we may safely infer that good taste was as rare in Bach's and Mozart's time as it is today.

Historians are able to examine changes in compositional styles and musical forms much more thoroughly than they can follow the prevailing performance tastes of a certain period at a certain location. We can describe the former quite accurately, but we know relatively little, and in some respects next to nothing, about the latter. The invention of Mälzel's metronome after 1800 allows us to document that during the nineteenth century tempo fashions changed with practically every generation;[8] and we may presume that the same was true during Bach's, Haydn's, and Mozart's time. This, however, is only an assumption. What exactly was the tempo Couperin or Bach preferred for a certain piece they had composed? What deviations from their own tempi did the composers still consider tolerable? At what point would they have protested? Would Bach have performed a work of Couperin's at the same tempo its composer would have chosen?

Not only personality but age, date, and place play a role as well. We can observe in our own century that composers frequently have changed their metronome markings—sometimes considerably—when they performed their own works in later years. (Compare, for example, Bartok's two recorded performances of his Suite for Piano op. 14.)

The eighteenth century made use of tempo indications such as adagio, largo, andante, allegro, presto; these are certainly helpful for modern performers. Indeed, they are our most important tools for finding the proper tempo. Studies of eighteenth-century barrel organs,[9] as well as the tempo indications based on the human pulse given by J. J. Quantz

in his flute treatise, are useful in this connection; the latter can be transferred into metronome values. These sources inform us that English,
North-, and Central-German musicians around 1740 apparently liked
rather fast tempi—much faster than most of us, at first encounter, would
believe possible. We read in Johann Sebastian Bach's obituary that his
tempi were "very lively." But this statement only compares Bach's tempi
to those of his contemporaries (and to what some of them *felt* about
tempi); it fails to tell us exactly what tempi are appropriate for his works.
Nevertheless, we do learn some valuable information from the statement: namely, that Bach's performances possessed a great deal of vitality
and that his sensitive, "*empfindsam*" son Philipp Emanuel felt that his father's tempi were rather fast.[10] Around 1750 there seems to have been
a general trend for tempi to have become slower—at least in Northern
Germany. There are also indications that the same trend was at work in
Vienna and Italy a decade earlier. But the evidence on that point is contradictory.

A few general hints provided by the theorists are helpful. Both
Quantz and Leopold Mozart advised their readers to search for the
smallest note values in a piece before starting to play. This admonition,
however, may have been meant primarily for sight readers and beginners. An experienced musician will not be tempted to take too fast a
tempo for a fast movement that begins with larger note values. For the
accomplished modern musician the danger of choosing a wrong tempo
is not so much one of stumbling over technical difficulties but of miscon-
struing the *affect* of a piece, of misunderstanding its character. Conversely, if he understands the meaning of a piece and perceives the
proper affect, he is not likely to miss the proper tempo. Leopold Mozart
writes that "one has to deduce [the tempo] from the piece itself, and it
is by this that the true worth of a musician can be recognized without
fail. Every melodious piece has at least one phrase from which one can
recognize quite surely what sort of speed the piece demands. Often, if
other points be carefully observed, the phrase is forced into its natural
speed. Remember this, but know also that for such perception long experience and a good judgment are required. Who will contradict me if
I count this among the chiefest perfections in the art of music?"[11] Leopold Mozart's statement that "long experience and a good judgment are
needed" is even truer today than it was in his own time. Young musicians
playing eighteenth-century music today who rely alone on their instinct
are even more likely to fail to catch the proper tempo.[12]

It is common knowledge that eighteenth-century musicians enjoyed
a large degree of interpretive freedom. (A work could be performed
in a variety of ways, not only with respect to the choice of instruments
for a continuo part or the embellishment of melodic lines, etc., but also
to such rhythmic modifications as over- or underdotting and the application of *notes inégales* in French repertoire.) Regarding the basic tempi,

however, musicians probably had very little freedom. Of course, it was no doubt easier for the eighteenth-century musician than it is for us to find the right, or at least a plausible, tempo. Performers (and listeners) were familiar with contemporary airs and dance tunes and could recognize the host of stylistic and performance conventions associated with them that are now unknown to us. Contemporaries of Bach or Mozart presumably could recognize allusions to popular dance types and were doubtless sensitive to their affective connotations.[13] Indeed, the tempo of a piece was often only implied by its inherent affect and not indicated explicitly with terms like "allegro" or "andante." At times the character of a piece, and its affect, were indicated by such terms as "affetuoso," "furioso," "amoroso," "gay," "dolce," "spirituoso," but such words are usually missing. Since neither Bach nor Haydn nor Mozart left any metronome markings, it is incumbent upon us, if we hope to discover their intentions with regard to tempo, to learn to recognize and understand these conventions and associations. Present-day performers have no other choice than to study the music, the titles, the few available tempo and affect indications and to ponder their meaning,[14] to search for possible underlying dance rhythms, to read contemporary reports about the specific virtues for which a certain composer became famous, and to look for performance hints in the prefaces or letters of composers and in the relevant treatises.

As stated earlier, conventions of musical performance often differed from one region to another. In certain regions the tempi of stylized dance movements evidently were determined by national dance traditions. Contemporary reports sometimes help us to learn more about such conventions. Mozart, for instance, wrote to his sister in 1770 from Bologna that minuets were generally performed more slowly in Italy than in Vienna. Reflecting on this remark we may consider the tempo of minuets in sonatas by Haydn or Mozart and the meaning of the indication *Tempo di menuetto.* When does it mean an andante, when an andantino or allegretto tempo? In any case, we must distinguish the *menuetti ballabile,* composed for instance for use in the Viennese *Redouten,* from the stylized minuet movements for keyboard works—the former certainly should not be played too fast.[15] Whether the latter were also performed more slowly than is usual today, is far less obvious and by no means clear. In older dictionaries minuets are sometimes characterized as fast dances. One reads in Brossard's *Dictionaire de Musique* (1703) that "the menuet is always a very lively and very fast" dance ("fort gay et fort vite"). There is also the question of accents and slight prolongations of certain beats. Curt Sachs wrote: "The novel dance of the day, the minuet, embodied a curious rhythmic anomaly. Its music was written in 3/4. But the regular step pattern consisted in a long bending step with the right foot, extending over two of the three quarter-notes, and another long bending step with the left foot, also extending over two quarters and therewith ignoring the bar line, plus two straight and shorter steps, coinciding with one quarter each. In notation:

music:

dance:

Hence the dancing master Giambattista Dufort felt compelled to recommend in his *Trattado del ballo nobile* (Naples, 1728) that the accompanying musicians should not stress the first beats of the even-numbered bars."[16]

Not only did minuets demand different tempi in various countries at various times; it is interesting to investigate the changing character of some other dances. For instance, different types of sicilianos evolved in the course of the eighteenth century: they could be performed either as fast as saltarellos or gigues in a presto or allegro tempo, as cantabile pastorales in an andante tempo, or they could demand the rather melancholy character of a forlane in an adagio tempo. This diversity may derive from the different traditions of Southern and Northern Italy. The easily recognizable rocking rhythm in 12/8 or 6/8 meter with its simple rhythmic patterns and repeated figures, often characteristically dotted (♪♫ ♪♫), was used for lively folk dances only in the South, but as a musical device it became fashionable everywhere, often under the name "siciliano." During the first decades of the eighteenth century the tempo was usually as lively as allegro. In Bach's ensemble works, however—for example, the aria "Erbarme dich," from the *St. Matthew Passion*, or the slow movement from the Clavier Concerto in E Major BWV 1053—we already find a tendency to prefer the slower, Venetian, type of melancholy siciliano in a minor mode (Ex. 2.4).

EXAMPLE 2.4. J. S. Bach: Clavier Concerto in E Major BWV 1053. Movement 2, beginning

This tendency is reflected more and more in the works of the Viennese Classical period: for example, in Haydn's F-major Sonata Hob. XVI/23, where the second movement, in F minor, is a siciliano (Ex. 2.5).

EXAMPLE 2.5. Haydn: Sonata in F Major Hob. XVI/23. Movement 2, beginning

In the middle movement of Mozart's sonata in F major K.280—a counterpart to Haydn's movement—we encounter the same key, rhythm, and tempo, but the mood here is probably more melancholy (Ex. 2.6).

EXAMPLE 2.6. Mozart: Sonata in F Major K 280. Movement 2, beginning

Even though both movements are marked *adagio*, these two sicilianos should not be played too slowly. As any good musician knows, one adagio is not necessarily as slow as another: the siciliano movement in Mozart's A-major Piano Concerto K.488, for example, is, if anything, a bit slower than the one in K.280. At all events, it is important to recognize that in the eighteenth century an "adagio" tempo, in general, was not as slow as we usually perceive it to be today. "Essere ad' agio" means literally "to be at ease"—not "slow." But tempo terminology, like so much else in the eighteenth century, was very much a regional, and a personal matter, changing with the generations. (In the case of J. S. Bach, for example, "adagio," along with its intensifiers, "molto adagio" and "adagiosissimo," evidently represented the slowest of the tempo markings.)[17]

Dance rhythms are found in many keyboard movements throughout the eighteenth century, from Domenico Scarlatti's sonatas to those of the Classical period, even though they are often not recognized as such today. This discussion of tempi in stylized dance movements demonstrates, on the one hand, the importance of recognizing the underlying dance character of a piece, if one is to capture its distinctive rhythmic quality and find its proper tempo. On the other hand, it should also reveal why composers increasingly felt obliged to add explicit tempo indications to a movement bearing the title *Menuet* or *Siciliano*.

Rhythm

Rhythm, as everyone knows, is the dimension of music that regulates the sequence of notes in time. Less well known is the fact that in the succession of time values a mathematically (metronomically) correct duration of the prescribed meter beats is hardly ever possible. It is simply human to introduce—intuitively or willfully—deviations from the aesthetically deadly strictness of the literal time values. An accented note is not only slightly louder than an unaccented one but often a tiny bit prolonged—especially in harpsichord music. A main characteristic of Baroque music is a steady rhythm. Even there, tiny prolongations or accelerations of the written time values are not only unavoidable but necessary to bring the music to life. Eighteenth-century theorists addressed this phenomenon in their elaborate discussions of "good" and "bad" notes, that is, accented and unaccented beats, within a measure. In 4/4 meter, for instance, the first and the third beats, or *buone note*, are "heavy," the second and the fourth are to be played more lightly. But the third beat is not as heavy as the first (and perhaps slightly shorter), and the fourth is lighter than the second, etc. These accents were compared to the accents in speech, and thus musical rhetoric was linked to rhetoric in speech. The concept of accent involves rhythmic as well as dynamic subtleties, and the realization of it requires musical taste. On the one hand, a musician has to avoid excess. in the application of expressive accents; on the other hand, he also has to avoid monotonous rhythmic regularity. (The latter extreme characterized many performances of Baroque music in the period shortly after World War II, when it was fashionable to play Bach in a "sewing machine style.") Especially on the harpsichord, on which the dynamic level can only be altered by increasing or decreasing the number of voices, small rhythmic irregularities are vital for an effective performance; moreover, the impression of dynamic shading is conveyed by means of these irregularities. In sum: although nearly all eighteenth-century theorists demanded that a musician keep an even rhythm (at least in the bass part), small deviations from metronomic regularity always occurred. Sometimes these deviations were deliberately exaggerated in melodic lines (but only there), in order to create the effects of rubato or *notes inégales*. Normally, however, the deviations were rather minimal and hardly noticeable.

With respect to changes of the basic tempo, on the other hand, the situation is different. Mattheson drew a distinction between meter and movement (*Takt* and *Bewegung*), associating them with the mathematical and emotional aspects of the tempo, and quoting from a French treatise published in 1687 by the viola-da-gamba player Jean Rousseau, he added: "It is insufficient, when playing a piece of music, to be able to beat and maintain the prescribed time. Rather, the conductor must as it were discern the composer's meaning, that is, must sense the various emotions that the piece wishes to have expressed."[18]

Mozart's remarks concerning both changes of tempo and smaller rhythmic alterations have a somewhat different emphasis. He once described the difficulties of the young Nannette Stein at the piano: "She will never acquire the most essential, the most difficult and the chief requisite in music, which is rhythm [time], because from her earliest years she has done her utmost not to play in time."[19] It seems evident that Mozart considered the most important virtue in music ("die hauptsache in der Musik") the ability to play "in time"—by which he surely meant with a steady rhythm and in a tempo that does not slow down at difficult places and rush elsewhere. In the same letter to his father Mozart continued: "Everyone is amazed that I can always keep strict time. What these people cannot grasp is that in tempo rubato in an Adagio, the left hand should go on playing in strict time. With them the left hand always follows suit."

Today we usually associate the freedom of agogic tempo changes with the so-called Romantic period. However, as Mattheson's comment reveals, deliberate changes of tempo were often desirable in earlier periods, too. We may assume that a composer's personal style played the more decisive role, and the period or local style perhaps a lesser one, in the use of such agogic changes. In other words: tempo changes are more appropriate for some composers than for others. In C. P. E. Bach's work they are essential. But in the music of J. S. Bach and Mozart, easily audible tempo changes are seldom necessary. Exceptions to this rule of course exist: in the music of Bach free rhythm is demanded, for example, in toccatas, fantasies, concertos, *recitativo* passages, and elsewhere. But they are nearly always indicated when desired. Bach explicitly prescribed such tempo changes, for example, in the first movement of the Violin Concerto in E major BWV 1042. Elsewhere, especially toward the end of pieces, a ritardando may have found his approval, and may be added even in the absence of an explicit indication. Likewise, there are several places in Mozart's concerti where a slight tempo change seems unavoidable or appropriate. But Mozart usually indicated any intended tempo change, and then may have changed the meter as well. We find such an instruction in the third movement of the Concerto in E-flat major K.482: the rondo marked *allegro* contains an episode marked *allegretto*. On the other hand, in the *Romanze* of the Concerto in D minor K.466, such indications are missing. Nearly every performer is tempted to play the main subject relatively slowly and the G-minor section somewhat faster. However, on January 4, 1786, Leopold Mozart wrote the following about this movement to his daughter: "I am sending you herewith a concerto. . . . [In the] Romance, the tempo is to be taken at the speed in which the noisy passage with the fast triplets just at the beginning of the third page of the Romance can be executed, and these must be properly practiced so that the theme is not too lifeless. In the same way the tempo of the first Allegro must be taken according to the fast passages." With this instruction, Leopold, who had heard his son perform the concerto in Vienna, makes clear that the basic tempo should not be altered, the intended tempo impression being written out in Mozart's notation. In Mozart's piano sonatas, too, there is rarely any reason to change the basic tempo audibly. Exceptions are those places where Mozart himself indicated such a change with a fermata sign.[20] In contrast to Mozart, there are rather many opportunities for slight ritardandos and accelerandos in the keyboard music of Haydn and Beethoven, though the general warning should be added that easily audible tempo changes, unless explicitly indicated, can be disturbing in Classical music.

The idiomatic style of a great performer, both in our time and in former centuries, has often been characterized by a less-than-strict observance of a steady rhythm. Indeed, such expressive freedom influences the taste and expectation of audiences. This was obviously true during the nineteenth century—for instance, in the case of Franz Liszt. During the seventeenth century Frescobaldi and his pupil Froberger were similarly influential keyboard players. In the eighteenth century C. P. E. Bach is supposed to have played his fantasies in a rhetorical, expressive, and liberal style. Only those who had actually heard him play his fantasies—or so it was said—could grasp his greatness.

With respect to rhythm and tempo the prevailing taste in the various parts of Europe apparently changed significantly after 1700, 1740, and again after 1780. After 1700 the preference, at least in Germany, seems to have changed in favor of stricter rhythmic discipline. Muffat (quite unlike the Italianized Froberger, but rather like Mozart) demanded that the tempo should not be changed within a piece. This attitude may have reflected the French-inspired classicism of the age of Louis XIV and may also have influenced the aesthetic outlook of the young J. S. Bach. Bach seldom wrote in fantasy style—the normal vehicle at the time for free rhythm and tempo. (The Chromatic Fantasy is one of the famous exceptions to this rule.) Bach's preference for strict forms—canons, fugues, Italian da-capo arias, and dance movements—points to a steady tempo, though a stiff or pedantic manner of performance should never be permitted.

The custom of *notes inégales*—the practice of French Baroque composers such as Couperin and Rameau of shortening the second of two notes in the proportions of 2 : 1, or 3 : 1, or in all possible proportions even up to 7 : 1—has been revived in our time. This performance habit was so widespread in France that in 1701 Marin Marais added the words *notes égales* or introduced signs (specifically, dots above the notes) whenever he wanted to avoid *inégalité*.

Although there is no question of the validity of *notes inégales* in the performance of French music, the discovery of the tradition at the beginning of the 20th century led to an overestimation of its use outside of France. Some German theorists who had been in France, such as Muffat and Quantz, described the practice; but its appropriateness for the works of German composers in general—and for J. S. Bach in particular—is sometimes disputable, and in most cases probably wrong. Italy exerted a much stronger influence on the musical life of Thuringia and Saxony than did France (but see chapter 4).

Like *notes inégales,* the "overdotting" of dotted figures is also of French origin. It is usually connected with the majestic style of the *ouverture* as performed at court festivities. The notation of double dots did not come into use prior to the middle of the eighteenth century. This historical fact explains why previously a single dot could have various meanings, depending on the context. Overdotting in the modern sense could only be notated correctly by means of an additive method, one employed on rare occasions by Bach, for instance at the end of the Allemande of the Partita in C minor, where he notated as in Example 2.7a rather than as in Example 2.7b.

EXAMPLE 2.7a. J. S. Bach: Partita in C Minor BWV 826. Allemande, mm. 31–32

EXAMPLE 2.7b.

That Bach felt it necessary to resort to such a notation here suggests that overdotting was not always intended by him. Overdotting, however, was practiced in Germany whenever performers wanted to imitate the majestic style of a French ouverture. Therefore it is more than likely that the opening movement of Bach's C-minor Partita needs a sharper rhythm than notated, since it is clearly in a French ouverture style (despite its Italian title, *Sinfonia*) (Ex. 2.8).

EXAMPLE 2.8. J. S. Bach: Partita No. 2 in C Minor BWV 826. Sinfonia. The circled notes should be played as thirty-seconds.

(continued)

EXAMPLE 2.8. (*continued*)

Ornaments

In his famous treatise C. P. E. Bach distinguished those ornaments indicated by symbols, which he called *wesentliche Manieren* ("essential graces"), from the unwritten, or improvised ornaments, which he called *willkürliche Manieren* ("arbitrary graces"). With respect to the former: French harpsichord music, in particular, poses relatively few problems, since numerous composers—among them, Jean-Henri D'Anglebert and François Couperin—published elaborate tables of ornaments indicating their execution. The most complete table of Couperin's ornament signs appears in the *Troisième livre de pièces de clavecin;* a shorter table is printed in the *Premier livre* and reprinted again in the *Deuxième livre.* (See chapter 4, Ill. 4.1 and 4.2.) These tables, like the French *agréments* in general, have been discussed in detail so often that it is unnecessary to review them again here.[21] More interesting for our purposes is J. S. Bach's opinion of Couperin, as related by his first biographer, Johann Nikolaus Forkel, for it vividly reveals Bach's independence in musical questions, including ornamentation: "Bach was acquainted with Couperin's works and esteemed them. But on the one hand he considered them as too affected in their frequent use of graces which goes so far that scarcely a note is free from embellishment. Besides, the ideas they contain were too flimsy for him."[22]

Bach, it is true, once copied D'Anglebert's ornament table, as published in his *Pièces de clavecin* (Paris, 1689). But this fact should not lead to the conclusion that Bach's ornament symbols invariably had the same meaning as they had in France. Bach's only authentic ornament table, the famous *Explication* written for his young son Wilhelm Friedemann (Ill. 2.2), is both incomplete and in various ways different from the table of D'Anglebert (Ill. 2.3), for example, in the nomenclature, which is not French but rather Italian and German.

In order to understand how a composer intended an ornament to be interpreted it is helpful if one can discover a parallel or corresponding passage in which the same ornament is written out in full. By so doing one can prove, for example, that Bach sometimes intended his short trills (*Pralltriller*) to be played with just three notes rather than the usual four. Among harpsichordists the execution of the *Pralltriller* with four notes was—until recently—one of those commonly accepted and

ILLUSTRATION 2.2. J. S. Bach: Ornament Table from the *Clavier-büchlein vor Wilhelm Friedemann Bach*, 1720. Yale University Library, New Haven.

ILLUSTRATION 2.3. Ornament Table from Jean Henri d'Anglebert, *Pièces de Clavecin,* as copied by J. S. Bach, ca. 1709/12. Stadt- und Universitätsbibliothek, Frankfurt am Main: *Mus. Hs. 1538.*

compulsory "rules" that was followed blindly (better: with closed ears). A musical ear, however, will readily determine whether, for example, the shape of the subject in Bach's two-part Invention in C major dictates that the *Pralltriller* should be played with three notes instead of four. The latter would demand a tone repetition that would disturb the melodic line and separate the eighth-notes that should belong together.

In Haydn's keyboard sonatas the *Pralltriller*, in almost all cases, are clearly intended to be played with only three notes. This is quite obvious, for example, in the second bar of Haydn's Piano Sonata in A-flat Hob. XVI/46 (Ex. 2.9a)[23]; for its execution as explained by C. P. E. Bach, see Ex. 2.9b.

EXAMPLE 2.9a. Haydn: Sonata in A-flat Hob. XVI/46. Movement 1, opening

EXAMPLE 2.9b.

Mozart made practically no use of the *Pralltriller* sign; he wrote **tr** instead. But his trill signs could have many more than one meaning.[24] In fast tempi one might even consider replacing a *Pralltriller* or a trill with a single-note appoggiatura, since the tempo often does not allow more notes. Such an execution is reasonable, for instance, in the main theme of the first movement of the Piano Concerto in G K.453, since it is important for the listener to notice that the first ornament is associated with a dotted figure. An ornament should always be an *abbellimento*. An execution as a very fast three-note *Pralltriller* will, if played properly (!), sound best here (Ex. 2.10).

EXAMPLE 2.10a. Mozart: Piano Concerto in G K. 453. Movement 1, opening

EXAMPLE 2.10b. Best Execution

Another indication that Mozart's *tr* sign can have different meanings is found in m. 12 of the second movement of the famous A-minor Sonata K.310 (Ex. 2.11).

EXAMPLE 2.11. Mozart: Sonata in A minor, K. 310. Movement 2, m. 12

The first **tr** might be executed as a *Pralltriller* with three notes, the second and third **tr** sound best if played as short appoggiaturas. A nearly identical passage at the end of the second movement in Mozart's Piano Sonata for Four Hands K.521, suggests the same kind of interpretation.

The common assumption that during the eighteenth century *all* trills began with the upper auxiliary note is based on quotations from North German treatises. Unfortunately, the North German theorists attempted to squeeze into rigid rules what Italian musicians were playing in a variety of ways—according to logic, convenience, and musical intuition. Vienna, for its part, was closer to Italy, both geographically and culturally, than to any Prussian city. And in Italy we find for instance, in Vincenzo Manfredini's treatise, *Regole Armoniche . . . per apprendere i Principii della Musica* (Venice, 1775), as the only explanation of the trill the following example (Ill. 2.4). This is not to dispute the common understanding that in the eighteenth century trills normally started on the

ILLUSTRATION 2.4. Realization of the trill according to Vincenzo Manfredini, *Regole Armoniche* (Venice, 1775).

upper auxiliary; but it is important to realize that many did not. In any event, unless there is an indication to the contrary, trills over notes in a descending scale should start on the main note.

Joseph Haydn's rather personal use of ornamentation signs, and the many meanings the same sign could have, is shown in his manuscript of the B-minor sonata Hob. XVI/32, where we find the following notation (Ex. 2.12).

EXAMPLE 2.12a. J. Haydn: Sonata in B minor, Hob. XVI/32

EXAMPLE 2.12b. Execution

In this case the so-called "Haydn ornament"   ∾   was possibly intended to have the same meaning as the written-out mordents in the previous bar.

Improvised Embellishments

In many works of the seventeenth and eighteenth centuries it is impossible to draw a clear distinction between composition and improvisation. Composers performed regularly, and performers nearly always composed. Vocalists and instrumentalists alike had to learn at the very beginning of their studies how to realize a figured bass and accompany a melody on the harpsichord; and organists seeking employment were supposed to improvise preludes and fantasies, making use of polyphonic devices. Every professional keyboard player acquired the ability to embellish simple melodies. Moreover he had usually developed early in his career an individual repertoire of *passaggii:* that is, a personal collection of melodic motives, figures, scales, arpeggios, runs, and trills, along with those ornaments that were most suited to his fingers and with which he was able to impress his audience. This repertory enabled him to improvise toccatas, preludes, capriccios, and fantasies; to invent embellished versions when repeating certain melodies or pieces; to vary common melodic figures such as triadic motifs or certain sequences; and to insert ad hoc shorter or longer improvisations at fermatas. Contemporary reports refer to the individual styles of great performers. Virtuosos were normally expected to establish a personal performance style, a *manner* of embellishing that could serve as a kind of trademark to distinguish them from their rivals. Repeated use of the same embellishments was sometimes criticized—especially when the performer failed to impress his audience in any other way. But so long as his imagination led him to vary details and avoid monotony, an idiomatic and judicious application of embellishments was apparently appreciated by most listeners. It is noteworthy that in the eighteenth century this *manner* or *method, taste, gusto,* or *goût* conceived of ornamentation in the broadest sense, so that it embraced not only rhythmic modifications such as rubato but also changes in articulation and dynamic shadings. Anything that enhanced the expression and impressed an audience seems to have been permitted in performances of music influenced by Italian *gusto*. As a consequence some Italian composers relied heavily (sometimes perhaps too heavily) on their performers and wrote down comparatively little. On the other hand, some performers took incredible liberties that were often disliked by the more competent and critical listeners. Contemporary reports contain complaints about both extremes.

We may distinguish three kinds of added notes or embellishments: those that are necessary because of incomplete notation; those that are permissible and a matter of taste; and finally, those that are tasteless, superfluous, or stylistically inappropriate. To the first group belong all additions needed to fill in various kinds of "shorthand writing," to which belong abbreviations such as figured bass numbers or da capo indications. Where numerous unaltered repetitions of a melody were written down by the composer, the performer was probably also expected to improvise little variations. Finally, fermata embellishments and cadenzas gave performers the opportunity to display their personal creativity.

To the second group of embellishments belong those additions by means of which a performer can "beautify" a simple melody. Uninteresting pieces by minor composers gain considerably when played by a fine performer capable of adding elaborate embellishments. But it is certainly dangerous to try to "beautify" a piece by one of the great composers. Small ornaments might sometimes be added in a J. S. Bach prelude, but it seems impossible to improve the quality of a Scarlatti sonata with additions. In Joseph Haydn's early sonatas the insertion of a short cadenza seems to be appropriate at a few fermatas (e.g., in the A-flat-major Sonata Hob. XVI/46). In general, however, it is seldom possible to add ornaments convincingly and with good effect in the sonatas of Haydn and Mozart, and nearly always unnecessary.[25] As for Beethoven, we know that he became furious when he heard Czerny embellish the piano part of his Quintet op.16, and when he learned that Nägeli printed some additional notes in one of his sonatas. The great Classical composers apparently did not trust the taste of their performers and decided to write down practically everything. J. S. Bach and Mozart, in fact, were accused by their critics of writing too many notes and leaving too little to the discretion of the performers.

Like every composer-performer, Mozart, too, developed a personal *manner* of embellishing his melodies and possessed a repertory of runs, scales, and trills that he often used in his cadenzas. An analysis of his ornamented versions of the adagio variation from the Sonata K.284, of the slow movements of the sonatas K.332 and K.457, and of his own concerto cadenzas and fermata embellishments enables us to reconstruct this repertory, at least in part, and thus to learn something about his style or *gusto*. A performer can then learn to add embellishments at the relevant fermatas or to vary a melodic line more or less in accordance with Mozart's own style. In contrast to most of the fermatas in Mozart's sonatas, practically every fermata sign over a note (not a rest!) in his concertos is an invitation for the soloist to invent a shorter or longer embellishment.[26] This fact is still unknown to many performers. A case in point is to be found in the second movement of the Piano Concerto in G major K.453. Hardly any performer dares to ornament the notes under the fermata signs in mm. 33 and 93. The orchestra understandably has no fermata sign on the corresponding notes in mm. 4 and 67. But when the pianist plays the same theme, we find fermata signs— clearly an invitation to the soloist to enrich the melodic lines. It makes little sense, then, for the soloist simply to prolong these notes as the orchestra does. Paul Badura-Skoda suggests the following embellishments (Ex. 2.13).

EXAMPLE 2.13. Mozart: Piano Concerto in G Major K.453. Movement 2, mm. 33 and 93, as performed by Paul Badura-Skoda

Of course, not all "improvisations" were in fact improvised. In his autobiography Karl Ditters von Dittersdorf confesses that he once secured the success of a new violin concerto by having prepared in advance a brilliantly varied repetition of the finale, counting on the audience's demand for an encore. It was demanded and he played the well-prepared "improvisation." As a result, he was considered a great improviser. Mozart, in one of his letters from Paris, reported a similar event. However, in view of Mozart's incessant activities in Vienna, we may assume that in his mature years he seldom had the time to prepare alternate versions. He reports in a letter of January 22, 1783: "I have not yet changed the *Eingänge* (lead-ins) in the Rondo [of the Concerto in E-flat K.271] because when I play the concerto I always do what comes to my mind."

In a certain sense, performances of all times involve an element of improvisation. But the eighteenth century expected more from a performer than just the more or less tiny rhythmic adjustments and dynamic shadings with which we grew up in the twentieth century. The addition of ornaments and embellishments was both accepted and expected. Slow movements, in particular, were expected to be quite lavishly embellished with passagework prepared in advance or improvised by the performer. Occasionally, compositions were published with both an unornamented and an embellished version of the melodic line, as in the following Adagio from a sonata by Pietro Nardini, published around 1760 (1765?) in Venice, reprinted by Cartier in 1798 (Ex. 2.14).[27]

EXAMPLE 2.14. P. Nardini: Sonata No. 1 in B-flat for Violin and Bass. Opening of Movement 1, with published embellishments. Paris: Cartier, 1798.

(continued)

EXAMPLE 2.14. (*continued*)

Mozart, we are informed, added some embellishments in the slow movements when he performed his own concertos. But we can observe the restraint with which he ornamented his original melodic lines from the embellished versions of his sonatas K.284, 332, and 457. At the other extreme, an example of the degree to which some instrumentalists increased the number and density of embellishments in the course of the eighteenth century is dramatically demonstrated by a chart, published in a late eighteenth-century reprint of Giuseppe Tartini's *L'Arte del arco,* showing seventeen different ways of playing an Adagio.[28]

When Tartini reached an older age, however, he completely changed his attitude toward such elaborate embellishment. A Swiss traveler who became Tartini's friend in Padua shortly before 1760 wrote the following report in his diary:[29]

> In his youth he [the famous violinist Tartini] had believed that beauty consisted of difficulty but he found he was wrong. He then threw himself into a highly ornamented style. A long time later, having found that he had erred again, he was truly puzzled for some time. There remained nothing but to try the very simple and unified style, but this did not seem to him to be capable of sustaining his reputation. Finally, he undertook to try it [the very simple style] in earnest. He perceived immediately that not only was true beauty and good taste to be found here, but also that this simplicity, this unity was deceptive; that it was even more difficult than all other styles. . . .
>
> He realized that when he had played very difficult pieces, the compositional defects were overlooked because of the difficulty; everyone considered him a great violinist, but he pleased very few [connoisseurs] or perhaps no one. In contrast to him, some musicians, without playing very difficult things, loaded their pieces with ornaments in such a way that they obscured the subject with so many embellishments that no one knew what was said. He compared such musicians to those authors who fill their writings with so many parentheses that the meaning of the text is lost. . . . In the end [he said] I am convinced that the only and true good taste is a simple and clear sound.

Authenticity and "Original" Sound

In debates about modern interpretations of eighteenth-century music, the issue often boils down to whether performers and their critics are confusing *Werktreue* (a faithful rendition of the work) with *Buchstabentreue* (a literal adherence to the text): and whether, in turn, the freedom that was permitted an eighteenth-century musician is curtailed today by adhering pedantically to rules postulated in theoretical treatises. It does not seem that our historical knowledge sufficiently addresses the complex interrelationships among local, period, and personal styles. In short, the debate raises the question whether a performer is primarily concerned about artistic quality or with the realization of academic theories. In any case, in his quest for authenticity a gifted and responsible performer must be able to distinguish between the letter and the sense of a musical text, and he will often have to rely on his artistically trained ear.

These considerations clearly affect the choice of instrument. It may well be desirable, and appropriate, under certain circumstances, to make use of a period instrument. On other occasions, however, it may be out of place. In a large auditorium, for example, the sound of a Silbermann or Stein fortepiano will simply not be loud enough to fill the hall: a modern piano is called for. But a good fortepianist who plays a Mozart or a Haydn sonata on a modern piano will nevertheless bring to his performance a "historically informed" rendition: the inevitable fruits of his experience with the fortepiano. For example, he will understand the need for lively articulation as well as a not-too-slow tempo and will incorporate this insight into his performance regardless of the momentary circumstances.

But the dilemma of authenticity involves yet another factor besides concert halls: namely, concert audiences. Even if we were able to reconstruct fully the acoustic conditions of eighteenth-century music we would still not be able to determine how differently audiences at the time of Haydn and Mozart responded to what they heard, compared with the response of modern audiences. Owing to certain inescapable facts of modern life performances of early music today are probably doomed never to be able to attract large audiences: for example, we are accustomed to a more hectic and presumably louder lifestyle, and concert halls, for purely economic reasons, have had to increase in size. Despite these unavoidable practical limitations to the complete attainment of historical "authenticity" in modern performance, old prejudices surrounding the revival of historic keyboard instruments have gradually been overcome.[30] Moreover, enlightened musicians today recognize that the best keyboard instruments from the age of Bach, Haydn, and Mozart—those built by Cristofori, Mietke, Hass, Silbermann, or the concert grands built by Gottfried Silbermann, J. A. Stein, Walter, Schantz, or Broadwood—are just as surely masterpieces as are the great violins of Amati, Stradivari, Guarneri, or Stainer—but, of course, only if they have been well restored and are sounding at their best.

To play early "hammer-harpsichords" (as pianos continued to be called as late as the 1780s) modern pianists must adopt a light-hand playing technique appropriate to the delicate eighteenth-century instrument. The lack of the appropriate technique may be the main reason why a recital on a fortepiano is not always an unqualified pleasure: the heavy modern piano touch leads to pounding. Curiously, modern harpsichordists and organists sometimes have more difficulty getting early fortepianos to sound well than do pianists. Evidently they have not practiced enough to master the touch needed for the proper treatment of the delicate instrument. This, in fact, was certainly the problem in the eighteenth century, too—one that proved to be the main stumbling block initially hindering the quick acceptance and triumphant progress of the fortepiano.

Until recently, museum instruments had often been imperfectly restored, and the resulting sound quality left much to be desired. In this connection the late director of the Instrument Collection of the Kunsthistorisches Museum in Vienna, Victor Luithlen, deserves special praise. During the 1950s Luithlen pioneered the effort to restore early keyboard instruments to their erstwhile perfection with the intention of making them not only playable but well-sounding. He understood that, just as in the case of violins, the wood of a keyboard instrument that has not been played for many years needs to become reaccustomed to sustaining vibrations—a process requiring time. Although the tone after a restoration is often disappointing at first, it gradually improves with use. Understandably, the prospect of protracted practice sessions on original instruments worries curators; but, properly played, an instrument will actually benefit from (reasonably limited) use. Luithlen understood this.

On the other hand, the argument made by some curators against restoration is certainly understandable. Apart from the risks attending any restoration effort, a number of historically valuable instruments should remain unrestored to enable future generations to study them, so to speak, in their "original state"—that is, with their original materials (though today they are anyway not absolutely in their original condition: materials such as wood and leather change with age). Many a well-meant restoration, particularly those undertaken prior to the last world war, resulted in the near or total destruction of authentic materials.

Early Use of the *Cembalo con martelli*

Of the leading keyboard composers of the eighteenth century—François Couperin, Domenico Scarlatti, J. S. Bach, Bach's sons, Haydn, Mozart, the young Beethoven—Couperin was presumably the only one not well acquainted with the *cembali con martelli* of Cristofori or Silbermann, their imitators, and successors. The other masters knew and played not only harpsichords and clavichords but *Hammerflügel* as well. This assertion clearly carries enormous implications for our understanding of eighteenth-century keyboard performance; accordingly, it is necessary to substantiate it at this juncture.

In 1702 the then seventeen-year-old Domenico Scarlatti arrived with his famous father at the court of the Medici at Florence. At the time he was already an accomplished harpsichordist and had been appointed organist at Naples. In Florence Domenico must have played one of the first of Bartolomeo Cristofori's *cembali che fa il piano e il forte*. He seems to have taken at least one of them with him to Lisbon in 1719, for the Tuscan composer Lodovico Giustini dedicated his set of sonatas—the first known keyboard works written expressly for the piano—to Scarlatti's royal student and patron in Lisbon, Don Antonio di Portogallo. Moreover, a piano-building tradition has recently been traced in Portugal.[31] Later on, in Spain, Scarlatti must have played both types of harpsichord: those with quills and those with hammers. In any event his pupil from Lisbon days and later his patron, the Portuguese Princess Maria Barbara, who eventually became Queen of Spain, bought five hammer-harpsichords in the course of her life.[32] Unfortunately, we have practically no information about Scarlatti's own instruments; but it seems safe to assume that he himself owned a "harpsichord with hammers," too.[33]

The *Hammerflügel* also played a greater role in the life of Johann Sebastian Bach than has hitherto been recognized.[34] We now know that the famous organ builder Gottfried Silbermann experimented with tangent and hammer actions from the turn of the century on, and we can reasonably assume that he constructed movable keyboards for *Pantalone* instruments. Later, at the same time that he built his first instruments with hammer actions modeled after Cristofori, he may already have installed a mechanism to lift all the dampers—a device lacking on Cristofori's pianos.[35] According to Zedler's *Universal-Lexicon* (1733), it was Gottfried Silbermann who gave the new *Hammerflügel* the name *Piano-Fort[e]*, though in later years he adopted the more cumbersome locution *instrument: piano et forte genannt.*[36] By 1732, at the latest, Silbermann had built such *Hammerflügel*, and it seems that he showed one to J. S. Bach and succeeded in obtaining the composer's full approval. In June 1733 a local Leipzig newspaper reported that at an upcoming concert of J. S. Bach's *Collegium musicum* one would hear "a new Clavicymbel, the likes of which have never yet been heard here."[37] This is most probably a reference to Silbermann's new pianoforte. It is possible that Bach acquired such a Silbermann piano in later years; and it is even conceivable that a two-manual compound instrument combining a *Kielflügel* with a *Hammerflügel* was ultimately in Bach's possession. Such instruments were sold in Leipzig from the 1730s on. They were also built in Italy, by Cristofori himself and by his pupil Giovanni Ferrini, among others.[38] Research into the use of compound instruments has only recently begun.[39]

Cristofori's invention obviously became known in Vienna at an early date. An announcement in the *Wiennerisches Diarium* in 1725 advertised *Flügel mit und ohne Kiele*—that is *Kielfügel* and *Hammerflügel* (harpsichords with quills and harpsichords with hammers). It was worded in a way that suggests that potential purchasers knew the difference between the two types in 1725. A recent discovery confirms this assumption.[40] The terms *pianoforte* or *fortepiano*, however, were certainly unknown in Austria at this time. The new instrument was still called *cembalo* or *clavecin*—sometimes, but not always, with attributes such as *con martelli* or *à maillet*.

We may conclude, then, that *claviere* with hammer mechanisms were known in the Imperial city during the first half of the eighteenth century. Joseph Haydn, therefore, could have encountered a *Hammerklavier* when still a child, as early as the 1740s or 1750s. He surely could not have owned such an expensive, delicate instrument in his student days, however, but rather would have practiced on an inexpensive clavichord. Moreover, at Eisenstadt he may not have had a *Hammerflügel* at his disposal before the late 1760s. In 1773, however, he was seen playing a fortepiano in Esterhaza.[41] This instrument may have been acquired by Prince Esterhazy shortly after the new castle, Esterhaza, was built and furnished in 1768. Therefore, Haydn's large-scale piano sonata in C-minor Hob. XVI/20, composed in 1771, was very likely inspired by the prospect of playing it on a new fortepiano grand. (Some of Haydn's earlier piano sonatas, too—for example, the Sonata in G Major Hob. XVI/6—sound better on a fortepiano than on a normal harpsichord.) His sonatas of the 1780s and 1790s are doubtless all intended to be played on fortepianos only. Haydn was explicit about this—as he was about his predilection for the Viennese fortepiano instruments of the brothers Schantz.

As for Mozart, practically all scholars concur that he composed his keyboard works for *Hammerflügel*, not for *Kielflügel*. We have reason to assume that Leopold Mozart made sure early on that both his children, Nannerl and Wolfgang, learned to play all the stringed keyboard instruments available at the time: clavichord, harpsichord, and piano; and Wolfgang also learned to play the organ. Later in Vienna, probably in the year 1782, Mozart acquired a fortepiano made by Anton Walter, a master instrument, which he afterward reinforced with a *fortepiano pedale*, a separate instrument placed underneath the *Hammerflügel*. The pedal keyboard probably had a range of two octaves. As we can prove from a concert announcement dated March 1785, Mozart used it in performances of free fantasies; he may also have called for it in his concertos. A trace of it is found in the autograph of the first movement of the Piano Concerto K.466 in D minor, mm. 88–90.[42]

The young Beethoven, finally, played pianos regularly and hardly ever used a harpsichord. In Bonn he had access to a Stein fortepiano; and in Vienna, before the turn of the century, he apparently preferred instruments by Anton Walter for his concert performances.

Good Execution: Music as Language and Rhetoric

Probably no eighteenth-century musician would have challenged the proposition that music expresses "something," that it is a language in its own right, a "language of sentiments," conveying certain feelings and concepts. The idea that the presentation of a speech has much in common with a musical performance is an old one. The eleventh chapter of Quantz's famous flute treatise entitled "Of Good Execution in General in Singing and Playing" (*Vom guten Vortrage im Singen und Spielen überhaupt*) begins with the following remarks:[43]

§ **1.** A musical performance may be compared with the delivery of an orator. The orator and the musician have, at bottom, the same aim in regard to both the preparation and the final execution of their productions, namely to make themselves masters of the hearts of their listeners, to arouse or still their passions, and to transport them now to this sentiment, now to that. Thus, it is advantageous to both if each has some knowledge of the duties of the other.

§ **2.** We know the effect in a lecture of good delivery upon the minds of the listeners; we also know how poor delivery injures the most beautifully written discourse; and we know again that a lecture delivered with the same words by two different persons will sound much better from one than from the other. The same is true of musical execution."

The validity of such a statement is certainly not restricted to the time of Quantz.

In the first part of the eighteenth century rhetoric was still a compulsory part of the *humaniora* studies taught at all Latin Schools and universities. Systematic studies of rhetoric comprised the invention, outline, and delivery of a discourse and discussed *Inventio, Dispositio* or *Elaboratio, Decoratio* or *Elocutio,* and *Pronuntiatio.* Only the last term was concerned with the delivery of the speech; the other terms referred to its outline and content. The most important books and treatises on rhetoric during the Baroque period were still based on writings from Classical antiquity, mainly on those of Quintilian. At the same time, Bach's younger contemporary Johann Christoph Gottsched was already famous in Germany for his books on rhetoric. Gottsched clearly influenced Mattheson; Quantz, too, was probably acquainted with Gottsched's writings, as was Leopold Mozart, who once asked his publisher in Augsburg to send him all the available books of Gottsched.[44] There is evidence that he instructed his son to rely on the famous rhetoric rules when composing and performing, and he probably shared Quantz's opinion that it is to the advantage of a musician to be acquainted with the *Ars rhetorica:*

§ **7.** . . . Now music is nothing but an artificial language through which we seek to acquaint the listeners with our musical ideas. If we execute these ideas in an obscure and bizarre manner which is incomprehensible to the listeners and arouses no feeling, of what use are our perpetual efforts to be thought learned?

Although not every poetic text was suitable for musical setting, the presence of a text in vocal music renders the content of a "musical speech" understandable. Precisely because comprehensive sentiments and ideas could not be equally clearly expressed in instrumental works, philosophers and theoreticians had long insisted on the supremacy of vocal music over instrumental music. The validity of this notion diminished toward the end of the century in the wake of the Enlightenment and changing aesthetic attitudes. Romantic ideas, for example, favored instrumental music, this time owing to the ambiguity of the sentiments aroused.

Quantz goes on in his Chapter on "Good Execution" to list the qualities necessary to be a good musician:

> § **10.** Good execution must be first of all true and distinct. Not only must each note be heard, but each note must be sounded with its true intonation, so that all will be intelligible to the listener. . . . You must try to make each sound as beautiful as possible. . . .
>
> § **13.** Execution . . . must be easy and flowing. . . .
>
> § **14.** No less must good execution be varied. Light and shadow must be constantly maintained. . . .
>
> § **15.** Finally, good execution must be expressive, and appropriate to each passion that one encounters. . . .

Conservative theorists in the eighteenth century often demanded that an instrumental work be governed by only one basic *affect* or passion—a rule that made sense particularly in connection with dance music. In general, the eighteenth-century *Affektenlehre* probably had a greater impact on North- and Central German musicians than on those living in the Catholic South or in Italy. As late as 1785 Ernst Wilhelm Wolff (1735–1790), Capellmeister to the Duke of Sachsen-Weimar, composed and published *Vier affectvolle Sonaten fürs Klavier*. At that time such a title for a keyboard work was hardly used south of the Danube, where, under the influence of Enlightenment individualism and rationalism, the attitude toward the affections had already begun to change during the 1740s. In the realm of music it was mainly the persuasiveness of *opera buffa* that led to a psychologically more realistic understanding of the function of the affections. Composers and performers adopted a more subjective, more "natural" attitude toward their creativity; and contrasting emotions were increasingly incorporated in a single piece of music. Quantz, the cosmopolitan mentor of Frederick II, demanded that performers carefully observe such changes:

> § **15.** The performer of a piece must seek to enter into the principal and related affections that he is to express. And since in the majority of pieces one passion constantly alternates with an-

other, the performer must know how to judge the nature of the passion that each idea contains, and constantly make his execution conform to it. . . .

As to how a musician was to grasp the meaning of the "language" of instrumental music, Quantz explains:

§ **16.** You can usually, if not always, perceive the dominant sentiment of a piece and in consequence how it should be performed. . . . (1) . . . Generally a major key is used for the expression of what is gay, bold, serious, and sublime, and a minor one for the expression of the flattering, melancholy, and tender. . . . This rule has its exceptions, however; thus you must also consider the following characteristics. The passion may be discerned by (2) whether the intervals between the notes are great or small, and whether the notes themselves ought to be slurred or articulated. Flattery, melancholy, and tenderness are expressed by slurred and close intervals, gaiety and boldness by brief articulated notes, or those forming distant leaps, as well as by figures in which dots appear regularly after the second note. Dotted and sustained notes express the serious and the pathetic; long notes . . . intermingled with quick ones express the majestic and sublime. (3) The passions may be perceived from the dissonances. These are not all the same; they always produce a variety of different effects. . . . This knowledge is indispensable not only to accompanists, but to all performers . . . (4) The fourth indication of the dominant sentiment is the word found at the beginning of each piece, such as Allegro, Allegro non tanto,—assai,—di molto. . . . In addition . . . each piece . . . may have in it diverse mixtures of pathetic, flattering, gay, majestic, or jocular ideas. Hence, you must, so to speak, adopt a different sentiment at each bar, so that you can imagine yourself now melancholy, now gay, now serious, etc. Such dissembling is most necessary in music. . . . One should not imagine, however, that this fine discrimination can be acquired in a short time. . . . It comes only with the growth of feeling and judgment.

Notes

1. Johann Mattheson, *Der vollkommene Capellmeister*, Hamburg, 1739 (facsimile edition, [Kassel, 1954], 484.)
2. See Eva Badura-Skoda, "Textual Problems in Masterpieces of the 18th and 19th Century," *The Musical Quarterly* 51 (1965): 301ff.

3. In those rare cases where the composer's ultimate version of a work is not the best version, it may be preferable to reproduce an earlier version. Editors of works by C. P. E. Bach and Schumann have occasionally reached this conclusion. These two composers constantly altered their works and sometimes returned to earlier versions after various attempts to solve a compositional problem. Re: C. P. E. Bach, see chapter 6.

4. Joseph Haydn, Sonata in E-flat Major, ed. Paul Badura-Skoda, *Diletto musicale* 168, (Vienna, 1958).

5. Joseph Haydn, *Haydns Klaviersonaten*, ed. Christa Landon, *Wiener Urtext-Ausgabe* (Vienna, 1966). The asterisks refer to footnotes that reproduce Haydn's original notation.

6. *Joseph Haydn Werke*, XVIII/3: *Klaviersonaten*, ed. Georg Feder (Henle-Verlag, Munich, 1966).

7. See also Max Rudolf, "Good Taste in Music and Related Matters," *Journal of the Conductor's Guild* 11 (1990): 2f.

8. See Rudolf Elvers, "Untersuchungen zu den Tempi in Mozarts Instrumentalmusik," Ph.D. dissertation (Free University of Berlin, 1953).

9. See the studies on this topic by David Fuller listed in the bibliography at the end of this chapter.

10. Robert L. Marshall has shown that Bach's *tempo giusto* or *tempo ordinario* was equivalent to an allegro. See his "Tempo and Dynamics: The Original Terminology," in Marshall 1989, 265.

11. Leopold Mozart, *Versuch einer gründlichen Violinschule* (Augsburg, 1756), Chapter I, Section 2, § 7, translation by Leo Black, quoted after Eva and Paul Badura-Skoda (1962), 9.

12. In connection with Mozart see the excellent book by Jean-Pierre Marty, *The Tempo Indications of Mozart* (New Haven, 1988).

13. See Wye J. Allanbrook and Wendy Hilton, "Dance rhythms in Mozart's arias," *Early Music* 20 (1992): 142–43.

14. Contemporary discussions of the meaning of the various tempo indications can be read in the treatises of Quantz and others. For modern discussions see inter alia the studies by Irmgard Hermann-Bengen, Eva and Paul Badura-Skoda, Robert L. Marshall, Jean-Pierre Marty, and Max Rudolf.

15. As the organizer of the 1982 International Joseph Haydn Congress in Vienna I tried to find suitable recordings of Haydn's *Menuetti ballabile* that could be used for a dance performance of minuets in historical costumes. The members of the *Danze Antiche-Ensemble*, directed by the dance historian Professor Eva Campianu, were all professional dancers of the Viennese *Staats-Opern Ballett*. In rehearsal tricots they could dance to the recorded minuet music; but as soon as the ladies put on rococo dresses all the recordings became useless: in all cases the tempi were too fast—and the robes hindered the ladies from making the proper turns in time. Thus, I was forced, in spite of my tight budget, to hire a small orchestra for the Redouten-Saal performance during the Haydn Congress.

16. Curt Sachs, Rhythm and Tempo (New York, 1953), 286. Uri Toeplitz quoted this passage in a paper delivered in 1991 at the London Mozart Conference of the Royal Music Association. Hemiolas were well known in dance movements of the time.

17. See Marshall, "Tempo and Dynamics," 266.

18. See § 26 of Der Vollkommene Capellmeister, 173.

19. Letter to his father dated 23 October 1777. Nannette was the daughter of the famous Augsburg piano maker Johann Andreas Stein.

20. Fermata signs had a number of different meanings in eighteenth-century music. See p. 53.

21. A recent large-scale discussion of French and German ornaments can be found in Neumann 1978 and Paul Badura-Skoda 1992. For the interpretation of Mozart's ornaments see Eva and Paul Badura-Skoda 1962 and Neumann 1986. See also Paul Badura-Skoda, "Mozart's Trills," in *Perspectives on Mozart Performance*, ed. Larry Todd and Peter Williams (Cambridge, 1991), 1–26, and relevant titles in the Bibliography.

22. Translation quoted after *The New Bach Reader: A Life of Johann Sebastian Bach in Letters and Documents*. Ed. Hans David and Arthur Mendel; rev. and enlarged by Christoph Wolff. New York, 1998, 434 (modified).

23. For an explanation of the proper execution of all ornaments in this sonata as well as in the sonatas in G major Hob. XVI/6, in C minor Hob XVI/20, and in F major Hob. XVI/23, see *Haydn, 4 Sonatas*, ed. Paul Badura-Skoda (Paris, 1982).

24. See Paul Badura-Skoda, "Mozart's Trills," 19.

25. Eva Badura-Skoda, "Über die Anbringung von Auszierungen in den Klavierwerken Mozarts," *Mozart-Jahrbuch 1957* and "Über nötige und unnötige Auszierungen in Mozarts Klavierwerken," *Kongreßbericht zum VII. Internationalen Gewandhaus-Symposium anläßlich der Gewandhaus-Festtage 1991*, 47–48.

26. In the revised edition of *Interpreting Mozart on the Keyboard* by Eva and Paul Badura-Skoda (in preparation) a list of all fermatas in Mozart's keyboard works that need to be embellished will be printed.

27. Cartier's print of Pietro Nardini's *VII SONATES POUR VIOLON ET BASSE par P. Nardini avec les Adagio Brodes. DERNIERE EDITION d'après les Manuscripts Originaux de l'Auteur* evidently appeared in 1798 and was reprinted in his treatise *L'ART DU VIOLON* of 1803.

28. See the reproduction in Hans-Peter Schmitz, *Die Kunst der Verzierung im 18.Jahrhundert* (Kassel, 1955), 131 (Beilage IIf).

29. This citation is part of the diary of a young Swiss art and music lover, Achilles Ryhiner of Basle (1731–1788), who made a two-year tour of Italy and France in the years 1758–1760. In his handwritten *Journal de voyage*, Ryhiner records the conversations he had with the great violinist during a three-week visit to Padua during the summer of 1758. See Martin Staehelin, "Giuseppe Tartini über seine künstlerische Entwicklung. Ein unbekanntes Selbstzeugnis," *Archiv für Musikwissenschaft* 35 (1978): 251–74. The present translation of the French document is by Rita Steblin.

30. I still recall the shock Paul Badura-Skoda created in 1955 when he requested permission from Westminster Recording Company to record Mozart's sonatas in the Viennese Kunsthistorisches Museum on an original Walter instrument. (The record appeared in 1956.)

31. See Stewart Pollens, "The early Portugese piano," *Early Music* 13 (1985): 18–27.

32. See Ralph Kirkpatrick, *Domenico Scarlatti* (Princeton, 1953), 178.

33. For a slightly different point of view, see chapter 5.

34. See Eva Badura-Skoda (1991), 159f.

35. Cristofori's pianos had dampers that could not be lifted. See Laurence Libin's discussion in this volume, chapter 1, pp. 18-20. Libin has also described early German square pianos, which were sometimes built without any dampers but had other coloristic devices, such as mute and harp stops. See Laurence Libin, "Early Pianos without Dampers," in *Atti del XIV Congresso della Società internazionale di Musicologia* (Bologna, 1990), 2: 287f.

36. That Silbermann invented this name as a noun is asserted in volume 5 of Zedler's *Universal-Lexicon*, at the end of the article on "Cembal d'amour."

37. Cited in Eva Badura-Skoda (1991), 163.

38. See Luigi Ferdinando Tagliavini, "Giovanni Ferrini and his harpsichord 'a penne e a martelletti,'" *Early Music* 19 (1991): 398-408.

39. See Eva Badura-Skoda (1994), (1998), also *The History of the Hammerflügel from Scarlatti to Chopin* (in press).

40. See Eva Badura-Skoda (1988), 37f.

41. See H.C. Robbins Landon, *Haydn: Chronicle and Works,* II: *Haydn at Eszterhaza 1766-1790* (Bloomington, IN, 1978), 343.

42. That Mozart did not write down any more notes for the pedal piano than those few found in these bars certainly had to do with his recognizing that he could not count on the availability of such a rare instrument. He probably found it useless—and for others perhaps even disturbing—to write notes that could not be realized on normal fortepianos.

43. The English translation of the Quantz quotations is taken—with very few alterations—from Johann Joachim Quantz, *on Playing the Flute*, trans. and ed. Edward R. Reilly (2nd ed., New York, 1985), 119-26, *passim.*

44. See Ellwood Derr, *Leopold Mozart, Wolfgang and Rhetoric: The Evidence of Application in Wolfgang's Viennese op. 2 (the so-called Aurnhammer-Sonatern.* In press.

Selected Bibliography

Note: Neither the well-known eighteenth-century treatises nor the large number of widely known older writings on the subject have been included, unless they are of special relevance.

Badura-Skoda, Eva. "Uber die Anbringung von Auszierungen in den Klavier-werken Mozarts." *Mozart-Jahrbuch 1957*: 186-98.

———. "Zur Fruhgeschichte des Hammerklaviers." In *Florilegium Musicolog-icum: Hellmut Federhofer zum 75. Geburtstag,* ed. Christoph-Hellmut Mahling. Tutzing, 1988, 37-44.

———. "Komponierte J.S. Bach 'Hammerklavier-Konzerte'?" *Bach-Jahrbuch 1991*: 159-71.

———. "Mozart and the Compound Piano." In *Musicologia Humana: Studies in Honor of Warren and Ursula Kirkendale,* ed. Siegfried Gmeinwieser, David Hiley, Jörg Riedbauer. Florence, 1994, 473-84.

———. "Vom Pedalcembalo zum Fortepiano pedale." *Cöthener Bach-Hefte* 8 (1998): 73-82.

———. *The History of the Hammerflügel from Scarlatti to Chopin* (in press).

Badura-Skoda, Eva und Paul. *Interpreting Mozart on the Keyboard.* London, 1962.

Badura-Skoda, Paul. *Interpreting Bach at the Keyboard.* Oxford, 1993.

Bonds, Mark Evan. *Wordless Rhetoric: Musical Form and the Metaphor of the Oration.* Cambridge, MA, 1991.

Buelow, George J., and Hans Joachim Marx, eds. *New Mattheson Studies.* Cambridge, 1983.

Derr, Ellwood. *Leopold Mozart, Wolfgang, and Rhetoric: The Evidence of Application in Wolfgang's Viennese op. 2 (the so-called Aurnhammer-SonateW.* In press.

Ferguson, Howard. *Keyboard Interpretation.* Oxford, 1975.

Fuller, David. "Analyzing the Performance of a Barrel Organ." *The Organ Yearbook* 11 (1980): 104–15.

———. "An Introduction to Automatic Instruments." *Early Music* 11 (1983): 164–66.

Haas, Robert. *Aufführungspraxis.* Potsdam, 1931.

Hosler, Bellamy. *Changing Aesthetic Views of Instrumental Music in 18th Century Germany.* Ann Arbor, MI, 1981.

Houle, George. *Meter in Music 1600–1800: Performance, Perception and Notation.* Bloomington, IN, 1987.

Kenyon, Nicholas, ed. *Authenticity and Early Music.* Oxford, 1988.

le Huray, Peter, ed. *Authenticity in Performance: Eighteenth-Century Case Studies.* Cambridge, 1990.

Marshall, Robert L. *The Music of Johann Sebastian Bach: The Sources, the Style, the Significance.* New York, 1989.

Marty, Jean-Pierre. *The Tempo Indications of Mozart.* New Haven, 1988.

Neumann, Frederick. *Ornamentation in Baroque and Post-Baroque Music.* Princeton, 1978.

———. *Essays in Performance Practice.* Ann Arbor, MI, 1982.

———. *Ornamentation and Improvisation in Mozart.* Princeton, 1986.

———. *New Essays in Performance Practice.* Ann Arbor, MI, 1989.

Performance Practice Review. 1988–.

"Proceedings of the Symposium on Authenticity in Performance." *Journal of the Conductor's Guild* 10 (1991).

Rosenblum, Sandra P. *Performance Practices in Classic Piano Music.* Bloomington, IN, 1988. *Studien zur Aufführungspraxis uud Interpretation von Instrumentalmusik des 18. Jahr-hunderts: Konferenzberichte,* especially vols. 10, 11, 25, 26, 34. Michaelstein/Blankenburg: 1979–1987.

Todd, R. Larry, and Peter Williams, eds. *Perspectives on Mozart Interpretation.* Cambridge, 1991.

CHAPTER THREE

Johann Sebastian Bach

Robert L. Marshall

Johann Sebastian Bach's reputation as one of the supreme figures of Western musical history rests primarily on the legacy of his keyboard music. Whereas the composer's church music and ensemble compositions, including such masterpieces as the Mass in B minor, the Passions, and the Brandenburg Concertos, fell virtually into oblivion after his death, the two- and three-part inventions, the harpsichord suites, the chorale settings, and the preludes and fugues of the *Well-Tempered Clavier* have been the objects of unbroken study, veneration, and emulation by generations of musicians—amateur and professional—from Bach's day to the present.

During his lifetime Bach had already been celebrated as the greatest living keyboard player. But it is essential to recognize that for Bach and his contemporaries, harpsichordists and organists were the same people. In the early eighteenth century, as throughout the seventeenth, the term "clavier" was generic and embraced all keyboard instruments, whether they were attached to strings or pipes. And it followed that a "clavier" player was equally at home on all the available keyboard instruments.

The Repertoire

Naturally enough, during the Baroque era the various keyboard instruments, including the organ, shared a common repertoire to a significant extent. This is true not only for the earlier masters but also—far more than has generally been acknowledged—for much of the "clavier" music of Bach. This means specifically that we must abandon the deeply entrenched "binary" categorization that is literally centuries old but nonetheless an anachronistic one[1] and recognize that with regard to performance medium, Bach's keyboard compositions do not fall into two strictly separated categories—consisting of works either for the organ or for the stringed keyboard instruments—but rather into three: works exclusively or primarily for organ, works exclusively or primarily for harpsichord, and works for "clavier," that is for any keyboard instrument. Only such a three-part division of Bach's keyboard repertory does full justice to the explicit designations contained in the sources and to the historical circumstances of keyboard performance in the Baroque era (Marshall 1986).

Compositions making use of preexistent sacred material (typically chorale settings) or calling for an obbligato pedal—and hence often designated *pedaliter*—were expected to be played primarily on the organ. Conversely, dance suites and variations on secular tunes were expected to be played primarily on the harpsichord. Not surprisingly, such works never have obbligato pedal parts. Finally, free keyboard compositions for manual(s) alone generally belonged to the common "clavier" repertory. The early sources for many of these compositions often carry the designation *manualiter* to indicate the absence of an obbligato pedal part—although in practice *manualiter* compositions occasionally contain isolated pedal points.[2] Since no other instrument but the organ was normally equipped with a pedalboard, the appearance of a *manualiter* indication in a work (by J. S. Bach or anyone else) would be redundant if applied to any other keyboard instrument and implies, at the very least, the acceptability of—if not a preference for—an organ rendition. The rationale for the existence of a *manualiter* (organ) repertoire is not hard to find: the organs in many small Thuringian churches often lacked pedals; moreover, many provincial organists often lacked the pedal technique for any real obbligato part, even if they could produce an isolated pedal point.

Most of J. S. Bach's "generic" clavier music dates from the first decade of his career and typically belongs to the genres of prelude (or toccata, or fantasia) and fugue, but it also includes keyboard transcriptions of ensemble compositions and presumably embraces not only the two-and three-part inventions but perhaps even the *Well-Tempered Clavier* as well.

This chapter will be limited to a discussion of Bach's keyboard works in the modern, more narrow, sense of compositions specifically for harpsichord and those more generally for "clavier" without pedals, that is, for harpsichord, clavichord, organ *manualiter*, or, indeed, fortepiano.

Bach's Instruments

The catalogue of Bach's estate refers to no fewer than eleven keyboard instruments: five harpsichords—including "1 veneered *Clavecin*, which if possible is to remain in the family" (valued at 80 thalers); two lute-harpsichords, a little spinet, and finally, "3 claviers with a set of pedals" that "the youngest son, Mr. Johann Christian Bach, received from the late departed during his lifetime" (NBR, 251, 256).[3] Nothing whatever is known about the specifications or builders of any of these instruments. Bach's pupil Agricola, however, reported that Bach had "required" that the "semitones" (i.e., the keys for the accidentals) on the harpsichord be "a little narrower at the top than at the bottom" and that he "also liked short keys on the organ."[4]

In recent years attention has focused on two surviving harpsichords evidently built by the Berlin court instrument maker, Michael Mietke, from whom, in March 1719, Bach had acquired a two-manual harpsichord for the Cöthen court (NBR, 87).   Both instruments—one single- and one double-manual, built around 1702–1703 and 1710, respectively—belong to the Charlottenburg Palace, Berlin (Ill. 3.1). They are "eclectic" instruments, sharing features of the Hamburg, Saxon, and South German schools—from South Germany (and Italy): thin cases and short string scale; from Hamburg (and France): large size and double bentside shape; from Saxony (and France): "classic" eighteenth-century dispositions (the single: 2 x 8'; the double: 2 x 8', 1 x 4', coupler), along with a narrow octave span and the short key heads preferred by Bach. Mietke, however, who died in 1719, also built harpsichords with 16' stops; and it is by no means inconceivable that contrary to prevailing wisdom, the "large" (and expensive: 130 thalers) instrument that Bach had brought back to Cöthen had a 16' disposition.[5]

The original compasses of the Charlottenburg instruments were FF to c''' (lacking FF♯ and GG♯) for the double, and GG to c''' (lacking GG♯), for the single. With some exceptions Bach's clavier compositions through the end of the Cöthen period generally observe a limit of AA to c'''. Beginning with the publication of the partitas in 1726, however, the normal compass extends from GG to d'''.[6]

Most significantly, Mietke's harpsichords evidently had brass strings, which, in combination with the short string scale, produced a relatively sustained, more "organ-like" sonority than is the case with the more usual iron alloys of the time.[7] Contemporary Thuringian organs were distinguished by a predilection for stops of the string family and, in general, for 8' and 4' registers (rather than mixtures and upper voices) that resulted in a light, delicate tone-quality.[8] This means that the characteristic timbres—and, by implication, the sound ideals—of the harpsichords and organs that were most familiar to Bach were by no means so different from one another as they are for the modern listener—a circumstance that must have made the idea of shared repertory for the two instruments all but inevitable, and by no means unnatural.

Agricola informs us, finally, that Bach had once examined one of the earliest pianofortes built by Gottfried Silbermann and had "praised, indeed admired, its tone; but he had complained that it was too weak in

ILLUSTRATION 3.1. Double Manual Harpsichord, Michael Mietke, ca. 1710. Charlottenburg Palace, Berlin. Reproduced by permission of the Verwaltung der Staatlichen Schlösser und Gärten, Berlin.

the high register, and was too hard to play." He adds that years later, Bach gave his "complete approval" to the improvements Silbermann had made to the instrument in order to correct these faults (NBR, 366). Most recently, Eva Badura-Skoda has argued persuasively that the original incident must have taken place around 1730/31 (about a year before Silbermann was to coin the term "Piano-Fort" to describe his instrument); moreover, that the reference to "a new Clavicymbel, the likes of which have not yet been heard in these parts? (NBR, 156) in a newspaper advertisement of June 1733 announcing the resumption of concerts by Bach's Collegium Musicum (following the end of an official mourning period) may also have been to a fortepiano. Given Bach's later unreserved praise of Silbermann's fortepianos and his documented per-

formance on one at the court of Frederick the Great, it is not unlikely—
as Badura-Skoda maintains—that the fortepiano is a plausible option for
much of Bach's later keyboard music.[9]

The First Decade, ca. 1703–1713: Apprenticeship and Early Mastery

According to the obituary of 1754, Bach had "laid the foundations
for his playing of the clavier" at Ohrdruf, under the guidance of his
elder brother Johann Christoph (1671–1721), with whom he lived from
1695 to 1700, following the death of their father. Although he does not
seem to have been a prodigy, and while nothing is known for certain
about when Bach began to compose, any instruction on the clavier at the
time invariably entailed not only the development of keyboard dexterity
but also a variety of compositional skills such as figured bass realization
and improvisation.

In any event, by the age of eighteen Bach had begun his career as
a musician and for the next ten years served as a professional organist:
first in Arnstadt (1703–1707), then Mühlhausen (1707–1708), finally
at the ducal court of Weimar (1708–1714). With his promotion to
Konzertmeister in March 1714 Bach's duties in Weimar took a new direction. In fact, however, Bach's music had already taken a profoundly
new direction during the summer of 1713—in the wake of his first extensive encounter with the modern Italian concerto, an event that decisively marked a new stage in the composer's artistic development. The
decade 1703–1713, then, despite the changing circumstances of his employment, is best regarded as constituting a single creative period in
Bach's life—the only period during which keyboard music was his central professional concern.

None of the early keyboard works reliably attributed to J. S. Bach
are precisely datable. Although some of them may have been written
before 1700, most were presumably composed in the decade 1703–1713.
Most survive in two manuscripts largely copied by, and originally in the
possession of, his older brother Johann Christoph. Both are identified
today by the names of early owners. The earlier of the two, the so-called
"Möller manuscript," is roughly contemporaneous with Bach's term in
Arnstadt; the second, the "Andreas Bach book," was evidently compiled
during the first years of Bach's service as court organist in Weimar. The
recent identification of the principal copyist of the volumes as Johann
Christoph Bach has inspired confidence in the attributions to J. S. Bach
(Schulze 1984). But the virtual absence of any sources in Bach's own
hand has inevitably led to problematic readings and at times conflicting
versions.

Besides Bach's music the two volumes preserve secular keyboard music by the principal German composers of the immediately preceding generations—chief among them the North Germans Böhm, Buxtehude, and Reinken and the Central Germans Kuhnau, Pachelbel, and Telemann—along with keyboard and ensemble works by leading French and Italian composers. This cosmopolitan repertoire clearly provided both the context and the stylistic models that helped shape Bach's early compositional development.[10]

Another important source for Bach's early keyboard music is the copies collected by the Thuringian organist Johann Peter Kellner (1705–1772).[11] The nature of Kellner's relationship to Bach is unclear, but he was probably never a student. For unlike Bach's known students, who apparently never made copies of these early works—a strong indication, incidentally, that the composer must have disowned them—Kellner was collecting them as late as the 1720s.

A hallmark of all of Bach's early compositions, an admittedly negative one, is the absence of any significant influence of the modern Italian concerto. The main influences rather are precisely those most highly represented in the Möller and Andreas Bach collections: the local traditions of Central and Northern Germany, whose keyboard forms and idioms are contrasted, and at times fused, with those of late seventeenth-century France. The early repertory in fact can be reasonably divided into two broad categories according to genre: (1) preludes (toccatas, fantasias) and/or fugues, and (2) a variety of multi-sectional, predominantly homophonic works: mostly suite-like collections, along with "sonatas," a set of variations, and a programmatic *capriccio* (Table 3.1).

Preludes, Fantasias, Toccatas, and Fugues

Nowhere is the evidence for a common keyboard repertory more compelling than in these interrelated genres. First of all, both *pedaliter* and *manualiter* compositions were notated in the original sources on two-stave systems; that is, there was never a separate staff for the pedal in this repertory. Moreover, several nominally *manualiter* fugues (BWV 949, 950, 955) conclude with pedal-like passages in the bass or with pedal points that not only imply organ performance but in fact are impossible to play on a harpsichord as written. More generally, there is no substantial difference between the keyboard styles of the *manualiter* and the *pedaliter* compositions belonging to this category. In illustration of this assertion Examples 3.1 through 3.4 juxtapose passages from the *manualiter* and *pedaliter* repertories, organized into four functional types: (1) opening gestures, (2) continuation patterns and sequences, (3) closing gestures, and (4) fugue themes (Exx. 3.1–4).

TABLE 3.1
J. S. Bach Early Keyboard Compositions
I. Preludes, Fantasias, Toccatas, and Fugues

Prelude and Fugue in A major BWV 896	Fugue in C after Albinoni BWV 946
Toccata in F♯ minor BWV 910	Fugue in A minor BWV 947
Toccata in C minor BWV 911	Fugue in A BWV 949
Toccata in D BWV 912/912a	Fugue in A after Albinoni BWV 950
Toccata in D minor BWV 913	Fugue in B minor after Albinoni BWV 951
Toccata in E minor BWV 914	
Toccata in G minor BWV 915	Fugue in B♭ after Reinken BWV 954
Toccata in G BWV 916	
Fantasia duobus subjectis BWV 917	Fugue in B♭ (after Erselius?) BWV 955
Prelude in C minor BWV 921	Fugue in G (Machs mit mir Gott) BWV 957
Prelude in A minor BWV 922	Capriccio in E *In Honorem J. C. Bachii* BWV 993

II. Suites, Sonatas, Ouvertures, Variations

Ouverture in F BWV 820	*Sonata* in D BWV 963
Suite in B♭ BWV 821	Sonata in A minor after Reinken BWV 965
Ouverture in G minor BWV 822	Sonata in C after Reinken BWV 966
Suite in F minor BWV 823	(Sonata in A minor BWV 967)
Partie in A BWV 823	*Capriccio* in B♭ BWV 992
Praeludium et Partita BWV 833	*Aria variata* in A minor BWV 989
	(Suite in E minor for lute BWV 996)

EXAMPLE 3.1. *Manualiter–Pedaliter.* Opening Gestures

    a. Toccata in E minor manualiter BWV 914—Prelude in G minor pedaliter BWV 535

BWV 914

(continued)

EXAMPLE 3.1. (*continued*)

BWV 535

(*continued*)

EXAMPLE 3.1. *(continued)*

b. Toccata in D minor manualiter BWV 913—Prelude in D minor
pedaliter BWV 549a

BWV 913

BWV 549a

c. Toccata in D manualiter BWV 912—Prelude in D pedaliter BWV 532

BWV 912

(continued)

EXAMPLE 3.1. (*continued*)

BWV 532

EXAMPLE 3.2. *Manualiter–Pedaliter.* Continuation Patterns and Sequences

   a. Toccata in C minor manualiter BWV 911—Toccata in D minor
      pedaliter BWV 565

BWV 911

(*continued*)

Example 3.2. (*continued*)

BWV 565

(*continued*)

Example 3.2. *(continued)*

b. Toccata in C minor manualiter BWV 911—Dorian Toccata pedaliter
   BWV 538

BWV 911

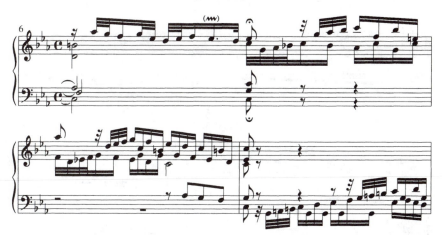

BWV 538

(continued)

EXAMPLE 3.2. (*continued*)

   c. Toccata in C minor manualiter BWV 911—Toccata in C pedaliter BWV
      564

EXAMPLE 3.3. *Manualiter–Pedaliter.* Closing Gestures

   Toccata in D minor manualiter BWV 913—Passacaglia in C minor
   pedaliter BWV 582

(*continued*)

EXAMPLE 3.3. (*continued*)

BWV 582

(*continued*)

EXAMPLE 3.3. (*continued*)

EXAMPLE 3.4. *Manualiter–Pedaliter.* Fugue Themes

a. Toccata in D manualiter BWV 912—Fugue in G pedaliter BWV 577–Toccata in G minor manualiter BWV 915

(*continued*)

EXAMPLE 3.4. (*continued*)

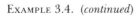

BWV 915

b. Toccata in F♯ minor manualiter BWV 910—Toccata in F pedaliter
   BWV 540

BWV 910

BWV 540

c. Toccata in G manualiter BWV 916—Toccata in C pedaliter BWV 564

BWV 916

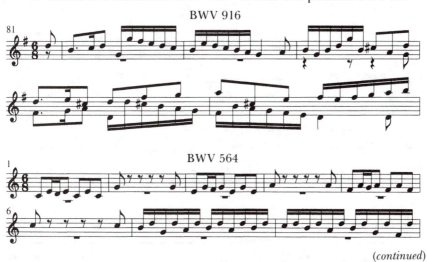

BWV 564

(*continued*)

EXAMPLE 3.4. (*continued*)

d. Toccata in E minor manualiter BWV 914—Toccata in D minor
   pedaliter BWV 565

In the final analysis, all of these compositions are works for "clavier." The particular medium of performance is a secondary consideration. They can be rendered appropriately, and for the most part, equally effectively, on either the organ or a stringed keyboard instrument.[12]

Bach's early preludes and fugues, whatever their medium of performance, document his emulation and assimilation of a wide range of styles from the archaic *stile antico* (in the Canzona BWV 588), to the rather mechanical "permutation" fugue on the Reinken model (the *Fantasia duobus subiectis* BWV 917), to rambling, quasi-improvisational *Spielfugen* in the manner of Bruhns and Buxtehude.

Although the terms *toccata, fantasia,* and *praeludium* were often used interchangeably in the seventeenth and eighteenth centuries, Bach and his contemporaries often seem to have recognized certain distinctions among them. *Praeludium* (with its French and Italian cognates *prélude* and *preludio*) and its synonym *praeambulum* are functional designations: they apply to any composition—short or long, simple or elaborate, homophonic or polyphonic—that serves as an introduction to another. Conversely, the terms *toccata* and *fantasia (fantaisie,* also *fantasie)* are, in principle, stylistic designations, frequently distinguishing two kinds of virtuosic display: keyboard virtuosity in the case of the toccata; compositional virtuosity in the case of the fantasia.[13]

The two surviving independent praeludia—the C-minor BWV 921, and the A-minor BWV 922—could have served either as introductions to specific fugues, from which they accidentally became separated during the source transmission, or as all-purpose preludes capable of being attached to any number of fugues sharing the same tonic. Their primitive features—repetitive, if flamboyant, keyboard-inspired formulas and sequences, short-breathed sections—suggest that they are among Bach's earliest keyboard compositions. Fugues surviving without preludes are far more numerous. With their striking subjects, characterized by repeated notes, rhetorical pauses, and uninhibited, if idiomatic, chains of melodic sequences, these compositions are often quite effective. Their stylistic limitations, however, are considerable. David Schulenberg calls attention to the rarity of real four-part writing, as well as to the "clumsy parallelisms, harsh passing dissonances, and excessively wide spacings," and suggests that these traits may be due "not so much to weak contrapuntal technique per se as to inexperience in the difficult art of writing meaningful counterpoint playable without pedals on a keyboard instrument" (Schulenberg 1992, 45).[14]

Of the three fugues on themes by Tomaso Albinoni (BWV 946, 950, 951),[15] the B-minor BWV 951—Bach's earliest fugue specifically designated as a harpsichord work—is the most impressive. To judge from the relatively numerous surviving copies and from its extensive reworkings, it is one of the few compositions from this period to which the composer remained committed. The formal and tonal refinements of the work in its final version—a richer and more balanced harmonic plan, the inclusion of a brief recapitulation—along with its chromaticism, argue that it stands at or over the threshold of Bach's second decade of keyboard composition.[16]

Bach's seven *manualiter* toccatas have been characterized as "*Sturm und Drang* products" (Keller 1950) and as "the culmination of Bach's early work for keyboard instruments without pedals" (Schulenberg 1992). Evidently written throughout the course of the first decade,[17] they are impressive (if at times problematic) compositions that attest not only to Bach's mastery of the keyboard but also to his command of a wide range of musical styles that he set down, for maximum effect, in striking juxtaposition. His primary concern in this regard was evidently to explore basic compositional principles: the opposition of the improvisational and the strictly composed, of rhapsodic unpredictability and self-conscious unity.

Like their North German models the *manualiter* toccatas consist, in principle, of five sections: three main parts separated (or linked) by two transitional episodes. The opening flourishes, or *passaggi*—which may well document actual improvisations—betray the young virtuoso composer's delight in digital virtuosity as well as coloristic and registral effect. Each toccata begins by opening the tonal space in a striking fashion: the D-minor and E-minor Toccatas with "pedal solos" in the bass; the G-major and G-minor Toccatas, in contrast, at the top of the keyboard, the former obsessed with repetitive scales and broken chord patterns, the latter cascading in a torrent of rapid triplets, and so on. Of the two transitional sections, the archaic style and relatively strict part writing of the first presumably form a deliberate contrast to the distinctly modern instrumental "recitative" style of the second. The fugal sections, for their part—the first normally in duple meter, the second quicker than the first and often in triple or compound meter—are rather old-fashioned: limited in harmonic scope, prone to motoric rhythms and extensive (at times excessive) sequential patterning, but also more concerned with obbligato countersubjects and double fugue techniques than would be the case later on.

Occasionally—in a manner reminiscent of the seventeenth-century variation suite—there are more or less obvious thematic or motivic similarities between the sections.[18] On other occasions the five-section schema is abandoned. In particular, the G-major toccata BWV 915 (like the C-major *pedaliter* toccata BWV 564) is in three movements, both compositions evidently the product of Bach's attempt to effect an accommodation between the stylistic worlds of the North German toccata and the Italian concerto.

Suites, Sonatas, Ouvertures, Variations

Whereas the *manualiter* preludes and fugues, at the very least, do not discourage organ rendition, there is little doubt that the works under this rubric were intended for the harpsichord. In contrast to Bach's early essays in the well-established styles and techniques of German keyboard music, the motley collection of suites and related compositions disclose his interest in more recent keyboard genres whose stylistic and formal conventions were by no means fully defined. Many of these efforts were to remain rather unsuccessful isolated experiments.

The compositions consisting largely of dances and related pieces are variously designated *Ouverture, Suite, Partie, Partita, Sonata*. The two ouvertures—in F major and G minor, respectively, BWV 820 and 822—begin, as expected, with introductory movements in the familiar orchestral style that may even be transcriptions for keyboard rather than original keyboard compositions. While both works conclude with the customary gigue, they omit the other dances increasingly standard at this time among German composers of keyboard suites—allemande, courante, and sarabande—substituting others in their place.

In the G-minor Ouverture BWV 822, French influence, as Schulenberg observes, is apparent from the rondeau form of the gavotte, the repetition of the final phrase (a *petite reprise*) in the bourrée, and from the dotted rhythms and homophonic texture of the gigue. Similarly, the three-measure phrases of the minuet from the F-major Ouverture BWV 820 are characteristically French.[19] The minuet also presents less than flattering testimony to the young composer's skill at this stage, with its inconsistent textures (two or three voices), stiff, unchanging rhythmic patterns, its melodic monotony (the first section consists of two virtually identical phrases, repeated: four statements in all), and its wavering tonal focus (Ex. 3.5).

EXAMPLE 3.5. Ouverture in F BWV 820. Menuet

The Sonatas in D major, A minor, and C major, BWV 963, 965, and 966, respectively—the last two arrangements of movements from Johann Adam Reinken's *Hortus musicus* (Hamburg, 1687)—are hybrid compositions that combine attributes of the toccata and the suite. They can be regarded perhaps as an early manifestation of the trend toward a *réunion des goûts*, here uniting the North German organ style with French dance music for *clavecin*. The D-major sonata is closest in style to the toccata, consisting of a pair of fugues separated by recitative-like transition sections. It begins, however, not with a virtuosic flourish but with a homophonic lyric movement. The final fugue, entitled "Thema all'Imitatio Gallina Cuccu," alludes to yet another keyboard tradition: the bird calls popular with seventeenth-century Italian and South German composers. The fugues in the "Reinken" sonatas, on the other hand, are sophisticated reworkings of the originals in which Reinken's "permutation" procedures of strictly invertible counterpoint are abandoned in favor of more flexible patterns.

The most well known of the early keyboard works, the *Capriccio sopra la lontananza de il Fratro dilettissimo* (Capriccio on the Absence of the Beloved Brother) BWV 992 and the *Aria Variata* in A minor BWV 989, fall, respectively, toward the beginning and the end of the first decade. Each is virtually in a class by itself within the Bach canon. The capriccio, copied into the Möller manuscript around 1705,[20] is the composer's only instrumental composition with an extramusical program—a conceit suggested by Johann Kuhnau's "Biblical" Sonatas (Leipzig, 1700)—but appropriated here to represent a purely secular, indeed mundane, event: the composer's separation from his beloved "fratro." The longstanding assumption, first advanced by Philipp Spitta, has been that the object of this distant precursor of the "Lebewohl" Sonata was Bach's older brother Johann Jacob. Both the identity of the "fratro" as well as the date, however, have recently been called into question.[21]

The capriccio is notable for the expressive intensity of the first half of the work, which reaches its climax in an effectively structured passacaglia on the famous *lamento* bass (perhaps Bach's very first passacaglia). This seriousness of tone contrasts sharply with the playful character of the last two movements: the brief "aria" and the quite difficult fugue, both of which, in the same spirit as the "cuckoo" fugue of the D-major Sonata, make use of "natural" sounds—here the octave leaps of the post horn.

The *Aria Variata*, presumably written toward the end of Bach's decade of apprenticeship, is his only set of secular variations before the Goldberg Variations. Among the numerous textual problems posed by this composition is one concerning its dimensions and organization. In one source the work consists of ten variations; in another, only eight, arranged in a different order. Each of the variations—all but the last of which is for two voices—is an exercise in motivic and textural consistency, while the composition as a whole explores an impressively wide range of contrasting styles and affects: a set of "character" variations, then, and a precocious harbinger of the Goldberg Variations.

The First Synthesis: 1713–1723

In the summer of 1713 Bach undertook a series of arrangements of Italian concertos. This activity did not coincide with any of the familiar changes of employment in the composer's biography; nonetheless, it was arguably the most significant artistic experience of his maturity—a "watershed" event that fundamentally transformed his approach to composition. As in the case of the early works, a revision of the time-honored periodization of Bach's career is once again in order. Rather than organized in terms of "the Weimar Period, 1708–1717," followed by "The Cöthen Period, 1717–1723," it is appropriate to conceive the decade 1713–1723 as a single, extraordinarily rich phase in Bach's artistic development—one marked at the beginning by the discovery of the Italian concerto and at the end by his departure to Leipzig, bringing with it the obligation to devote himself exclusively, at least temporarily, to the composition of church music. Such a division is further justified by the fact that many of Bach's keyboard compositions cannot be precisely dated either to the Weimar or the Cöthen years, while work on others, though begun in Weimar, continued on into the Cöthen period (and perhaps beyond).

Among the new duties connected with Bach's promotion to Konzertmeister in March 1714 was the obligation to compose a church cantata every four weeks. He continued in his post as court organist, however, and evidently managed, before leaving Weimar three years later, not only to prepare keyboard transcriptions of concertos in the Italian style but to compose several large-scale preludes and fugues, the English Suites, and, apparently, much of the *Well-Tempered Clavier*. At Cöthen the composition of solo keyboard music evidently had nothing to do with Bach's official duties as court Kapellmeister. For the most part Bach's Cöthen keyboard works belonged to the private sphere: to domestic music-making with his family and especially to his activities as a teacher. His keyboard compositions thereafter took on an explicitly didactic function and were increasingly organized into sets or cycles.

In the final analysis, however, the period of artistic maturity that began about 1713 lasted in fact not for ten but rather some thirty years, during which Bach largely concentrated his efforts as a keyboard composer on the genres of the suite and the fugue. His most important contributions were to be consolidated in six substantial collections, three volumes of suites—the English and French Suites, and the Partitas (along with the *Ouverture* BWV 831)—and three of fugues—the *Well-*

Tempered Clavier (WTC) 1 and 2, and the *Art of Fugue* (along with the Two- and Three-Part Inventions). Bach regarded the two contrasting genres as forming a single integrated pedagogical program. According to Heinrich Nicolaus Gerber, a pupil of Bach's in Leipzig from 1724–1727, the composer started him off on the Inventions. "When he had studied these through to Bach's satisfaction, there followed a series of suites, then the *Well-Tempered Clavier*. . . . The conclusion of the instruction was thorough bass" (NBR, 322). In terms of chronology the English and French Suites, along with WTC 1 and the Inventions, belong mainly to the decade 1713–1723; the remaining compositions belong to Bach's Leipzig years.

The Concerto Transcriptions

Bach's keyboard arrangements of twenty-one concertos in the Italian style—five *pedaliter* (BWV 592–96), and sixteen *manualiter* (BWV 972–87)[22]—evidently were prepared during the period from July 1713 to July 1714 in fulfillment of a request from the young Weimar Duke Johann Ernst (Schulze 1984). Whether prepared primarily for practical performance by the duke or himself, or for purposes of study, the transcriptions represent the composer's first known sustained encounter with the modern Italian concerto style.[23]

The formal and tonal principles Bach discovered in the Italian concertos of Vivaldi, Torelli, and the two "Marcello"s—in particular the age-old principles of ritornello form now immeasurably enriched by the vastly expanded harmonic resources of functional tonality—would inform almost every work he wrote henceforth. Mastering and expanding on them and exploring their almost infinite capacity for combination with other principles of musical structure and design were destined to become a constant challenge and preoccupation in his future agenda as a composer. There were, for example, obvious correspondences between the Italian concerto and the German keyboard prelude, and between the Italian concerto and the fugue. Like many preludes, the style and the very ethos of the concerto provided an opportunity for the display of virtuosity; like many fugues, the form of the concerto was based on a principle of alternation between thematic and comparatively nonthematic sections: in the concerto between ritornello and solo, in the fugue between exposition and episode. Bach, characteristically, was interested in the potential for synthesis suggested by these connections.

Even more fundamentally, however, he was attracted to the rational tonal design and ritornello organization of the concerto that enabled the creation of unified, continuous instrumental movements on a hitherto unprecedented scale, avoiding, on the one hand, the tonal monotony and short-breathed sectionalism of, say, the variation set or the passacaglia, and on the other, the tendency, observable at times in the early toccatas—and even the early fugues—toward excessive variety and contrast at the cost of any sense of a compelling underlying unity.

Four "Great" Preludes (Fantasias) and Fugues

Among the first original fruits of Bach's study of the Italian concerto are three large-scale concertante *manualiter* works—all (coincidentally or not) in the key of A minor: the Fantasia and Fugue BWV 904, the (Fantasia and) Fugue BWV 944, and the Prelude and Fugue BWV 894. *Pedaliter* organ works like these—grand in scale, virtuosic in character, concertante in style—have come to bear the epithet "great," a designation just as appropriate for their presumably contemporaneous *manualiter* counterparts.[24]

Like the toccata, the *fantasia* is a subcategory of prelude insofar as it usually denotes a movement preceding a fugue. But the emphasis this time is typically on compositional rather than keyboard prowess. In the Fantasia in A minor BWV 904/1, for example, Bach is concerned with creating an unlikely hybrid that unites the ritornello design of the modern concerto with archaic suspension-based counterpoint (*durezze e ligature*) of the *stile antico*.

The Fugue in A minor BWV 944—preceded in its earliest source by a miniature, ten-measure *Fantasia pour le Clavessin* in arpeggio style—is the *manualiter* counterpart of the *pedaliter* Fugue BWV 543. Despite its enormous length and unbroken, potentially monotonous, sixteenth-note motion throughout, it succeeds on account of its obvious virtuosity and owing to an effective concertante distinction between thematic and episodic figuration. Bach's indebtedness to the concerto is particularly clear in the ritornello structure of the Prelude in A minor BWV 894. Both the prelude and the fugue were later reworked as the outer movements of a true concerto: the Triple Concerto BWV 1044 (whose authenticity as a work by Bach, however, has been challenged).[25]

The keyboard fantasia as a display of both technical and compositional virtuosity reaches its zenith in the Chromatic Fantasia for harpsichord BWV 903. As with the early fantasia BWV 944 there is no ambiguity here about the intended instrument. The heading in one of the earliest copies reads *Fantasie* [*sic*] *chromatique pour le Clavecin* (Ill. 3.2).[26] What defines both fantasias specifically as harpsichord compositions is no doubt their extensive, and specifically marked, *arpeggio* writing.

Undoubtedly Bach's best-known single keyboard composition, the Chromatic Fantasia has been endlessly performed (and analyzed) for more than two hundred years. In expression and technique it is his most extravagant keyboard work, in harmony his boldest. Forkel's assertion that "the fantasia is unique and never had its like" is routinely invoked. The composition, however, as Spitta was the first to observe (3: 181–2),

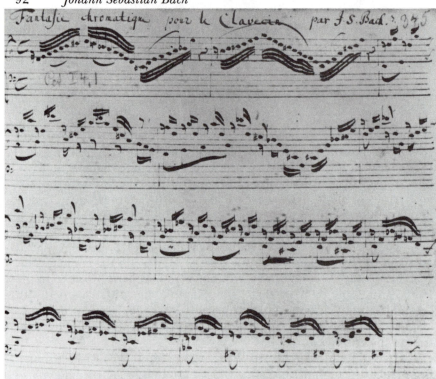

ILLUSTRATION 3.2. Chromatic Fantasia BWV 903, Intermediate Version. Copy by Johann Tobias Krebs, after 1974. *Mus. ms. Bach* P. 803, p. 345. By courtesy of the Staatsbibliothek zu Berlin—Preußischer Kulturbesitz, Musikabteilung.

is not altogether unlike the organ Fantasia in G minor BWV 542, insofar as both are unparalleled harmonic tours de force, whose seemingly spontaneous, "improvisational" flights of "fantasy"—rhapsodic passage work, enharmonic experimentation—are in fact subjected throughout to formal discipline of unparalleled subtlety.

It is not inconceivable that both works, as Spitta suggested, were composed at about the same time—around 1720.[27] George Stauffer has pointed out similarities between the keyboard figuration preserved in an early version of the Chromatic Fantasia (BWV 903a) and in an early version of the fifth Brandenburg Concerto (BWV 1050a).[28]

The form of the Fantasia has been variously described as a two-part, three-part, or four-part design. A three-part "dialectical" conception seems most persuasive, consisting of a tempestuous opening toccata (to m. 49), an introspective central section, designated *Recital*[*ivo*] in the early sources (mm.49–61), and a final peroration in which the opening passage work returns and is ultimately reconciled (m. 68) with the pathos-laden rhetorical gestures of the central recitative.[29] Harmonically, the first section moves from tonic to dominant, the central section "prolongs" the dominant by means of an arpeggiation (A - E - C♯), the final section returns to the orbit of the tonic in order to express a full authentic cadence: subdominant-dominant-tonic (Ex. 3.6).

EXAMPLE 3.6. Chromatic Fantasia BWV 903. Tonal Plan

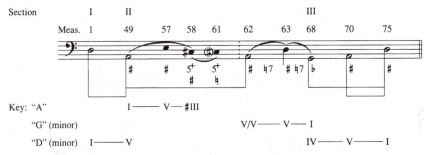

In its harmony the Chromatic Fantasia can be understood as an inquiry not only into the behavior of chromatic and enharmonic relations but into the problematic nature of the minor mode itself, whose elusiveness resides in the instability of its upper tetrachord.[30] Bach presents the issue programmatically at once in the two flourishes that open the work, which state the "melodic," "natural," and "harmonic" forms of the minor scale in close order. As a consequence of the changing inflections of the sixth and seventh scale degrees—the constantly changing combinations of half-steps and whole steps, with their attendant changes in harmonic orientation—the interval of a second emerges as a unifying thematic motif, most conspicuously as a recurring, poignant "sigh" figure but also concentrated into an ornamental mordent or shaping the outline of entire phrases (Ex. 3.7).

EXAMPLE 3.7. Chromatic Fantasia BWV 903. Motivic Seconds

(continued)

94   *Johann Sebastian Bach*

EXAMPLE 3.7. (*continued*)

The fugue, though less celebrated than the fantasia, is as monumental in conception as the great organ fugues. For the sake of dramatic effect it abandons strict part-writing at the end and indulges in massive chordal sonorities and "organistic" octave doubling in the bass. The unusually long and complex subject, quite unlike the opening of the fantasia, is harmonically ambiguous at first and seems to contain its own answer (Ex. 3.8).[31]

EXAMPLE 3.8. Chromatic Fantasia BWV 903. Fugue Subject

As Hermann Keller has observed, the harmonic treatment of the subject is extraordinary, too, in that it is used to effect modulations. The statement in m. 76, for example, begins in A minor, and ends, after passing through E minor, in B minor [32]—a most uncommon choice of tonal goals for a composition in D minor. No less than the fantasia, then, the fugue "is unique and never had its like."

The English Suites

Forkel's comment that these compositions "are known by the name of English Suites because the composer made them for an Englishman of rank" has not received much credence,[33] but it should not be dismissed out of hand. A copy once belonging to Johann Christian Bach carries the remark: "Fait pour les Anglois" [*sic*]; moreover, in most early sources the upper stave is notated in the treble rather than the soprano clef—counter to Bach's norm in both Weimar and Cöthen but conforming with English practice at the time.[34] At all events, the English Suites are the earliest of Bach's three collections of keyboard suites. Considerations of style—and the existence of an early version of the "first" suite (the Suite in A BWV 806a) in the hand of Bach's Weimar colleague Johann Gottfried Walther—suggest that Bach had begun to compose the suites at Weimar.[35]

The order of the dances is typical of a particularly German manifestation of the suite tradition that extends back to Johann Froberger. It begins with an uninterrupted succession of the "core" dances—allemande, courante, sarabande—and concludes with the gigue that is preceded by one or more optional dances. Bach's immediate model for the English Suites, however, was almost certainly the six suites by Charles François Dieupart published in Amsterdam in 1701, which have the same order and, like Bach's, begin with an introductory movement. (Bach made copies of all six Dieupart suites in Weimar, between ca. 1710 and 1714, that is, at about the time that he seems to have been composing the English suites.)[36]

With the exception of the A-major Suite, the English Suites are distinguished by their stylistic and formal consistency.[37] The most conspicuous hallmark of the set is the presence of a substantial prelude that is balanced, as a rule, at the end by a correspondingly large-scale, contrapuntal, gigue. Bach's recent study of the latest Italian instrumental styles is reflected in the virtuosic and concertante style of the preludes and in their imaginative combination of fugal procedures with ritornello and da capo designs. The treatment of the core dances, on the other hand, is rather old fashioned: the allemandes are serious and essentially polyphonic; the courantes all belong to the French form—in 3/2 meter with extensive cross rhythms; and the sarabandes closely observe the traditional rhythmic conventions of the dance, most notably the characteristically pervasive short-long rhythms.

The French Suites

The history of the French Suites is extraordinarily complex. Not only are there at least two versions of each of the six standard suites, BWV 812–17, but two further suites—the A-minor BWV 818, and the E-flat major BWV 819—are occasionally transmitted together with the French Suites in some early sources—either instead of or in addition to one or the other of the traditional six.[38] Later, more ornamented versions of the six suites are scattered in numerous eighteenth-century manuscripts of varying degrees of authority. Many of these changes and additions may reflect revisions made over time by J. S. Bach during the course of instruction, but it is impossible to determine whether all of them are authentic. Yet another version, indeed the earliest of all, has survived—at least for the first five suites. It was entered by J. S. Bach himself at the beginning of the 1722 *Clavierbüchlein* for Anna Magadalena Bach.[39]

Not even the intended order of the French Suites is altogether certain. In contrast to Bach's other collections of keyboard pieces, there is no compelling logic to the succession of keys in the standard sequence (D minor, C minor, B minor, E-flat major, G major, E major) or in any of the other successions represented in the early sources—apart from the binary division into three minor keys followed by three in the major and the scalewise descent of the first three keys. On the other hand, the number of movements increases from five (Suite 1), to six (Suites 2 and 3), to seven (Suites 4 and 5), to eight (Suite 6).

Dispensing with an opening prelude the French Suites begin directly with the three traditional dances. The courante is represented, despite the uniformly French designation throughout, in its two opposing national styles: the older, more complex French form, with its characteristic 3/2 meter (Suites 1 and 3), and the more recent, simpler Italian form, notated in 3/4 (Suites 2, 4, 5 and 6). The collection is distinguished, finally, by the inclusion of unusual dances: the loure and the polonaise, both of which occur in none of Bach's other keyboard suites,[40] and even a nondance movement: the air.

In contrast to the six "great" English Suites, Forkel describes these as the six "little suites" and remarks that "they are generally called French Suites because they are written in the French taste. By design, the composer is here less learned than in his other suites, and has mostly used a pleasing, more predominant melody" (NBR, 468–69). We may assume that by "the French taste" Forkel had in mind precisely the lighter, more homophonic textures as well as the more *galant* melodic writing that are the hallmarks of these suites. This style—virtually the antithesis of the English Suites—no doubt reflected the taste, and very likely the influence, of the owner and dedicatee of the notebook in which the French Suites were originally inscribed: Anna Magdalena Bach.[41] In particular, the French Suites testify to her evident enthusiasm for the minuet. The dance appears in five of the French Suites—in three of them (Suites 2, 3, and 4) as a later addition. The sixth suite, for its part, includes both a polonaise and a minuet; moreover, the minuet appears after the gigue as the concluding dance of the suite—a formal device familiar from the first Brandenburg Concerto and another reflection of the French taste.[42]

The Clavierbüchlein vor Wilhelm Friedemann Bach

Exactly two months after his eldest son's ninth birthday Bach began a small compilation of short keyboard pieces for him and inscribed them in a small oblong volume to which he gave the title *Clavierbüchlein vor Wilhelm Friedemann Bach*.[43] The volume enables us to reconstruct some of the first steps of Bach's pedagogical method. It begins with the rudiments—the names of the clefs and pitches—but then proceeds at once (omitting any discussion of rhythmic notation, for example) to the famous ornament table, the *Explication,* for a demonstration of how the ornament symbols are to be "properly" (*artig*) played.[44] The (rather conservative) principles of keyboard fingering are explained next with the aid of an *Applicatio,* an extensively fingered composition, in C major and in binary form, consisting mainly of scale patterns and accompanying chords (Ex. 3.9).

EXAMPLE 3.9. Applicatio BWV 994

Over the course of the following year or two the father, and occasionally the son, entered some two dozen compositions into the *Clavierbüchlein*—dances, chorale preludes, and, above all, fifteen keyboard preludes, eleven of them representing an early version of preludes from the *Well-Tempered Clavier* (see below).

Inventions and Sinfonias

After an interruption of more than a year, during which he had been preoccupied with the *Well-Tempered Clavier,* Bach returned to Friedemann's *Clavierbüchlein* and, along with his son, entered into it the two- and three-part Inventions and Sinfonias.[45] The purpose of these new pieces, as Gerber's report makes plain, was to prepare the student for the preludes and fugues of the *Well-Tempered Clavier.*

In the *Clavierbüchlein* the fifteen two-part compositions are each designated *Praeambulum,* the three-part pieces *Fantasia.* Moreover, both series begin on C and are arranged as an ascending succession of seven natural keys, with natural thirds, followed by a descending succession of the eight remaining familiar keys C, d, e, F, G, a, b; B-flat, A, g, f, E, E-flat, D, c. The major and minor keys on C-sharp, F-sharp, and A-flat, as well as any calling for more than four accidentals, are missing.[46]

Shortly afterward—certainly during the year 1723—Bach wrote out a new copy, renaming the two-part compositions *Inventio* and the three-part pieces *Sinfonia*, and reordering the keys of each series into a single ascending scale with the major mode consistently preceding the minor. Bach is thought to have taken the term *Inventio* from the *Invenzioni da camera*, op. 10, by Francesco Antonio Bonporti (Bologna, 1712), several of which Bach had copied out, evidently for use as figured bass exercises.[47] But Bach's Inventions have little in common with Bonporti's Corellian *sonate da chiesa* for violin and accompanimental continuo, for they are premised on the fundamental equality of two voices and explore the various manifestations of imitative polyphony, canon, and invertible counterpoint. The designation *Sinfonia* for the three-part pieces is similarly curious, since it was most commonly associated at this time with instrumental ensemble music. It may have been intended to evoke its Latin cognate *Symphonia* in its archaic and most generalized sense as a concord of multiple parts. Bach also provided an elaborate title page (Ill. 3.3):

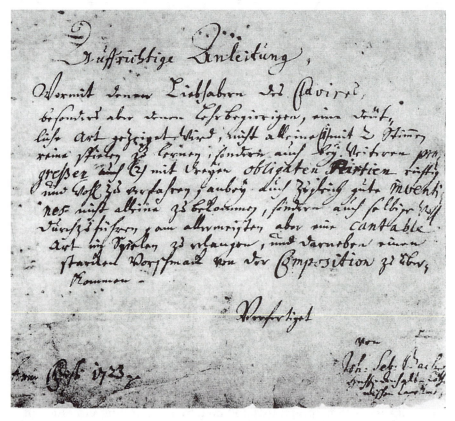

ILLUSTRATION 3.3. Inventions and Sinfonias BWV 772–801. Autograph Title Page. *Mus. ms.autogr. Bach* P 610. By courtesy of the Staatsbibliothek zu Berlin—Preußischer Kulturbesitz, Musikabteilung.

UPRIGHT INSTRUCTION [AUFFRICHTIGE ANLEITUNG],

wherein the lovers of the clavier, and especially those desirous of learning, are shown a clear way not only (1) of learning to play clearly in two voices, but also, after further progress, (2) of dealing correctly and well with three obbligato parts; furthermore, at the same time not only of having good inventions [*inventiones*] but of developing the same well [selbige wohl durchzuführen], and above all of arriving at a singing style in playing [*cantable* Art im Spielen], all the while acquiring a strong foretaste of composition.[48]

The idiosyncratic terminology of this text has been extensively interpreted. The reference to a "cantabile style" of playing, in particular, has been variously interpreted as "lyric" and "expressive" (Spitta), "song-like" and "legato" (Keller), as well as clearly articulated, like the words of a sung text (Butt 1990). Given the strict part-writing in these compositions, Bach may have had in mind a polyphonically conceived rendition, that is, one concerned primarily with the independence of each of the constituent "singing" voices.

The entire text invites exegesis. The moral tone resonating at once in the initial word "auffrichtig" ("upright," "candid," "honest," or "straightforward") is no less apparent than the intensity of the pedagogical commitment that informs the whole. Although Bach's formulations about having good "inventions," "developing" them well, and playing them in a "singing style" have obvious corrollaries in classical rhetoric— *Inventio, Elaboratio* (or *Dispositio*), and *Elocutio* (or *Executio*)—precisely what Bach meant by his terms has been a matter of controversy.

Is the "invention," of the C-major Invention, for example, the opening seven-note motive or the contrapuntal framework in which this motive is embedded?[49] Similarly, is the generating idea of the C-minor its complex theme or the technique of strict canonic imitation that is almost invariably associated with it? The "idea" of the E-major Invention, for its part, is surely the two-part contrary motion model that embraces both the ascending scale in the bass and the descending scale in the treble.

Apart from their observance of conventional tonal plans, the two-part Inventions are formally unpredictable. In all cases, the initial "invention," once formulated, is transposed, contrapuntally recombined, and extended by sequential patterning and repetition—in a word, "developed"—the artful disposition of these essentially mechanical procedures constituting, in effect, the composition.[50] Perhaps Bach called these pieces "Inventions" precisely because they largely avoid predictable formal schemata. (A traditional binary form with repeated sections appears only in the E-major Invention.)

The three-part Sinfonias manage to combine fugal texture with that of the contemporary Italian instrumental trio sonata, insofar as the bass occasionally functions as a continuo-like support for two closely related treble parts. The sonata style is most pronounced in the E-flat Sinfonia, whose duetting upper parts survive in several different ornamented versions. Its rococo elegance and fundamentally homophonic texture stand in the strongest imaginable contrast to the F-minor Sinfonia—a strict triple fugue combining *empfindsam* sigh figures, chromatic ostinati, and intensely dissonant combinations.[51]

In their stylistic and expressive range as well as their extensive appropriation of fugal procedure the three-part Sinfonias undeniably succeed in leading "those desirous of learning" to the threshold of the *Well-Tempered Clavier*. They fulfill this purpose so well, however, that their own claim to the status of serious artworks often remains unrecognized.

The Well-Tempered Clavier I

Bach's self-imposed pedagogical mission reached its first artistic culmination with the completion, in Cöthen in 1722, of the first volume of the *Well-Tempered Clavier*. Ernst Ludwig Gerber, the son of Heinrich Nicolaus, relates that, "According to a certain tradition [Bach] wrote his Tempered Clavier . . . in a place where annoyance, boredom, and the absence of any kind of musical instrument forced him to resort to this pastime" (NBR, 372). E. L. Gerber presumably had this account from his father, who presumably had heard it directly from Bach during his years of tutelage.

The disagreeable place where Bach "wrote" the WTC—or, more likely, as Alfred Dürr has suggested, the place where he conceived the plan of gathering together a number of existing preludes and fugues and augmenting them to embrace the twenty-four keys—was presumably not Cöthen but Weimar, where Bach spent the last four weeks of his tenure under arrest for having "insisted too stubbornly" on his release from the ducal service.[52] Earlier conjecture had posited that Bach had composed, or worked on, the *Orgel-Büchlein* during his Weimar detention; but it is now clear that most of the *Orgel-Büchlein* chorales had been completed years earlier, perhaps 1708–1710 (Wolff 1988); and it is equally clear that work on the WTC must have begun long before 1722, the date on the title page of Bach's famous autograph score, a handsome manuscript that was obviously intended to be a fair copy.

In fact, no fewer than three preliminary versions of the work survive, whose readings antedate the earliest readings of the autograph.[53] These early versions reveal that the fugues were originally designated *Fughetta;* that compositions in the minor mode with a natural third occasionally preceded their counterparts in the major mode (d-D, e-E, a-A); that several compositions (the Preludes and Fugues in C minor and F minor, the Preludes in A-flat major and B-flat minor) originally had "Dorian" key signatures; and that the D-sharp-minor fugue, along with the prelude and fugue in G-sharp minor, were originally in D minor and

G minor, respectively—a strong indication that they were probably composed before Bach had conceived the idea of the WTC, and were later
transposed by a half-step in order to represent the more exotic keys in
the collection.

The most significant differences of musical substance between the
familiar and the preliminary versions of the WTC concern the preludes.
New coda-like sections were added to the preludes in c, C-sharp, d, and
e (in the latter the subsequent addition of an arioso melody in the right
hand as well). Other preludes, too, were substantially expanded—none
more dramatically than the C-major, which increased in three stages
from 24 to 35 measures.[54] The revisions bear witness, above all, to a new
conception of the prelude as a genre and of its relationship to the fugue.
Whereas the early versions of the preludes typically consist of undifferentiated figuration patterns that betray their origin as technical exercises, the revised versions are formally articulated by means of sectional
contrasts or the introduction of subtle recapitulations of earlier passages.
They are independent, self-sufficient movements and not merely prefaces to more substantial compositions.[55]

In the year 1722 Bach wrote out a complete copy of the *Well-Tempered Clavier* that, to judge from the handsome script and the elaborate
title page, was intended to be a clean, "fair copy" of the work. Over the
course of time, however, and most likely in conjunction with his teaching
activities, Bach repeatedly entered corrections into the fair copy. It is
possible, in fact, to identify at least four later stages in the evolution of
the work, extending over close to a twenty-year period, into the early
1740s.[56] What Bach meant by "well-tempered" in his title will probably
never be definitively resolved. The only reasonably authentic opinion
regarding keyboard temperament attributed to Bach is Kirnberger's
comment that Bach "expressly required of him that he tune all the thirds
sharp."[57] For the rest, it is likely that Bach did not have strict equal temperament in mind but was only concerned that it be possible to play in
all twenty-four major and minor keys.[58]

The *Well-Tempered Clavier* marks the culmination of a keyboard tradition that can be traced to the Renaissance practice of performing the
verses of the magnificat in alternation between the chorus and the organ. Since the magnificat was sung in each of the eight church modes,
the *alternatim* practice precipitated the composition for the organ of
cycles of magnificat "versets" in the eight modes or "tones." The opening
section of such an organ magnificat was typically in the style of a free
"intonation," or prelude, with the following versets set as brief fugues or
"fughettas." The genre was particularly cultivated during the seventeenth century among South German composers. Over time the number
of keys represented increased, while the number of versets or fughettas
for each key decreased. By the end of the seventeenth century the number of versets was reduced to a single prelude and fughetta in each key

(Constantini 1969). The immediate model for the WTC was Johann Kaspar Ferdinand Fischer's *Ariadne Musica* (1702–1715), a collection of preludes and fugues in twenty keys.[59] Bach's use of Fischer's model is evident not only in the overall plan but also in the close resemblance of several fugal subjects in the two collections.

Bach's volume, however, is far more than a collection of well-crafted preludes and fugues. It is a comprehensive survey of the most important and disparate forms and styles of the era, all developed in accordance with a single unifying compositional principle. The juxtaposition of diametrically contrasting styles and structures at the outset—in the first two fugues—can be regarded as programmatic for the entire collection. The Fugue in C major is a "strict fugue"—a *fuga obligata*—a continuous succession of expositions without the relief of intervening episodes.[60] The diatonic subject is reminiscent of a renaissance hexachord theme, and the conjunct linear writing generally suggests the vocal style and texture of a motet. The C-minor Fugue, in contrast, with its clear alternation of expositions and episodes, is an example of a "free fugue," a *fuga libera*. Its disjunct melodic writing and motivic upbeat patterns are "instrumental" rather than "vocal" in style and evocative of the dance— a bourrée, perhaps,—while the episodes maintain the texture of a baroque trio sonata.

Other styles and genres represented, or at least suggested, among the fugues include bourrée (C$\sharp$), seventeenth-century *stylus gravis* ricercar (c$\sharp$), French ouverture (D), sixteenth-century *stile antico* motet (d$\sharp$), passepied (F), and gigue (G). With respect to contrapuntal technique we find not only fugues for three or four voices but for two (e) and five (c$\sharp$) as well; stretto fugues (C, b$\flat$), a triple fugue (c$\sharp$), and a *fugue d'artifice* (d$\sharp$), with its ingenious combinations and recombinations of augmentations, diminutions, strettos, and inversions.

Among the preludes, the stylistic models and allusions extend from the Renaissance *intonazione* (C) to the Corellian trio sonata (b), and encompass the *perpetuum mobile* (c), two-part invention (C$\sharp$, F), loure (c$\sharp$), toccata (E$\flat$, B$\flat$), sarabande (e$\flat$), pastorale (E, also a binary sonata), aria (e), Italian concerto (A$\flat$), and finally, the remarkable B-flat minor prelude, with its relentless motivic consistency and altogether original and forward-looking climactic design (Besseler 1955).

The volume is also an encyclopedia of musical *affects* (in the vocabulary of the Baroque era), offering what a later age would describe as "character pieces" in which are represented every shade of expression: the playful (fugue in C$\sharp$), the witty (fugue in E$\flat$), the cheerful (fugue in F), the serene (fugue in d$\sharp$), the sombre (fugue in f), the tragic (prelude in b$\flat$, fugue in b).

As to "form," the only valid generalization is that a fugue will maintain a strict number of voices and, rather like a chess game, will begin almost ritualistically with the constituent parts entering one by one with a statement of the subject in alternation on the tonic and its upper or lower fifth. When a fugue, like the C-minor, is based on the alternation of tonally static expositions and modulating episodes between them, then the connection with the formal rationale of the modern ritornello concerto is clear. A fugue like the F-major, on the other hand, adopts not only the rhythm and meter of a Baroque dance (passepied) but its regular phrase periodicity and even something like its binary tonal division—if not its repetition scheme.

For all their stylistic and formal variety, however, the compositions of the WTC are based on a modern tonal structure ultimately reducible to an archetypal cadential pattern: typically I-V-vi-IV (or ii)-V-I in the major mode, or i-III-V-i in the minor. Perhaps the most impressive achievement of the work, in fact, is its fusion of the potentially antithetical principles of functional tonality and linear counterpoint.

The Second Synthesis: Leipzig, 1726–1741

The Partitas

During his first three years in Leipzig Bach was completely preoccupied with the composition of church music. But by 1726 he had begun to turn his attention once again to keyboard music, proclaiming the event with the inauguration of an ambitious publishing venture. Bach evidently took both the title *Clavierübung* (Keyboard Exercise) as well as the designation "partita" from a publication of his Leipzig predecessor, Johann Kuhnau, who published two volumes of seven suites (or *Parthien*) each, under the title *Neue Clavierübung* (Leipzig, 1689, 1692).[61] Bach's partitas were issued singly from 1726 to 1731, the serial publication concluding in 1731 with the appearance of the collected edition, designated "OPUS 1."[62]

The key succession of the six partitas—B-flat, c, a, D, G, e—is ingenious (Ex. 3.10).

EXAMPLE 3.10. *Clavierübung*, Part One. The Tonics of the Six Partitas

It consists of three major and three minor keys organized into two symmetrical groups of three (major-minor-minor, major-major-minor) and arranged as a succession of ascending tonics, B-flat-c-D-e, intertwined with a descending series (B-flat-)-a-G, the intervallic distances between adjacent keys growing, accordingly, from a second to a sixth, and the tonal extremities from the first partita to the last (B-flat–e) separated by a tritone and belonging to different modes. Attesting to the same systematic mentality, each partita begins with an introductory movement bearing a different genre designation, the second half of the series, that is, Partita 4, initiated with an ouverture. (Bach would repeat this symbolic formal gesture at the midpoint of the Goldberg Variations.) The dances proper begin each time with the traditional allemande. In Partitias 1, 3, and 5 it is followed by a corrente, in Partitas 2, 4, and 6, by a courante. This time, in contrast to the French Suites (see above), the national distinction is properly designated throughout. The sarabandes, for their part, largely ignore the typical rhythmic patterns of the traditional dance, while the familiar optional dances (bourrée, gavotte, minuet)—a constituent of all the English Suites and half the French Suites—have been almost entirely eliminated. They have been replaced in effect by "character" pieces in binary or rondo form: rondeau, capriccio, burlesca, scherzo, aria, air.

The Italian Concerto and the French Ouverture

In 1735, four years after the appearance of the collected edition of the partitas, Bach published Part Two of the *Clavierübung*, "consisting," according to the title, "in A Concerto after the Italian Taste and an Ouverture after the French Manner for a Harpsichord with Two Manuals."[63] Bach demonstrated the link between this volume and its predecessor not only by retaining the series title but by continuing the succession of ascending tonics represented by the first, second, fourth and sixth partitas—B-flat, c, D, e—to the first piece in the new volume: the Italian Concerto is in F major. Although the ouverture—perhaps planned at first in emulation of Kuhnau's collection) as the seventh of the suites promised for the first volume—was originally in C minor,[64] it was now transposed to B minor, obviously in order to form a tritone with the F-major tonality of the concerto symbolizing the diametric opposition of the two national styles. In thus juxtaposing the Italian and French styles Bach may have been following the example of François Couperin, whose *Les goûts réunis* and *Les nations* had been published in the mid 1720s. Bach's concerto and ouverture represent not only the opposition of national traditions but of generational styles, as well, that is, of new and old.

The national identify of the Italian Concerto BWV 971 is established at once by its genre; its modernity—and to a large extent its lasting appeal—resides in its accessibility: its formal clarity and textural simplicity. The numerous two- and four-measure phrases, small-scale repetitions, frequent and emphatic cadences, contrasting solo theme, "drum bass" accompaniments, along with regular ritornello designs and recapitulations in the outer movements, are all hallmarks of the pre–Classical concerto style, as it was cultivated in the 1730s and 1740s in both Italy and Germany.

Bach's last contribution to the genre of the keyboard suite, the Ouverture BWV 831 on the other hand, is deliberately retrospective— as representative of the French rococo as the concerto is of the Italian pre–Classical style. Like Bach's early keyboard ouvertures of some thirty years before, the composition dispenses with the allemande: its traditional introductory function—as in the four orchestral ouvertures BWV 1066–1069—rendered superfluous by the presence of the ouverture movement. The composition also follows older French practice in its separation of the remaining core movements (eliminated altogether in the early keyboard ouvertures BWV 820 and 822) from one another and in its systematic reinstatement of paired dances in alternation, a feature increasingly neglected by Bach after the English Suites. Both the courante and the gigue reflect the characteristic rhythms of the French manner; but the ubiquitous influence of the concerto principle is evident in this work, too, specifically, in the two outer movements—the ouverture and the concluding "echo" (see Dreyfus 1987).

Most of Bach's Leipzig keyboard music was written over the course of approximately fifteen years, from about 1726 to about 1741, either in conjunction with the ongoing publication of the four volumes of the *Clavierübung* or with the compilation of the second *Well-Tempered Clavier* and the *Art of Fugue*. More precisely, with the exception of Part Two of the *Clavierübung*, Bach's involvement with keyboard music seems to have been concentrated at the beginning (1726–1731) and the end (ca. 1738–1742) of this fifteen-year period. Much of the seven-year interim was absorbed by Bach's duties in connection with the Leipzig Collegium musicum (whose direction he had assumed in 1729) as well as by his increasing connections with Dresden.

Between the appearance of Part Two of the *Clavierübung* and the publication of Part Three in 1739 Bach completed seven clavier concertos BWV 1052–1058. Whether they—along, perhaps with the concertos for multiple claviers—were written primarily for performance by the Leipzig Collegium musicum or for Bach's recitals at Dresden is not clear. They may well have been performed at both venues. In any event, Bach's renewed interest at just this time in the genre of the concerto— specifically the then fashionable keyboard concerto—is attested both by the completion of the accompanied concerti and by the publication of the unaccompanied Italian Concerto BWV 971.[65] Characteristically, at just about the same time that Bach was revisiting the ever-modern genre of the keyboard concerto, he also was preparing Part Three of the *Clavierübung* for publication, a collection mainly of *stile antico* chorale settings explicitly (according to the title page) "vor die Orgel." Nonetheless, the volume contains four *Duetti* BWV 802–805 that do not require pedals, along with eight chorale settings explicitly designated *manualiter* and hence playable on any keyboard instrument. Understandably, however, the entire volume, with the exception of the duetti, has been regarded as the exclusive province of organists.

The Well-Tempered Clavier II

Like its counterpart of 1722, the second *Well-Tempered Clavier,* compiled between 1738 and 1740, stands at the end of a period of wide-ranging stylistic assimilation that may be characterized this time as a "second synthesis," one that extended even farther afield historically, on the one hand engaging in an ever deeper exploration of the music of the past, and on the other, embracing the latest stylistic developments as advanced by a younger generation of composers. The development had begun with Bach's assumption of the directorship of the Leipzig Collegium musicum in 1729 and with the intensification of his contacts with the Dresden court shortly thereafter (Marshall 1976). The two powerful centers of musical activity in the Saxon capital, in particular—the Roman Catholic church and the Italian opera—exerted a two-pronged influence on Bach's artistic development hardly less profound than that engendered by his exposure to the Italian concerto some two decades earlier. Through the church Bach intensified his longstanding historicizing interest in the *stile antico;* through the opera and its attendant concert life at court he expanded his familiarity with the latest musical fashions.

Bach's flirtation in WTC 2 with music written "according to the latest taste" (in the words of his one-time pupil Lorenz Mizler)[66] is most apparent in the preludes. Whereas only one prelude in WTC 1—the last—is set with two repeated halves; ten in WTC 2 are so designed. Half of these (D, d♯, f, g♯, B♭), along with nine further preludes without a central double bar repetition (C, c♯, E♭, F, F♯, f♯, A♭, A, b♭)—in all more than half the preludes of the volume—are precocious explorations of the emerging pre–Classical sonata design. That is, they include clear recapitulations of the opening material, usually in the tonic, occasionally (the preludes in C, A♭, b♭) in the subdominant. The full "three-part" sonata form—exposition, development, recapitulation—is articulated with emphatic clarity in the orchestral D-major prelude: a veritable opera Sinfonia for keyboard alone and hence in its own way a counterpart to the presumably contemporaneous Italian Concerto BWV 971. Considering that some of these compositions must have been composed before 1740—that is, well before the publication of such landmarks in the early history of the sonata as Giovanni Platti's Sonatas op. 1 or C. P. E. Bach's "Prussian" Sonatas—then it does not seem to be an exaggeration to place J. S. Bach in the vanguard of sonata composers.

Bach's indebtedness to the music of his sons' generation is apparent, too, from his appropriation of such characteristically *empfindsam* features as the expressive ornamentation of the preludes in C-sharp minor and G-sharp minor, and the "sigh" figures of the F-minor. Other preludes remain within the stylistic orbit of the first WTC. The G-major and B-major preludes exploit concertante writing, while the preludes in E, F, A-flat, and B-flat evoke the pastoral style. As before, many take the two- and three-part inventions as their model, united at times with allusions to traditional dance rhythms (the allemande in the c and d♯ preludes, the corrente in the E-minor).

Curiously enough, the "rhetorical frame" of the collection seems to be inverted in comparison with that of its predecessor. WTC 1 begins with an intimate *arpeggiando* prelude; WTC 2, in stunning contrast, opens with a monumental pedal point. But the style of the second C-major prelude soon evolves into decorated broken-chord patterns reminiscent of the *style brisé*. This striking *réunion*, at the outset, of the quintessential organ and harpsichord idioms can be taken, perhaps, as emblematic for the entire collection.[67] No less remarkable are the contrasting conclusions of the two volumes: the somber, tragic, B-minor fugue of WTC 1 vis-à-vis the playful B-minor fugue of WTC 2, with its humorous octave leaps—an anticlimactic *dénouement* not unlike that produced by the last of the Goldberg Variations.

Modern elements are occasionally evident in the fugues as well. Schulenberg (203, 217) refers to the *galant* qualities of those in C, F, f, and F-sharp and the sonata-like design of the B-flat major. Their concentration at the midpoint and endpoints of the collection is noteworthy. For the most part, however, the fugues of WTC 2 hold the stylistic balance to the preludes by virtue of their more conservative posture and their frequent indulgence in contrapuntal artifice. There are no fewer than three stretto fugues (D, E, b♭), four double fugues (c♯, A♭, g♯, and B), and one triple fugue (f♯). In addition, the declamatory rhetoric of several subjects—especially those in G minor and A minor—reflects Bach's extensive experience with choral fugues in the church cantatas of the early Leipzig period (Ex. 3.11).

EXAMPLE 3.11.

a. *Well-Tempered Clavier* 2. Fugue in G minor BWV 885

b. *Well-Tempered Clavier* 2. Fugue in A minor BWV 889

On the other hand, the archaic stance of the fugues in D, E-flat, E, and B attests to the composer's intensified interest during the 1730s in the pseudo-Renaissance *stile antico,* the pendant to his experiments at just the same time with the *style galant* and pre–Classical style.

The history of Bach's second series of preludes and fugues in all the major and minor keys is, if anything, even more complex, its pre-history even longer, than that of the first. No fewer than nine of the forty-eight compositions from WTC 2 survive in discrete, earlier versions (Brokaw 1985). Copies of some of them, prepared by members of Bach's circle during the 1720s, suggest that Bach was contemplating a "simple" series of preludes and three-voiced fugues, perhaps limited to the "white" keys with natural thirds: C, d, e, F, G, and a (Hofmann 1988). Moreover, unlike the first compilation, we cannot be certain that WTC 2 ever received its final form. Evidently working from earlier copies of the individual pieces, Bach, along with his wife, prepared a score over a period of some two or three years extending from about 1738/39 to about 1740 (Franklin 1989). This source, however, the so-called "London autograph," is not an integral volume but rather an incomplete set of separate, unbound sheets, one for each prelude and fugue pair. This organization would have made it an easy matter for the composer to substitute individual items, if he so decided, without disturbing the whole.

The Fantasia in C minor BWV 906

On two separate occasions—the first between 1726 and 1731, the second between circa 1738 and 1740—Bach took the unusual pains of writing out a fair copy of this well-known composition. The time periods of these activities, along with aspects of the notation and the style of the composition, are suggestive.[68] In the first instance, the fantasia could have been intended to serve as the opening movement of the second partita of the *Clavierübung,* the C-minor BWV 826. If so, then the flamboyant technique of hand crossing that had been introduced in the concluding gigue of Partita 1 would have carried over to the opening movement of Partita 2. In the second instance, the bipartite sonata form of the fantasia would have recommended it as the representative of C minor in WTC 2. In fact, the second autograph of the fantasia appends to the fantasia the fragment of a fugue BWV 906/2. Assuming this conjecture is correct, it is not clear why Bach then decided to remove BWV 906 from the WTC in favor of the present C-minor prelude and fugue, but the reasons may be the same as those that prompted him to abandon the highly (perhaps overly) chromatic fugue altogether, before he had finished copying it.[69]

The Final Decade

The Goldberg Variations

It is odd that the *Clavierübung*, Bach's *magnum opus* of keyboard music, does not contain a volume of fugues. Given the composer's lifelong cultivation and supreme mastery of the form—a supremacy recognized and appreciated by his contemporaries—a fugue collection certainly would have made an obvious, and fitting, conclusion to the series. In fact, during the late 1730s and early 1740s Bach was occupied not only with the compilation and composition of the *Well-Tempered Clavier II* but with the *Art of Fugue* as well (see below). The thought is hardly outlandish that he may have intended to include one or the other (or both of them) in the *Clavierübung*. (The inclusion of both, along with the Goldberg Variations, would have brought the number of parts of the *Clavierübung* to the traditional six.) For some reason, however, completion of both WTC 2 and the *Art of Fugue* was interrupted—perhaps, among other things, by the commission of the Goldberg Variations—and neither work reached final form.

The *Keyboard Practice Consisting in an ARIA with Divers Variations,* universally known as the Goldberg Variations, was published (most probably in the year 1741)[70] as the final volume of the *Clavierübung*, but the composition is more usually regarded as marking a new beginning, standing at the threshold of Bach's last creative period, and initiating the series of formidable, austere instrumental cycles that include the *Art of Fugue*, the *Canonic Variations on "Vom Himmel hoch,"* and the *Musical Offering*. According to Forkel, the work was commissioned by the Russian ambassador to the Dresden court, Baron Hermann Carl von Keyserlingk, for his harpsichordist, Johann Gottlieb Goldberg, a former Bach pupil.

The Goldberg Variations constitute the largest single keyboard composition published at any time during the eighteenth century. The work is another grand Bachian synthesis, one that this time, as Manfred Bukofzer suggested, "sums up the entire history of Baroque variation" (Bukofzer 1947). The theme—a sarabande of sorts—and all thirty variations are built on the same thirty-two measure ground bass:[71] nine variations are in the form of strict canons, each appearing (as every third number) at a different interval of imitation and systematically proceeding from the unison to the ninth. Among the remaining variations we find an ouverture, a fugue, a trio sonata, several different dances, and a quodlibet, or medley of popular tunes.

We also find keyboard writing of the most extravagant sort—hand-crossings, passages in thirds, trills in inner parts, rapid arpeggios and runs. Demanding and idiomatic keyboard writing at this level of difficulty can be found, if anywhere, in the works of only one other composer of the time: Domenico Scarlatti. Indeed, there are striking similarities between the title of Scarlatti's *Essercizi per gravicembalo,* consisting of thirty virtuoso sonatas, and that of Bach's synonymous *Clavierübung . . . vors Clavicimbal,* consisting of thirty virtuoso variations.[72]

What is most striking about Bach's composition, however, is not its compositional or keyboard virtuosity but its modernity. Departing from the practice of his predecessors, Bach not only rigorously retains the regular phrase structure of the theme throughout the work but reinforces it with his variation patterns and figurations. This is accomplished, for the most part, by the direct replication of phrase units. In the first section of the first variation, for example, the pattern of the first four bars is repeated in the next four, with the right and left hands exchanging their parts. Then a new four-measure pattern is introduced at the beginning of the second eight-measure period. This, too, is repeated after four measures, again with the parts of the right and left hands exchanged. This persistent four-measure organization is maintained even in the tenth variation, the Fughetta.

But the phrase structure could be projected just as well by juxtaposing to the first idea another—perhaps completely contrasting—idea, of equal length. In Variation 14, for example, a long trilled note in various registers is followed by running arpeggio patterns in eighths and sixteenths (Ill. 3.4). These in turn are followed by an outburst of mordents alternating between the hands. There is then a rush of thirty-second-notes combined with a crossing of hands, and the section ends with a flurry of thirty-second-note mordents for both hands together. Such "disorderly, excessive" variety, such sudden, capricious shifts of ideas and patterns are altogether "un-Bachian"—and altogether modern.

Even more than the keyboard virtuosity, then, the thoroughgoing periodicity constitutes a "progressive" element in the Goldberg Variations. In fact, Bach's rekindled interest in the variation form at this time, at the beginning of the last decade of his life and for the first time since his youth, could well have been stimulated by his interest in exploring the compositional potential of this time-honored, but suddenly modern, principle of musical organization.

The Art of Fugue

The *Art of Fugue* owes its reputation as Bach's final composition to the circumstance that it was published posthumously and was unfinished at his death. In fact, however, the surviving autograph score reveals that most of the work had been composed by 1742, that is, within about a year of the publication of the Goldberg Variations.[73] Moreover, in its conception, the *Art of Fugue* represents the next logical step for Bach, following on the WTC and the Goldberg Variations, for it unites the

Illustration 3.4. Goldberg Variations BWV 988. Beginning of Variation 14. Original Edition (Nuremberg, ca. 1741).

basic compositional premises of both. Like the former it is a collection of fugal compositions surveying a variety of contrapuntal styles and techniques. Like the latter it not only introduces the technique of strict canon but, most significantly—and unlike all previous didactic collections of contrapuntal models (for example, Johann Theile's *Musikalisches Kunstbuch* of fifty years earlier and Johann Mattheson's quite recent *Wohlklingende Fingersprache*)[74]—it, too, is designed as a set of "variations." That is, all the contrapuncti and canons make use of the same subject, melodically embellished or contrapuntally altered though it may be from one movement to the next.

The *Art of Fugue* is not just an anthology but quite literally a *Gradus ad Parnassum* of counterpoint. In contrast to the *Well-Tempered Clavier* the fourteen untitled movements of the original autograph version were arranged not by key, in the neutral "alphabetical" manner of an encyclopedia, but in order of increasing complexity or contrapuntal rigor: simple, double, and counter fugues, followed by a canon at the octave, then triple fugues and mirror fugues (along with an arrangement of the mirror fugue for two claviers) followed by an augmentation canon.[75'] The inclusion, specifically, of triple fugues in the collection—the first for three voices, the second for four—may have been Bach's response to a published challenge issued to him by Johann Mattheson in his *Vollkommener Kapellmeister* to produce such a composition (Butler 1983a).

Owing to its tonal and thematic unity and, above all, its overarching concern with contrapuntal artifice, the style of the *Art of Fugue*, in contrast to Bach's earlier fugal collections, is relatively uniform, and frequently reminiscent of the *stile antico* (particularly so in the large note-values chosen for the notation of several movements in the published version). As Schulenberg remarks with reference to the opening movements, "many passages lack the well-defined harmonic rhythm and strong sense of harmonic directionality one expects in a late-Baroque work, and the modulatory range is very limited" (p. 352). Yet there are modern touches even here, for example, the "sigh" figures in the augmentation canon, and the pervasive dotted rhythms in Contrapunctus 6, designated "in Stylo Francese" in the original print. Moreover, it may well be that the intense chromaticism, dissonance, and tonal obscurity of many passages in the *Art of Fugue* (for example, in Contrapuncti 3 and 13) were just as deliberately intended to be demonstrations of harmonic speculation as the elaborate canonic combinations were of contrapuntal ingenuity. They should be understood, accordingly, not as archaic relics but as a decidedly modern, even "visionary," experiment, one that Bach would resume—in the B-A-C-H episode of the unfinished fugue—when he returned to the work at the end of his life.

The Musical Offering

On July 7, 1747, some five years after he had penned much of the score of the *Art of Fugue,* Bach published a *Musical Offering to His Royal Majesty in Prussia.* The story of the work's origin is well known. In May 1747 Bach had given a command performance at the court of Frederick the Great in Potsdam, on which occasion the king played a peculiar theme, purportedly of his own invention, on his Silbermann fortepiano and requested that Bach improvise a fugue on the subject. He also asked the composer to improvise a fugue in six parts. According to the newspaper account, Bach fulfilled the task to the king's satisfaction and to everyone's astonishment and promised to "set it down on paper in a regular fugue and have it engraved on copper."[76]

The engraving, however, not only included the three-voiced fugue but also a new six-part fugue—this one, too, unlike the one he had performed in Potsdam, based on the king's subject—along with ten canons and a trio sonata, all making use of the royal theme. Bach's decision to expand the publication in this way may have been influenced by his induction, in June 1747, into the erudite Society of the Musical Sciences, founded by his former pupil Lorenz Mizler. For that occasion, too, Bach had produced a learned work, the *Canonic Variations on the Chorale Vom Himmel hoch* BWV 769. Both prestigious events, then—occurring in rapid succession—would understandably have provoked a renewed interest in the compositional problems first explored in the Goldberg Variations and the *Art of Fugue:* contrapuntal artifice and thematic unity.[77]

The two keyboard fugues of the *Musical Offering* are both designated *ricercar* in the original edition, even though the two compositions could hardly be more different.[78] Bach's interest, as so often before, was evidently in juxtaposing opposites: the three-part composition is a quite loose-textured work, intended, perhaps, to capture the character of the original improvisation. By the same token, it is also modern in style, roughly binary in form (Schulenberg 1992, 341) and alluding at times— as a gesture perhaps to the royal taste—to popular *galant* mannerisms such as triplets and sigh figures. The six-part setting, on the other hand, conforms to the more traditional understanding of *ricercar.* It is uncompromisingly contrapuntal, although lacking the traditional artifices of canon and stretto. Except for its chromaticism, dictated by the royal subject, it is distinctly old-fashioned.[79] Finally, the three-part ricercar, with its "sighs," arpeggios, and broken chords, is clearly music for stringed keyboard instrument—the harpsichord, if not, indeed, the fortepiano on which it originated; just as clearly, the monumentality and massive sonorities of the six-part ricercar, strongly encourage, even if they do not mandate, performance on the organ.

B-A-C-H: *The Revision of the* Art of Fugue

Membership in Mizler's Society, along with the publication of the *Musical Offering*, may have prompted Bach's decision in the last years of his life to return to the *Art of Fugue* and to prepare it for publication.[81] In the spring of 1751 a revised and expanded version of the work was published posthumously, the task apparently carried out by Bach's son Carl Philipp Emanual and Johann Friedrich Agricola. The edition includes four new constituent movements: a second simple fugue with inverted subject, two canons (one at the tenth and one at the twelfth), and a fragmentary fugue *a 3 soggetti;* five movements are substantially expanded, while others appear in revised form. In addition, each movement is designated either *contrapunctus* or *canon* and in most cases carries a verbal indication of its principal contrapuntal device. Finally, the movements appear in a new sequence, and the publication ends with a completely unrelated composition—the chorale prelude on the tune "Wenn wir in höchsten Nöthen sein" BWV 668a, offered by the editors in compensation for the incomplete fugue.

As it appears in the print, the new order is at least partially corrupt, but it is clear that the expansion and the reorganization of the work reflected a new conception of its purpose, which is now more concerned, perhaps, with the representation of fugal categories than with demonstrating degrees of contrapuntal complexity (Wolff 1991).

Altogether new is the addition of a fugal category that represents the *ne plus ultra* of contrapuntal complexity. Although the *Art of Fugue,* as a whole, can no longer be considered Bach's final work, that distinction may well still belong to the fugue *a 3 soggetti.* The autograph of the legendary unfinished fugue survives on a separate sheet, written at the very end of Bach's life: sometime between August 1748 and October 1749 (Kobayashi 1988). The fragment, which breaks off after a remarkably chromatic section based on the subject B-A-C-H, has been recognized for over a hundred years as the quadruple fugue mentioned in the composer's obituary, whose missing final section was to reintroduce the main theme of the work in combination with the previous three subjects of the movement, whereupon the entire complex would be inverted (NBR, 304).[82]

Moreover, Bach's "final fugue" may not have been left unfinished by the composer. Recent speculation has plausibly suggested that Bach, contrary to the testimony of the obituary, in fact completed the final section, that it was relatively short, and was probably written on a separate sheet of paper that was lost by his heirs.[83] In its uniqueness the quadruple fugue—Bach's only fugue with four themes—has an obvious counterpart in the six-part ricercar from the *Musical Offering,* his only fugue for six voices; and it may well have been his work on the latter that prompted Bach to add a similarly unique, similarly monumental, contrapuntal tour de force as the capstone—if not necessarily the conclusion[84]—of what the ailing master must have understood would be his *opus ultimum*.

Notes

1. It is datable to the obituary for Bach published in 1754 by Carl Philipp Emanuel Bach and Johann Friedrich Agricola. See the English translation in NBR, pp. 297–307, especially pp. 303–4.

2. This can be the case in harpsichord pieces, as well, as the sustained bass notes in the opening measures of the sarabande from the third English Suite attest.

3. The last reference, presumably, is not to three "pedal harpsichords," as sometimes asserted, but to three manuals—perhaps clavichords, otherwise unmentioned in the estate catalogue—along with a separate pedal board. See Marshall 1986.

4. Agricola's comments appear in his published annotations to Jacob Adlung, *Musica Mechanica Organoedi* (Berlin, 1768). He also mentions that the builder Zacharias Hildebrand, "about the year 1740," had constructed a lute-harpsichord, or *Lautenclavicymbel,* according to Bach's instructions, "which was of smaller size than the ordinary harpsichord . . . [and] had two sets of gut strings, and a so-called little octave (*Octävchen*) of brass strings (NBR, 366). See also chapter 1.

5. This paragraph is based on Germann 1985, which argues compellingly that the two unsigned harpsichords at Charlottenburg are in fact by Michael Mietke. Germann emphasizes Mietke's indebtedness to the seventeenth-century French school and credits him with being the first to introduce many of its features into Germany.

6. The pitch e''' appears in the mirror fugue of the *Art of Fugue;* e''' and f''' in the second movement of the Triple Concerto BWV 1044. See Dürr 1978.

7. The use of brass strings throughout the compass implies tuning at a low chamber pitch of about a' = 392. Personal communications from Paul Guglietti and Mark Kroll. See also note 4.

8. See Faulkner 1991, also Cornell 1991.

9. Badura-Skoda 1991. See also chapter 2, above.

10. See Hill 1987 and Hill 1991. The secular repertory of the Möller and Andreas Bach volumes was surely complemented by a similar collection of chorale settings. Some of its contents may survive in the so-called "Neumeister collection," containing thirty-eight chorale preludes by the young Bach (thirty-three hitherto unknown), along with chorale settings by Bach's ancestors and others. See Wolff 1985.

11. Many survive in a single large volume, evidently gathered and bound together only after Kellner's death. See Stinson 1989a.

12. The strongest argument for a preferred harpsichord rendition can be made in the case of the Toccata in G major BWV 916. An early copy, now lost but attributed to Bach's pupil Heinrich Nicolaus Gerber, bore the title *Concerto seu Toccata pour le Clavecin.* In addition, the first movement contains some written-out octave doublings for tutti effects in the opening movement that, as Schu-

lenberg remarks (p. 76), "would be superfluous on the organ." On the other hand, not only does the work contain numerous formal and textural affinities with the C-major *pedaliter* Toccata BWV 564, but written-out octave doublings can be found in bona fide organ works such as the Toccata in D minor BWV 565.

13. The use of the term *Capriccio* for BWV 993 is an anomaly; the work is a fugue and altogether different in design from the *Capriccio on the Absent Brother* BWV 992. See below.

14. See also Stauffer 1980 regarding Bach's early organ preludes.

15. The subjects are all taken from Albinoni's trio sonatas op. 1 (Venice, 1694).

16. See the analysis of the two versions in Schulenberg 1992, 54–57.

17. It is tempting to connect the individual toccatas, on the basis of their ranges, with Bach's organs at Arnstadt, Mühlhausen, and Weimar and thus create the framework for a chronology. But such an enterprise is ultimately inconclusive. See the argumentation in Marshall 1986.

18. For example, between the two fugues of the D-minor, between the "arioso" and final fugal sections of the F♯-minor, or the characteristic neighbor-note pattern in three of the four sections of the E-minor toccata.

19. They are an example of the so-called *Menuet de Poitou*. See Little 1991, 71–72.

20. Hill 1987, 126.

21. Hill 1987, and especially Wolff 1992.

22. Seventeen, if one includes the questionable Concerto in G major BWV 592a.

23. Only shortly before, in February 1713, Bach had begun to employ the latest Italian operatic forms in his vocal music; the recitative and the da capo aria make their first appearance in the "Hunting" cantata, *Was mir behagt*, BWV 208.

24. Schulenberg plausibly suggests that the *manualiter* compositions may all date from the late Weimar period. For other datings see Stinson 1989b.

25. NBA VII/3, KB 47–48.

26. As copied by Johann Tobias Krebs, a Weimar pupil of Bach's. A second copy in the same ms. (Berlin State Library *mus. ms. Bach* P 803) has the same title. See Zietz 1969, 67, 71, 94–98.

27. Peter Williams has noted stylistic similarities between the opening flourishes of the organ fantasia and those found in the unaccompanied violin sonatas of 1720 (Williams 1:118–22). But George Stauffer has suggested a considerably earlier dating for BWV 542/1, namely, ca. 1708–1712. Curiously enough, Stauffer's argument, though based entirely on stylistic analysis, does not mention the work's astonishing enharmonic writing. See Stauffer 1980, 109–110.

28. The date of the early version of the concerto has been associated with the purchase of the Mietke harpsichord in 1719. See Stauffer 1989, especially pp. 175–81.

29. Bach may have borrowed the idea of an instrumental recitative from the slow movement of Vivaldi's "Grosso Mogul" Concerto, a work that he had transcribed for organ, BWV 594. See Schulenberg 1992, 118.

30. This may also explain the absence of a flat in the key signature of the original manuscripts of the Fantasia—but not the fugue.

31. See Marshall 1976 for more on the theme's complex structure.

32. Keller 1950, 161.

33. As translated in NBR, 468.

34. NBA V/7, KB, 86–91.

35. NBA V/7, KB, 85–86. On Dieupart see chapter 4.

36. See NBA IX/2, especially pp. 38, 45.

37. Whether the Suite in A, even in its revised form, was conceived from the outset as part of the set is not altogether certain. Not only is it the only suite to make use of the contra octave, it is also superfluous to the key scheme of the remaining suites: A minor, G minor, F major, E minor, D minor. See Eppstein 1976, especially pp. 36 and 48. Moreover, in the earliest known copy the Suite in A minor, i.e., the second suite, originally bore the designation "Svit. 1re." See NBA V/7, KB, 86.

38. See NBA V/8.

39. See NBA V/4, KB, and Dadelsen 1957.

40. The loure appears in an unaccompanied violin partita in E BWV 1006, the polonaise in the first Brandenburg Concerto BWV 1046 and the Orchestral Suite in B minor BWV 1067.

41. Both of Anna Magdalena's notebooks in fact bear witness to her decidedly French taste in music. See Marshall 1990.

42. On the numerous special problems posed by the minuet movements in the French Suites see NBA V/8, KB, 81–84.

43. The entire volume has been published in a facsimile edition, edited by Ralph Kirkpatrick. See also the critical edition in NBA V/5.

44. See the facsimile reproduction in chapter 2, above.

45. Since Forkel the three-part pieces are usually referred to as Inventions as well.

46. As Don Franklin has pointed out, except for the absence of F ♯ minor, the keys are the same as those described by Johann Mattheson in *Das neu-eröffnete Orchestre*, published in 1713. See Franklin 1989, 225. The seven ascending two-part inventions may well all have been composed at an earlier time than the remaining compositions. See NBA V/5, KB.

47. See Schulenberg 1992, 407, n. 50.

48. Based on the translation in NBR, as emended in Dreyfus.

49. Dreyfus 1996, Chapter 1.

50. Ibid.

51. An allegorical interpretation of this extraordinary composition is offered in Chafe 1991, 43–51.

52. Dürr 1984, 7. Another possibility suggested by Dürr is Carlsbad, where Bach sojourned with Prince Leopold for about five weeks in 1718 and again in 1720.

53. See Dürr 1984, and NBA V/6.1, KB.

54. See White 1992.

55. See Dürr 1984, also Riedel 1969, and Brokaw 1986.

56. See the commentary by Walter Dehnhard, in his 1973 edition of the work, also Dürr 1984.

57. Cited by Friedrich Wilhelm Marpurg. See NBR, 368.

58. A number of possible systems have been proposed. For an overview, see Lindley 1980.

59. See the modern edition, edited by Ernst von Werra. Fischer omits five keys: C♯, e♭ (d♯), F♯, a♭ (g♯), and b♭—that is, all keys of five or more accidentals, with the exception of B major. On the other hand, he includes E-Phrygian as the twentieth key.

60. Friedrich Wilhelm Marpurg, *Abhandlung von der Fuge* (Berlin, 1753). See NBR, 359.

61. Bach, too, it seems, may have planned to include a seventh suite. According to a newspaper announcement published in 1730 for the fifth partita, two more were to follow. See BD, 202.

62. The composition of the partitas, however, may well have antedated their publication considerably. This is known to be the case for Partitas 3 and 6, for which early versions were entered by J. S. Bach—as fair copies—at the beginning of the 1725 *Clavier-Büchlein* for Anna Magdalena Bach.

63. For the date see NBA V/2, KB, 17.

64. See NBA V/2, KB.

65. See Wolff 1985, also Schulze 1981. Jane R. Stevens argues plausibly that several of Bach's accompanied concertos for one or more harpsichords—in addition to the C major Concerto for two harpsichords BWV 1061, for which the fact is established (see NBA VII/5, KB)—may, at some earlier stage, have been unaccompanied keyboard concertos. See Stevens 2001, 48.1.

66. See NBR, 350. Although Mizler was specifically refering to a secular cantata (now lost) it is worth noting that this remark in defense of his teacher was made in 1738, i.e., at just about the time Bach was assembling WTC 2.

67. Bach may originally have planned to open WTC 2 with a surviving version of the prelude in C♯ major BWV 872a/1, notated in C major and in *arpeggiando* style quite similar to that of BWV 846/1. It is published in NBA V/6.2, 344–45.

68. See the commentary in the facsimile edition.

69. For two interesting completions of the fugue see Cone 1974 and Schulenberg 1992.

70. For the problems of dating the publications see NBA V/2, KB, 94.

71. Bach's authorship of the theme has been challenged in Neumann 1985. But see Marshall 1989, 54–58, and Schulenberg 1992, 326.

72. Historical and geographical conditions by no means preclude Bach's having known Scarlatti's music. See Marshall 1976.

73. Specifically, the first nine pieces were entered by 1742, the five remaining pieces by 1746. See Wolff 1983, also Kobayashi 1988.

74. Re Theile, see Carl Dahlhaus's preface to the modern edition; re Mattheson, see Stauffer 1983. See also Snyder 1980 for a possible precedent in Buxtehude for Bach's mirror fugue.

75. Wolff 1991, 274, and Schulenberg 1992, 348.

76. See NBR, 224, 302–3, for the original newspaper account and the obituary report of 1754.

77. Whether the constituent movements of the collection were intended to be arranged in a specific order, however, has been a matter of controversy. See Kirkendale 1980, Christoph Wolff 1991, and Marissen 1994a.

78. On the contemporary definitions of ricercar, see Wolff 1991, 324–29.

79. For an opposing analysis of the ricercars, see Marissen 1994b, 92–94.

80. In addition to the two ricercars, the NBA suggests realization of two two-part canons on the harpsichord. See NBA VIII/1, pp. 48, 54, 70, 78.

81. The title *Kunst der Fuge* may not have been Bach's; it appears on the title page of the autograph in the hand of his son-in-law, Johann Christoph Altnikol. Conceivably, Bach's own title could have been *Clavierübung letzter Teil!*

82. The nineteenth-century Beethoven scholar Gustav Nottebohm was the first to recognize the true nature of the fugue. See Wolff 1975.

83. Wolff 1975 and Butler 1983b. For a recent completion, see Schulenberg 1992, 369.

84. Gregory Butler has suggested that the quadruple fugue would have been the fourteenth and final fugue followed, in the publication, by the four canons. See Butler 1983b.

85. The author is indebted to George Stauffer, Mark Kroll, and Maynard Solomon for a number of helpful suggestions.

Significant Musical Editions and Facsimiles

BG. *Johann Sebastian Bach's Werke.* Complete edition of the Bach-Gesellschaft. 46 volumes. Leipzig, 1851–1900. Especially volumes 3, 13/2, 14, 25, 31/2, 36, 43/2, 45.

NBA. *Johann Sebastian Bach. Neue Ausgabe sämtlicher Werke.* Ed. the Johann-Sebastian-Bach-Institut, Göttingen, and the Bach-Archiv, Leipzig. Kassel and Leipzig, 1954–2000. Volumes V/1–10; VIII/1–2.

NBA . . . KB. The volumes of critical reports (*Kritische Berichte*) for the edition.

Bach, Johann Sebastian. *Aria mit 30 Veränderungen.* Ed. Ralph Kirkpatrick. New York, 1938.

———. *Clavierbüchlein vor Wilhelm Friedemann Bach.* Facsimile edition with a preface by Ralph Kirkpatrick. New Haven, 1959.

———. *Clavier-Übung. Teil I–IV.* Facsimile edition, after copies in the Music Library of the City of Leipzig, with a commentary by Christoph Wolff. 4 volumes. Leipzig, 1984.

———. *Das Wohltemperierte Clavier.* Ed. Walter Dehnhard. 2 vols. Vienna, 1977–1983.

———. *Das Wohltemperierte Clavier.* Facsimile edition, ed. Hans Pischner. Leipzig, [1965].

———. *Das Wohltemperierte Clavier II.* Facsimile of the autograph manuscript in the British Library. *Add. MS. 35021,* with an introduction by Don Franklin and Stephen Daw. London, 1980.

———. *Fantasia per il cembalo.* BWV 906. Facsimile edition with an introduction by Robert L. Marshall. Leipzig, 1976. Reprinted in Marshall 1989.

———. *Fantasien, Präludien und Fugen.* Ed. Georg von Dadelsen and Klaus Rönnau. Munich, 1969–1970.

———. *Kunst der Fuge, BWV 1080. Frühere Fassung.* Ed. Christoph Wolff. Leipzig, 1986.

———. *Kunst der Fuge, BWV 1080. Spätere Fassung.* Ed. Christoph Wolff. Leipzig, 1986.

———. *Kunst der Fuge, BW 1080. Autograph: Originaldruck.* Facsimile edition, edited with a study by Hans Günter Hoke. Leipzig, 1979.

———. *Musicalisches Opfer. BWV 1079.* Facsimile edition, edited with commentary by Christoph Wolff. Leipzig, 1977.

Literature Cited and Selected Bibliography

Note: A comprehensive bibliography is published in Schulenberg 1992.

BD. *Bach-Dokumente H: Fremdschriftliche und gedruckte Dokumente zur Lebens-geschichte Johann Sebastian Bachs.* Ed. Werner Neumann and Hans-Joachim Schulze. Kassel, 1963

NBR. *The New Bach Reader: A Life of Johann Sebastian Bach in Letters and Documents.* Ed. Hans David and Arthur Mendel; rev. and enlarged by Christoph Wolff. New York, 1998.

Badura-Skoda, Eva. "Komponierte J.S. Bach 'Hammerklavier-Konzerte'?" *Bach-Jahrbuch* (hereafter *BJ) 1991,* 159–71.

Badura-Skoda, Paul. *Interpreting Bach at the Keyboard.* Oxford, 1993.

Besseler, Heinrich. "Bach als Wegbereiter." *Archiv fur Musikwissenschaft* 12 (1955): 1–39.

Bodky, Erwin. *The Interpretation of Bach's Keyboard Works.* Cambridge, MA, 1960.

Breig, Werner. "Composition as arrangement and adaptation." In *The Cambridge Companion to Bach,* ed. John Butt. Cambridge, 1997, 154–70.

Brokaw, James A. "Recent Research on the Sources and Genesis of Bach's *Well-Tempered Clavier,* Book II." *Bach* 16/3 (1985): 17–35.

———. "Techniques of Expansion in the Preludes and Fugues of J.S. Bach." Ph.D. dissertation, University of Chicago, 1986.

Bukofzer, Manfred. *Music in the Baroque Era.* New York, 1947.

Butler, Gregory. *"Der vollkommene Capellmeister* as a stimulus to J. S. Bach's late fugal writing." In *New Mattheson Studies,* ed. George J. Buelow and Hans Joachim Marx. Cambridge, 1983, 293–305. [Butler 1983a]

———. "Ordering Problems in J. S. Bach's *Art of Fugue* Resolved." *The Musical Quarterly* (hereafter *MQ*) 69 (1983): 44–61. [Butler 1983b]

Butt, John. *Bach Interpretation: Articulation Marks in Primary Sources of J. S. Bach.* Cambridge, 1990.

Chafe, Eric. *Tonal Allegory in the Vocal Music of J. S. Bach.* Berkeley, 1991.

Cone, Edward T. "Bach's Unfinished Fugue in C Minor." In *Studies in Renaissance and Baroque Music in Honor of Arthur Mendel,* ed. Robert L. Marshall. Kassel, 1974, 149–55.

Constantini, Franz-Peter. "Zur Typusgeschichte von J.S. Bachs Wohltem-periertem Klavier." *BJ 1969: 31–45.*

Cornell, Robert. "The Development of String Sound in the Thuringian Organ of the Eighteenth Century." *Early Keyboard Studies Newsletter,* 5/4 (1991): 6–7.

Dadelsen, Georg von. *Bemerkungen zur Handschrift Johann Sebastian Bachs, seiner Familie und seines Kreises.* Trossingen, 1957.

Dreyfus, Laurence. "The Kapellmeister and His Audience: Observations on 'Enlightened' Receptions of Bach." In *Alte Musik als asthetische Gegenwart: Kongressbericht Stuttgart 1985,* ed. Dietrich Berke and Dorothee Hanemann. 2 vols. Kassel, 1987, 180–89.

———. *Bach and the Patterns Invention.* Cambridge, MA, 1996.

Durr, Alfred. "Tastenumfang und Chronologie in Bachs Klavierwerken." In *Festschrift Georg von Dadelsen zum 60. Geburtstag,* ed. Thomas Kohlhase und Volker Scherliess. Stuttgart, 1978, 73–88. Reprinted in Durr 1988.

———. *Zur Fruhgeschichte des Wolhtemperierten Klaviers I von Johann Sebastian Bach.* Gottingen, 1984.

————. *Im Mittelpunkt Bach: Ausgewahlte Aufsatze und Vortrage.* Kassel, 1988.

————. *Johann Sebastian Bach: Das Wohltemperierte Klavier.* Kassel, 1998.

Eisert, Christian. *Die Clavier-Toccaten BWV 910–916 von Johann Sebastian Bach: Quellenkritische Untersuchungen zu einem Problem des Frühwerks.* Mainz, 1994.

Eppstein, Hans. "Chronologieprobleme in Johann Sebastian Bachs Suiten fur Soloinstrument."BJ *1976:* 35–57.

Faulkner, Quentin. "Some Characteristics of Eighteenth-Century Thuringian Organs." *Early Keyboard Studies NewsleUer,* 5/4 (1991): 3–5.

Fischer, Johann Kaspar Ferdinand. *Siimtliche Werke fur Klavier uud Orgel.* Ed. Ernst von Werra. Leipzig, 1901. Reprint. New York, 1965.

Forkel, Johann Nicolaus. *Ueber Johann Sebastian Bachs Leben, Kunst und Kunstwerke.* Leipzig, 1802. Translation in *BR,* 295–356.

Franklin, Don O. "Reconstructing the Urpartitur for WTC II: a Study of the 'London Autograph' (BL Add. MS 35021)." In *Bach Studies,* ed. Don O. Franklin. Cambridge, 1989, 240–78.

Germann, Sheridan. "The Mietkes, the Margrave and Bach." In *Bach, Handel, Scarlatti: Tercentenary Essays,* ed. Peter Williams. Cambridge, 1985, 119–48.

Hill, Robert. "The Möller Manuscript and the Andreas Bach Book: Two Keyboard Anthologies from the Circle of the Young Johann Sebastian Bach." Ph.D. dissertation, Harvard University, 1987.

————, ed. *Keyboard Music from the Andreas Bach Book and the Möller Manuscript.* Cambridge, MA, 1991.

Holmann Klaus. "'Fünf Praludien und fünf Fugen': Über ein unbeachtetes Sammelwerk Johann Sebastian Bachs." In *Bericht über die Wissenschaftliche Konferenz zum V. Internationalen Bachrest der DDR ... 1985,* ed. Winfried Hoffmann and Armin Schneiderheinze. Leipzig, 1988, 227–35.

Keller, Hermann. *Die Klavierwerke Bachs.* Leipzig, 1950.

Kirkendale, Ursula. "The Source for Bach's *Musical Offering:* the *Institutio oratoria* of *Quintilian." Journal of the American Musicological Society* (hereafter *JAMS)* 33 (1980): 88–141.

Kobayashi, Yoshitake. "Zur Chronologie der Spätwerke Johann Sebastian Bachs: Kompositions- und Aufführungstätigkeit von 1736 bis 1750." *BJ* 1988: 7–72.

Koster, John. "The Harpsichord Culture in Bach's Environs." In *Bach Perspectives IV: The Music of J. S. Bach: Analysis and Interpretation,* ed. David Schulenberg. Lincoln, NE, 1999, 57–77.

Lindley, Mark. "Temperaments" and "Well-tempered Clavier." In *The New Grove Dictionary of Music and Musicians,* ed. Stanley Sadie. London, 1980. 18: 660–74; 20: 337–38.

Little, Meredith, and Natalie Jenne. *Dance and the Music of J. S. Bach.* Bloomington, IN, 1991.

Löffier, Hans. "Die Schüler Joh. Seb. Bachs." *B J 1953:* 5–28.

Marissen, Michael. "More Source-Critical Research on J. S. Bach's *Musical Offering." Bach* 25/1 (1994): 11–27. [Marissen 1994a]

————. "The Theological Character of J. S. Bach's *Musical Offering.*" In *Bach Studies* 2, ed. Daniel Melamed. Cambridge, 1994, 85–106. [Marissen 1994b]

Marshall, Robert L. "Bach the Progressive: Observations on His Later Works." *MQ* 62 (1976): 313–57. Reprinted in Marshall 1989, 271–93.

————. "Organ or 'Clavier'? Instrumental Prescriptions in the Sources of Bach's Keyboard Works." In *J. S. Bach as Organist: His Instruments, Music, and Perfor-*

mance Practices, ed. George Stauffer and Ernest May. Bloomington, IN, 1986, 212–39. Reprinted in Marshall 1989, 271–93.

————. *The Music of Johann Sebastian Bach: The Sources, the Style, the Significance.* New York, 1989.

————. "The Notebooks for Wilhelm Friedemann and Anna Magdalena Bach: Some Biographical Lessons." In *Essays in Musicology: A Tribute to Alvin Johnson,* ed. Lewis Lockwood and Edward Roesner. Philadelphia, 1990, 192–200.

Neumann, Frederick. *Ornamentation in Baroque and Post-Baroque Music, With Special Emphasis on J. S. Bach.* Princeton, 1978.

————. "Bach: Progressive or Conservative and the Authorship of the Goldberg Aria." *MQ* 71 (1985): 281–94.

Riedel, Herbot. "Recognition and Re-cognition: Bach and the Well-Tempered Clavier." Ph.D. dissertation, University of California, Berkeley, 1969.

Schmieder, Wolfgang. *Thematisch-systematisches Verzeichnis der musikalischen Werke Johann Sebastian Bachs: Bach-Werke-Verzeichnis.* Second revised and expanded edition. Wiesbaden, 1990.

Schulenberg, David. *The Keyboard Music of J. S. Bach.* New York, 1992.

————. "Composition and Improvisation in the School of J. S. Bach." In *Bach Perspectives I,* ed. Russell Stinson. Lincoln, NE, 1995, 1–42.

————. "Versions of Bach: Performing Practices in the Keyboard Works." In *Bach Perspectives IV: The Music of J. S. Bach: Analysis and Interpretation,* ed. David Schulenberg. Lincoln, NE, 1999, 111–35.

Schulze, Hans-Joachim. "Johann Sebastian Bachs Konzerte—Fragen der Überlieferung und Chronologie." *Beiträge zum Konzertschaffen Johann Sebastian Bachs (Bach-Studien 6),* ed. Peter Ansehl, Karl Heller and Hans-Joachim Schulze. Leipzig, 1981, 9–26.

————. *Studien zur Bach-Überlieferung im 18. Jahrhundert.* Leipzig, 1984.

Snyder, Kerala J. "Dietrich Buxtehude's Studies in Learned Counterpoint." *JAMS* 35 (1980): 544–64.

Spitta, Philipp. *Johann Sebastian Bach.* 3 vols. Leipzig, 1873–1880. English translation, reprint. New York, 1952.

Stauffer, George. *The Organ Preludes of Johann Sebastian Bach.* Ann Arbor, MI, 1980.

————. "Johann Mattheson and J.S. Bach: The Hamburg Connection." In *New Mattheson Studies,* ed. George J. Buelow and Hans Joachim Marx. Cambridge, 1983, 353–68.

————. "'This fantasia ... never had its like.' On the Enigma and Chronology of Bach's Chromatic Fantasia and Fugue in D minor, BWV 903." In *Bach Studies,* ed. Don Franklin. Cambridge, 1989, 160–82.

Stevens, Jane R. *The Bach Family and the Keyboard Concerto: The Evolution of a Genre. (Detroit Monographs in Musicology, Studies in Music, 31.)* Warren, MI, 2001.

Stinson, Russell. *The Bach Manuscripts of Johann Peter Kellner and his Circle: A Case Study in Reception History.* Durham, NC, 1989. [Stinson 1989a]

————. "Toward a Chronology of Bach's Instrumental Music: Observations on Three Keyboard Works."*Journal of Musicology* 7 (1989): 440–70. [Stinson 1989b]

Theile, Johann. *Musikalisches Kunstbuch.* Ed. Carl Dahlhaus. Kassel, 1965.

White, Andrew. "The Prelude and Fugue in C major from Bach's *Well-Tempered Clavier* [Book I]: Notes on the Compositional Process," *Bach* 23 (1992): 47–60.

Williams, Peter. *The Organ Music of J. S. Bach.* 3 vols. Cambridge, 1980–1984.

Wolff, Christoph. "The Last fugue: Unfinished?" *Current Musicology* 19 (1975): 71–77. In Wolff 1991, 259–64.

——. "Zur Chronologie und Kompositionsgeschichte von Bachs Kunst der Fuge." *Beiträge zur Musikwissenschaft*, 25 (1983): 130–42. Translated as "The Compositional History of the Art of Fugue." In Wolff 1991, 265–61, 424.

——, ed. *The Neumeister Collection of Chorale Preludes from the Bach Circle: Facsimile Edition of the Yale Manuscript LM 4708.* New Haven, 1985. "Introduction" reprinted in Wolff 1991, 107–28, 406–8. [Wolff 1985a]

——. "Bach's Leipzig Chamber Music." *Early Music* 13 (1985): 65–75. Reprinted in Wolff 1991, 223–38. [Wolff 1985b]

——. "Zur Problematik der Chronologie und Stilentwicklung des Bachschen Frühwerkes, insbesondere zur musikalischen Vorgeschichte des Orgelbüchleins." In *Bericht über die Wissenschaftliche Konferenz Leipzig 1985*, ed. Winfried Hoffmann and Armin Schneiderheinze. Leipzig, 1988, 449–455. Translated as "Chronology and Style in the Early Works: A Background for the Orgelbüchlein." In Wolff 1991, 297–305, 426–27.

——. *Johann Sebastian Bach: Essays on His Life and Music.* Cambridge, MA, 1991.

——. "The Identity of the 'Fratro Dilettisimo' in the Capriccio B-Flat Major and Other Problems of Bach's Early Harpsichord Works." In *The Harpsichord and its Repertoire: Proceedings of the International Symposium. Utrecht 1990*, ed. Pieter Dirksen. Utrecht, 1992, 145–56.

Zietz, Hermann. *Quellenkritische Untersuchungen an den Bach-Handschriften P 801, P 802 und P 803.* Hamburg, 1969.

CHAPTER FOUR

French Masters

Mark Kroll

The French harpsichord tradition spans a period of almost 200 years: from the first decades of the seventeenth century to the last years of the eighteenth. Although the music evolved and changed dramatically, the essential core of the French harpsichord style remained remarkably consistent throughout the entire period. Such a statement would be difficult to support with reference to any other period or genre in the history of keyboard music. The harpsichord works of Handel bear little resemblance to those of Purcell or Byrd, and there are few similarities between the music of the seventeenth-century Spanish composers Cabanilles and Correa de Arauxo and the sonatas of Domenico Scarlatti. But a harpsichord composition written in 1655 by Chambonnières and one composed by Balbastre in 1787, although profoundly different in many details, would both be immediately recognizable as French.

Elements of the Style

Texture

In the French harpsichord style a two-voice texture prevails: an elegant, richly ornamented melody in the right hand is typically supported by a simple accompaniment in the left. Intricate contrapuntal writing and full-voice chordal homophony are both avoided. Consequently, many compositional forms cultivated in other national traditions of the period—fugues, ricercars, fantasias, sonatas—are rare in France. Moreover, virtuoso keyboard display was kept to a minimum, as well. Neither extensive arpeggiation (as in J. S. Bach's *Chromatic Fantasia* and Handel's *Lessons*) nor rapid scale passages and repeated notes (as in the sonatas of Domenico Scarlatti) appear in the French repertory until the end of the century. The French harpsichord composer was interested in obtaining maximum expressive effect by different means altogether, through resonant spacing of parts, subtle sonority, and a rich harmonic vocabulary.

One well-known manifestation of the French approach to keyboard writing was the *style-luthée* (lute style) or *style-brisé* (broken style), an arpeggiated texture that produces a kaleidoscopic palette of shifting sonorities as well as the suggestion of an implicit polyphony. As the name of the technique suggests, it acknowledges the compositional style of the lutenists, such as Charles Mouton (b. 1626, d. after 1699) and Denis Gaultier (1603–1672). The *style-luthée* is idiomatic to no other keyboard instrument but the harpsichord (Ex. 4.1):

EXAMPLE 4.1. Gaspard Le Roux. *Courante luthée*, mm. 1–5, from Suite No. 1 (*Pièces de clavessin*, 1705)

Close stylistic links between the music of the clavecinistes and the lutenists is evident in other respects as well, particularly in the notation of mandatory ornaments and in the use of descriptive or fanciful titles. Whether the French harpsichord tradition developed directly from the lute school or whether both shared a common heritage and aesthetic remains an open question.

Ornamentation

The elaborate ornamentation of French harpsichord music is perhaps an even more unmistakable hallmark of the style than its texture. Listeners past and present have expressed astonishment (or chagrin) at the number and variety of French ornaments. Charles Burney's description of François Couperin's music is indicative: "The great Couperin . . . was not only an admirable organist but, in the style of the times, an excellent composer for keyed instruments . . . tho' his pieces are so

ILLUSTRATION 4.1. François Couperin: *Pièces de clavecin*, Book One (Paris, 1713). From the Table of Ornaments.

crowded and deformed by beats, trills, shakes, that no plain note was left to enable the hearer of them to judge whether the tone of the instrument on which they were played was good or bad" (Burney 2:976).

The manner in which ornamentation was applied to keyboard music in France distinguishes it from all other keyboard music of the Baroque era. Unlike English divisions or Italian embellishments consist-

ing of notes and figurations spontaneously added to a simple melodic line by the performer, the French *agréments* are neither optional nor improvisatory. On the contrary: they are an integral part of the composition. (One has only to play a French melody with the ornaments removed to understand fully their indispensability.) On one level,

French ornaments are melodic decorations, similar to the ornate decorations added to French furniture and architecture of the period. But there was nothing superficial about their function: the *agréments* were meticulously notated and applied to exploit the astonishing range of nuance, color, and dynamic resources available on the French harpsichords of the period. These instruments, with their sensitive keyboards, are marvels of construction and refinement—the perfect vehicles for the execution and realization of the *agréments*.

Most composers developed personal systems for the notation of ornaments and usually included an explicatory table at the beginning of their publications. The tables from Couperin's first book of harpsichord pieces and from Rameau's 1724 publication are representative (Ill. 4.1 and 4.2).

Notes Inégales

One of the most misunderstood aspects of French Baroque music is the tradition of *notes inégales:* the practice of performing passages written in equal note values in unequal rhythm. There is no doubt that the application of *inégales* was standard practice in the performance of eighteenth-century French harpsichord music. Its use is corroborated by numerous sources. We cite three: François Couperin, the theorist M. de Saint-Lambert, and the flute composer Jacques Hotteterre.

Couperin:
We do not notate as we perform, which is the reason why foreigners perform our music less well than we perform theirs. For example, we perform as dotted a succession of eighth-notes moving by step; yet we notate them as equal (Couperin 1717, 49).
Saint-Lambert:
The equality of movement that we require in notes of the same value is not observed with eighth-notes when there are several in a row. The practice is to make them alternatively long and short, because this inequality gives them more grace (St. Lambert 1702, 46).
Hotteterre:
When this (the number of eighth-notes) is even, the first is to be taken long, the second short, and so on (Hotteterre 1707, 24).

In sum, a step-wise succession of apparently equal note values in French harpsichord music must be played with some degree of inequality. The crucial question is: to what degree? This is the issue that has led to great confusion and misinterpretation. The most common misconception is the assumption that inequality calls for the performance of uniform dotted rhythms. Uniform dotting is certainly one possible realization of *inégalité,* but it is only one of a vast range of rhythmic inter-

ILLUSTRATION 4.2. Jean-Philippe Rameau: *Pièces de clavecin* (Paris, 1724). From the Table of Ornaments.

pretations. Composers, after all, were obviously able to notate dotted rhythms without ambiguity whenever that is what they wanted. Indeed, dotted notes sometimes appear side-by-side in the same composition with evenly notated passages (Ex. 4.2).

EXAMPLE 4.2. François Couperin. *La Bersan*, mm. 23–25, from Ordre No. 6. (*Pièces de clavecin*, Book Two, 1716/17)

Understood properly, the *notes inégales* convention represents an exceedingly refined form of rubato, one of such subtlety that it cannot be adequately notated. It is an expressive device that must be applied with the greatest artistry. This is clear both from the theoretical sources and from the music itself; and it is testimony to the subtlety of the French style. Bacilly writes: "Although I say that alternate dots are implicit in divisions (that is to say that of two notes one is commonly dotted), it has been thought proper not to mark them for fear of getting used to performing them by jerks" (Bacilly 1668, 232–33).

This is amplified by Saint-Lambert: "The decision as to whether they should be more or less unequal is a matter of taste. There are some pieces in which it is appropriate to make them very unequal and others in which they should be less so. *Taste is the judge of this,* as it is of tempo" [emphasis added] (St. Lambert 1702, 25).

The proper application of *inégales,* then, defies a strict or simple arithmetical realization; rather, it varies subtly according to the character of a piece. One of the most enlightening discussions of *inégales* is found in a treatise on mechanical instruments. The author, Marie Dominique Joseph Engramelle, was challenged to devise a system for producing an accurate mathematical representation of *inégales,* one that would enable him to play it on his mechanical organs. Engramelle introduces a large number of ratios to represent uneven notes (such as $2 : 1, 3: 1, 3 : 2$, and even $7 : 5$), but he ultimately concedes that his mathematical and mechanical constructs at best can only approximate the subtleties of the art. He complains bitterly that his model performers are rarely consistent in their use of inequality but rather continually change and adjust its application in their performances. In the end Engramelle admits that: "Inequalities ... in many places vary in the same piece; it is left to fine taste to appreciate these variations of inequality" (Engramelle 1775, 230).

The Keyboard Genres

Almost the entire repertory of the clavecinistes belongs to one of three categories: dance music, character or descriptive pieces, and dedicatory works.

Dance Suites

During the early eighteenth century the French suite consisted of a core of four dances—allemande, courante, sarabande, and gigue—although their order could vary. The dances generally resembled their seventeenth-century counterparts, but they encompassed a wider stylistic range. The sarabande, for example, was no longer necessarily a slow dance: Gaspard Le Roux composed a sarabande in D major marked "gaye." And the gigue now appears in two distinct types: the Italian form, in rapid 6/8 or 12/8 time, with prevailing rhythmic motion in equal eighth-notes, and the somewhat slower French form, in 6/4 time, and more complex in rhythm (Ex. 4.3).

EXAMPLE 4.3a. Charles Demars. Gigue, mm. 1–3, from Suite No. 3 (*Ier Livre de pièces de clavecin*, 1735)

EXAMPLE 4.3b. Louis-Nicolas Clérambault. Gigue, mm. 1–4, from Suite No. 1 (*Pièces de clavecin*, 1704)

In the early decades of the eighteenth century the dances are usually preceded by a prélude, or by an *ouverture*. The préludes employed both whole-note, (i.e., unmeasured) and rhythmic notations. During the seventeenth century the prélude, in its purest form, had been written out entirely in whole-notes and the performer was given complete liberty to interpret the harmonic and melodic implications of the notation (Ex. 4.4).

EXAMPLE 4.4. Louis Couperin. Beginning of the Prélude from Suite [No. 8] in D

The very nature of the unmeasured prélude, then, assured that every performance would be, in effect, improvisatory. During the course of the eighteenth century, however, prélude composers increasingly imposed more constraints on the performer's freedom until the form itself was eventually abandoned. A variety of dances and other movements were often added to the basic core. The most common additions were menuets and gavottes; other movements included chaconnes, passacailles, rigaudons, and rondeaux. Like the four core dances, they are usually in simple binary form, but examples of rounded binary, ternary, rondeau, and even sonata form are also represented.

Character Pieces

Programmatic by definition, character pieces appealed to the expectation, popular in eighteenth-century France, that music should express or represent something other than itself. By means of the imaginative use of keyboard figures, distinctive rhythms, or unusual harmonies, composers attempted to suggest natural phenomena, scenes from the theatre or from the folk heritage, emotions or states of mind, paintings and other works of art, even political or social situations. Couperin's *Les ondes* (*ordre* no. 5), for example, creates the impression of waves with gently undulating scale passages. Similarly, his *Les fastes de la grande et anciénne-Mxnxstrxndxsx* (*ordre* no. 11), represents the chaotic disruption of a troupe of entertainers by means of a rapid tremolo figure in the left hand; and *La marche des gris-vêtus* (*ordre* no. 4) imitates the pompous march of a noble order with thick chords and square rhythms.

Character pieces appeared only infrequently in the early part of the century, but became increasingly common after 1730.

Dedicatory Pieces

Dedicatory pieces were written to honor famous or influential persons whose names appeared in the title. Jean-Philippe Rameau's *La Forqueray* (*Pièces de clavecin en concerts*) is a typical example. The musical content of dedicatory compositions was usually abstract rather than representational, but they were occasionally programmatic and could even take the form of a dance movement.

History to about 1750

The first decade of the eighteenth century was a period of intense activity for the composers of *pièces de clavecin*. Important collections were published by François (Charles) Dieupart, Louis Marchand, Louis-Nicolas Clérambault, Jean-François Dandrieu, Gaspard Le Roux, Jean-Philippe Rameau, and Elizabeth Jacquet de la Guerre. These works represent a transition from the idiom of the seventeenth-century masters—Jacques Champion Chambonnières, Louis Couperin, Jean Henri-D'Anglebert—to the styles and genres of the new century.

The end of the eighteenth-century harpsichord tradition is difficult to identify precisely. The problem, in brief, is to determine when the harpsichord was decisively supplanted by the piano. According to David Fuller, Jean-François Tapray's four *Symphonies concertantes*, published between 1778 and 1783, "were the last French music in which harpsichord was indispensable" (Gustafson/Fuller 1991, 1). Fuller also remarks that "pianos were rare in France in the 1760's and relatively uncommon in the seventies. In the eighties . . . pianos were overtaking the older instrument in the esteem of players . . . and by the nineties they had fully caught up and were rapidly passing it in manufacture. . . . After about 1780 it makes little sense to speak of 'French harpsichord music' because . . . the piano was by then established as the modern medium" (p 15).

On the other hand, many harpsichords were found in the workshop of the illustrious maker Pascal Taskin as late as 1793—a strong indication that the instrument was still being played toward the end of the century. Moreover, the harpsichord evidently appeared as a solo instrument in programs of the famous Concert Spirituel during the decade from 1777 to 1787.[1] It is true, however, that the use of the term *clavecin* or *cembalo* in the title of a piece after 1770 by no means indicates that the work was intended exclusively for the harpsichord.[2] Nonetheless, a work like Balbastre's *La d'Esclignac*, which appeared as late as 1787, still retains idiomatic harpsichord figuration.

All in all, it seems reasonable to consider Louis Marchand's *Pièces de clavecin* of 1699 as marking the beginning of eighteenth-century French harpsichord music and the death of Balbastre in 1799 as marking its end. The first significant collection of harpsichord music literally published in the new century, however, was Charles Dieupart's *Six suittes de clavecin*, which appeared in print in 1701.

Charles Dieupart (166?–1740) was born in Paris (with the Christian name François) sometime after 1667, but he spent most of his professional life in England (where he was known as Charles Dieupart). In addition to his keyboard music he composed instrumental ensemble works and songs. He also participated in many English productions of Italian opera.

The *Six suittes* were never published in France but rather in Amsterdam; they are listed in Estienne Roger's catalogue of 1702. Nevertheless, they are unmistakably French harpsichord music, although with strong German and Italian elements. They are also the first examples of French-style suites in which the number and order of dance movements are fixed and uniform throughout. Each suite begins with an *ouverture*, followed by allemande, courante, sarabande, optional dance, and gigue. In fact, Dieupart was the first French keyboard composer to write Lullian-style overtures rather than preludes—a practice that occurs rarely later on. Dieupart's allemandes, courantes, and sarabandes resemble their French antecedents in character, texture, and rhythm, but his gigues belong to the Italian type. The contrapuntal quality of Dieupart's writing in general, however, attests to his familiarity with German models.

Dieupart's suites are also the first to have been published in an alternative ensemble version (previous publications merely suggested that option). The upper part of the harpsichord part was assigned to the "violin or flute" and a simplified figured version of the bass line to the "bass viol and arch lute." The names of the ornaments appear in both English and French.

Although Dieupart's suites contain many atypical features, they were more widely known outside France than other French harpsichord music and therefore were sometimes taken as the model of the French style. J. S. Bach, for example, came to know and admire Dieupart's suites and even copied out some of the pieces. The striking similarity between the theme of the prelude from the first English Suite BWV 806 and Dieupart's gigue in A major is one indication of Bach's interest in the French composer.[3] The reason for Dieupart's fame and influence abroad, no doubt, is that he lived in England and had an influential publisher in Amsterdam.

Louis Marchand (1669–1732) was one of the great keyboard virtuosos of his time, not only in France but throughout Europe. Marchand began an extensive tour of Germany in 1713 and in September 1717 arrived in Dresden for the now-famous noncompetition with J. S. Bach. Despite the debacle in Dresden, Marchand's fame and popularity as a virtuoso and teacher remained throughout his life.

Marchand published two books of *Pièces de clavecin*. Both appeared together in 1702, although Book One was first published in 1699. Each book contains only one suite (although the term "suite" is not actually used). These works belong more comfortably than Dieupart's to the seventeenth-century clavecin tradition, but there are a number of progressive features in Marchand's work. Book One begins with the expected prélude, but it is not written completely in the traditional whole-note style: it also makes use of notated rhythmic values. The dances conform to French practice: an allemande is followed by two courantes, a sarabande, gigue, chaconne, gavotte, and menuet. But the writing throughout is notable for the skillful use of *style-brisé,* and for the sensitivity to texture and sonority. Book Two (which contains an elegant poetic dedication by Saint-Lambert) is more conservative, and the individual dances are on a smaller scale. The prélude combines both notated rhythms and whole-note style but remains improvisatory and unmeasured. The allemande, courante, sarabande, gigue, gavotte, menuet, and menuet rondeau that follow feature a simpler and thinner texture than is found in Book One.

Louis-Nicolas Clérambault (1676–1749) was a member of a distinguished family of musicians. He occupied numerous organist positions, and served as supervisor of the concerts of Mme. de Maintenon for Louis XIV. In addition to his keyboard music, he wrote solo and trio sonatas, songs, and motets, but he is particularly well known for his cantatas.

In 1704 Clérambault published his only book of *Pièces de clavecin,* consisting of two suites: one in C major, the other in C minor. The opening prélude of the first suite is *non-mesuré* and uses a combination of whole-notes and notated rhythms similar to Marchand's Book Two prélude. Moreover, Clérambault also employs vertical dotted lines to indicate when the right and left hands should play together (Ex. 4.5).

EXAMPLE 4.5. Clérambault. Beginning of the Prélude from Suite No. 1 (*Pièces de clavecin,* 1704)

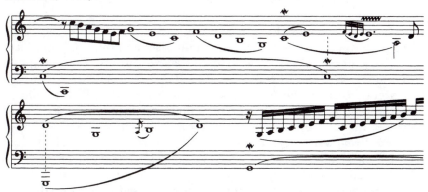

The allemande contains some notable features: the **C** time signature is modified by the marking "gay," it includes a *double,* and it is surprisingly homophonic. The suite concludes with a courante, two sarabandes, gavotte (also with *double*), gigue, and two menuets. The appearance of the movement order of the C-minor suite seems quite odd: it begins with an allemande, which is followed in turn by a gigue, an unmeasured prelude, a courante, and a *sarabande grave*. This unusual order, however, does not prescribe a unique performance practice, but evidently reflects either a misunderstanding or a technical difficulty on the part of the publisher. The composer's printed explanations in the score before the prelude clarify the issue: "Prélude qui doit se jouer devant l'Allemande," and after that movement: "La Courante et la Sarabande doivent se Jouer devant la Gigue immediatement apres l'Allemande." In other words: normal order.

Jean-François Dandrieu (ca. 1682–1738) was often compared favorably with Couperin and Rameau. A significant problem for any consideration of Dandrieu's harpsichord works is their complicated chronology. The first book was published around 1704; the second and third appeared between 1710 and 1720 but were probably written earlier. Dandrieu then published three more books of harpsichord pieces, calling them *Premier livre* (1724), *Second livre* (1728), and *Troisième livre* (1734). His intention evidently was either to replace or to repudiate the three earlier harpsichord volumes, perhaps finding their style too youthful or archaic. Many of the works in these last three books are simply reworkings of the earlier pieces, the change often amounting to no more than the addition of descriptive titles.

Dandrieu's compositional style is similar to that of his contemporaries, and he generally follows common practice. Most of his pieces in fact are rather uninspired and lightweight and cannot stand comparison with the masterpieces of Clérambault, Couperin, or Rameau. For example, his attempts at the expressive use of *style-luthée* in *La lyre d'Orphée* or at descriptive writing in *Le turbulent* (both from Book Two, 1728) seem facile when compared with Couperin's *Les baricades mistérieuses* (*ordre* no. 6) or *Le turbulent* (*ordre* no. 18).

Dandrieu's suites do contain some interesting features, however. Two préludes are included for the D-minor suite of the 1704 collection, and Book Three (1734) has a declared didactic purpose—the composer even going so far as to add fingerings. The gigues in the fourth suite apparently contain the first known *fort-doux* indication of the century. Dandrieu thus exploits the expressive potential of the dynamic contrast between the two keyboards of eighteenth-century French harpsichords.

Elizabeth-Claude Jacquet de la Guerre (1666/67–1729) was a child prodigy as well as a favorite of Louis XIV. She remained an active figure in the Parisian musical scene until she retired from the public in 1717.

It is not surprising that Jacquet's work fits comfortably into the continuum of the clavecin traditions of both centuries: her first book of harpsichord pieces (now lost) appeared in 1687; Book Two was published in 1707. The arrangement of the dances and the use of *style-brisé* is fairly conventional, but Jacquet calls for three- and four-part chordal textures more often than most of her contemporaries. A good example of this is provided by the allemande in G major. The chaconne in D major, cast in the form ABACADAEA, is one of the longest examples of the genre from the early part of the century. Jacquet and Dandrieu were the only eighteenth-century composers before Couperin to treat the rigaudon as a separate form, although Jacquet was alone in treating the rondeau in this manner. In conformity with common practice, she indicates in the preface that the works may be performed with instrumental accompaniment (in this case a violin); however, a separate part is not provided for that instrument.

Gaspard Le Roux (b. mid-seventeenth century–d. 1705/7). Little is known about Le Roux's life. His *Pièces de clavessin* were written at the end of the seventeenth century, but their 1705 publication date, along with a number of stylistic features, allows us to include Le Roux among the eighteenth-century composers. The lack of a dedication in his *Pièces* suggests that he may have been independent of means and did not need patronage.

Le Roux follows seventeenth-century practice insofar as a large number of his dance movements are randomly grouped by tonality into suites (though without using the term). The préludes also look backward: they are all in the whole-note style. On the other hand, Le Roux's compositional technique is exceptionally sumptuous and presages some of the best writing of Couperin and later composers. Particularly striking are the rich harmonic language of the sarabande in G minor (with its twelve couplets) and the textural subtlety of the *Courante luthée* (Ex. 4.1, p. 125). The gigues, for their part, reflect an Italian influence.

Three of Le Roux's compositions—*La pièce sans titre, La favoritte,* and *La bel-ebat*—are the first known examples of nondance pieces with fanciful titles. Most of Le Roux's harpsichord pieces appear in alternative arrangements for two melody instruments and figured bass. This practice again follows common procedure, but Le Roux exploits it to a greater extent than other composers. He goes even further by suggesting that these pieces may also be played by two harpsichords.

François Couperin (1668–1733) represents the ultimate expression of the art of the French harpsichord tradition. His music encompasses all the elements of the national style raised to an unequaled level of refinement. Couperin's achievement towers over those of his predecessors and successors. Acknowledged as "le Grand" in his own lifetime, he enjoyed the most esteemed reputation among his contemporaries as a performer and composer.

Couperin occupies a central position both chronologically and stylistically. His career unfolded at the middle of the 200-year tradition of clavecinistes. He was witness to the last twenty years of the reign of Louis XIV and to the beginning of the gradual dissolution of the French absolute monarchy. Couperin's music was not only a synthesis of all that had come before, it profoundly influenced all that would follow. Couperin drew upon the French opera as epitomized by Lully, upon Italian chamber music and the sonatas of Corelli, on the commedia dell'arte and the *tragédies lyriques,* French folk songs, and the paintings of Watteau. All these traditions left their imprint on Couperin's harpsichord music, where they were imbued with delicacy, passion, humanity, and *bon goût.*

A member of a distinguished musical dynasty, François "le Grand" was born on November 10, 1668. His uncle was Louis Couperin. His father, François, from whom he most probably received his early training, was organist at St. Gervais. Couperin's appointment as "organiste du roi" in 1693 allowed him to come in close contact with many members of the aristocracy. During the last fifteen years of the reign of Louis XIV Couperin significantly expanded his activities. He participated in concerts at Versailles and Fontainebleau, wrote many chamber works, and established his reputation as a composer and teacher. His fortunes continued to improve even after the death of Louis, and he maintained his preeminence as a composer of harpsichord and chamber music. In addition to four published volumes of harpsichord music, Couperin's works include two organ masses, secular and religious vocal music, chamber music (including *Les nations, Concerts royaux,* two viola da gamba sonatas and *L'apothéose de Corelli* and *L'apothéose de Lully*), and the didactic works *L'art de toucher le clavecin* and *Regle pour l'accompagnement.*

Couperin's first book of harpsichord music was published in 1713, but many of the pieces had been written earlier, and they contain features that look back to the seventeenth century. Four of the five suites (or *ordres,* as Couperin preferred to call them) are loose collections of movements reminiscent of the works of D'Anglebert and Louis Couperin. The composers of these multimovement suites did not intend that all the pieces should be played consecutively at a single performance but rather that the performer would select several contrasting movements and group them together to form a suite. The number of pieces in Couperin's *ordres* range from four (in no. 4) to twenty-three (in no. 2).

Most of these pieces are dances, but there is already a substantial number of character and descriptive pieces. The use of genre pieces became the norm in Couperin's next three books, and in the work of all future clavecinistes. Couperin's belief that music should inspire the deepest feelings and thoughts and should be expressive or represent something specific may account for his preference for character and descriptive music over conventional dance pieces. As he remarks in the preface to the 1713 collection: "In composing these pieces, I have always had an object in view. . . . Thus the titles reflect ideas which I have had. . . . The pieces which bear them are a kind of portrait which, under my fingers, have on occasion been found fair enough likenesses."

Even though Book One is the product of a youthful composer, it already contains several masterpieces. The allemande *La ténébreuse* (*ordre* no. 3) is notable for its magnificent use of *style-luthée* and the brilliant exploitation of the dark, sonorous lower register of the French harpsichord; the chaconne *La favorite* in the same *ordre* is an equally skillful blend of the lute style, expressive harpsichord writing, and large formal structure. *Le réveil-matin ordre* no. 4), in which a tremolo figure graphically depicts the alarm of a morning wake-up call, reveals Couperin's humor and descriptive skill.

Book Two (1716–1717) displays a fully developed Couperin style; it also attests to changing tastes in France. Not only has the average number of pieces in each *ordre* fallen from fifteen to eight, but only one *ordre* (no. 8) retains the traditional core of dances. Some of Couperin's most refined writing appears in Book Two, where a perfect balance is achieved between a simple but elegant melodic line, rich and poignant harmonies, and the skillful use of ornaments to create nuance and the effect of dynamic contrast. The volume contains a number of masterpieces. *Les bergeries* (*ordre* no. 6) evokes the dream-like world of Watteau. The famous *Les baricades mistérieuses* in the same *ordre* is a marvel of sonorities and the exploitation of *style-luthée*. The power and scope of the B-minor *passacaille* (*ordre* no. 8) suggested to Wilfrid Mellers "the rigidity of a social and technical convention . . . [which] . . . only just succeeds in holding in check a passion so violent that it threatens to engulf both the personality and the civilization" (Mellers 1987, 193). But Book Two also attests to Couperin's sympathy for popular music and for everyday life, and to his conviction that the popular and the serious can easily intermingle.

The level of artistry is maintained in Book Three (1722). In the eighteenth *ordre* alone one encounters harmonic language of power and pathos (*Allemande La verneüil*), elegant simplicity (*Soeur Monique*), vivid intensity (*Le turbulent*), the humor of the commedia dell'arte (*Le galliard boiteux*), and brilliant descriptive writing (*Le tic-toc-choc, ou Les maillotins*) (Ex. 4.6).

EXAMPLE 4.6. F. Couperin. Beginning of *Le Tic-Toc-Choc*, from Ordre No. 18 (*Pièces de clavecin*, Book Three, 1722)

Book Four was published in 1730, but according to Couperin himself, most of its music had been completed three years earlier. (There is also some indication that Couperin had composed many other pieces that did not appear in this or the previous volumes, and that are now lost.) In this final book Couperin achieves a mature balance between simplicity and sophistication, or as Mellers puts it, "between the claims of the individual, society and God" (Mellers 1987, 211). A fine example of this is *L'arlequine* (*ordre* no. 23): its deceptive simplicity and subtle chromaticism recall the innocent complexity of Watteau's painting *Gilles*.

There are no préludes in any of the four books of *ordres*, although Couperin suggests in *L'art de toucher le clavecin* that the préludes published there could be used before an *ordre* in the corresponding key. (Couperin, incidentally, never used the whole-note style in his préludes. They were all written in notated rhythmic values, with the addition of the modifying word *mesuré* or *non-mesuré* to indicate the relative freedom of the performance.)

Couperin's *L'art de toucher le clavecin* (1716; revised 1717) is a slim volume. It contains only eight préludes, along with informative and instructive suggestions about the performance of his harpsichord music, and about style in general. Among his precepts we read:

> On technique: "In order to be seated at the correct height, the underside of the elbows, wrists and fingers must all be on one level. . . . Sweetness of touch depends, moreover, on holding the fingers as closely as possible to the keys."
>
> On fingering: "I do not allow the old fingering other than in places where the hand must play two different parts (at the same time)."
>
> On instruments: "One must always play very delicately on the keyboard and always have a very well-quilled instrument. I understand that, nevertheless, there are those people who are quite indifferent; perhaps they play equally badly on any instrument at all."[4]

Couperin's influence outside of France was much less extensive than it was at home. He was not well known in England, and Burney's comment about the ornaments cited earlier gives an indication of the prevailing critical view in that country. Couperin's influence in Germany can be discerned in Telemann's "Paris" quartets and in the works of Georg Muffat and Johann Mattheson. Among German keyboard compositions Friedrich Wilhelm Marpurg's *Clavierstücke* (1762) are most deeply indebted to the French masters. Marpurg transcribed *Le réveil-matin* along with works by Clérambault and others and wrote his own pieces with titles in the style of Couperin.

J. S. Bach knew some of Couperin's work. The aria for organ, BWV 587, is a transcription of *L'imperiale* from *Les nations*.[5] The version of *Les bergeries* (Book Two, *ordre* no. 6), which appears as rondeau in the *Clavierbüchlein vor Anna Magdalena Bach* of 1725, was probably not transcribed from the Couperin publication but based on one of the many copies of the original made in Holland, Great Britain, or Belgium.[6] Substantial differences in the notation of the lefthand figure between the Bach and Couperin versions raise important questions about the possible differences in the way the harpsichord was played in France and in Germany. Briefly, Bach does not preserve Couperin's complicated system of notation for the lefthand figure, with its carefully indicated ties and held notes. Rather, he uses a simple pattern of eighth- and sixteenth-notes. Does this imply that Bach preferred a more detached style of harpsichord playing, or should such figures (which appear throughout Bach's harpsichord music) be realized with the notes held, regardless of the notation? The divergent notation in the two versions also raises questions about the intended execution of some of the ornaments (Ex. 4.7).

EXAMPLE 4.7a. F. Couperin. Beginning of *Les Bergeries,* from Ordre No. 6 (*Pièces de clavecin,* Book Two, 1716/17)

EXAMPLE 4.7b. F. Couperin. *Les Bergeries,* as notated in the 1725 *Clavierbüchlein vor Anna Magdalena Bach*

Jean-Philipe Rameau (1683–1764) received his early musical training at his birthplace, Dijon, from his father and the Jesuits. In 1706 he moved to Paris, and owing to the success of his first book of harpsichord pieces, succeeded Marchand as organist of the Jesuit College. From 1709 to 1715 he was again in Dijon where he succeeded his father at Notre-Dame. From 1715 to 1722 he served as organist at Clermont Cathedral. At this time he wrote his organ works as well as his epochal *Traité de l'harmonie.* Rameau returned to Paris in 1722 but was still unable to secure a suitable organist position even after the publication of his harpsichord collections.

Although Rameau's reputation as a composer is based primarily on his operas, his three solo harpsichord collections (1706, 1724, 1729, or

1730), the transcriptions from his operas *Les Indes galantes* (1735) and *La dauphine* (ca. 1747), and the ensemble compositions of the *Pièces de clavecin en concerts* (1741) contain some of the most important and exciting French harpsichord music of the eighteenth century.

Book One (1706) fits comfortably into the stylistic tradition of Marchand and Clérambault. The opening prélude is unmeasured, written in both whole-note style and notated rhythms; it also includes a gigue-like section in 12/8 meter. The remaining pieces are traditional dances and include two allemandes (the first in *style-luthée*, the second more Italianate), two sarabandes (in minor-major modalities), and a single character piece: *La Vénitiénne*.

The 1724 collection contains two suites (without using that term) in the keys of E and D, respectively. The suite in E maintains an equal balance between dances and descriptive pieces. Included among the latter is the remarkable portrayal of the warble of birds, *Le rappel des oiseaux*. Rameau was introduced to birdsongs by the Jesuit mathematician Père Louis-Bertrand Castel, who also claims to have given Rameau "the outlines of pieces which imitate the truths of nature" (Girdlestone 1957, 30). The pieces in D include some of the century's finest descriptive and most idiomatic harpsichord music, among them compositions inspired by natural phenomena (e.g., *Les tourbillons*, or whirlwinds), or by the theatre (*Les cyclopes*),[7] as well as others that evoke moods or states of mind (*Les tendres plaintes, Les soupirs*). Rameau made his intentions explicit in a letter of October 25, 1727: "You have only to come and hear how I have characterized the song and dance of the savages who appeared at the Theatre Italien two years ago, and how I have rendered the titles *Les soupirs, Les tendres plaintes, Les cyclopes, Les tourbillons* (that is to say the swirls of dust raised by high winds)." The 1724 collection also features some of the most virtuosic and progressive keyboard writing in the history of French harpsichord music. The revolutionary lefthand figure in *Les cyclopes*, which Rameau called "batteries" (Ex. 4.8), and the

EXAMPLE 4.8. Jean-Philippe Rameau. *Les cyclopes*, mm. 32–37 (*Pièces de clavecin*, 1724)

cross-rhythms and lefthand passages of *Les niais de Sologne* make these works two of the most challenging pieces in the Baroque keyboard literature.

Rameau returns again to dance movements in the collection of 1729/1730. The allemande is notable for its soaring lyricism and poignant suspensions, and the powerful sarabande features dramatic chromatic modulations. *Les trois mains* is an appropriate title for this virtuoso tour de force. The theme and keyboard style of the gavotte with *doubles* reveals Rameau's familiarity with Handel's Air with Variations in the E-major Suite published in the latter's 1720 collection.

Of the miscellaneous pieces, *La poule* is one of Rameau's best known. The repeated notes and keyboard figures graphically depict the barnyard sounds of chicken (Rameau even writes beneath the opening notes the onomatopoetic "co co co co co co co dai"). In addition to its intrinsic beauty the reputation of *L'enharmonique* rests on its daring notation and its implications for harmonic theory. In this work Rameau uses enharmonic spellings of chords to create startling chromatic modulations (Ex. 4.9).

EXAMPLE 4.9. Jean-Philippe Rameau. *L'enharmonique*, mm. 13–20 (*Nouvelle Suites*, 1729)

Rameau was well aware of the didactic and revolutionary potential of *L'enharmonique*. He writes in the preface to the volume: "The harmony which creates this effect has by no means been thrown in haphazardly; it is based on logic and has the sanction of Nature herself." In other comments he offers remarkably specific suggestions concerning the proper rendition of the piece: "Its performance must bring out the composer's intention through a softening of the touch and by suspending the appoggiaturas more and more as one approaches the thrilling passage where a momentary stop is indicated by the sign ⌒ ."[8]

The art of transcription was a common practice during the Baroque era, and Rameau was particularly fond of the genre. Many of his harpsichord pieces have their counterparts in his own operas and instrumental ensemble works. In 1735 Rameau published a large collection of transcriptions entitled *Les Indes galantes, ballet réduit à quatre grands concerts.* The publication effectively doubles the number of harpsichord works by Rameau. In the preface he writes: "As the public have appeared less satisfied with the recitatives of *Les Indes galantes* than with the rest of the work, . . . I offer here the instrumental music only, mixed with some vocal numbers and choruses." Not all the transcriptions are entirely idiomatic, and a few of the works are clearly intended for ensemble performance. The *Tambourin,* for example, is unplayable by a single harpsichordist.

The arrangements from *Les Indes galantes* are not Rameau's only transcriptions, but they are his most extensive and provide an informative glimpse into his compositional technique. In the *Quatre grands concerts* no piece is left unchanged, the changes range from minor details to complete alterations of texture, harmony, form, and ornamentation. Not surprisingly, the most common procedure is a thinning of the texture, although the occasional use of thick block chords in the left hand has no precedent in Rameau's earlier harpsichord music. Passages are sometimes transposed to avoid hand-crossing or too large a gap between treble and bass; inner parts are added to enrich the harmony, and the bass line is simplified in faster movements. Occasionally the material of two bars is compressed into one. But Rameau here rarely uses some of his favorite idiomatic devices, such as *style-brisé,* "batteries," virtuoso hand crossings, and arpeggiation. Finally, these pieces contain about two or three times as many ornaments as are found in the originals. This, again, is not surprising: it demonstrates Rameau's sensitivity to the role of ornaments in achieving gradations of sound and color on the harpsichord.

Rameau's *Pièces de clavecin en concerts* (1741) deserve inclusion in this survey. Most Baroque chamber music calls for one or more melody instruments accompanied by a basso continuo. Obbligato keyboard parts are sometimes prescribed, but the typical role of the harpsichordist is to realize a figured bass. French music for accompanied harpsichord represents a complete reversal of this practice. Here the harpsichord is the principal soloist, accompanied by the melody instruments. This mode of performance was an option often implied by early clavecin composers, but the appearance in 1734 of Jean-Joseph Mondonville's *Sonates pour le clavecin avec accompagnement de violon* immediately and decisively established the genre. Numerous similar publications followed; indeed, almost all chamber music composed in France after 1750 adopted this format.

Rameau, too, wrote his *Pièces de clavecin en concerts* in direct response to Mondonville's publication, as he acknowledges in the preface: "The success of recently published sonatas, which have come out as harpsichord pieces with a violin part, has given me the idea of following much the same plan.... I have given them the form of little concerts for harpsichord, violin or flute, and viol or second violin."[9]

The composer also maintains, however, that "these pieces lose nothing by being played on the harpsichord alone." Rameau in fact did transcribe four pieces for the solo instrument: *La livri, L'agaçante, La timide,* and *L'indiscrète.* The new genre did not always meet with uniform approval or complete understanding, as Mathon de la Cour observed: "It would seem that sonatas of this kind ought to be classified as trios; they nevertheless retain the name of sonatas because the harpsichord part predominates, and the accompanying parts are not obbligato—or at least they are only written to make the harpsichord shine."[10] The problems of balance inherent in accompanied harpsichord music inspired the same commentator to make this amusing observation on music and society:

> We cannot resist pointing out here that the harpsichord is the only creature in this world that has been able to claim sufficient respect from other instruments to keep them in their place and cause itself to be accompanied in the full sense of the term. Voices, even the most beautiful ones, lack this privileged position; they are covered mercilessly and all the nuances are hidden from us without scruple; but as soon as it is a question of accompanying a harpsichord, you see submissive and timid instrumentalists softening their sounds like courtiers in the presence of their master, before whom they dare not utter a word without having read permission in his eyes.[11]

French music for accompanied harpsichord was to have a significant influence on later chamber music. The roots of the Classical sonata for violin and piano, for example, can be traced in great part to this tradition.

In addition to his harpsichord compositions, Rameau's instructions on playing the instrument command our attention, for their remarkably practical advice is still valid today. In the *Méthode pour la mécanique des doigts* (attached to the first edition of his second collection of *Pieces de clavecin),* for example, he writes: "As one acquires assurance, the height of the seat should be lowered till the elbows are a little below the level of the keyboard; thus will the hands remain as it were glued to the keyboard and acquire a desirable legato."[12]

After Mid-Century

The harpsichord composers of the generation after Couperin and Rameau continued to be productive and to publish an impressive quantity of music for the instrument. Unfortunately, the range in quality was wide and extended from the highest artistic level to crude amateurism. Mellers considers the composers of this final period to be "musical Bouchers" for whom "emotional indulgence reduces the art to (very charming) sensory titillation .... They write to please."[13] Although there is some truth to this verdict, it is too harsh. French society itself was rapidly changing. With the aristocracy in decline, it was altogether natural for composers to write to suit the tastes of a growing, increasingly heterogeneous middle class.

Music style was also undergoing natural evolution. Couperin's refinement and economy of expression were often replaced by extroverted virtuosity and broad humor. "Alberti" basses and other Italianate figuration appeared more frequently, as did sonata form—not surprisingly, in conjunction with the growing influence of the fortepiano. Nevertheless, outstanding harpsichord music worthy of inclusion in the classical literature of the French clavecinistes was still being written by Michel Corrette (1709–1795), Jean-François Tapray (1738–1819), Jean-Jacques Beauvarlet-Charpentier (1754–1794), Nicolas Siret (1663–1754), and Armand-Louis Couperin (1727–2789). The most significant composers of the period, however, were Jacques Duphly, Claude Balbastre, and Joseph Nicolas Pancrace Royer.

Jacques Duphly (1715–1789) settled in Paris in 1742 and earned his living there as a respected teacher. He published four books of harpsichord pieces (1744, 1748, 1758, 1768). Several dances appear in the first three books, but the vast majority of pieces are descriptive or dedicatory. The quality of this music is high, and pieces like *La Felix* and *La Pothoüin* deserve a place in the classic clavecin tradition. *La Forqueray,* with its masterful use of *style-luthée* and the lower registers, captures the spirit of Couperin's *Les baricades mystérieuses.* The virtuosity of *La Médée* and *La victoire* recalls Rameau's *Les cyclopes* and *Les niais de Sologne.* In the tender mood piece *Les graces,* Duphly strives for maximum expressivity, and even lapses into mannerism by notating passages where the harpsichordist's hands should be uncoordinated—the right hand being played slightly after the left. This technique was commonly employed during this period, and is well-known to harpsichordists, but it was rarely notated.

Duphly's music earned him a small international reputation. His music was published in Germany by Marpurg and in England by Walsh.

Claude-Bénigne Balbastre (1717–1799), a native of Dijon, studied composition in Paris with Rameau and went on to achieve fame as an organist and harpsichordist. Balbastre was also an early champion of the piano, even though he was once quoted as saying that it would never replace the "majestic" clavecin. In 1776 he was appointed organist to the king's brother (the future Louis XVIII). Among his students were Marie-Antoinette and Thomas Jefferson. Until 1782 he frequently appeared at the Concert Spirituel. The Revolution, however, treated Balbastre poorly and he lived his last years in poverty.

Balbastre published his first book of *Pièces de clavecin* in 1759. Several other harpsichord pieces—including one of the last unmeasured preludes of the century—appeared later in miscellaneous collections. He also wrote music for organ and for piano. Among his piano pieces we find a *Marche des marseillais . . . arrangés pour le forte piano/par le citoyen C. Balbastre/aux braves défensers de la république.* In 1779 Balbastre also published a collection of *Sonates en quatuor* for harpsichord/fortepiano, two violins, bass, and two horns ad libitum.

As with Duphly, Balbastre's harpsichord publications contain some of the best and some of the weakest music written for the instrument. Even more than his older colleague, Balbastre attempted to accommodate a wide diversity of approaches, including French, Italian, and the nascent Classical piano styles. *La d'Hericourt,* a grand *tombeau* in C minor, skillfully exploits the lower register of the harpsichord and is worthy to be mentioned together with Couperin's *La ténébreuse* in the same key. Italian influence manifests itself in *La Lugeac,* an irrepressible gigue-like piece in the spirit of Domenico Scarlatti. *La Suzanne* is a character portrait with virtuoso keyboard figuration reminiscent of Rameau. *La Malesherbe* brings us almost into the world of early Mozart, complete with an "Alberti" bass and a periodic phrase structure in the *galant* style.

Joseph-Nicolas-Pancrace Royer (c. 1705–1755) was born in Turin and was trained for a career in the military. He moved to Paris in 1725 and was master of music at the Opéra from 1730 to 1733. In 1748 he took over the direction of the failing Concert Spirituel. His own compositions include operas, ballets, and vocal instrumental works.

Royer published one book of *Pièces de clavecin* (1746), although there are reports of additional harpsichord works that are now lost. Some of these pieces are among the most attractive in the literature—and also the most eccentric. Royer's keyboard music retains all the characteristics of the French clavecin tradition but also clearly shows the change in style and taste that occurred after the death of the Sun King. A work such as *Les tendres sentiments* continues in the Couperin mold, with its eloquent simplicity, expressive harpsichord writing and poignant harmonies. The character pieces *Les matelots, Tambourin,* and *La remouleuse* exude the spirit of the vaudeville and the commedia dell'arte. The most striking works of the collection are *La vertigo* and *La marche des Scythes.* One can imagine, however, that the repeated chords and dramatic leaps of *Le vertigo,* or the slapstick humor and outrageous hysteria of *La marche des Scythes,* would not have found an appreciative audience in Versailles (Ex. 4.10).

EXAMPLE 4.10. Joseph-Nicolas-Pancrace Royer. *Le vertigo*, mm. 11–27 (*Pièces de clavecin*, 1746)

Influence and Legacy

The dissemination of French harpsichord music throughout Europe was quite uneven. Handel, for example, may have been directly familiar with French harpsichord music, but if so, it had little effect on his compositions, other than the use of styl-luthée. Domenico Scarlatti almost certainly had no more than a casual acquaintance with this repertoire; his music, at all events, reveals no trace of its influence. But while many French composers were unknown outside of Paris, others did enjoy international renown. Dieupart's reputation benefited from the publication of his music in London and Amsterdam. Walsh printed one book by Duphly and three by Rameau, and Roger published pieces of Le Roux in Amsterdam. François Couperin's music was never printed outside of France, but copies of the books were widely distributed. German composers, including Johann Sebastian Bach, also copied the music by hand.

The impact of French music was more extensive in Germany than elsewhere. Cultural connections between the two countries were already well established by the beginning of the century, and the interest in French music was stimulated further by the sojourns in Germany of eminent French virtuosi such as the famous flautist Pierre-Gabriel Buffardin.

Bach's numerous keyboard suites, his *Ouverture nach Französischer Art* BWV 831, and the Aria from the Goldberg Variations BWV 988 testify to his intimate knowledge of the French style. A number of collections of miscellaneous French pieces appeared in Germany. Works by Couperin, Rameau, and Royer were published in the *Nebenstunden der berlinischen Musen in kleinen Clavierstücken* (1762), and works by Clérambault, Couperin, and Dandrieu in Marpurg's *Clavierstücke mit einem practischen Unterricht für Anfänger und Geübtere* (1762–1763).

French harpsichord music continued to exert an influence in the francophile atmosphere of the Saxon court at Dresden and especially the Prussian court of Frederick the Great. Moreover, the keyboard works of C. P. E. Bach and those of the following generation—including Haydn and Mozart—are indebted to the French tradition to a greater extent than has generally been recognized. The Classical piano style has much in common with French harpsichord music, for example, the preference for two-voice textures, the stock of melodic and accompaniment figures, and periodic phrase structure.

Over a century later Claude Debussy was eager to acknowledge his admiration and his debt to the keyboard masters of the French Baroque. In 1915 he was tempted to dedicate his *Études pour le piano* to Couperin.[14] Two years earlier he had already wondered: "Why are we so indifferent toward our own great Rameau? And toward Destouches, now almost forgotten? And to Couperin, the most poetic of our clavecinistes, whose tender melancholy is like that enchanting echo that emanates from the depths of a Watteau landscape filled with plaintive figures?"[15]

Notes

1. See Constant 1975, 167, 172, 216.

2. A stunning example of this can be found on the title page of Beethoven's "Moonlight" Sonata: *Sonata quasi una Fantasia per il Clavicembalo o Piano-Forte* (Vienna, 1802).

3. There is an even closer similarity, however, to an A-major gigue by Gaspard Le Roux.

4. Couperin 1717, 29, 37, 50.

5. Whether Bach was in fact the author of this arrangement is far from certain. See Karl Heller's review of the evidence in the critical report (KB) of the *Neue Bach-Ausgabe* (NBA), IV/8, 95. Wilfrid Mellers claims that there is evidence that Bach and Couperin exchanged letters, but legend has it that the letters were later used to cover jam pots and were subsequently lost (Mellers 1987, 12). Mellers notes that this story was related to Charles Bouvet by Mme. Arnette Taskin.

6. Thurston Dart maintains that Bach could never have afforded to buy even one of Couperin's elegantly engraved books. See Dart 1969, 591ff. The rondeau was copied into the *Clavierbüchlein* by Anna Magdalena Bach sometime before 1733. See NBA V/4, KB, 71, 81–82.

7. This number may have been inspired by the one-eyed giant in Lully's *Persée*, which was revived in 1722.

8. Jean-Philippe Rameau, *Pièces de clavecin,* ed. Erwin R. Jacobi (Kassel, 1960), 58.

9. Jean-Philippe Rameau, *Pièces de clavecin en concerts,* ed. Erwin R. Jacobi (Kassel, 1976), xv.

10. C.-J. Mathon de la Cour in *Almanach Musical 1777* (for 1776), 79–80, cited in Gustafson and Fuller 1990, 5.

11. *Ibid.,* p. 5

12. Rameau, *Pièces de clavecin en concerts,* 19.

13. Mellers 1987, 248–49. The reference is to François Boucher (1703–1770), the Rococo painter and decorator.

14. In a letter of 28 August 1915 addressed to Jacques Durand, Debussy asked: "You haven't given me an answer about the dedication: Couperin or Chopin?" See *Debussy Letters,* selected and edited by François Lesure and Roger Nichols, trans. Roger Nichols (Cambridge, MA, 1987), 300–01.

15. In the Bulletin of the *Société Internationale de Musique* for 15 January 1913. See François Lesure, ed., *Debussy on Music,* trans. and ed. Richard Langham Smith (New York, 1977), 273.

Selected Facsimile and Modern Editions

Balbastre, Claude-Bénigne. *Pièces de clavecin, premier livre* (1759). Facsimile edition. Courlay, 1990.

———. *Pièces de clavecin, d'orgue et de fortepiano.* Ed. Alan Curtis. Paris, 1974.

Clérambault, Louis-Nicolas. *Pièces de clavecin, premier livre.* Facsimile editions. Geneva, 1982. New York, 1986.

Couperin, François. *Pièces de clavecin.* Facsimile edition. New York, 1973.

———. *Pièces de clavecin.* Complete edition. Ed. Kenneth Gilbert. Paris, 1969–1972.

Dandrieu, Jean-François. *Trois Livres de clavecin.* Ed. Pauline Aubert and Brigitte François-Sappey. Paris, 1973.

Dieupart, Charles. *Six Suittes de clavessin.* Ed. Paul Brunold. Paris, 1934. Rev. Kenneth Gilbert. Paris, 1979.

Duphly, Jacques. *Pièces de clavecin, premier livre* (1744). Facsimile edition. Courlay, 1986–1987.

———. *Pièces de clavecin, second livre* (1748). Facsimile edition. Courlay, 1986–1987.

———. *Pièces de clavecin, troisième livre* (1756). Facsimile edition. Geneva, 1986.

———. *Pièces de clavecin.* Ed. Françoise Petite. Paris, 1967.

Jacquet de la Guerre, Elizabeth. *Pièces de clavecin.* Ed. Carol Henry Bates. Paris, 1986.

LeRoux, Gaspard. *Pièces de clavecin.* Facsimile edition. Geneva, 1982.

———. *Pièces de clavecin.* Ed. Albert Fuller. New York, 1959.

———. *Pièces de clavecin.* Complete edition. Ed. Albert Fuller and Andrew Appel. New York. Forthcoming.

Marchand, Louis. *Pièces de clavecin.* Facsimile editions. Geneva, 1982. New York, 1985.

———. *Pièces de clavecin.* Ed. Thurston Dart. Paris, 1960.

Rameau, Jean-Philippe. *Pièces de clavecin* (1706). Facsimile edition. Ed. R. Peter Wolf. New York, 1986.

———. *Pièces de clavecin* (1724). Facsimile edition. New York, 1967.

———. *Pièces de clavecin* (1729). Facsimile edition. New York, n.d.

———. *Pièces de clavecin.* Complete edition. Ed. Kenneth Gilbert. Paris, 1979.

———. *Pièces de clavecin.* Ed. Erwin R. Jacobi. Kassel, 1960.

———. *Pièces de clavecin en concerts.* Ed. Erwin Jacobi. Kassel, 1961.

Royer, Joseph-Nicholas-Pancrace. *Pièces de clavecin.* Ed. Lisa Crawford. Paris, 1990.

———. *Pièces de clavecin.* Facsimile edition. Geneva, 1982.

Literature Cited and Selected Bibliography

Anthony, James R. *French Baroque Music from Beaujoyeulx to Rameau.* Revised and expanded edition, Portland, 1997.

de Bacilly, Benigne. *Remarques curieuses sur l'art de bien chanter.* Paris, 1668. Facsimile of Paris, 1670 edition. Geneva, 1971.

Bates, Carol Henry. "French Harpsichord Music in the First Decade of the Eighteenth Century." EM 18 (2), 1989): 184–196.

Baumont, Olivier. *Couperin, Le musicien des rois.* Paris, 1998.

Beaussant, Phillipe. *Francois Couperin.* Paris, 1980.

Burney, Charles. *A General History of Music,* 2 vols. London, 1776–1789. Reprint. New York, 1957.

———. *The Present State of Music in France and Italy.* London, 1771–1773. Reprint. New York, 1969.

Correspondance littéraire, philosophique et critique par Grimm, Diderot, Raynal, Meister, etc. Ed. Maurice Tourneux. Paris, 1879–1892. Reprint. Nendeln/Liechtenstein, 1968.

de Chabanon, Michel-Paul. *Eloge de M. Rameau*. Paris, 1764.

D'Aquin de Chateau-Lyon, Pierre-Louis. *Lettres sur les hommes célèbres . . . sous le regne de Louis XV*. Paris and Amsterdam, 1752. Revised 1753 as *Siècle literaire de Louis XV, ou Lettres sur les hommes célèbres*.

Clark, Jane. "Les folies françoises." *Early Music* (hereafter *EM*) 8 (1980): 163–69.

Cohen, Albert. *Music in the French Royal Academy of Sciences*. Princeton, 1981.

Constant, Pierre. *Histoire du Concert spirituel, 1725–1790*. Paris, 1975.

Couperin, François. *L'Art de toucher le clavecin*. Paris, 1716. Revised 1717. Modern edition. New York, 1974.

Dart, Thurston. "On Couperin's Harpsichord Music." *Musical Times* (hereafter *MT*) 110 (1969): 590–94.

Denis, Jean. *Traité de L'Accord de L'Espinette*. Paris, 1650. Facsimile edition. New York, 1969.

Donington, Robert. *The Interpretation of Early Music*. New York, 1974.

Engramelle, Marie-Dominique-Joseph. *La Tonotechnie, ou l'art de noter les cylindres*. Paris, 1775. Facsimile edition. Geneva, 1971.

Fuller, David. "Les petits marteaux de M. Rameau." *EM* 11 (1983): 516–17.

———. "Eighteenth-Century French Harpsichord Music." Ph.D. dissertation, Harvard University, 1965.

———. "Accompanied Keyboard Music." *The Musical Quarterly* 60 (1974): 222–45.

Gilbert, Kenneth. "Les Livres de clavecin de François Couperin: note bibliographique." *Revue de Musicologie* (hereafter *RM*) 58 (1972): 256–57.

Girdlestone, Cuthbert. *Jean-Philippe Rameau: His Life and Work*. London, 1957. Revised edition. New York, 1969.

———. "Rameau's Self-borrowings." *Music and Letters* 39 (1958): 52–56.

Gustafson, Bruce. *French Harpsichord Music of the 17th century: a Thematic Catalogue of the Sources with Commentary*. Ann Arbor, MI, 1979.

Gustafson, Bruce, and David Fuller. *A Catalogue of French Harpsichord Music, 1699–1780*. Oxford, 1990.

Hawkins, John. *A General History of the Science and Practice of Music*. London, 1776. Reprint. New York, 1963.

Hefling, Stephen E. *Rhythmic Alteration in Seventeenth- and Eighteenth-Century Music: Notes Inégales and Overdotting*. New York, 1993.

Hotteterre le Romain, Jacques Martin. *Principes de la Flute Traversiere, ou flute d'Allemagne; de la flute à bec, ou flute douce, et du haut-bois*. Paris, 1707. Trans. P. M. Doublas. New York, 1968. Trans. David Lasocki. London, 1968.

Ledbetter, David. *Harpsichord and Lute Music in 17th-Century France*. Bloomington, IN, 1987.

Lesure, François. *Bibliographie des éditions musicales publiées par Estienne Roger et Michel-Charles le Cène*. Paris, 1969.

Marpurg, Friedrich. *Historisch-kritische Beytrage zur Aufnahme der Musik*. Berlin, 1754. Reprint. Hildesheim, 1970.

Mellers, Wilfred. *François Couperin and the French Classical Tradition*. London, 1950. Reprint. London, 1987.

Mercure de France, 1672–1825.

Sadler, Graham. "Rameau's Harpsichord Transcriptions from '*Les Indes galantes.*'" *EM* 7 (1979): 18–24.

de Saint Lambert, Monsieur: *Les Principes du Clavecin.* Paris, 1792. Trans. Rebecca Harris-Warwick. Cambridge, 1984.

Tessier, André. "L'oeuvre de G. Le Roux." RM 3 (1922): 168.

Tilney, Colin. *The Art of the Unmeasured Prelude for Harpsichord: France, 1660–1720.* London, 1991.

Titon du Tillet. *Le Parnasse françoise.* Paris, 1732, 1743, 1755, 1760.

Zaslaw, Neal. "The New Rameau Edition." *MT* 124 (1983): 28.

CHAPTER FIVE

Domenico Scarlatti

Frederick Hammond

for Roberto Pagano

Domenico Scarlatti's changing reputation has reflected the depictions of his successive biographers. For the eighteenth-century music historian Dr. Charles Burney, Scarlatti was a keyboard composer of "original and happy freaks," a judgment the nineteenth century confirmed by limiting performances of Scarlatti to a few sonatas at the beginning of a piano recital. A more serious evaluation began in 1935 with a monograph on Scarlatti by Sacheverell Sitwell, reflecting Sitwell's pioneering interest in southern Baroque art. In 1953 the distinguished harpsichordist Ralph Kirkpatrick published the first full-scale study of Domenico Scarlatti as a major composer of keyboard music. Employing new biographical material, Kirkpatrick presented an evocative picture of Scarlatti's life and surroundings, a survey of his output as then available, an analytical model for the sonatas, an examination of Scarlatti's instruments, a discussion of performance and performance practice, a detailed enumeration of the musical sources, and a catalogue of works (amplified to a thematic catalogue of the sonatas in the German edition of the book). As a musician, Kirkpatrick was able to embody his knowledge in editions, performances (including a series of all-Scarlatti recitals), and recordings that established Scarlatti as perhaps the greatest idiomatic composer for the harpsichord, influencing two generations of players, scholars, and listeners.

Every icon sooner or later arouses an iconoclast, and Kirkpatrick's work eventually found one in the musicologist Joel Sheveloff. Sheveloff's doctoral dissertation (Sheveloff 1970) and subsequent publications (Sheveloff 1980, 1985), based on a close analysis of the manuscript and printed sources of the sonatas, called into question several of Kirkpatrick's fundamental assumptions and conclusions. This revaluation continued in two monographs on Scarlatti inspired by the tricentenary celebrations in 1985. Roberto Pagano's *Scarlatti, Alessandro e Domenico: due vite in una* (1985) (an English translation is forthcoming, took as its point of departure the most mysterious aspect of Domenico's life, his relationship with his father. Working within the cultural context of southern Italy, Pagano employed Sicilian archival material to provide a new reading of the relationship between the two Scarlattis. Malcolm Boyd's general account of Domenico's life and work (1986) summarized the newest scholarly information and placed a more balanced emphasis on the vocal component—especially the newly discovered operas——in the development of Scarlatti's musical style.

The Career

Domenico Scarlatti was born in Naples on October 26, 1685, the sixth of ten children of the composer Alessandro Scarlatti (1660–1725). Although Domenico's mother was Roman, Alessandro and his family were Sicilian—an inheritance that shaped Domenico's musical career. Like other southern Italian families, the Scarlattis formed an extended professional clan, of which Alessandro had become the "boss" at an early age. He firmly directed the musical and personal lives of his two brothers, his two sisters and their husbands, and three of his own children—not always to his satisfaction or their own best advantage (Pagano 1985).

Domenico was born into a golden age of Neapolitan music. Southern Italy and Sicily formed part of the kingdom of Spain and were ruled from Naples by viceroys, Spanish grandees whose courts emulated those of their royal masters. Under the patronage of the viceroys and the great aristocracy, opera had been introduced into Naples in the mid-seventeenth century and flourished along with instrumental music and vocal serenades. The fervent piety of southern Italy made the viceroyal chapel and other Neapolitan churches centers for the composition and performance of sacred music. To supply this diverse musical market, Naples imported leading foreign composers (Alessandro Scarlatti had been brought from Rome in 1684 to direct the viceroyal chapel) and supported four conservatories for training local musicians.

The first forty years of Domenico Scarlatti's life were dominated and overshadowed by his father. Alessandro had become the leading exponent of Neapolitan opera, receiving commissions for well over a hundred staged works from Naples, Rome, Florence, and Venice, as well as producing sacred works, keyboard and orchestral music, and over six hundred secular cantatas, all under the highest aristocratic patronage. Alessandro shaped Domenico's career to the same pattern so closely that it assumed a kind of *Doppelgänger* relationship with that of his father.

Nothing is known of Domenico's earliest musical education, except that he did not attend any of the Neapolitan conservatories. Probably, as is often the case in professional families, much of his training was absorbed from his immediate environment. By the age of fourteen he had produced a chamber cantata, and in 1701, not yet sixteen, he was appointed organist and composer to the viceroyal chapel under his father's direction. Domenico's precocious abilities as a keyboardist were recognized in his additional appointment as chamber harpsichordist to the Viceroy. Nonetheless, a year later the Scarlattis visited the melomane Prince Ferdinando de'Medici in Florence in search of better jobs (Holmes 1987).

The Grand Prince had no permanent employment for father or son, and the "numerosa famiglia" of Scarlattis returned to Naples. During his father's absence in Rome the following year Domenico achieved a degree of independence with his first two operas, commissioned for the 1703–1704 Neapolitan season. (Domenico's independence need not be exaggerated: his brother Giuseppe painted the scenery, uncle Tommaso sang tenor, the theatre was managed by the husband of one aunt, and another uncle by marriage played double bass in the orchestra.)

With the extinction of the Spanish Hapsburgs in 1700 the crowns of Spain and Naples had passed to the French Bourbons in the person of Louis XIV's grandson the Duc d'Anjou, whose accession as Felipe V precipitated the War of the Spanish Succession (1702–1714). In the ensuing confusion Alessandro Scarlatti lost his post as *maestro di cappella* in Naples in 1703; Domenico failed to succeed his father and followed him to Rome. In the spring of 1705 Alessandro sent Domenico off to Venice, the musical capital of Europe, under the tutelage of the celebrated castrato Nicolini (Nicolo Grimaldi, 1673–1732). Alessandro summed up Domenico's early career in a well-known letter commending him to Ferdinando de'Medici in Florence (Rome, May 30, 1705): "I have detached him by force from Naples, where although there was a place for his talent, it was not a talent for that place. I am sending him away also from Rome, because Rome has no roof to welcome Music, which here lives as a beggar. This Son, who is an Eagle whose Wings are grown, must not remain idle in the nest, and I must not impede his flight."[1]

The Grand Prince ignored this broad hint and forwarded Domenico and his companion on to Venice. His prediction that there Domenico's ability "should meet with better acceptance and favor" was fulfilled. We do not know whether Domenico studied in Venice with Francesco Gasparini, greatly esteemed by Alessandro, but during his sojourn in the "Serenissima" (1705–1708) he had the opportunity to hear five of Gasparini's operas and to read (and perhaps collaborate on) the important treatise *L'armonico pratico al cimbalo* (The practical harmonist at the harpsichord) (Gasparini 1708).[2] Domenico encountered George Frideric Handel, who spent the winter of 1707–1708 in Venice "at a Masquerade, while he [Handel] was playing on a harpsichord in his visor. Scarlatti happened to be there, and affirmed that it could be no one but the famous Saxon, or the devil."[3] Domenico also participated in the performances of an oratorio and two new operas by his father—the latter, resounding fiascos.

In 1707 Alessandro was rescued from his difficulties by an appointment as *maestro di cappella* at the basilica of Santa Maria Maggiore in Rome, where Domenico again followed him. In 1708 or early 1709 Cardinal Ottoboni arranged the famous keyboard contest between Handel and Domenico at his palace of the Cancelleria. Since Scarlatti's keyboard music seems to grow out of his improvisatory performances, the few surviving descriptions of his playing are of particular interest. Although the account in John Mainwaring's biography of Handel may be suspect as having been written a half-century after the event, it deserves to be quoted in full.

> When [Handel] came first into Italy, the masters in greatest esteem were Alessandro Scarlatti, Gasparini, and Lotti. The first of these he became acquainted with at Cardinal Ottoboni's. Here also he became known to Domenico Scarlatti, now living in Spain, and author of the celebrated lessons. As he was an exquisite player on the harpsichord, the Cardinal was resolved to bring him and Handel together for a trial of skill. The issue of the trial on the harpsichord hath been differently reported. It has been said that some gave the preference to Scarlatti. However, when they came to the Organ there was not the least pretence for doubting to which of them it belonged. Scarlatti himself declared the superiority of his antagonist, and owned ingenuously, that till he had heard him upon this instrument, he had no conception of its powers. So greatly was he struck with his peculiar method of playing, that he followed him all over Italy, and was never so happy as when he was with him.

At this stage of his career, according to Mainwaring, "the characteristic excellence of Scarlatti seems to have consisted in a certain elegance and delicacy of expression."[4]

The War of the Spanish Succession resulted in the momentary cession of southern Italy to Austria, and Alessandro Scarlatti found himself reinstated as *maestro di cappella* in Naples, where he returned in 1708 and remained for the rest of his life except for a visit to Rome in the years 1718 to 1721. Domenico was left in Rome without stable employment or the direction of his overpowering father. He seems to have returned to Venice from 1709 to 1710, where he encountered the young Dublin organist Thomas Roseingrave. Domenico had reacted to his contest with Handel by developing the demonic qualities in his own playing. Upon Roseingrave's arrival in Venice, the young Irishman was invited to an "academy" in a noble house, where he was requested to perform a toccata. "And, says he, 'finding myself rather better in courage and finger than usual, I exerted myself ... and fancied, by the applause I received, that my performance had made some impression on the company.'. . . A grave young man dressed in black and a black wig, who had stood aloof in one corner of the room, very quiet and attentive while Roseingrave played, being asked to sit down at the harpsichord, when he began to play Rosy said, he thought ten hundred d Is had been at the instrument; he never had heard such passages of execution and effect before."[5]

In 1709 Domenico acquired his own aristocratic patroness, becoming *maestro di cappella to* the exiled ex-queen of Poland, Maria Casimira. During the next five years he composed a number of outdoor serenades and at least seven operas for her palace theatre, with sets by Filippo Juvarra, the greatest scene designer of the period. Of the operas (which are still coming to light), a risque farce, *La Dirindina,* has been rediscovered and published (Scarlatti, ed. Degrada 1985). In a composer of such wit as the keyboard sonatas of Scarlatti display, the sense of the comic— the "ingenious jesting of the Art" that he claimed for his *Essercizi*— revealed in *La Dirindina* adds a stroke of color to Domenico's sometimes monochromatic portrait.

By the age of thirty, Domenico Scarlatti had demonstrated his father's competence in all areas of composition and seemed headed for a conventionally successful career as a composer of opera and sacred vocal music. From 1713 to 1719 he occupied a notable place in Roman music as composer and director for the Cappella Giulia, the resident choir of St. Peter's. After the departure of Maria Casimira from Rome in 1714 he also became *maestro di cappella* to the Portuguese ambassador. In 1715 he was commissioned to set Apostolo Zeno's *Arableto* for the Teatro Capranica, the principal Roman public opera theatre.

Domenico's success as an independent artist in Rome during his father's absence in Naples may have brought "all the knots to the comb," as the Italians say, in their relationship. On January 28, 1717, Alessandro was forced to grant his son freedom from "all paternal control and obligations"—the ancient Roman *patria potestas*—in an extraordinary legal document whose significance is still debated. Recent research has revealed that the supposed reference to an imprudent first marriage by Domenico in fact concerns Domenico's attempt to forbid the marriage of his son Alexandro (Kenyon 1988). In 1718 what was to be Domenico's last opera was presented at the Capranica. In February of 1719 he resigned from St. Peter's to travel to London for a reworking of an earlier opera. His actual movements are uncertain: he may in fact have visited London, but journeys to Portugal and a possible sojourn in Palermo are also documented; in 1724 and 1725 he visited Paris.[6]

Other newly discovered documents show that Domenico also made a crucial visit to the Portuguese court in 1719, where King João V appointed him court composer, *Mestre de capela,* and music master to king's daughter, Princess Maria Barbara (1711–1758), and his younger brother, the Infante Don Antonio. Between 1720 and 1722 Scarlatti, who had become a member of the Confraternity of Santa Cecilia in Lisbon, produced sacred pieces and six serenatas for court celebrations (Doderer 1991). Italian musicians were no novelty in Portugal: in 1728 the royal chapel at Lisbon under Scarlatti's direction employed some forty Italian singers and instrumentalists.[7] The organist of the royal chapel, however, was Portuguese, the young Carlos de Seixas (1704–1742). Seixas composed some seven hundred keyboard sonatas, 105 of which survived the Lisbon earthquake of 1755 (Seixas 1965). He was sent by Don Antonio to Scarlatti for keyboard lessons and is said to have received Scarlatti's accolade, "It is you who should give me lessons."

Domenico's departure from Italy and his break from his father's domination proved to be the watershed of his career. Of his two new pupils, Don Antonio was proficient enough to receive the dedication of the first collection published explicitly for the fortepiano, Lodovico Giustini's twelve *Sonate* of 1732. But it was the corpulent Maria Barbara, "extravagantly fond of dancing and music," who became the center of Scarlatti's musical life (Ill. 5.1).[8] To her we owe the transformation of Domenico Scarlatti from a vocal composer of talent to a keyboard composer of genius, the germination of his 500 keyboard sonatas, and their preservation for posterity. If she was able to perform adequately the corpus of music that she called into being, she also must have been one of the most extraordinary keyboard players of the eighteenth century.

In 1725 Domenico made a last visit to his dying father in Naples, where he met Alessandro's true artistic heir, Johann Adolf Hasse, who later recalled to Burney Domenico's "wonderful hand, as well as fecundity of invention." (Frederick the Great's flautist and composer J. J. Quantz, who heard Alessandro play in 1725, remembered his "learned style of playing, although he did not have as much facility in performance as did his son.")[9] Alessandro's death completed the emancipation begun by Domenico's legal exemption from the *patria potestas* and his removal to Portugal. In 1727 Domenico traveled to Italy on a subsidy of 1,000 scudi from the king, and in 1728, at nearly forty-three, he sealed his independence by marrying a sixteen-year-old Roman girl.

In January of 1729 a double marriage united the houses of Bourbon and Bragança. Maria Barbara married the heir to the Spanish throne, Fernando, Prince of the Asturias, and her brother Don José was joined with Fernando's sister Maria Vitoria. When the new Princess of the Asturias traveled to Spain, her suite included her music master and his new wife. Presumably she needed the solace of her music and some reminder of her relatively carefree earlier life on sinking into the miasma of the Spanish court. Her new father-in-law, Felipe V, had aged from a charming young prince into a manic-depressive worn out by alternate indulgences in the bedchamber and the confessional. His psy-

ILLUSTRATION 5.1. Farinelli presents a manuscript to Maria Barbara and Fernando VI (1758). Biblioteca Real, Palacio de Oriente, Madrid.

chotic depression inverted the normal daily routine of the Spanish court and virtually paralyzed the administration of the state; he even abdicated briefly. After the weddings the court remained stranded at the Alcázar in Seville for four years, when the king was finally roused sufficiently from his lethargy to move to Castile, and a yearly cycle of royal progresses was established among his various residences.

In 1737 Felipe V's melancholy received its definitive treatment with the arrival of the great castrato Farinelli (Carlo Broschi 1705–1782). The king was so enraptured by Farinelli's singing that he allowed himself to be bathed and dressed, and consented to function again as nominal head of state. For the next ten years Farinelli kept the king compliant by performing the same four songs every evening. In 1738, perhaps as a compensation for the favors that were being showered on Farinelli by the king and queen, Scarlatti was made a knight of Santiago by Maria Barbara's father. (Domingo Antonio de Velasco's portrait of Scarlatti commemorates this halcyon period in Domenico's life [Ill. 5.2].) In return, Domenico dedicated to João V the handsome volume of thirty *Essercizi per gravicembalo* issued at London or Venice in 1738, with a title page by Jacopo Amiconi (Ill. 5.3). The following year Thomas Roseingrave published in London a pirated edition of the *Essercizi,* plus twelve additional sonatas, laying the foundations for the "English cult of Scarlatti." With the death of his wife in 1739 Scarlatti's last tie with Italy was broken, and three years later he completed his hispanization by marrying a young woman from Cadiz.

The Princes of the Asturias succeeded to the Spanish throne in 1746, inaugurating a reign of brilliant artistic activity under the supervision of Farinelli—splendid operatic productions, sacred music, instrumental music, and ephemeral diversions such as embarkations and illuminations. Fernando VI and Maria Barbara maintained the routine set up by Felipe V, and Scarlatti and the Queen's instruments followed their yearly itinerary. Each of the royal palaces had a different attraction, whose echoes can be heard in Scarlatti's music: the hunting lodge of the Pardo; Buen Retiro on the outskirts of the capital; Aranjuez, a garden-palace on an island in the Tagus where Scarlatti composed a set of sonatas; and the grim monastery-mausoleum of the Escorial.

Although Farinelli was an intimate and admirer of Scarlatti, Domenico did not flourish conspicuously under his newly enthroned pupils. Perhaps this was by choice; his few written remains from this period suggest that he lived a retired life in Madrid. Already in 1749, eight years before his death, Scarlatti executed his testament, which mentions neither instruments nor scores. His one surviving letter, written in Italian to the Duke of Huescar in 1752, implies that the writer was in poor health: "I cannot go out of my house." Like some of his Spanish contemporaries, Scarlatti also may have been out of sympathy with musical

ILLUSTRATION 5.2. Domingo Antonio de Velasco: Domenico Scarlatti. Alpiarça, Portugal. Bequest of José Relvas.

developments at court (Pennington 1981). He sent Huescar two sixteenth-century motets that he had scored up from parts, assuring the Duke that they would serve not only to celebrate the praise of his ancestor the Duke of Alba, but also so that "many modern theatrical composers may observe and profit (if they wish to) by the true manner and true law of writing in counterpoint, which I observe in few today, and yet I hear them praised."[10]

Scarlatti devoted his last years to arranging and supervising the copying of his keyboard sonatas in two series of manuscript volumes executed between 1752 and 1757. A set bearing the queen's arms was copied perhaps in gratitude to Maria Barbara, who—Farinelli told

ESSERCIZI PER GRAVICEMBALO
di
Don Domenico Scarlatti
Cavaliero di S. GIACOMO e Maestro
de'

SERENISSIMI PRENCIPE e PRENCIPESSA
delle Asturie &c.

ILLUSTRATION 5.3. Domenico Scarlatti: Essercizi per Gravicembalo (1738). Title page. Courtesy of Library of Congress.

Burney—often paid Domenico's gambling debts. Domenico returned to vocal music for a series of six important solo cantatas (perhaps for Farinelli) and the copying of a *Missa quatuor vocum* in *stile antico* (1754). He took his farewell in a moving *Salve Regina* for soprano, strings, and continuo, which bears the notation "the last of his compositions written in Madrid shortly before dying"—July 23, 1757.

The Sources of the Scarlatti Sonatas

Domenico Scarlatti's keyboard sonatas are transmitted in three major sources, none of them autograph. These comprise the printed *Essercizi per Gravicembalo* of 1738 (see Ex. 5.8, p. 182); a set of fifteen manuscript volumes in Venice, Biblioteca Nazionale Marciana, Mss. 9770–9784 (see Ex. 5.4, p. 174); and another manuscript set of fifteen volumes in Parma, Conservatorio Arrigo Boito, A G 31406–31420 (see Ex. 5.5, p. 175). All three collections are organized in units of thirty sonatas. They are laid out neatly with one-half sonata to each opening, necessitating only a single page turn per work, and in a format so large as to suggest that they were intended for a nearsighted player.

The Venice set consists of thirteen volumes copied between 1752 and 1757 and numbered I–XIII, plus two unnumbered volumes copied in 1742 and 1749 by various hands, totaling 496 sonatas; additional volumes contain a copy of the printed *Essercizi* and sonatas by Sebastian Albero, organist of the Royal Chapel in Madrid, copied by the main scribe. The collection was purchased in 1835 from the Contarini, a family of Venetian patricians who also assembled the greatest surviving collection of Venetian Baroque opera scores for the theatre of their miniature Versailles on the Brenta. It is bound sumptuously in red leather, and the gold-tooled arms of Portugal and Spain on the covers indicate that it was the personal property of Maria Barbara. The Parma volumes, acquired from a Bologna antiquary in 1899, are more simply bound. They contain 463 sonatas, including fourteen that do not appear in Venice (K.356–357, K.544–555). In a secondary manuscript, K.544–555 bear the notation "Last sonatas of D. Domenico Scarlatti, composed in the year 1756 and 1757, in which he died" (Pagano 1988). The Parma manuscripts are copied largely in the hand of the main scribe of the Venice source. (In Parma XIV–XV the initials "S" or "SA" appear, perhaps indicating Sebastian Albero or Scarlatti's pupil Antonio Soler as the copyist.) Presumably one or both of the sets comes from the estate of Farinelli, to whom Maria Barbara left "all my books and papers of music" (Kirkpatrick 1953), but their history until their arrival at their present domiciles is still untraced (Alvini 1986).

Kirkpatrick took the Venice collection, since it was the queen's series, as the primary source for his catalogue despite its discrepancies with the Parma manuscripts. Although this judgment was challenged by Sheveloff, the K. numbers in the order of the Venice manuscripts remain the standard identification of the Scarlatti sonatas.

Secondary sources add a few *unica* to the contents of Venice and Parma. The most important manuscripts consist of five volumes in Münster containing 349 sonatas; seven volumes in Vienna, once the property of Johannes Brahms, containing 308 sonatas; and a collection of manuscript copies in Vienna whose importance has only recently been noted (Choi 1974). Given the troubled history of Spain in the nineteenth and twentieth centuries, the scarcity of Spanish Scarlatti manuscripts is not surprising, but even there a few new sources have appeared. Some of these contain original works, others present existing sonatas butchered to fit the limited compass of the Spanish organ keyboard. A *Fandango del S.gr Scarlate* discovered in 1984 might furnish a link between the Scarlatti sonatas and Spanish folk music, but its authenticity is doubtful (Editions: Martinez 1984; Discography: Puyana).[11]

Much of the problem in accepting Scarlatti as a major keyboard composer was created by the first complete edition of his works (Editions: Longo 1906–1908), for nearly fifty years the only one available. The editor, Alessandro Longo, disregarded completely the chronologi-

cal order of the manuscripts and the original arrangement of many of
the sonatas in pairs; he rearranged them into suites of his own consti-
tution, catalogued the sonatas in this order, bowdlerized the texts, and
disfigured them with pianistic performing indications. The violence
done the originals is evident even in Longo's nos. 1–5, which correspond
to K.514, 384, 502, 158, and 406 in the Venice manuscripts. The main
task of subsequent publications of Scarlatti has been to reconquer the
purity of the original sources.

As a model, Kirkpatrick (1953) presented clean texts for sixty of the
sonatas. Thirty years later a modern edition of the Venice manuscripts
was completed (Editions: Gilbert 1971), and a comprehensive critical
edition based on all the surviving sources is in progress (Editions: Fadini
1978); unfortunately, this adds a third numbering system to the Longo
and Kirkpatrick catalogues. The sonatas are also available in facsimiles
of the *Essercizi,* the Parma manuscripts (rearranged in the Venice-
derived order of Kirkpatrick's catalogue) (Editions: Kirkpatrick 1971),
and some of the Venice manuscripts (Editions: Alvini 1985). These facsimile editions are particularly important because the principal manuscript sources have deteriorated perceptibly in the last forty years
(Kirkpatrick 1971), and their accessibility presumably will be restricted.

Modern editions of Scarlatti, including Kirkpatrick's, often omit an
important notational feature of the Venice and Parma manuscripts.
Scarlatti distinguished the first and second endings of the first half of a
sonata not by marking them as such but by setting off the first ending
with slurs in both hands, indicating that it was to be omitted in the repeat
(Ex. 5.1, Parma XV 22). Thus, example 5.1 is not to be performed with
the descending arpeggio both ending the repeat of the first half and
beginning the second half, as I did for several years, having first learned
the sonata from the Longo edition. The first time through the first half,
the arpeggio cadence is played; at the end of the repeat it is omitted to
dovetail into the second half.

EXAMPLE 5.1. Sonata in D Major K.535, mm. 34–36

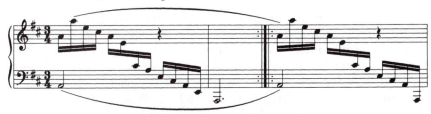

No autograph manuscript of a keyboard piece by Scarlatti has been identified, but Scarlatti studies are haunted by the possible existence of his
"original manuscripts," the scores he supplied to the copyists of the Venice and Parma series. Their recovery might solve many of the fundamental problems of Scarlatti scholarship exemplified in the opposing

hypotheses of Kirkpatrick and Sheveloff: the dating, the original arrangement, and the instrumental medium of the sonatas. Attempts to create a chronology of the sonatas on the basis of style have failed (Pestelli 1967), but a documented chronology would provide the basis for a valid stylistic analysis.

The discovery of the lost Scarlatti manuscripts indeed might accomplish all these wonders and more. But it seems increasingly unlikely that the manuscripts ever existed as a unified corpus even at the time of Scarlatti's testament. The fact that the Venice and Parma collections, although containing the same repertory and copied mostly by the same scribe, do not always duplicate each other in the arrangement and sometimes even the pairing of the sonatas, scarcely suggests that the copyist was working from a single coherent source. As Malcolm Boyd has pointed out, some lapses in the copying of the sonatas suggest that the scribe was actually transcribing sketches written in musical shorthand, possibly even dictated improvisations.[12] If, as seems to have been customary in Spain, the scribe was a pupil of the composer (as Soler was), this would be a sensible and practical system. The examples in Boyd's own book show how simple it is, in the case of a composer who depended so much on repetition and sequential procedures as Scarlatti did, to devise a shorthand notation for his music. Eighteenth-century sketch and printers' manuscripts were apparently regarded as not worth keeping, as witness J. S. Bach's practice of retaining only a final printed copy or *Handexemplar* of his published works in which to enter subsequent corrections and additions. Therefore, it is possible that the scribes of Venice and Parma were given not complete scores but sketches in some kind of abbreviated notation; these they simply discarded once they had written out the fair copies, just as a secretary would throw away the shorthand notes of a meeting after typing up the minutes.

Scarlatti's Instruments

The keyboard instruments available in the first half of the eighteenth century comprised the organ, which dominated the ecclesiastical repertory as solo and continuo instrument; the harpsichord, which held a similar position in the secular realm; the comparatively new fortepiano with little specific literature of its own; and the clavichord, largely an instrument for domestic practicing and pedagogy. In Italy during Scarlatti's youth the harpsichord was by far the most common domestic keyboard instrument. In eighteenth-century Spain, harpsichords, fortepianos, and clavichords, of both Spanish and foreign manufacture, were available in many types and models. Their identification is further complicated by the fact that in Spain plucked stringed keyboards were called *clavicordio*, *clavicimbalo*, or *espineta*, while the clavichord was *mon-*

acordio. (To add a final twist of confusion, in present-day Spanish the clavichord is *clavicordio,* the harpsichord *clavicémbalo* [Kenyon de Pascual 1992].)

Except in a few cases, it is impossible to assign Scarlatti sonatas to a specific instrument. The eighteenth-century accounts of Domenico's keyboard playing all describe him as a harpsichordist, only once as an organist, and never as a performer on the fortepiano or clavichord. The titlepage of the *Essercizi per Gravicembalo,* "written to accommodate [the player] to the Mastery of the Harpsichord," clearly shows a two-manual harpsichord, reversed in the engraving. Domenico's portrait (Ill. 5.2) shows him resting his right hand on a one-manual harpsichord. (The genre painting by Louis Michel Van Loo, now in the Hermitage, depicting Maria Barbara performing on a two-manual French harpsichord [Dowd 1986] is invalid evidence since it is an idealized representation commissioned by Catherine the Great after the Queen's death.) While Domenico ventured at the organ in his contest with Handel, he was clearly less at home there, although at least three of his sonatas—K.287, 288, 328, and possibly K.255—were written for organ (Tagliavini 1985; Discography: Sacchetti). Some important Spanish manuscript sources assign sonatas to the harpsichord ("clavicordio" or "clave"), others to the organ (Kirkpatrick 1953; Boyd 1986). Although the clavichord flourished in Spain well into the nineteenth century and was produced in formats capable of dealing with the largest of the Scarlatti sonatas, it does not appear to have been employed at the Spanish court (Kenyon 1982).

It is an open question as to when and where Scarlatti first encountered the fortepiano—on his visits to Florence in 1702 or 1705, in Portugal (Pollens 1985), or in Spain. However, for the performance of Scarlatti, Pagano accurately characterized the harpsichord as a certainty, the fortepiano as an hypothesis. Physically, the Florentine fortepiano was unimpressive; mechanically, it was complex, delicate, and unreliable, and it was limited both in range and in tone color. Scarlatti might have conceived a few monochromatic sonatas for the early piano, but there is no reason to suppose that a composer already acknowledged in his youth as a master of the visually and aurally splendid harpsichord should have taken any more interest in the fortepiano than Artur Rubinstein took in the clavichord.

Stringed keyboard instruments of the eighteenth century differed not only in their various means of tone production, but also in their national traditions of construction: Italian, Franco-Flemish, German, English, Spanish. All of these were known in Spain. The Italian harpsichords that Scarlatti played in his early years were light, resonant, one-manual instruments whose single keyboards of box naturals and ebony sharps controlled two registers of strings, both at 8-foot or unison pitch (8-foot = normal pitch, 4-foot = an octave higher, 16-foot = an octave below). (Cardinal Ottoboni, however, was the proud owner of a transposing harpsichord with two keyboards and three registers [Piperno 1981].) For protection, these light instruments were placed in a heavier decorated outer case (Ill. 5.4). The standard string scaling of the Italian harpsichord was short in the treble and doubled the string length well down into the tenor register, producing a characteristic sharp curve at the treble end of the bentside tapering off to a sharply angled tail. (An outline in which the bass angle is also rounded is called a double bentside.) The sound is rather brittle in the treble, full and rich in the tenor and bass, and is marked by a strong attack and a relatively quick decay.

Until the publication of Kirkpatrick's book, the Spanish harpsichords of Scarlatti's later years were virtually unknown except for casual observations such as those of Burney, who reported that "the natural keys are black, and the flats and sharps are covered with mother of pearl; they are of the Italian model, all the wood is cedar, except the bellies, and they are put into a second case." Farinelli's Spanish instrument had "more tone" than any of his Italian ones.[13]

The inventory of instruments belonging to Maria Barbara at her death in 1758 gives an idea of the instruments available to Scarlatti at the Spanish court. Its value rests on two assumptions, neither of them verifiable: first, that the Scarlatti sonatas were intended only for the Queen's instruments; second, that the contents of Maria Barbara's collection did not vary significantly throughout her adult life. The inventory lists three Florentine fortepianos, nine harpsichords, and an organ.

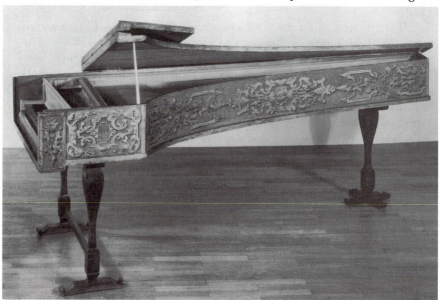

ILLUSTRATION 5.4. Italian harpsichord, ca. 1700. Staaliches Institut für Musik forschung, Berlin.

The fortepianos were built of cypress with box and ebony keyboards ranging from four to four and one-half octaves, suggesting the work of the inventor of the piano, the Florentine Bartolomeo Cristofori, or his pupil Giovanni Ferrini (Montanari 1991; Tagliavini 1991). One instrument was kept at Aranjuez, one at the Escorial, and the third presumably at Buen Retiro. Two instruments of fifty and fifty-six keys in ebony and bone had started life as fortepianos but subsequently had been converted into one-manual harpsichords, perhaps because of the difficulty of repairing the fiendishly delicate Florentine action.

Of the seven remaining harpsichords in the queen's possession, the most elaborate had five registers and four sets of strings (probably $2 \times 8'$, $8'$, $1 \times 4'$, with either a 16-foot, a 2-foot, or a third 8-foot as the fourth choir and some form of lute or nasal stop as the fifth register) with a range of fifty-six ebony and mother-of-pearl keys. From Farinelli's biographer Giovenale Sacchi we learn that Maria Barbara had expressed a wish for a harpsichord with "more varied sounds." Farinelli secretly arranged for such an instrument to be built by the obscure maker Diego Fernandez. The specifications of this amazing object have recently come to light in an inventory of Farinelli's possessions (Cappelletti 1995). It was furnished with no less than ten different registers, activated by pedals. The instrument had three types of strings: brass, steel, and gut, with at least one 4' register. Some of the registers covered the entire keyboard, others were divided for left or right hand so as to produce solo and accompaniment in different timbres. It should be noted, however, that this Pleyel before the fact was an anomaly among the queen's harpsichords and cannot be considered normative for Scarlatti's sonatas. Three of the queen's harpsichords, one identified as Flemish and all keyed in ebony and bone, had three registers (probably $2 \times 8'$, $1 \times 4'$), with fifty-six, fifty-eight, and an unidentified number of keys. These may have had either one or two keyboards.

The crucial element in relating these instruments to Scarlatti's sonatas is not the number of keyboards, however, but the range. A two-manual harpsichord is not necessary for the performance of Scarlatti's almost dyslexic hand crossings. On eighteenth-century instruments the equivalence of sound between the two manuals necessary for the free exchange of material between the hands, as in the Goldberg Variations or François Couperin's *pièces croisées,* could be achieved only with the lightest registration, one 8-foot stop on each manual. This is inappropriate for Scarlatti, whose crossed-hands passages do not employ identical notes and often demand the full instrument. However, thirty-four Scarlatti sonatas do require another special feature: a full five-octave range; and K.485 requires five octaves and a note. (For a full tabulation of the sonatas by range see Rousset 1986.)

Only the three remaining instruments in Maria Barbara's collection possessed a compass of sixty-one keys or five octaves (FF–f‴, GG–g‴ or perhaps FF–g''' without an F-sharp). All three were harpsichords, with two sets of strings—most likely 2 × 8′—specified in one instance. Like the fortepianos, one of these five-octave harpsichords was kept at Aranjuez, one at the Escorial, and one apparently at Buen Retiro. That they were of Spanish manufacture is shown by the agreement between Burney's description and a bill presented in May 1757 from Diego Fernandez charging the imposing sum of 9,600 reales for constructing the harpsichords housed at the Escorial and Aranjuez. These were double, on the Italian model, with outer cases of white poplar and inner cases, music desks, and jackrails of cedar and cypress; they had one manual with keyboards of sixty-one keys of ebony and mother-of-pearl, endblocks of ebony, mother-of-pearl, and bone, and stands of turned beechwood with iron plates and bolts for dismantling (Kenyon 1987). A superb pair of sonatas "Per Cembalo espresso" in C major (K.356–357), transmitted only in a volume of the Parma collection copied in 1754, displays an almost orgiastic delight in the possibilities of a five-octave GG-g'''—harpsichord—so much so that the copyist has had to lay the music out on four rather than the customary two staves to accommodate the constant juxtapositions of contrasting registers (see Ex. 5.5, p. 175). It is tempting to speculate that the sonatas were commissioned by Maria Barbara to celebrate the arrival of a new five-octave instrument like the one furnished by Fernandez in 1757.

On the basis of the queen's inventory, Kirkpatrick described the ideal Scarlatti instrument as "a sonorous harpsichord in cedar and cypress, with one keyboard and two stops at eight-foot pitch, one of the stops ... voiced very delicately to permit the performance of *cantabile* pieces, and the other ... voiced strongly in order to lend brilliance and power to the *tutti*."[14] In the forty years since Kirkpatrick's researches, Iberian harpsichords, fortepianos, and clavichords have been recovered and examined, and the names and personalities of makers and even the outlines of various local Spanish traditions of construction have begun to emerge. Spanish harpsichords from the first half of the eighteenth century often differed significantly from those in the queen's inventory and represented types other than Kirkpatrick's normative one. They deviated from Italian constructional models in merely decorating a singlecase instrument to suggest a double case ("false inner-outer"); they lacked the five-octave compass; walnut was the favored wood; their registers often included a 4-foot stop; and they often displayed the non-Italian feature of a double bentside. Three-manual harpsichords were on sale in Madrid, and the Spanish made five-octave pianos that differed significantly from Florentine instruments (Kenyon 1982, 1987, 1987bis).

The acoustical results of these differences are uncertain, since only one recording of a historical Spanish harpsichord apparently exists, and modern makers do not seem to have attempted reproductions. The recorded instrument is dated circa 1720 and appears to have box naturals

ILLUSTRATION 5.5. Spanish harpsichord, ca. 1720. Collection of Rafael Puyana, Paris.

and ebony accidentals. It has an outer case, a double bentside, two 8-foot registers, and a four-and-one-half-octave range of G/B-c''' (Discography: Puyana) (Ill. 5.5). Italian harpsichords may have been tuned in some variety of meantone, limiting the range of available keys, but the Spanish seem to have practiced equal temperament (a feature of guitar tuning), which would have facilitated the tonal extensions of Scarlatti's mature keyboard style (Barbieri 1987; Pennington 1981).

Of the various types of keyboard instruments available to Scarlatti, only the fortepiano and the clavichord permit the player any real control over dynamics. Not only is the sound of the harpsichord incapable of extensive dynamic variation by touch, but on all of the harpsichords available to Scarlatti the knobs controlling the registers were located either in the righthand cheek or above the keyboard. Stops, and therefore dynamics, could be altered only where the player had at least one hand (and in the case of a manual coupler where one keyboard is pushed in like a drawer, both hands) free. The most likely places for such changes are the prolonged bars of rests in both hands that punctuate many Scarlatti sonatas, although this is by no means their only significance.

As Kirkpatrick pointed out, Scarlatti's employment of the resistant medium of harpsichord sound for his sonatas allowed him to write his dynamics and orchestration into the music without the necessity of impracticable register changes. On the harpsichord, increasing the number of voices and the level of dissonance and concentrating the parts toward the center of the keyboard gives an impression of greater volume. Decreasing the number of voices and the dissonance and spacing the parts wider at the ends of the instrument produces a decrescendo (Ex. 5.2).

EXAMPLE 5.2. Sonata in D Major K.119, mm. 56–65

(Sheveloff advocated the employment of the fortepiano precisely because its flexible dynamic can emasculate these distinctions.) These devices are employed in creating the harmonic and motivic structure of the Scarlatti sonatas, where the point of greatest intensity and volume is found not at the end, as in much nineteenth-century music, but immediately preceding the final establishment of the key in each of the two halves of the sonata, the "crux" of Kirkpatrick's analytical model. The ending releases the tension in repeated cadential figures (Ex. 5.3).

EXAMPLE 5.3. Sonata in D Major K.119, mm. 176–90

(continued)

EXAMPLE 5.3. (*continued*)

Aspects of Performance Practice in Scarlatti

Owing to Ralph Kirkpatrick's experience as a virtuoso harpsichord-ist, his chapter on performance (Kirkpatrick 1953) and the preface to his edition of sixty sonatas (Editions: Kirkpatrick 1953), whose principles are embodied in his two recordings (Discography: Kirkpatrick Sixty So-natas, Sonatas), still provide the best introduction to Domenico Scarlatti's keyboard music. Perhaps because improvisation was crucial to its crea-tion, Scarlatti's keyboard music lies beautifully under the hand, and it can be known most completely only by the performer because Scarlatti's sense of the relation between finger and keyboard informs every aspect of the sonatas—fingering, ornamentation, memorization. Burney re-ported that Scarlatti "used to say that the music of Alberti, and of several other modern composers, did not in the execution want a harpsichord, as it might be equally well, or perhaps, better expressed by any other instrument; but, as nature had given him ten fingers, and his instrument has employment for them all, he saw no reason why he should not do so" (Pagano 1990). The subject of eighteenth-century keyboard finger-ings is far too complex to embark upon here. Fortunately, no authentic keyboard fingerings by Scarlatti exist, and attempts to derive them from the fingerings in a toccata of Alessandro (written when Domenico was thirty-five) are unconvincing (Lindley 1985).

The meaning of Scarlatti's ornaments is still controversial. Kirk-patrick based his discussion (Kirkpatrick 1953: Appendix IV) on a com-prehensive examination of eighteenth-century performance practice materials, employing Germanic sources—especially C. P. E. Bach's *Essay on the True Art of Playing Keyboard Instruments*—to organize and supple-ment more fragmentary material from France, Italy, and Spain. Certain details of this mid-eighteenth-century German tradition, such as the prevalence of long appoggiaturas, the placement of ornaments on the beat, and the commencement of trills on the upper auxiliary, became articles of faith as rigid as the diametrically opposed nineteenth-century practices that they supplanted. However, all of these conventions were challenged with copious historical evidence by Frederick Neumann (Neumann 1978). The following discussion does not pretend to supplant Kirkpatrick's source study of mordents, acciaccaturas, trills, appoggiaturas, and other ornaments in their various forms and combinations, but rather indicates specific cases in which the argument has evolved in the intervening forty years.

Tremulo

Neumann's most positive contribution to the discussion of Scarlatti's keyboard ornamentation was an explanation of the "puzzling consistency of differentiation between the trill sign [⚡] and that for the tremulo [*Tremulo, Tre., Trem^{lo}., Trem.*]" (Kirkpatrick 1953), which can appear in the same passage (Ex. 5.4, Venice I 28).[15] He suggested that the trill sign indicated a trill with the conventional upper auxiliary while the tremulo denoted a continuous mordent with the lower auxiliary (the French *pincé continu*).[16] (Sachs 1991 ignored the distinction between the two indications and proposed either repeated notes or a combination of trill and repeated notes.)

EXAMPLE 5.4. Sonata in A Minor K.175, mm. 23–29, Venice I 28

Appoggiatura/Trill

As Kirkpatrick himself recognized from Neumann's work, there is ample evidence that C. P. E. Bach's long appoggiatura was not necessarily the most appropriate resolution of the diversely notated appoggiaturas in earlier and non-German eighteenth-century keyboard music, nor were ornaments invariably played on the beat. Even regarding the short appoggiatura, Kirkpatrick eventually distinguished between the appoggiatura played before the beat and thus accenting the on-beat note, the appoggiatura played on the beat but still accenting the main note, and the conventional on-beat accented appoggiatura: ♪♩ ♩♩ ♩♩

Neumann also challenged the primacy of upper-note trills, encouraging performers to consider the effect of the initial appoggiatura on the line that it decorates and to decide on musical grounds between two equally "authentic" alternatives, upper- or main-note trills. The trills of K.357, for example, function as dominant pedal-points; therefore, the main note should be stressed, whether by a main-note trill or by an unaccented upper auxiliary (Ex. 5.5, Parma IX 30).

EXAMPLE 5.5. Sonata in C Major K.357, mm. 62–69, Parma IX 30

Scarlatti's sense of the finger on the keyboard is apparent here in his direction, "Continuous trill, and where the hand does not reach the fingers that form it are changed." Eighteenth-century authorities agree that the best fingers for trilling are 2–3. Here the player can make a fine effect by beginning with these; the entry of the top voice, necessitating a change to 1–2, also masks the less facile fingering. Other sonatas contain directions for special effects such as changing fingers on repeated notes or executing a glissando with a single finger, "Con dedo solo," an Italian ornament known as a *sdrucciolato* (Sachs 1991).

Improvised Ornamentation

In the performances of the last few decades the question of improvised ornamentation has largely superseded the problem of realizing notated ornaments. The practice of Scarlatti's own contemporaries in this respect covered the entire spectrum of possibilities. François Couperin directed that his keyboard music be performed exactly as written, J. S. Bach provided decorated *doubles* for some of his courantes and sarabandes, and Handel notated only the merest skeleton of what he actually performed. The only Scarlatti sonatas that might be ornamented would seem to be slow *arioso* movements like K.208 or unadorned passages whose parallels in the other half of a sonata are embellished. And yet the melodic line of K.208 needs no further elaboration, and the heavier decoration at the end of the second half of K.519 suggests that it is deliberately applied to reinforce the closing. In music as in theology,

"'Orthodoxy,' a real Alice once said of a bishop, 'is reticence'" (W. H. Auden).

The Sources of Scarlatti's Keyboard Style

In his letter to the Duke of Huescar, Scarlatti expressed his respect for solid traditional counterpoint. His father voiced the same opinion, and their friend Gasparini summed up the requirements for becoming "a true and practiced Organist" as making "a particular study of *intavolatura,* and especially of the Toccatas, Fugues, Ricercares etc. of Frescobaldi and of other Excellent Men" and having "Instruction from good, and learned Masters."[17]

Perhaps the most influential of the "Excellent Men" for Domenico was his own father, with his "learned style." The keyboard pieces that so impressed the Romans at Domenico's performance in 1708 may have resembled the toccatas of Alessandro, although the surviving manuscripts of these works date from Alessandro's last years. The opening with a phrase in the treble repeated immediately in the bass that is a hallmark of Domenico's sonatas recurs throughout his father's keyboard toccatas, ultimately derived from the openings of cantatas and arias. The formal variety of Alessandro's operatic arias and his chromatic and major-minor shadings also may have influenced his son. In Naples Domenico may have learned from the keyboard music of Gaetano Greco (particularly Greco's fugues) and Francesco Durante. The dense acciaccaturas that became a hallmark of Domenico's style were widely practiced in the musical circle of the Grand Prince in Florence (Silbiger 1987). In Rome and Venice Scarlatti was certainly exposed to the music of Bernardo Pasquini, Corelli, Gasparini, and Handel, and probably that of Vivaldi and the Marcellos as well; Gasparini provided a possible point of contact with the music of Frescobaldi. In Lisbon the keyboard music of Seixas may have contributed to Scarlatti's later style, especially in the assimilation of folkloric materials.

The deeper sources of Scarlatti's keyboard idiom lie in the voice, the dance, the eighteenth-century orchestra, continuo playing, and popular music: Burney tells us that in Spain Scarlatti "imitated the melody of tunes sung by carriers, muleteers, and the common people."[18] From the voice (and from its analogues, stringed and wind instruments) Scarlatti learned the sense of a phrase based on a finite amount of breath, as opposed to the theoretically infinite extension of the keyboard phrase. Scarlatti's vocal sense is sometimes that of the *cante jondo,* sometimes that of the operatic aria (although with a melodic purity recalling the Emperor Charles VI's celebrated advice to Farinelli to mix "the pathetic with the spirited, the simple with the sublime").[19]

From the dance Scarlatti learned to shape rhythmic phrases and to vary their relationships of length: see, for example, the opening of the second half of the Sonata in F minor K.519, where the successive phrases describe roughly the same harmonic pattern, but their length decreases as their intensity increases (a subtlety lost on the keyboardists who chop up Scarlatti's groups of repeated phrases into banal echo effects). With his feeling for the extended dance phrase, Scarlatti often establishes a pattern under the hand and then carries it beyond the confines of the individual fingers (Ex. 5.6).

EXAMPLE 5.6. Sonata in C Major K.159, mm. 17–19

Spanish dance stimulated the rhythmic counterpoint characteristic of Scarlatti's keyboard style, as Manuel de Falla recognized when he evoked Scarlatti in the last movement of his harpsichord concerto. The simplest kind of rhythmic counterpoint is *hemiola,* the imposition of a 3/4 rhythm on two 3/8 units or their equivalent, which Scarlatti sometimes pushes to the point of dissolving the underlying meter (Ex. 5.7).

EXAMPLE 5.7a. Sonata in A Minor K.532, mm. 140–55

EXAMPLE 5.7b. Sonata in C Major K.464, mm. 32–37

The moments where long harmonic sequences, animated by a rhythmic pulse rather than by a directional movement, oscillate around a tonal center like a top on its axis also have a clear choreographic analogue.

The orchestra and other instrumental reminiscences inspired much of Scarlatti's extension of keyboard sound beyond its normal limits of reference. Unison passages recall the Corellian or Vivaldian string concerto; trumpets and horns are clearly distinguishable, as are bells, guitars, mandolins, drums, artillery salvoes or fireworks, and the castanets and heel-stamps of Spanish dance.

Scarlatti, Bach, Handel, and their less illustrious contemporaries shared a common training as continuo players. Accompanying was regarded by Gasparini as the culmination of keyboard training, demanding not only "the command of all the good rules of Counterpoint, but also good taste, naturalness, and freedom to recognize immediately the quality of the Composition, in order to be able besides playing in Concert, to accompany the Singer with accuracy and discretion, to animate, satisfy, support him."[20] The daily exercise of continuo playing furnished the performer/composer with an unfailing inner compass for harmonic direction, goals, and extensions. It also provided a context for harmonic orientation and a sense of underlying bass movement, whether explicit or implied (see Kirkpatrick's analysis of K.394, where what sounds like a succession of parallel fifths is revealed as the skeleton of a perfectly orthodox chord progression).

Although continuo playing is based on textbook harmony, observance of the rules was subordinate to the musical goals articulated by Gasparini and C. P. E. Bach. Scarlatti "was sensible he had broke through all the rules of composition in his lessons; but asked if his deviations from these rules offended the ear? and, upon being answered in the negative, he said, that he thought there was scarce any other rule, worth the attention of a man of genius, than that of not displeasing the only sense of which music is the object."[21]

All of these musical influences Scarlatti had in common with most of the composers of his time, but his experience of the Iberian peninsula seems to have added a new element and acted as a catalyst. Until we know more about eighteenth-century Iberian folk music, detailed documentation of its influence on Scarlatti is impossible. Yet no one who has played Scarlatti and who has visited Spain or heard Spanish popular music can deny the elements of Spanish dance and song that seem to pervade many Scarlatti sonatas (Sitwell 1935; Sitwell 1967; Clark 1976; Vitucci 1991). Like Haydn at Esterháza, in the isolation of Spain Scarlatti was forced to become original.

The Structure of the Scarlatti Sonata

A few maverick Scarlatti sonatas display either multimovement or continuous structures, most notably the fugues. (For an example both of how different and how effective a Mediterranean keyboard fugue can be by comparison with the familiar Bachian type, see K.417.) The overwhelming majority of Scarlatti sonatas, however, are in binary form with each half repeated. The form is defined both by harmonic structure and by the treatment of motivic material. The first half of the sonata establishes the key, often with a statement in the right hand repeated in the left. It moves from the tonic to the dominant or some other related key (the relative minor of the dominant, for example) and closes there. The second half opens in the new key (or at any rate away from the tonic), reestablishes the original tonic, and closes there. The closings of each half, reiterated affirmations of the secondary and primary tonic, are almost always essentially identical or at least closely related to each other, although the second closing may be extended or emphasized. The opening of the sonata may be cited at the beginning of the second half (Kirkpatrick's "closed" sonata), or the second half may open with new or different material (the "open" sonata), often an extended modulatory passage in block chords animated only by a persistent rhythmic pulse. The point of greatest rhythmic, harmonic, and motivic intensity in each half—the "crux"—is reached, not at the end, but at the point immediately preceding the establishment of the final key of the half and its confirmation in the various sub-elements of the closings.

Such an outline, however, tells us as much about the Scarlatti sonata as "it begins with meeting someone" tells about a love affair. The possibilities of this framework are many, and Scarlatti exploited them fully. The mature sonatas vary in length from sixteen to some 160 measures (K.431, K.460). A continuous texture in each half produces a two-unit structure. Sections of violent contrast in each half (usually preceded by a dramatic silence indicated by a corona, i.e., fermata) subdivide each half of the form (K.402, K.478, K.518); a three-unit shape is created when the contrast is confined to one section at the beginning of the second half (K.235, K.261, K.394, K.461).

The single movement is not the largest constructional unit of the Scarlatti sonatas. The Venice and Parma manuscripts present many of the sonatas grouped on the same tonic in pairs or in occasional triptychs. Kirkpatrick's insistence on these previously ignored pairings was attacked by Sheveloff, since the pairings are not invariably the same between the two sources, or different pairings may exist in earlier manuscripts.[22] Certain indications of pairing are unequivocal: a calligraphic hand pointing to the next sonata or the even more explicit direction, "At the Falling [cadence] of the last ending of this Sonata, immediately attack the Following, as the Hand directs," resulting in the *enjambement* of one sonata with the next (K.347–348); the cancellation of the flats in the minor tonic of the first sonata of a pair at the beginning of the second in the major (K.526–527); or the copyist's note that he has written two sonatas in the wrong order and that the second of the pair is to be played first (K.517). Certain frequent pairing types are equally convincing. A duple-meter andante or allegro may be followed by a faster sonata in triple meter, or a minuet may appear as the second sonata of a pair (a combination frequent in Iberian keyboard music and in *galant* music in general). Common motivic or harmonic procedures may unite both sonatas, as in K.402–403, K.514–515, or the shifts between major and minor that dapple K.443–444.

Many writers on Scarlatti have attempted to define his style in relation to the development of Classical sonata form. Is Scarlatti, the exact contemporary of Bach and Handel, really a "Baroque" composer? Scarlatti himself was aware that he had chosen a different compositional path from a rococo composer such as Alberti; do his sonatas therefore "prefigure" the Classical sonata? As Kirkpatrick noted, Scarlatti was inventive enough to have conceived the Classical sonata form (as he did in at least one case, K.159) and to have discarded it. That these questions remain unanswered suggests that "if there is no answer, there is no question," to paraphrase Gertrude Stein. Even if the Scarlatti sonatas really influenced Viennese Classicism (and despite Choi 1974 there is still much research to be done on the manuscript dissemination and influence of Scarlatti in Vienna), the fact remains that they belong to a different formal world from the Viennese sonata. As Charles Rosen has demonstrated, Classical sonata form is defined above all by gesture functioning in a tonal context. The reestablishment of the opening tonic is as important an event in a Scarlatti sonata as it is in a Classical work, but it occurs in the context of closing gestures, not of opening ones. The reader need merely imagine a Mozart piano concerto in which the recapitulation in the first movement is accomplished only by the return of the closing material to feel the difference between Scarlattian and Classical concepts of musical structure.

The Development of Scarlatti's Style

In the absence of a reliable chronology of Scarlatti's keyboard sonatas it is difficult to formulate an account of his development as a keyboard composer. Nonetheless, there exist a few chronological parameters. According to their dedication, the thirty sonatas comprising the 1738 *Essercizi* (K.1–30) were written while Domenico was in the service of the King of Portugal, between 1719 and 1728. The twelve sonatas added to Roseingrave's pirated edition of the *Essercizi* were composed before its publication in 1739, some of them probably collected during

Roseingrave's visit to Italy in 1709–1715. Other chronological limits are set by the copying dates of Venice and Parma: K.43–93, 1742; K.98–138, 1749; K.148–201 and K.202–205 (only in Parma), 1752; K.206–323, 1753; K.326–417, 1754 (including K.356–357, unique to Parma); K.418–451, 1755; K.454–513, 1756; and K.514–555, 1756–1757 (from K.544 on in Parma only). The Santini manuscripts (Münster) date K.374–379 to 1754 at Aranjuez and K.544–555 to 1756–1757. If the inscription on the manuscript Bologna, Civico Museo Bibliografico Musicale FF 232, "Per studio di Francesco Gasparini," is correct, then the Scarlatti works that it contains, K.426 and K.430, were written before Gasparini's death in 1727. On the basis of K.426, which is a mature sonata stylistically and calls for a top g‴, this seems unlikely, since the construction of the queen's five-octave harpsichord in 1757 suggests interest in extended ranges was a late development. However, the work has close affinities with K.148, and in the Bologna version the g‴ appears only at the end. The Worgan manuscript, British Library Add. 31553, which contains forty-four sonatas ranging between K.43 and K.144, dates from about 1749.

Kirkpatrick believed that the sonatas were composed in roughly the same order in which they were copied in Venice and Parma, from which he inferred that the dates of copying and composition were the same. This led him to the astonishing hypothesis that the sonatas represented the final flowering of a composer between sixty-seven and seventy-two years old. Although the first conclusion is generally accepted, the second has been questioned by Sheveloff and others except in the case of the dated late sonatas.

The sonatas of the *Essercizi*, the earliest datable source, show the fully developed Scarlatti style, as we might suspect from Domenico's urbane address to the reader: "Do not expect, whether you are Amateur or Professional, in these Compositions deep Understanding, but rather the ingenious jesting of the Art, to train you in the Mastery of the Harpsichord. Neither Visions of Interest, nor Aims of Ambition, but Obedience moved me to publish them. Perhaps they will be pleasing to you, and more willingly then will I obey other Commands to oblige you in an easier and more varied style. Show yourself therefore more human, than critical; and thus you will increase your own Delight."

The thirty *Essercizi* are homogeneous in character and consistent in style. They are arranged more or less progressively as binary sonatas—all allegro or presto—of successively greater difficulty and length culminating in a fugue. The sonatas tend to be rhythmically continuous and do not show the dramatic contrasts of harmony and character that occur in the later works, except for abrupt juxtapositions of major and minor. The traditional imitative beginning between the hands occurs in eleven of the sonatas. In form, all but three are "closed" sonatas. Pairings (or at least successive sonatas on the same tonic) occur twice. The harmonic language of the *Essercizi* is recognizably kin to that of the later sonatas. K.26 displays a basic feature of Scarlatti's harmonic style, the acciaccatura—dissonant tones filling up the intervals of a chord (Ex. 5.8).

EXAMPLE 5.8. Sonata in A Major K.26, mm. 36–42 (*Essercizi XXVI*)

(See also Exx. 5.2, 5.4 above, and Ex. 5.9 below.) These were employed extensively in continuo playing and were treated by Gasparini in chapter 9 of *L'Armonico pratico*. (They also may owe something to Spanish guitar strumming.) The *Essercizi* abound in other elements of Scarlatti's mature style: the sense of keyboard spacing (cf. the octave displacements in the second half of K.1), the juxtaposition of a melody with a rich chordal accompaniment (K.6), the movement that seems a chain of harmonic progressions dissolved into a continuous figuration (K.27), the raucous accompanied Iberian song of K.29, as well as the overall virtuosity, the command of harpsichord sonority, and an almost obsessive interest in hand crossings.

Scarlatti's prefatory note to the player, "To explain to you the disposition of the hands, I advise you that by the D is indicated the right, and by the M the left," was no mere formality. Beginning with the *Essercizi*, his fascination with hand-crossing went far beyond creating a "three hands" texture of alternating soprano and bass around a moving middle voice (cf. Rameau's "Les trois mains" or the Gigue of Bach's first Partita). In many cases, Scarlatti even crosses the hands in passages that could be rewritten in normal position without losing a note. What he gains is a sense of danger, the destruction of the normal relation between hand and keyboard to create a new kind of choreography. (Despite many recent recordings, hand-crossing leaps should not be split into two gestures, one on either side of the leap: the challenge to the performer is to make the musical phrase move *across* the leap.)

A suggestive but flawed account by Dr. Burney connects Scarlatti's hand crossings with his early keyboard works. In Vienna Burney had met Alexander Ludwig L'Augier, "a living history of modern music."

In Spain [L'Augier] was intimately acquainted with Domenico Scarlatti, who, at seventy-three [Scarlatti in fact died at seventy-two], composed for him a great number of harpsichord lessons which he now possesses, and of which he favored me with copies. The book in which they are transcribed, contains forty-two pieces, among which there are several slow movements, and of all these I, who have been a collector of Scarlatti's compositions all my life, had never seen more than three or four. They were composed in 1756, when Scarlatti was too fat to cross his hands as he used to do, so that these are not so difficult, as his more juvenile works, which were made for his scholar and patroness, the late queen of Spain, when princess of Asturias.[23]

(If any one had to forego hand crossings it was probably not Domenico, whose portrait reveals him as slender, but Maria Barbara or L'Augier, who was "of uncommon corpulency.")

In the twelve sonatas that Roseingrave appended to the *Essercizi*, although their dating is uncertain, we find both stylistically coherent works such as K.33, K.36, K.38–39, K.41, and sonatas in which elements of Scarlatti's mature style as represented in the *Essercizi* seem unassimilated: reminiscences of the Italian concerto grosso (K.31, K.37, later transfigured in K.347), simple melody-bass settings of arias and minuets (K.32, K.34, K.40, K.42), and a bustling melody-bass sonata movement (K.35). The miscellaneous early sonatas copied into the Venice manuscripts in 1742 and 1749 (K.43–93, 98–138) similarly range from rather crude and stylistically uncertain essays to sonata-pairs of a breadth and sophistication greater than those of the *Essercizi*. (In addition to binary keyboard sonatas there appear dance movements intended for a melody instrument and figured bass, K.88–91, and an Italianate figural variation set, K.61, reminiscent of Alessandro Scarlatti's keyboard variations on the *Follia*.). K.77 is a very stiff example of a texture that Scarlatti later managed with great subtlety, the accompanied cantabile melody (cf. K.208).

Along with these old-fashioned and tentative works there appear others that point to the later sonatas. A clear reference to the pairing of sonatas occurs in the Parma version of K.53 ("Before this sonata one must play the one which follows [K.258], which is its Companion, and before it"), which contradicts the pairing of K.52–53 in Venice. An early example of the typical D-major hunting-horn sonata (K.140) changes key drastically—D major to C major—after a caesura and cadences in the minor despite the opening fanfare in the major. The technical demands on the performer here are sometimes extreme, not only in terms of the hand-crossings of the *Essercizi* but also in extensive leaps within a hand, chains of thirds and sixths, pedal-point trills, repeated notes, rapid scales, and arpeggiated bass passages requiring wrist rotation. In general, the latest of these sonatas show a clearer delimitation of sections, and Scarlatti's power to extend and sustain them is such that by comparison with a work like K.126 some of the *Essercizi* seem short-breathed.

The sonatas in the first two volumes of the 1752 sets (K.148–205) seem to be the works "in an easier style" promised by Scarlatti in the preface of the *Essercizi*. Technically, these sonatas are as simple as the preceding ones were virtuosic; hand crossings, for example, occur only in K.182. Although the sonatas of this group are not as dramatic as their predecessors, they do consolidate certain stylistic gains. Scarlatti's command of figuration becomes virtually absolute in terms of sonority and the avoidance of routine formulas. Dramatic shifts of mode are more frequent (K.151, K.167), and slow movements occur more often. The treatment of dissonance, as well, is frequently more intense, as in the minor seconds of K.193 or the unprepared acciaccaturas (excised in the Longo edition) that open K.175 (Ex. 5.9).

EXAMPLE 5.9. Sonata in A Minor K.175, mm. 1–6

The second half of K.180 is a good example of the degree of suspense that Scarlatti achieves by oscillating harmonies around a throbbing pedal point.

A heightened intensity, fostered by the Spanish penchant for equal temperament, is apparent in the opening sonata of the first two Venice volumes copied in 1753, K.206. Starting from E major, within seventeen measures Scarlatti arrives in E-flat minor. The whole sonata is a study in the management of harmonic color, modal ambiguity, and unexpected inflections (see also K.215). In K.212 the wider employment of the open form encourages harmonic excursions at the beginning of the second half, and in K.260 the constant yet subtly varied eighth-note motion outlines a wonderful succession of slow-moving harmonies. In some cases, the relation between the two sonatas of a pair is brought into sharper focus than in the earlier sonatas, especially where Scarlatti follows a work of harmonic intensity with a 3/8, 6/8, or 12/8 movement of more discursive character. Technically, these sonatas are more difficult than the ones immediately preceding them, but generally because of purely musical demands such as the expansion of figures beginning under the hand to the point where they can be negotiated only by a leap.

The sonatas of K.266–355 were copied into the Venice manuscripts in 1753 and 1754. Some of these sonatas are less demanding than their predecessors, but the repeated notes of K.298 and the wild leaps of K.299 are as daunting as anything in Scarlatti. Pairs of sonatas opening with a slow movement now occur with some frequency, and many of these slow movements have a remarkable tonal range. K.296, for example, begins in F major; by the time it reaches the cadencing material of the first half (in the relative minor of the dominant), it has traversed F minor, D-flat major, and B major. (Kirkpatrick used to say, "Suddenly you realize that for the first time in a recital you're playing G-flat.") Again, the second sonata of a pair is often less complex in harmonic character, more regular in figuration, and is set in triple or compound meter. K.297, in 3/8, contrasts the wide-ranging modulation of K.296 with an insistence upon the tonic and dominant areas (emphasized by the employment of the closed form), but echoes the first-half minor cadence of its partner by cadencing both halves in the minor.

Of the last sonatas, K.358–543 were copied into the queen's manuscript from 1754 to 1757 and K.544–555 appear to have been composed and were copied into Parma in 1756–1757. The set of sonatas K.374–379, written at Aranjuez in 1754, consists of three pairs: a cut-time andante and 6/8 allegro in G, a 3/4 allegro and 2/4 allegrissimo in B minor, and a cut-time allegro and unmarked minuet-like 3/8 in F. All are rather modest works. No extended range is called for, the basic texture is two-voice, and no dramatic changes of key or mood occur. The one extravagance of the group is a series of one-finger glissandos in K.379. These relatively sober works might have been written for one of Maria Barbara's Florentine fortepianos.

To the player who has been reading through the Scarlatti sonatas in chronological order, the most striking aspect of these last works is the degree to which they intensify and transfigure the language of the earlier sonatas. In general, the texture of these works is sparser but with no loss of richness; a single chromatic inflection here may have the weight of a chord or an entire measure in an earlier work—the final distillation of the harmonic sense inculcated by continuo playing. It is possible to isolate in the late sonatas virtually all the procedures characteristic of their predecessors: hand-crossings (K.529, K.554), dramatic silences (K.478), abrupt explosions (K.394), wild leaps (K.509–510), long, richly modulating movements (K.402), and sudden and distant key changes (K.491, K.510). On the other hand, Scarlatti can construct a sonata of 134 measures—K.493—out of nothing but the progressions I-V/V-I. In the drone-basses of the *Pastorale* K.513 (one of the few sonatas whose descriptive title derives from Scarlatti), the thoroughly hispanized "Domingo Escarlatti" recalled the land of his birth for the last time, evoking the sheepskin-clad shawm-and-bagpipe players who still come down to Rome from the Abruzzi at Christmas to play before the crib of the Christ Child.

Writers on Scarlatti seem compelled to debate rather nervously whether he is indeed a Top Composer like his two great contemporaries, or whether his output of miniature works dooms him as "a dwarf among giants," in Schumann's unkind phrase. Perhaps literature provides a more illuminating parallel than music. One of the monuments of nine-teenth-century Italian poetry is a collection of some two thousand son-nets in Roman dialect by Giuseppe Gioachino Belli. As sonnets they are miniatures even more circumscribed formally than the Scarlatti sonatas, and their limitation to *romanaccio* dialect rivals Scarlatti's limitation to the harpsichord as a medium. The effect of Belli's work is achieved not so much by the individual sonnet—although there are examples of pathos, obscenity, crystalline purity, and breathtaking virtuosity—as by their to-tality, which paints nineteenth-century Rome from the Pope in his golden coach to Santaccia, the prodigious whore of Piazza Montanara. In a nonverbal way, Scarlatti's sonatas constitute the same kind of pan-orama, with the same transcendent gift of seeming to observe and report without intellectual, emotional, or moral judgment and editing.

Notes

This essay reflects above all my thirty years as a pupil and friend of Ralph Kirkpatrick, and my equally valued association with Roberto Pagano. David Montgomery, Isabel and Laurance Roberts, and Howard Schott have read various drafts, and with Malcolm Boyd and Sibyl Marcuse have contributed numerous helpful suggestions. For permission to reproduce illustrations I am indebted to the distinguished harpsi-chordist Rafael Puyana; the Biblioteca Real, Madrid; the bequest of José Relvas, Alpiarça, Portugal; and the Library of Congress, Washington, DC. Translations are my own.

1. Quoted in Kirkpatrick 1953, 21–22; further letters are given by Boyd 1986, 10–14.

2. The Grand Prince is quoted in Boyd 1986, 12. According to Burney, Ales-sandro "had so high an opinion of Francesco Gasparini, then a composer and a harpsichord master of great eminence in Rome, that he placed his son, Domen-ico, while a youth, to study under him in that city." Burney 1776/1935, 2: 635; quoted in Kirkpatrick 1953, 25–26.

3. Mainwaring 1760, 51–52; Kirkpatrick 1953, 32.

4. Mainwaring 1760, 59–62; Kirkpatrick 1953, 32–33.

5. Burney 1776, 2: 703–4; Kirkpatrick 1953, 30–31.

6. Revised version of Pagano 1985, 354–55.

7. Walther 1732, original in Kirkpatrick 1953, 334; quoted in Boyd 1986, 97–98.

8. Coxe 1815, 3: 18–19, quoted in Boyd 1986, 99–100.

9. Boyd 1986, 100–01.

10. Kirkpatrick 1953, 121 and plate 39; translation of Scarlatti's Testament in Boyd 1986, 236–38.

11. For the most recent account of manuscript discoveries, including eight sonatas attributed to Scarlatti, see Boyd 1986, 148–57, 190–94, and Appendix III, containing the two unpublished sonatas. The *Fandango del S.gr Scarlate* was discovered in a late eighteenth-century manuscript (Editions: Martinez 1984).

12. Boyd Review 1989. In K.516–517 the scribe was already in some confusion from his original since he writes at the beginning of K.517, "What follows should be played first." A four-measure passage at the end of the second half is marked for repetition, while the previous occurrence is written out. The recurrence of the same mistake in two successive bass passages suggests that the passage occurred only once, in a defective version, in the original, and that the repetition was indicated in shorthand. The same appears in K.532, where an F-sharp is missing in the bass in both measures 31 and 40. See Hammond 2001.

13. Burney 1771, 1: 203–04; Kirkpatrick 1953, 176.

14. Kirkpatrick 1953, 180.

15. Kirkpatrick 1953, 390.

16. Neumann 1978, 352–55.

17. Gasparini 1708, (V); Kirkpatrick 1953, 27.

18. Burney 1771, 1: 247–49; Kirkpatrick 1953, 82.

19. Quoted by Kirkpatrick 1953, 95.

20. Gasparini 1708, (V).

21. Burney 1771, 1: 248.

22. A Madrid manuscript (Conservatory MS 3/1408) containing archaic notational features pairs K.160 and K.333, whereas in Venice the pairing is K.160–161, in Parma K.161–160, and in both K.333 is unpaired (Boyd 1986, 162–63).

23. Burney 1771, 1: 247–49; Kirkpatrick 1953, 170–71.

Bibliography

EDITIONS

Alvini, Laura, Castellani, M., and P. Paolini eds. *Domenico Scarlatti. Sonate per Cembalo.* Florence, 1985–. [Facsimile of the Venice manuscript]

Fadini, Emilia, ed. *Domenico Scarlatti: Sonate per clavicembalo.* Milan, 1978–.

Gilbert, Kenneth, ed. *Domenico Scarlatti: Sonates.* Paris, 1971–1984.

Kirkpatrick, Ralph, ed. *Sixty Sonatas.* 2 vols. New York, 1953.

———, ed. Domenico Scarlatti: *Complete Keyboard Works in Facsimile.* New York, 1971. [Facsimile of the *Essercizi*, the Parma manuscript, and manuscript and printed unica]

Longo, Alessandro, ed. *Opere complete per clavicembalo di Domenico Scarlatti. Criticamente rivedute e ordinate in forma di suites da Alessandro Longo.* Milan, [1906–]; *indice tematico.* Milan, 1937.

Martinez, Rosario Alvarez, ed. *José Herrando, Doménico Scarlatti, Francisco Courcelle, José de Nebra y Agustino Massa: Obras ineditas para tecla.* Madrid, 1984. [Contains an unpublished manuscript sonata and Fandango ascribed to Scarlatti]

LITERATURE CITED

Alvini, Laura. "Les certitudes ambiguës: Farinelli et les manuscrits italiens des sonates." *Domenico Scarlatti: 13 recherches. Actes du colloque international de Nice.* Nice, 1986, 36–42.

Barbieri, Patrizio. *Acustica accordatura e temperamento nell'illuminismo veneto.* Rome, 1987.

Bogiankino, Massimo. *L'arte clavicembalistica di Domenico Scarlatti.* Rome, 1956.

Boyd, Malcolm. *Domenico Scarlatti—Master of Music.* New York, 1986.

——————. Review of Scott Ross, recording of Domenico Scarlatti, *Complete Keyboard Works. Early Music* (hereafter *EM)* 17 (1989): 267–74.

Burney, Charles. *A General History of Music,* 2 vols. London, 1776–1789. Reprint. New York, 1957.

——————. *The Present State of Music in France and Italy.* London, 1771–1773. Reprint. New York, 1969.

Cappelletto, Sandro. *La voce perduta: Vita di Farinelli evirato cantore.* Turin, 1995.

Choi, Seunghyun. "Newly Found Eighteenth Century Manuscripts of Domenico Scarlatti's Sonatas and their Relationship to other Eighteenth and Early Nineteenth Century Sources." Ph.D. dissertation, University of Wisconsin, 1974.

Clark, Jane. "Domenico Scarlatti and Spanish Folk Music." *EM* 4 (1976): 19–21.

——————. "His own worst enemy." *EM* 13 (1985): 542–47.

Coxe, William. *Memoirs of the Kings of Spain.* London, 1815.

Doderer, G. "Aspectos novos em torno da estadia de Domenico Scarlatti na corte de D. Joao v (1719–1727)." Preface to facsimile ed. of Scarlatti, *Libro di tocate per cembalo, e tutti.* Lisbon, 1991, 7–53.

Dowd, William. "Le clavecin de Domenico Scarlatti." *Domenico Scarlatti: 13 Recherches. Actes du colloque international de Nice.* Nice, 1986, 88–95.

Gasparini, Francesco. *L'armonico pratico al cimbalo* (1708). Translated by David Burrows as *The Practical Harmonist at the Keyboard.* New Haven, 1963.

Hammond, Frederick. Review of Boyd 1986. *Notes* 43 (1988): 476–77.

——————. Review of Fadini 1978. *Music and Letters* 69 (1988): 563–65.

——————. Review of Pagano 1985. *Music and Letters* 69 (1988): 519–22.

——————. "Domenico Scarlatti: A la recherche des autographes perdus." *Fiori Musicologici: Studi in onore di Luigi Ferdinando Tagliavini,* ed. François Seydoux. Bologna, 2001, 275–295.

Heartz, Daniel. "Farinelli and Metastasio: Rival twins of public favour." *EM* 12 (1984): 358–66.

Holmes, William C. "Lettere inedite su Alessandro Scarlatti." *La musica a Napoli durante il Seicento.* Rome, 1987, 369–78.

Kenyon de Pascual, Beryl. "*Clavicordios* and clavichords in 16th-century Spain." *EM* 20 (1992): 611–30.

——————. "The five-octave compass in 18th-century Spanish harpsichords." *EM* 15 (1987): 74–75.

——————. "Francisco Perez Mirabal's harpsichords and the early Spanish piano." *EM* 15 (1987): 503–13 [1987bis].

——————. "Harpsichords, Clavichords and Similar Instruments in Madrid in the Second Half of the Eighteenth Century." *The Royal Musical Association Research Chronicle* 18 (1982): 66–84.

——————. "Domenico Scarlatti and his Son Alexandro's Inheritance." *Music & Letters* 69 (1988), 23–29.

Kirkpatrick, Ralph. *Domenico Scarlatti.* Princeton, 1953. 3rd revised edition, 1968. German translation. Horst Leuchtmann. Munich, 1972, 2 vols.

——————. "Scarlatti revisited in Parma and Venice." *Notes* 28 (1971): 5–15.

——————. "Who wrote the Scarlatti sonatas? A study in reverse scholarship." *Notes* 29 (1973): 426–31.

Lindley, Mark. "Keyboard Technique and Articulation: Evidence for the Performance Practices of Bach, Handel, and Scarlatti." In *Bach, Handel, Scarlatti: Tercentenary Essays,* ed. Peter Williams. Cambridge, 1985, 207–43.

Mainwaring, John. *Memoirs of the Life of the Late George Frederic Handel.* London, 1760.

Montanari, Giuliana. "Bartolomeo Cristofori: a list and historical survey of his instruments." *EM* 19 (1991): 383–96.

Neumann, Frederick. *Ornamentation in Baroque and Post-Baroque Music. With Special Emphasis on J. S. Bach.* Princeton, 1978.

Pagano, Roberto. "Alessandro et Domenico Scarlatti: biographie assortie de quelques considerations musicales." *Domenico Scarlatti: 13 Recherches. Actes du colloque international de Nice.* Nice, 1986, 8–15.

––––––. "Piena utilizzazione delle dieci dita: una singolare applicazione practica della parabola dei talenti." *Gli Atti del Convegno Scarlatti e il suo tempo, Accademia Chigiana, 1985.* Florence, 1990.

––––––. *Scarlatti Alessandro e Domenico: Due vite in una.* Milan, 1985.

––––––. "Scarlatti, Domenico." In LE BIOGRAFIE, vol. 6 of *Dizionario Enciclopedico Universale della Musica e del Musicisti.* Turin, 1988.

––––––, Lino Bianchi, and Giancarlo Rostirolla. *Alessandro Scarlatti.* Turin, 1972.

Pennington, Neil D. *The Spanish Baroque Guitar: With a Transcription of De Murcia's* Passacalles y obras. 2 vols. Ann Arbor, MI, 1981.

Pestelli, Giorgio. *Le sonate di Domenico Scarlatti: Proposta di un ordinamento cronologico.* Turin, 1967.

Piperno, Franco. "Il restauro di Giovanni Antonio Alari ad un 'cembalo a tre registri con la variazione de'tuoni' del Cardinale Ottoboni." *L'organo* 19 (1981): 175–78.

Pollens, Stewart. "The early Portuguese piano." *EM* 13 (1985): 18–27.

Rousset, Christophe. "Approche statistique des sonates." *Domenico Scarlatti: 13. Recherches.* Nice, 1986, 68–87.

Sachs, Barbara. "Scarlatti's tremulo." *EM* 19 (1991): 91–93.

Scarlatti, Domenico. La *Dirindina.* Ed. Francesco Degrada. Milan, 1985.

Seixas, Carlos de. *Sonatas. Portugaliae Musica X,* 1965.

Sheveloff, Joel. "Domenico Scarlatti: Tercentenary Frustrations." *The Musical Quarterly* 71 (1985): 399–436; 72 (1986): 90–118.

––––––. "The Keyboard Music of Domenico Scarlatti: A Reevalnation of the Present State of Knowledge in the Light of the Sources." Ph.D. dissertation, Brandeis University, 1970.

––––––. "Scarlatti, [Giuseppe] Domenico." *The New Grove Dictionary of Music and Musicians.* London, 1980.

Silbiger, Alexander. Introduction to Florence, Biblioteca del Conservatorio di musica Luigi Cherubini, MS D. 2534. *17th Century Keyboard Music* 10. New York, 1987.

Sitwell, Sacheverell. *A Background for Domenico Scarlatti.* London, [1935].

––––––. *Baroque and Rococo. [Southern Baroque Revisted].* New York, 1967.

Sutherland, David. "Domenico Scarlatti and the Florentine fortepiano." *EM* 23 (1995): 243–56.

Tagliavini, Luigi Ferdinando. "Remarks on the Compositions for organ of Domenico Scarlatti." In *Bach, Handel, Scarlatti: Tercentenary Essays,* ed. Peter Williams. Cambridge, 1985, 321–25.

————. "Giovanni Ferrini and his harpsichord 'a penne e martelletti.'" *EM* 19 (1991): 398–408.

Van der Meer, John Henry. "A curious instrument with a five-octave compass." *EM* 14 (1986): 397–400.

————. Communication. *EM* 15 (1987): 75–76.

Vidali, Carole F. *Alessandro and Domenico Scarlatti: A Guide to Research*. New York, 1993.

Vitucci, Matteo Marcellus. *The Language of Spanish Dance*. Oklahoma City, 1991.

Walther, Johann Gottfried. *Musicalisches Lexicon*. Leipzig, 1732.

SELECTED DISCOGRAPHY

Kirkpatrick, Ralph. *Domenico Scarlatti. Sixty Sonatas*. Columbia (1954); harpsichord by John Challis.

————. *Domenico Scarlatti. Sonatas*. Deutsche Grammophon 2544–072 (1970); harpsichord by Rainer Schutze.

Pinnock, Trevor. *Domenico Scarlatti. Sonatas for Harpsichord*. CRD 3368 (1981); harpsichord by Clayson and Garrett, 1972, after Dulcken.

Puyana, Rafael. *Virtuoso Sonatas and Fandangos from Eighteenth-century Spain*. L'Oiseau Lyre 417 341–2; three-manual harpsichord by Hieronymus Albrecht Hass, 1740; one-manual anon. Spanish harpsichord, ca. 1720; two-manual harpsichords after Blanchet (Willard Martin) and Taskin (David Rubio).

Ross, Scott. *Domenico Scarlatti. Complete Keyboard Works*. Erato ECD 75400 (1984–1985), 34 CDs; one Italian and four French harpsichords.

Rowland, Gilbert. *Domenico Scarlatti. Sonatas for Harpsichord*. Keyboard Records, KGR 1026 CD (26 vols. as of 1989); harpsichord by Michael Robertson, 1974, after Taskin.

Sacchetti, Arturo. *Domenico Scarlatti and Domenico Zipoli. Works for Organ* (including the fugues K.41, 58, 93). Radio Vaticana 061.004, Frequenz 1989 (Ancient Organs of Rome).

Valenti, Fernando. (Over three hundred sonatas). Westminster ABC (reissue), recorded in Vienna; harpsichords by Ammer and Neupert.

CHAPTER SIX

Carl Philipp Emanuel Bach

David Schulenberg

We are accustomed to dividing the music of eighteenth-century Europe into two convenient categories, the late Baroque and the early Classical, with the division falling neatly at the middle of the century, coinciding with the death of J. S. Bach. Yet the death of an obscure German cantor was an event of very little consequence as far as most European musicians were concerned. Even for Bach's two eldest sons, who in 1750 were already among the leading musicians in Europe, the stylistic transition that we place at the middle of the eighteenth century was by then an accomplished fact; as for us, we might better view it as an ongoing process that had been underway for at least several decades and would continue for several more.

Of the elder Bach's five sons who became professional musicians, the most important, both for the size and for the consistent quality and originality of his output, is now generally acknowledged to have been Carl Philipp Emanuel (1714–1788). While one might have expected the musical personalities of the Bach sons to have been entirely dominated by that of the father, the one common trait they seem to have inherited was a certain stubbornness, an insistence on going their own ways, which in Emanuel led to the creation of a large and varied oeuvre that greatly expanded the expressive and technical vocabulary not only of the keyboard but of all the other major idioms of the time as well, excepting opera. Emanuel Bach's works include over three hundred distinct pieces for solo keyboard, among them some of the most profound as well as some of the wittiest, most engaging keyboard music ever written. About half of the keyboard works are sonatas, a type of piece that Bach, more than any other composer, helped shape at a time when the very idea of a three-movement solo keyboard sonata was new. Bach was also the author of one of the most influential writings on keyboard playing ever written, the *Versuch über die wahre Art das Clavier zu spielen* (Essay on the

191

True Manner of Playing the Keyboard), which remains an essential guide to the performance of mid-eighteenth-century music, above all his own works.

Born in Weimar in 1714, Emanuel moved with the rest of the Bach family to Cöthen in 1717 and to Leipzig in 1723. In 1734 he left for the university at Frankfurt on the Oder, ostensibly to study law but probably intending to pursue a musical career and hoping to take advantage of the city's proximity to Berlin, the political and cultural center of northeastern Germany. Indeed, in 1738 he entered the service of Crown Prince Frederick of Prussia—from 1740 King Frederick the Great— serving him as one of several court harpsichordists until early 1768. In that year Bach moved to Hamburg, where he spent the last twenty years of his life as director of music at the city's five principal churches. All told, Emanuel Bach's career was somewhat longer than Haydn's—dated works are known from 1731 to 1788—and the sheer quantity of solo keyboard music is probably greater than for any other major contemporary. He composed for the keyboard throughout his career, and together with his fifty-two keyboard concertos, the solo keyboard works, especially the sonatas, form the most important part of his output.

Of Bach's works for solo keyboard, the best known are the pieces, mostly sonatas, that appeared in a number of famous collections that Bach either published himself or had issued with his authorization and supervision. Among these are the six Prussian and six Württemberg sonatas of 1742 and 1744, respectively; the *Probestücke* issued in conjunction with the first volume of the *Versuch* in 1753; three further sets of six sonatas published during the early 1760s, the first of these including varied reprises; and six collections published during the period 1779– 1787 and bearing the subtitle *für Kenner und Liebhaber*, that is, for "experts" (or "connoisseurs") and "amateurs." During the 1760s Bach also published three sets of *Clavierstücke*, the first of which is an ambitious collection including a concerto, a symphony, and several other substantial pieces, while the two subsequent collections are made up of smaller pieces suitable for teaching. As numerous as they are, these publications include at most only about half of Bach's output for solo keyboard. Many pieces were issued individually in the popular anthologies that began to appear shortly after the middle of the century, and a large number of works, including some of Bach's most distinctive contributions to the keyboard repertory, were left unprinted during his lifetime.

Bach's Keyboard Style

Bach has often been regarded as a transitional figure. In a purely chronological sense his music indeed stands between the Baroque and the Classical, and it contains elements of both styles. But music historians have largely discarded the view of Bach's music as an evolutionary link—in particular, between the music of J. S. Bach and that of Haydn. There is no direct line of stylistic inheritance from J. S. to C. P. E. Bach, or from Emanuel Bach to Haydn; Emanuel's keyboard works represent a distinct style best understood on their own terms, not those of an earlier or a later period.

Attempts have been made to see Bach's own music as evolving from an additive, freely developmental (*fortspinnungshaft*) compositional style characteristic of the Baroque toward a more symmetrical or regular type of writing sometimes regarded as "Classical."[1] Indeed, in many later works—especially those for amateur players (*Liebhaber*)—Bach employs periodic rondo-like themes, avoiding the asymmetrical, even fragmented phrasing found in some early pieces. But the apparent increase in the use of periodic symmetry represents not a development toward Viennese Classical style—simple symmetry in any case being far from typical of Haydn or Mozart—but a borrowing from certain French dances and other late-Baroque genres characterized by simple symmetrical themes. This, like Bach's occasional use of recitative or fantasia style in sonatas, represents not a development toward Classical (or even Romantic) style but a conscious continuation of stylistic strands already present in early eighteenth-century music. Thus it is problematic to see Bach's keyboard works as manifestations of a new interest in "expression" or "contrast"; the music of Corelli, Vivaldi, Telemann, and above all J. S. Bach is full of surprises that contradict the modern notion of Baroque music as characterized by thematic or rhythmic "unity." Emanuel's true innovations lay in his incorporating such elements as chromatic harmony and recitative-like melody into genres—especially the emerging keyboard sonata—that had not previously seen them, at least not in such concentration and in so many remarkable juxtapositions with other special devices.

Empfindsamkeit, Sturm und Drang, *and* Galant

Despite the potential problems with seeing him as a composer obsessed with musical expression, Emanuel Bach has long been recognized as the chief exponent of the so-called *empfindsamer Stil*, an "expressive" or "sensitive" manner cultivated in northern Germany during the mid-eighteenth century. While it has never been clear precisely what makes a piece "*empfindsam*," important elements are probably a more or less homophonic texture and a gently expressive melodic line broken up by rests into many small motives, including "sigh" figures (descending appoggiaturas). Sometimes confused with *Empfindsamkeit* but in fact quite distinct is the so-called *Sturm und Drang*, the more violently emotional strain in German eighteenth-century music characterized by unusual melodic intervals and sudden and unprepared shifts of texture or rhythmic character. Chromatic harmony plays a role in both types of piece, but notwithstanding the use of some highly elliptical progressions, Bach practically never departs from the harmonic language of his Baroque predecessors; even in the late rondos and fantasias, his most consistently chromatic pieces, progressions through the circle of fifths predominate, while the third-relation, which would become so important in the later Classical and Romantic styles, is rare if not unknown. ·

It is no doubt the *empfindsam* and *Sturm und Drang* works that kept Bach's name alive during the nineteenth and early twentieth centuries, in part because they were thought to have anticipated and even directly influenced the emergence of Romantic style. But it is hard to find concrete musical parallels between the music of Bach and, say, Mendelssohn, and at any rate the *empfindsam* works represent only a fraction of Bach's output. Far from being a composer of quirky music of limited appeal, Bach possessed a stylistic range of considerable breadth. Nevertheless, expression was clearly the essence of music for members of Bach's generation. Admiring accounts of Bach's clavichord playing, written by several younger contemporaries, noted such things as the "cry of sorrow and complaint" or the "vehement fire" (*heftiges Feuer*) that he drew from the instrument in performing his own works.[2] From this has emerged the view of Bach as a sort of pre–Romantic; yet it is the accounts themselves, not Bach's music, that are truly Romantic in character. His direct influence is clear only in certain works by a few north-German contemporaries, and even with these—notably Johann Gottfried Müthel, composer of a few extraordinary keyboard sonatas, variations, and concertos—the music of other composers, especially J. S. and W. F. Bach, seems to have been at least equally influential.

The *Essay* makes it quite clear that Bach himself valued clarity and precision in performance even as he called for passionate musical expression. In a famous sentence he pronounced, "Since a musician can move [others] in no other way, let him [first] move himself."[3] Taken out of context, this seems to reduce music (or musical performance) to a reflection of the player's momentary emotional state. In fact, however, Bach states just the opposite; the player must evaluate the spirit of the piece and then enter into it.[4] Moreover, Bach's statement occurs in the course of enumerating many other specific technical requisites of good performance. Some of these would be necessities in any type of music— fidelity to the score, steady tempo, and so forth—but other parts of Bach's discussion, such as his emphasis on the clear and correct execution of ornaments, or the detailed rules given concerning articulation, apply especially to his own music, and have nothing to do with an arbitrary "Romantic" type of performance.

Yet it is difficult to hear certain works of Bach, such as the A-minor Württemburg sonata or the F-minor sonata from the third collection *für*

Kenner und Liebhaber, without sensing a fiery expressive power that we normally associate with Beethoven and later composers. Bach's expressive agitation is of a very different kind, however. For one thing, the music operates within much narrower temporal boundaries; the pieces are shorter, though hardly miniatures. They often contain dramatic contrasts in expressive character (or "affect"), but rather than occupying distinct sections of a movement the contrasting segments usually alternate in rapid succession, sometimes within a single phrase (as in Ex. 6.1, p. 198). Indeed, one well-known feature of Bach's style is the use of sudden changes of pacing, unprepared pauses, and other dramatic gestures. Only in recitative was such writing previously the norm, and not surprisingly, efforts have been made to see Emanuel's style as obeying a "rhetorical principle."[5]

But while there are one or two close imitations of recitative in Emanuel's keyboard works, it would be a mistake to make too much of some vaguely "rhetorical" aspect of his style. The interruptions, digressions, parentheses, and other "rhetorical" effects found in some (not all) of Bach's works are also musical ones, even if theorists have delighted in applying to such things Greek and Latin terms that originally applied to certain figures of speech.[6] The "rhetorical" labeling is really a rudimentary form of musical analysis, an attempt to explain the construction of the music out of a large number of small, distinctly articulated segments, just as language is comprised of individual words and phrases. This sort of structure is typical of eighteenth-century music in general, but in Bach's music the relationships between adjoining segments are often not what we would expect them to be—hence the occasional impression that his music is fragmented or disjointed, though always on the surface, never at larger levels of construction. Even where the musical surface seems to be unusually fragmented, one must beware of taking the "rhetoric" too seriously, of assuming it to be hyper-expressive. It is just as likely to be a product of Bach's sense of humor; wit is as much a part of his musical personality as is *Empfindsamkeit.*

In fact, the famous irregularities of Emanuel's style are entirely absent from many pieces, perhaps the majority. Many of the slighter pieces fall into the unruffled periodic phrasing that was the norm for light keyboard music throughout the eighteenth century; some adopt a homogeneous, sequential style reminiscent of his father's preludes.[7] But Emanuel seems, even in his earliest works, to have had as little to do with his father's style as possible, instead modeling his pieces on those of other, more consistently *galant* composers such as Telemann. Indeed, while only a fraction of Bach's music is *empfindsam* or *sturm-und-drangisch,* virtually all of it can be described as *galant.* Today the term is most often used to refer to the bland, emotionally neutral style of such minor contemporaries as Quantz and Heinichen. But for Bach it meant something more specific: a style that eschewed complex polyphony in order to emphasize an expressive or engaging melody.[8]

It is possible that Bach's sometimes strident advocacy of expression in music and his belittling of mechanical or merely fashionable performance and composition reflected a distinction between what he regarded as an older, less personal style, and a newer, expressive one. The two styles correspond roughly with what we would call Baroque and *galant,* respectively, although Bach would have counted his father as one of the chief exponents of the *later* style. For, in eighteenth-century terms, Sebastian Bach was very often a *"galant"* composer; Emanuel himself counted Sebastian among the composers of the new idiom, explaining his father's use of "difficult keys" and his system of fingering as products of the "far-reaching change in musical style" that was taking place during Sebastian's lifetime.[9] But there is clearly a wide stylistic gulf between Emanuel's music and that of his father. For one thing, the genres in which they wrote are quite different; where Sebastian wrote praeludia (preludes and fugues) and suites, Emanuel specialized in three-movement sonatas and various types of single-movement piece. Sequences and other types of patterned repetition are common in the music of both composers, as is true throughout the eighteenth century, but Emanuel was much more likely to embellish the subsequent statements of a passage. And only in a small number of pieces did Emanuel systematically employ his father's contrapuntal texture: in a few sonata movements resembling two- and three-part inventions, and about a half-dozen fugues.

Texture, Dynamics, and Instrumentation

Emanuel himself is supposed to have said that he and his older brother Friedemann adopted their highly original styles because they recognized the futility of imitating that of their father.[10] Yet, as one examines the music of the two composers, it becomes clear that Emanuel— and also Friedemann, though in different ways—owed a considerable debt to Sebastian Bach. There is, to begin, an absolutely sure command of harmony and voice-leading, sometimes manifested in progressions that are as chromatic (and as effective) as any by Sebastian Bach. Moreover, while Emanuel's keyboard music is often described as having a homophonic texture, it is in fact fundamentally polyphonic, if rarely in more than two real voices. The bass is almost always subordinate to the melody, but it remains a true *line,* one to which a sensitive performer or listener must attend as carefully as to the upper part. The melody itself often implies several distinct voices, and, except in Bach's earliest works, it usually contains an abundance of ornament signs as well as more complex, written-out embellishments, products of the tradition, handed down by Sebastian Bach, of specifying details of performance that many other composers still left to the performer's discretion.

In Emanuel's music those details included dynamic markings, which, over the course of his career, gradually increased in number. This would seem to reflect the gradual replacement of harpsichord and organ by fortepiano and clavichord as the chief keyboard instruments. But it may reflect merely an increasing precision of notation on Bach's part, for there are signs that at a relatively early date Bach was already composing his solo keyboard works primarily for the clavichord—this despite the fact that only a few pieces, all composed after 1750, specifically call for *Bebung* or the *Tragen der Töne*, techniques available only on that instrument.[11] Indeed, while Bach expressed a clear preference for the clavichord in the *Versuch,* an unambiguous indication of instrument occurs in only a few scores, such as the rondos from the collections *für Kenner und Liebhaber.* The latter are for fortepiano; there are also a few sonatas for organ. There are many *Clavier-Sonaten* and *Clavierstücke,* but while the word *clavier* was often used specifically for the clavichord during the later eighteenth century, it also seems to have retained the more generic meaning of "stringed keyboard instrument"—as did the word *cembalo,* which appears often in Bach's autograph manuscripts.

In fact, most of Bach's solo pieces were written in such a manner as to permit performance on any instrument with a sufficient compass; for instance, only one of the organ works requires pedal.[12] Although some works of the 1740s already contain dynamic indications that can be executed only on an instrument capable of free dynamic graduations—that is, the clavichord or fortepiano—in the first volume of the *Versuch,* published in 1753, Bach counsels harpsichordists to ignore closely spaced dynamic markings, and he suggests that players be able to play everything on both clavichord and harpsichord.[13] No doubt he would have added the fortepiano as well, had the instrument been as widespread and as free of technical imperfections as it eventually became; he himself owned good examples of all three instruments at his death.[14]

This does not mean that all works will be equally effective on all instruments; for most pieces the clavichord probably remains the instrument of choice, although for public performances today the fortepiano may be more effective. While most works are of course playable on the modern piano, the different registers of the latter are not so distinct in timbre as on the older instruments; Bach draws on this effect in numerous passages that are repeated in a higher or lower octave. On the modern piano it is also relatively difficult to attain the crisp articulation and precise ornamentation so highly valued by Bach—who noted the difficulty of obtaining these things on eighteenth-century fortepianos as well.[15] Bach generally avoided idiomatic types of keyboard scoring such as the Alberti bass that were coming into use during the eighteenth century and that seem particularly well suited to the piano. But in other respects he gradually left behind the traditional idiom of the harpsichord, and later pieces include such things as legato octaves for the right or the left hand, or opening crescendos and closing diminu-endos.[16]

Thus, there was a certain freeing of the keyboard idiom in the course of Bach's career. This included a tendency away from strict po-lyphony in two or three parts, and with it a gradual increase in the va-riety of figuration and rhythmic motives coexisting within a single movement. Yet most individual movements possess a more consistent rhythmic manner or affect than do later Classical and Romantic com-positions. Contrast, where it occurs, is a *local* phenomenon, as in Exam-ple 6.1, where a single eight-bar phrase shifts rapidly from one "affect" to another (Ex. 6.1).

EXAMPLE 6.1. Sonata in C (*Damen-Sonaten*, No. 2) H. 205. Movement 1, mm. 24–31a

Despite the swift changes in motivic material and the sudden shifts in register, the harmonic rhythm remains fairly constant, and the passage even concludes with a conventional cadential formula.

Structure and Material

Bach's tendency to pack many imaginative details into short and, from a structural point of view, rather simple pieces has earned him the label "mannerist."[17] The term is not unjustified so long as it is under-stood in a strictly technical sense: Bach's works often acquire their indi-viduality through complex or variegated *Manieren* (ornaments) that are applied to a relatively simple underlying structure. Bach himself seems to have viewed the themes, motives, and other elements of his keyboard music as arising through the elaboration or "variation" of an underlying harmonic progression—more precisely, of a hypothetical figured bass.

This is clear from the many diverse passages that all derive from simple bass lines (Ex. 6.2).

EXAMPLE 6.2a. Rondo in G (Pieces for *Kenner und Liebhaber,* fifth set) H. 268, mm. 138–39

EXAMPLE 6.2b. Fantasia in C (Pieces for *Kenner und Liebhaber,* fifth set) H. 284, second Andantino, mm. 3–8

EXAMPLE 6.2c. Rondo in C (Pieces for *Kenner und Liebhaber,* second set) H. 260, m. 137

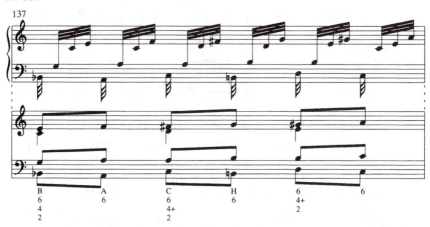

EXAMPLE 6.2d. Sonata in B Minor (Pieces for *Kenner und Liebhaber,* first set) H. 245. Movement 2, mm. 9–16, with original fingering

The sequential figuration of Example 6.2a and the cantabile melody of Example 6.2b—both equally characteristic of Bach's late style—were composed over and presumably received their initial impulse from the same chromatic ascent. Example 6.2c is composed over a variant of the same bass, a line that happens to be a form of the B-A-C-H motive (B-flat, A, C, B-natural); the figure occurs so often in Bach's bass lines that it cannot have been accidental.[18] The chromatic modulations of Examples 6.2b can be (somewhat laboriously) analyzed in terms of functional harmony, and this will show that despite frequent elided progressions and unusual pivot chords, all the relations are of the dominant/tonic variety. But it is perhaps more useful to understand such a passage in terms of its underlying voice-leading, which is most easily revealed by reducing it to its underlying figured bass progression, as shown. This is not always easy. Especially in the cadenza-like passages found in the fantasias and many of the later sonatas and rondos, the rhythmic shape of the figuration is often such as to obscure the true bass line. Thus in Example 6.2d, another variation on the "BACH" line, one must take care not to confuse chord tones with *acciaccature* and other embellishments.

Figured-bass realization was the subject of the second volume of the *Essay*, which ends with a demonstration of how to create a keyboard fantasia out of a bass line (Ex. 6.3).

EXAMPLE 6.3. *Versuch,* Part 2. The first thirteen notes of a figured bass line and their realization in the Fantasia H. 160

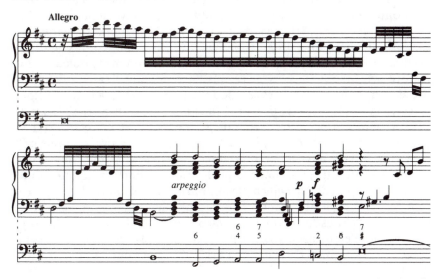

(continued)

EXAMPLE 6.3. (*continued*)

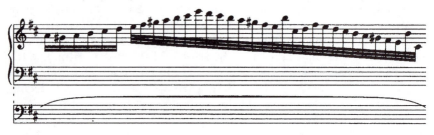

Of course, one might compose or improvise many different pieces over a single bass line; indeed, some of Bach's works demonstrate precisely this point. Chief among these is an entire three-movement sonata that was, in Bach's words, "afterwards twice varied throughout."[19] In the later versions, the harmonic progressions and, in general, the phrasing of the original remain intact, but the thematic material and many details of the texture are rewritten. This piece was an exceptional case, a compositional tour de force, but Bach applied the same technique in many other pieces, in particular those provided with what are termed *varied reprises*.

In eighteenth-century terminology the word *reprise* seems to have meant any repeated section, in particular one of the two portions of a dance or sonata movement preceding and following the double bar. When repeating these sections, a performer customarily added embellishments, a practice of which Bach approved, but only when applied with restraint and intelligence.[20] Bach took the unusual step of writing out varied reprises for many of his own works, but in doing so he went beyond mere embellishment, for the "varied" passages are often recomposed, the original thematic material disappearing almost entirely (Ex. 6.4).

EXAMPLE 6.4. Passages in original and varied forms

a. Sonata in D Minor H. 139 (*Reprisen-Sonaten*, No. 4). Movement 1, mm. 16b–20 and 42b–46

b. The same. Movement 3, mm. 1–2 and 21–22

c. Sonata in G, H. 137 (*Reprisen-Sonaten*, No. 2). Movement 3, mm. 1–4 and 17–20

Bach did not invent varied reprises; they also occur in the last movement of one of his father's concertos after Vivaldi (BWV 975) and in the second movement of a trio-sonata attributed to J. S. Bach as BWV 1038.[21] Emanuel himself has been suggested as the real author of the latter; in any case, only he wrote a large number of keyboard pieces exploiting the idea.[22]

Form

Bach's use of varied reprises, with their seemingly arbitrary alterations of thematic material, seems to suggest that he lacked discipline, an impression that might be reinforced by the fantastic juxtapositions of contrasting material in certain pieces (as in Ex. 6.1). But Bach's "manneristic" detail is usually contained within exceptionally well-defined formal schemes, most of which are varieties of sonata form. Bach's sonata form was not the complex type familiar from the works of the Viennese Classical composers and codified by nineteenth-century theorists, but rather a simpler sort closely related to the binary forms of the Baroque suite; indeed, a few movements by Sebastian Bach show all the salient features of Emanuel's sonata forms.[23] Such a movement falls into two or three main sections, with a double-bar often placed after the first. There is a single main theme, usually stated at the beginning of each section; each section continues with a modulating passage, usually sequential, and eventually a closing passage.

It used to be customary to see Bach's version of sonata form as a direct ancestor of the type employed by Haydn, Mozart, and Beethoven. But it remains unclear how much of Bach's music would have been known in Vienna during the formative years of the Classical style, and at any rate, there are substantial differences between sonata form as found in the music of Bach (and other north Germans) and the forms employed in the slightly later Viennese Classical style. While the sections in the three-part version of Bach's form correspond with the exposition, development, and recapitulation of a Classical sonata-allegro, those terms are best avoided when discussing Bach's music. All three sections tend to be comparable in style, material, and internal structure, save for the tendency toward more frequent and more distant modulation in the second section. Nor is there likely to be a major formal articulation *within* any of these sections, like that separating the first and second thematic groups of a Classical sonata form—even though Bach may insert at any point a brief digression or interruption, such as a *piano* passage in a foreign mode, or even a fermata. There are, to be sure, a number of movements that anticipate later "textbook" sonata form, even including a distinct "second" theme. But this theme is not necessarily recapitulated in the last section; indeed, while all three sections generally employ the same motives in roughly the same order, only the first and last few bars of the first section are likely to be recapitulated literally.

Bach found numerous ways of embellishing this basic design, especially by tinkering with the beginning of the last section. That point is the so-called double return, the crucial moment at which the opening theme returns along with the original key. Bach's earliest sonata movements, even those falling into three sections, often lack such a return; most later ones prepare it with a short retransition. The latter is often merely a brief sequence, but Bach occasionally employs quite extraordinary routes to the return, sometimes generating considerable dramatic force.[24]

Bach's most important discoveries in the realm of form, however, concern the three-movement sonata as a whole. Bach was already treating the sonata as a unified cycle in a few works from the mid-1740s, and increasingly thereafter. Unification is achieved not through the use of common thematic material in different movements, but rather by modulating transitions that link two or sometimes all three movements. Particularly in the later works, the middle movement may itself be reduced to a short bridge, a coda to the first movement; when all three movements are connected the sonata may resemble a multisectional fantasia. The idea of unifying the cycle in this manner probably stemmed from the Italian sinfonia or overture of the early eighteenth century. A number of Bach's sonatas closely imitate the style of such orchestral pieces, and the coda at the end of the first movement often resembles the modulating bridge found at the corresponding point in his own symphonies. This sort of cyclic unification may seem fairly superficial; nevertheless it implies that each sonata represents a unique, integrated sequence of musical affects or characters, unlike the more loosely constructed *suite de pièces*.

Revisions and Alternate Versions

One last general aspect of Bach's keyboard works remains to be discussed, and that is his penchant for revision. Throughout his life he continued to return to existing works, editing and sometimes substantially altering them. One reason may have been an obsessive perfectionism, but practical considerations were also involved; since only a fraction of the music was ever published, by frequently updating his music Bach made it necessary for buyers to purchase copies (that is, manuscripts) from himself, at least if they wished to be certain of acquiring the most recent versions. Usually Bach revised his works through essentially the same process used in composing a varied reprise or improvising a fantasia over a bass line. At times, especially in the earliest works, the revisions seem to have included more substantial alterations—substitutions or insertions of phrases or larger passages. Unfortunately, the original versions of Bach's earliest keyboard works have mostly been lost; Bach himself seems to have destroyed many of them near the end of his life.[25]

Organization and Editions of Bach's Keyboard Works

The large number of works and their frequent revisions have provided ample work for many musicologists, and before proceeding to a detailed look at the individual works it will be necessary to consider briefly how scholars have organized Bach's music. There have been at least six major attempts to catalogue Bach's keyboard music, beginning with a list apparently drawn up by Bach himself and published after his death as part of what scholars refer to as the *Nachlassverzeichniss* ("estate catalogue").[26] The latter gives dates and places of composition, even indicating when most of the earliest pieces were revised; all subsequent lists derive directly or indirectly from this one. Best known are the turn-of-the-century thematic catalogue by Alfred Wotquenne and the more recent one by E. Eugene Helm.[27] The "W" (or "Wq") numbers assigned to individual works by Wotquenne have entered general use, like the "K" numbers used for the works of Mozart. But since the Helm catalogue provides a more complete listing of Bach's works, Helm ("H") numbers are employed here. Solo keyboard works make up the first 334 entries in the Helm catalogue; unlike Wotquenne, Helm lists the keyboard works in a single roughly chronological sequence.

Older studies of Bach's music focused on what was understood as its transitional position between Baroque and Classical music. More recent writings have been concerned with understanding the works within their musical and cultural context, and with tracing their compositional history, especially in the many works known to exist in multiple versions. An effort to publish the complete works, known as The Carl Philipp Emanuel Bach Edition, was launched in the early 1980s but has produced only a few volumes. A reliable critical edition is sorely needed, since, while about half of Bach's keyboard works have appeared in modern editions, the editions are not always dependable, and editors have not always been aware of the existence of alternate versions. Hence, while readers should consult the Helm catalogue for modern editions of the pieces mentioned here, many of these editions are to be used with caution.

Nevertheless, most of the important works, including all of those that appeared in Bach's own printed collections (with the exception of the *Clavierstücke* of 1765), are available in reasonably accurate modern editions. And nearly all of the known keyboard works can be consulted in an edition consisting of facsimiles of eighteenth-century prints and manuscripts.[28] With a little practice even nonspecialists can use these facsimiles, since the notation employed is essentially the same as that used today; the only unfamiliar aspect is the frequent use of the soprano clef (C-clef on the bottom line) for the upper staff.

While sonatas make up only about half the total number of Bach's solo keyboard pieces, most of the remainder are relatively short one-movement pieces. Thus, the sonatas are by far the largest portion of Bach's keyboard output, and they will be our main concern in what follows. More than half of the sonatas appeared in print during Bach's lifetime, some of them in collections put together by Bach himself and containing only his own works, others as individual pieces in anthologies. In general, the most important sonatas are those that appeared in Bach's own publications; these form the basis of our discussion. Variations, rondos, fantasias, and other genres tended to occupy Bach's attention only during certain periods, and thus will be considered last.

The concertos for keyboard and orchestra are the only other group of pieces that rival the solo sonatas in importance and that similarly occupied Bach throughout his long career. These pieces, the first of which were written at Leipzig in apparent imitation of Sebastian's concertos, underwent a development roughly paralleling that of Bach's sonatas, with particularly striking innovations taking place in the 1740s. Those years saw the creation of one of the most profound concertos of the entire century, the D-minor Concerto of 1748 (H. 427). But thereafter Bach's imagination seems to have slackened until the Hamburg period, when he again produced a number of notable works, such as the 1788 double concerto for harpsichord and fortepiano H. 479. Other categories of Bach's music, such as the duo sonatas for keyboard and flute or violin and the piano trios, include some major works but are on the whole of lesser importance.

Bach's Keyboard Works

Most of Bach's earliest works are probably no longer extant, either lost or intentionally destroyed by the composer in an effort to prevent the dissemination of compositions he considered unrepresentative of his mature work. Nevertheless, recent scholarship suggests that the young Emanuel once owned a "Little Clavier Book" that, like the extant *Clavierbüchlein* of his older brother Friedemann, might have included his own early efforts. A number of keyboard pieces surviving elsewhere have been tentatively traced to this lost manuscript or identified as possible early works of the young Emanuel Bach; the music in question consists largely of suites and individual dance movements.[28] As one might expect in works possibly composed by young members of the Leipzig Bach household, these contain echoes of Sebastian's Partitas, Goldberg Variations, and other mature keyboard music. Yet, whether or not actually composed by Emanuel, they share with his later keyboard works an emphasis on elaborate, sometimes idiosyncratic soprano melody, while avoiding imitative counterpoint.

One of the few assuredly authentic early pieces that survives in its original form is a little minuet with crossing hands (H. 1.5), which was printed in 1731 from a plate engraved mainly by the teenaged Emanuel himself.[30] The music, composed in imitation of similar pieces by Sebastian,[31] is attractive but shows no real sign of what was to come. Nor do the four pieces (H. 1) that Emanuel himself copied into the *Clavierbüchlein vor Anna Magdalena Bach* of 1725, that is, the second Little Keyboard Book of his stepmother, Anna Magdalena Bach (Berlin, Deutsche Staatsbibliothek, Mus. ms. Bach P 225). These pieces—two marches and two polonaises—have been studied by generations of young pianists as works of Sebastian Bach; more recently they have been assigned to Emanuel.[32] While they form a pleasant series of movements in *galant* style, they fall in different keys and probably do not constitute a suite in the modern sense.

Early Sonatas

A polonaise and a march from the Little Keyboard Book recur as sonata movements that, if indeed by Bach, must be very early works.[33] The same Little Keyboard Book also contains a more substantial "Solo" known from other sources as the opening Allegro of the sonata H. 16. Like most of the works composed at Leipzig and Frankfurt, the sonata was revised at Berlin—rather heavily, at least in the first two movements.[34] Even in their earliest known forms, however, these movements are finely crafted works. While lacking the overt dramatic gestures of works of a few years later, they contain a number of small harmonic surprises and reveal a mastery of the simple sonata form described above.

It is possible that the movements of this sonata were at first separately composed, and that the date given for the composition of the sonata (1736) was that of their organization into a three-movement cycle. Sebastian Bach never composed multimovement keyboard sonatas in the modern sense, and the idea of writing such pieces would not have been self-evident to his sons, despite the model furnished by the concerto or by certain types of chamber sonata. While the Bach family might have known multimovement keyboard sonatas by Marcello or other Italian composers, the idea might equally well have originated in their own impromptu transcriptions of ensemble sonatas at the keyboard; the two-voice texture of many of Emanuel's early keyboard sonatas is close to that of a work for flute and continuo.[35]

Only one of the Leipzig and Frankfurt sonatas was printed during Bach's lifetime: H. 2 in B-flat, which appeared in 1761 in what was probably a heavily revised version (Ex. 6.5).

EXAMPLE 6.5. Sonata in B-flat H. 2

a. Movement 1, mm. 1–2

b. Movement 2, mm. 1–2

c. Movement 2, mm. 28–32

The reason for selecting this work for publication might have been the fact that the first movement (Ex. 6.5a) is based on thematic material from one of Sebastian's two-part inventions.[36] This is Emanuel's only keyboard work to quote directly from his father, although many other works from as late as the early 1750s include material reminiscent of J. S. Bach. Indeed, the second movement of H. 2 also owes much to Sebastian; for example, the closing passage (Ex. 6.5c) employs a type of figuration obviously derived from Sebastian's preludes, and the harmonic progression is nearly identical to one in the Saint John Passion (first chorus, mm. 16–19). This passage may have survived the revisions of the 1740s relatively untouched, but the opening of the movement (Ex. 6.5b) employs a more irregular type of florid melody that seems likely to be the product of embellishments added to a simpler original. In its present form the movement also includes a fixture common to many slow movements by Berlin composers: a cadenza to be improvised by the player, signified by a fermata over the final 6/4 chord (see Ex. 6.5c).

Such cadenzas raise questions of performance and interpretation that merit a brief digression. Bach employed them until the end of the Berlin period, although many sonatas written after the 1740s dispense with them, and they seem always to have been regarded as optional. The cadenza in the slow movement of a solo piece may seem out of place today, but the type of cadenza called for is more lyrical than virtuosic; Bach provided written-out examples in some works, and these show that he followed the tradition of a short cadenza as illustrated by the flutist Quantz.[37]

The Prussian and Württemberg Sonatas and Other Sonatas of the 1740s

Bach's first decade in Berlin coincided with an astonishing burst of creativity. His best-known works of the decade are the six Prussian and six Württemberg sonatas, which appeared in 1742 and 1744, respectively. Even the earlier set reveals great genius, although the Prussian sonatas inevitably appear a bit simple by comparison with later works. Sonata 1 opens with one of several rather restrained movements of the 1740s that retain the invention style found in the early sonata in B-flat. But the second movement mimics recitative, making a more literal imitation than in some earlier pieces (such as Sebastian's Chromatic Fantasia), since Emanuel includes some of the familiar formulas of operatic recitative while notating the accompaniment as a figured bass.[38] Even more remarkable is the fact that the passages in recitative alternate with an entirely different type of texture; indeed, they enter as interruptions of the arioso that opens the movement (Ex. 6.6).

EXAMPLE 6.6. Sonata in F H. 24. ("Prussian" Sonata No. 1). Movement 2, mm. 1–6, with suggested realization of the figured bass. (The original print gives only the figured bass in the section labeled *Recit.*)

The inclusion of recitative might have been a gesture toward King Frederick, to whom these sonatas were dedicated (hence their designation as "Prussian" sonatas). The Berlin opera house opened under his patronage late in 1742, and scenes in which recitative and arioso alternate are a familiar if exceptional type in opera seria. Bach never again made so direct an imitation of recitative, but the idea of alternating regularly between sharply differentiated types of texture, rhythm, and thematic material recurs in many other pieces.[39]

As published, the order of the Prussian sonatas seems to reflect that of their composition, but the pieces also increase in length and complexity. Indeed, Sonata 6 H. 29 is comparable stylistically with the sonatas of the Württemberg set, which are more homogeneous and also more evenly divided between witty works in major keys and stormy ones in minor keys (the Prussian set has only one of the latter). The sixth Prussian sonata (H. 36) also includes a type of slow movement that Bach repeated several times in the later set and in other works of the 1740s: a sort of imitative "trio" comparable to Sebastian's three-part inventions (sinfonias). But imitative polyphony is not very well suited to the *empfindsam* style of Bach's slow movements, and he rarely used it afterward.

Probably the most arresting movements in the Württemberg set are the fiery Allegros of the three sonatas in minor keys, which share a *sturm-und-drangisch* quality with several concertos of the same period (e.g., H. 427 in D minor).[40] But other movements are equally remarkable; for example, the slow movement of Sonata 3 is a sort of rondo that finds wonderfully eloquent ways of answering the question posed in the opening gesture, the last appearance of which leads directly into the final cadence (Ex. 6.7).

EXAMPLE 6.7. Sonata in E Minor H. 33 ("Württemberg" Sonata No. 3). Movement 2.
    a. Mm. 1–4

    b. Mm. 24–27

(continued)

Example 6.7. (*continued*)

c. Mm. 52–55

NOTE: In the original print (Nuremberg: Winter, 1744) the turn sign (in the old vertical form) appears directly over the first note in m. 1, slightly to the right of it in mm. 24 and 52. It should probably be placed between notes 1 and 2 as shown.

Sonata 6, in B minor, is notable for the extreme fragmentation of its first movement, which seems to borrow from the vocabulary of accompanied recitative. But a good player will make it clear that the seemingly isolated gestures are parts of larger phrases, which in turn cohere into what was already by this date Bach's normal, that is, ternary, type of sonata form. Bach later wrote out embellishments for the first two movements, including a cadenza for the Adagio; the embellishments for the first movement might be played as varied reprises, even though Bach probably intended them as replacements for the original readings.[41]

There are, besides the Prussian and Württemberg sonatas, a number of equally important works from the 1740s that remained in manuscript or were published only later. Among these are several sonatas that might be described as "symphonic," since they not only incorporate the drum basses of contemporary orchestral writing but also tend to adopt a relatively heavy chordal texture as well as imitations of string figuration (tremolos and the like).[42] Also notable are two remarkable sonatas in C (H. 46) and in G minor (H. 47), which may have been the ones Bach later described as resembling fantasias.[43] But during the same decade a distinction becomes clear between works of great originality, which usually require considerable skill of the performer, and more routine pieces presumably written on commission or intended for students. The existence of the two categories of pieces might be related to the differing needs of experts and amateurs—in German, *Kenner und Liebhaber,* a phrase that Bach would use in the titles of his Hamburg keyboard publications. In his autobiography he wrote that in all but the fraction of his works written "for himself" he had been constrained (*gebunden*) by the demands of "certain persons" or "the public."[44] As early as the 1740s, then, the need to satisfy his patrons seems to have prevented Bach from writing music that was as difficult or, perhaps, as expressive as he might have wished it to be.

The Probestücke

The first volume of Bach's *Essay* appeared in 1753. It is not a primer for the beginner or amateur, but rather was directed toward the professional performer and teacher. Nevertheless, the first volume was accompanied by a set of six rather special sonatas (H. 70–75). Each is in the usual three movements, but all eighteen movements are in different keys, and the sonatas are of increasing length, difficulty, and musical sophistication. The idea of combining a keyboard treatise with a series of pedagogic pieces came from several sources—among them Couperin's *L'Art de toucher le clavecin* (Paris, 1717), in which the preludes are, like Bach's sonatas, supplied with copious ornaments and fingerings; and Mattheson's *Grosse General-Bass-Schule* (Hamburg, 1731), from which Bach borrowed the title given to the individual movements of the sonatas: *Probestücke* or "test pieces." As in a number of other pieces for which Bach provided fingerings, modern pianists will find few surprises here (Ex. 6.8).

EXAMPLE 6.8. From the *Probestücke*

   a. Sonata 4 (H. 73). Movement 1, mm. 17–19

   b. Sonata 3 (H. 72). Movement 2, mm. 22–26

(continued)

EXAMPLE 6.8. (*continued*)

c. Sonata 2 (H. 71). Movement 3, mm. 33–34

d. Sonata 4 (H. 73). Movement 1, mm. 9, 16

But Bach's fingerings aim more at lightness and clear articulation than at a seamless legato, and one might note the use of fingerings that force articulations at leaps, before appoggiaturas, or for other reasons (Ex. 6.8a); the restrained use of finger substitution on sustained notes (Ex. 6.8b, left hand) and of changing fingers on repeated notes (Ex. 6.8a, right hand); and the preference for crossing the thumb under the second finger, especially in the left hand (Exx. 6.8c–d).

Despite the modest title, the *Probestücke* are far more than simple teaching pieces. None of the movements, not even the initial Allegretto in C, is really easy; even the simplest repays careful study. By the fourth sonata the player is faced with an opening movement replete with Bach's trademark changes of pace, as well as a florid Largo that includes a written-out cadenza. The crown of the set has always been recognized as being the final sonata, which proceeds from a fiery Allegro in F minor **with extensive hand-crossings (a device that Bach used hardly anywhere else) to a famous free fantasia in C minor.**

Despite their unconventional key structures, the *Probestücke* do form true three-movement sonatas. While only two movements are actually linked by a modulating transition (the last two movements of Sonata 4), the keys of the three movements in each sonata are closely related, and, especially in the last sonata, the three movements form as satisfactory a cycle as in any of Bach's other works from the same period. Bach's decision to close the set with a free fantasia presumably reflected the exalted place that that genre occupied in Bach's mind; free improvisation, not fugue, was for him the highest form of solo keyboard music. The *Essay* itself closes with a discussion of the free fantasia, although the chapter describing the improvisation of such pieces appeared only in part 2, published in 1762. The C-minor fantasia was later republished— without Bach's authorization—in a version that included a vocal setting of Hamlet's soliloquy (in German).[45] Needless to say, the original version of the "Hamlet" fantasia, as it is sometimes called, has nothing to do with Shakespeare—and since Bach discouraged programmatic interpretations of his instrumental works, it is equally unlikely to be a lament for Sebastian Bach, as has also been argued.[46]

Later Berlin Sonatas, including the Sonatas with Varied Reprises

During the remaining fifteen years at Berlin, Bach's keyboard output continued to reflect the distinction between "serious" and simpler sonatas. But even among the "serious" works there seem to be few that challenge convention or introduce genuine innovations. For those who prize the fire of some of the earlier sonatas, or the distilled eloquence of the Hamburg ones, the later Berlin works are likely to represent a diminishing of vitality. Many movements open with conventional *galant* ideas, and while some eventually introduce surprises, in others—especially those published outside of Bach's own collections—even the surprises seem routine: pale reflections of the *empfindsam* gestures of Bach's more serious works. The A-minor sonata of 1758 (H. 131), one of the relatively few works in a minor key, is nevertheless typical; it opens with a striking unison gesture but at once relaxes into *galant* formulas: "sigh"-motives in parallel thirds, and already in bar 3 a routine sequence (Ex. 6.9).

EXAMPLE 6.9. Sonata in A Minor H. 131. Movement 1, mm. 1–4

The most important sonatas from this period, however, were those published in three of Bach's own collections. The first of these, the sonatas with varied reprises (*Reprisen-Sonaten*), appeared in 1760 and were intended to illustrate the practice of embellishing repeated passages. Bach was no doubt serious about the pedagogic intent avowed in the preface to the set, for it contains characteristic examples of most of the types of sonata movements that a player was likely to encounter in the prints of the 1750s and 1760s. Indeed, the *Reprisen-Sonaten* are more representative in this regard than the *Probestücke,* since the latter do not include any real examples of symphonic style, such as occurs here in the first movement of Sonata 3, or any of the frankly bland *galant* type represented by the last movement of Sonata 2, in which Bach's variations seem intended to show what can be done when the composer has provided relatively meager material. Rondo forms, simple and not so simple, are also present, as they were not in the *Probestücke.*

One lesson gained from the *Reprisen-Sonaten* is that "variation" of some sort could be applied to practically any type of keyboard music. Bach included examples of many different types of variation: not only the traditional addition of ornament signs and embellishments, but more elaborate and expressive types of florid variation as well, for example, his peculiar variety of *tempo rubato* consisting of quintuplets, septuplets, or other unusual divisions of the beat, as in Example 6.4a.[47]

Two subsequent sets of six sonatas were published as "continuations" (*Fortsetzungen*) of the *Reprisen-Sonaten,* even though between them they contain only two sonatas with varied reprises.[48] Particularly notable in the first set (published in 1761) is the imaginative treatment of the three-movement cycle; for example, in Sonata 1 H. 150 all three movements are connected by short modulating passages. This is the sonata that was afterward twice "varied," and while Bach did not write the later versions in order to supply varied reprises for H. 150, one might use them for this purpose.[49] Sonata 2 also has an interesting cyclic organization; it opens with a short adagio introduction whose rhythm and tempo return in the slow movement, though without repeating any of the actual motivic material.

The second *Fortsetzung,* published in 1763, differs from Bach's earlier collections in including several sonatas that had been composed much earlier. One of these, H. 37 in F-sharp minor, had been written at about the same time as the Württemberg sonatas; its first movement is notable for the frequent alternation between two types of passage, distinguished by rhythm, motivic content, and dynamic level (Ex. 6.10).

EXAMPLE 6.10. Sonata in F♯ Minor H. 37 (*Zweyte Fortsetzung,* No. 4). Movement 1, mm. 13–23

(continued)

EXAMPLE 6.10. (*continued*)

As in the slow movement of the first Prussian sonata, this type of alternation should not be confused with the contrast between "first" and "second" themes in a Classical sonata form; the alternation operates at a local
level, with frequent changes of character occurring even within phrases.
As in a few of the Prussian and Württemberg sonatas, the slow movement is an imitative trio, somewhat like Sebastian's sinfonias (three-part
inventions).

Two further collections of sonatas composed at Berlin are much less
significant. The "Six Easy Clavier Sonatas" (*Sechs leichte Clavier Sonaten*)
published in 1766 are not, in fact, particularly easy, but they are relatively short and cannot have given Bach much trouble. Even more routine are most of the *Sonates à l'usage des Dames*, composed at Potsdam in
1765 and 1766 though not published until 1770, after Bach had moved
to Hamburg. Some of these sonatas seem almost perfunctory; presumably their brevity and simplicity were meant to appeal to the fashionable
ladies mentioned in the title—though one would think the rapid changes
of character in the first movement of Sonata 2 to have been rather un-
ladylike by eighteenth-century standards (see Ex. 6.1, p. 198).

The Sonatas für Kenner und Liebhaber

Six sonatas composed in the later part of the Berlin period were
eventually included in the Hamburg collections *für Kenner und Liebhaber*,
which Bach began to issue at one- or two-year intervals starting in 1779.
Only the first is a conventional set of six sonatas; the next two sets introduce a special type of rondo, and these are joined by free fantasias in
the last three collections. Any suspicions that Bach's inspiration might
have been flagging would have been put to rest by the first set, which is
as varied and original as any that Bach wrote. It includes two short sonatas that open, or seem to open, in the "wrong" key (Nos. 3 and 5, H.
245 and 243). There is also a splendid sonata in symphonic style (No. 4,

H. 186). Some of these sonatas are practically fantasias, the movements being played without a break or otherwise closely linked. For example, the idea of opening in the "wrong" key is repeated in the last two movements of Sonata 5. Each opens with an unstable harmony that can be heard in relation to the end of the previous movement, so that the sonata consists in effect of an unbroken succession even though there are no connecting bridges as such between the movements.

In the later sets the conception of the sonata as a continuous succession of related movements grows even clearer. For example, the opening work of the fifth set (H. 281) is one of only a few instances in which Bach begins a work in a minor key and closes in the parallel major. But while later composers tended to make the entry of the major mode a moment of blazing triumph, this sonata, after opening with a fiery movement in E minor, proceeds to a delicate rondo in E major that ends *pianissimo,* with a gesture of the most astonishing simplicity. The first sonata of the fourth set (H. 273) even goes so far as to begin and end in virtually unrelated keys, G and E, but the modulation does not seem entirely cogent and this may be one of the rare cases in which Bach has miscalculated.

In general, however, the quality of these sonatas is so consistently high that it is somewhat arbitrary to single out any of them for special mention. Even in the second set, where the three short sonatas might seem to be in danger of being outshone by the rondos, the last sonata (H. 270) is an ingenious two-movement work that rounds out the set in a blaze of harmonically inspired figuration. The sonatas of the following set, on the other hand, are all lengthy and in minor keys; the third is one of Bach's greatest sonatas, an F-minor work (H. 173) that Forkel compared to an ode, seeing in it what James Webster describes as "a reflection of the natural process of the soul's changing passions."[50]

Rondos

The rondos and fantasias included in the collections *für Kenner und Liebhaber* are Bach's most important keyboard works outside the realm of the sonata. The eleven rondos in these sets are, like the Classical rondo, descended from the rondeau of the French clavecinistes, but they are a very different sort of piece. Bach had previously included simple rondos—often really variants of da capo form—as movements in keyboard sonatas; a number of Bach's character pieces (see below) are also of this type. But occasionally Bach elaborated the design by varying the restatements of the theme (as in the *Reprisen-Sonaten*), or more significantly, by introducing it in different keys. One early example of the latter type is the character piece *L'Aly Rupalich,* H. 95, and 1755, an odd but highly imaginative example of the *murky,* a type of piece—evidently a dance—characterized by octave leaps in the bass.[51] The piece lacks, however, one of the salient characteristics of the rondos *für Kenner und Liebhaber,* in which the episodes alternating with the statements of the theme include lengthy modulating passages containing arpeggiated figuration. Most of the latter pieces, even the one in E (H. 265), which opens with a delicate *pianissimo* four-bar theme, gradually turn into concerto-like display pieces.

Bach must have invented this type of rondo specifically for inclusion in the sets for *Kenner und Liebhaber;* the only comparable movements are one or two rondos in the piano trios, all written at Hamburg in the 1770s. The rondos *für Kenner und Liebhaber* were intended specifically for the fortepiano, presumably on account of the lively figuration. Another late rondo, however, bears the title "Departure of my Silbermann Clavichord" (*Abschied von meinem Silbermannischen Clavier* H. 272), and Bach is supposed to have composed it in 1781 upon giving up a favorite instrument; in it he demonstrates the possibility of writing a serious, expressive rondo.[52] While the title was probably not meant to be taken seriously, the piece itself is indeed sad and expressive, and lacks the concerto-like episodes of the other late rondos. Both types of rondo resemble Bach's fantasias in their use of sudden and often disconcerting shifts in tonality and rhythm; only two of the rondos, those in B-flat and C minor (H. 267 and 283), come close to what might be called a Classical type of form or modulation, and some of the others, such as the one in G (H. 268)—the longest and most wandering—raise serious questions of musical coherence.[53]

Fantasias

Similar questions arise in connection with some of Bach's fantasias. Like his father, Bach used the term *fantasia* for different sorts of pieces. Some, such as those included in the three Berlin collections of *Clavierstücke* (discussed below), are brief improvisations resembling a prelude; they are close to the short pieces that Bach called *solfeggi*. Of the latter, the most famous, H. 220 in C minor, has become known under the inauthentic title "Solfeggietto" but is typical in its construction out of arpeggiation in sixteenths. A *free* fantasia, on the other hand, is a longer piece that modulates to relatively remote keys and (usually) includes passages notated without the use of bar lines.[54] The lack of bar lines does not imply a complete absence of meter; most unbarred passages can be interpreted in common time.[55] Bach's earliest such piece is now thought to be one in E-flat (H. 348), preserved in an autograph manuscript written in the 1740s.[56] Much better known are the C-minor fantasia that concludes the *Probestücke* (H. 75/3) and the smaller one in D (H. 160) included at the end of the *Essay* to demonstrate the improvisation of fantasias.

Besides explaining the fantasia as an elaboration of a figured bass, the *Essay* describes a formal plan based on a somewhat circuitous route away from and back to the tonic key.[57] Such a plan is already clear in the C-minor fantasia, which, after an initial unbarred section—whose opening progression can be found in any number of earlier improvisatory pieces—proceeds to a measured largo in the relative major. While the final section in some of the later fantasias restates substantial portions of the opening section, that is not the case here; nevertheless the unbarred notation does return, as do a few motivic ideas.

Four of the six fantasias from the collections *für Kenner und Liebhaber* follow the same general plan, although it is considerably altered in several. These pieces are all in major keys, and on the whole they have a light, fantastic quality very different from that of the earlier C-minor work. Bach felt that publishing another "dark fantasia" would not help sales,[58] and these, like the rondos, are essentially comic in style—though this does not preclude many wonderfully expressive, even mysterious passages, as in the middle sections of the first C-major fantasia H. 284. But two other fantasias from the Hamburg period are considerably darker in character; one is a short but intense work in G minor (H. 225), while the other is a powerful piece in F-sharp minor (H. 300) to which Bach afterward added a violin accompaniment and the title *C. P. E. Bachs Empfindungen* (Bach's Sentiments).[59]

The F-sharp-minor fantasia was composed in 1787 and is apparently Bach's last work for solo keyboard. Moreover, it seems to quote from two earlier pieces concerned with death and resurrection, inviting further programmatic interpretation.[60] At the very least, one is reminded of a letter in which Bach explained that his published fantasias were meant to reveal to posterity what an improviser (*Fantast*) he had been.[61] This work contains an even greater number of indirect harmonic progressions and startling juxtapositions of contrasting material than do the published fantasias, further obscuring its essential ternary design.

The fact that even this piece can be understood as falling into a sort of elaborated ternary form does not, of course, assure its coherence. Nor can the quest for ever more intense musical expression suffice as an explanation for some of the more puzzling moments in such a work. It is difficult to escape the conclusion that in these late fantasias and rondos (and in some of the sonatas as well) Bach was consciously skirting the boundaries of musical intelligibility. While there is rarely any question about the immediate, moment-to-moment connection between musical events, even that minimal standard of coherence seems to be breached in a passage such as that shown in Example 6.11.

EXAMPLE 6.11. Fantasia in F♯ Minor H. 300. First Largo, mm. 8–10

EXAMPLE 6.11. (*continued*)

While the drift of the passage as a whole is clear enough—a modulation from D to V of G minor—the sudden juxtaposition of B-minor and G-minor chords is practically a denial of functional harmony. It can be explained in terms of secondary functions, or by surface voice-leading (bass B moves by half-step and octave transferral to B-flat). But its real function is to lift the music momentarily out of one tonal realm and into a seemingly disconnected one; the octave transfer and the change in dynamic level confirm this.

Other Pieces

Bach's remaining keyboard works fall into a wide variety of genres. Most were written during the 1750s and 1760s. This was the period of the *Essay*, and like the easier sonatas of the period, many of the pieces were probably written for Bach's students. The best of these were published in three collections of keyboard pieces (*Clavierstücke*), of which the first and largest appeared in 1765. The "Keyboard Pieces of Various Types" (*Clavierstücke verschiedener Art*) is a virtual concert or recital program incorporating examples of most of the common types of instrumental pieces, including two imitations of orchestral genres.[62] The set is built around four large pieces—a concerto, a symphony, a sonata, and a fugue—interspersed with dances and other smaller works.

The symphony (H. 191) is a transcription of a work composed a few years earlier (H. 655), while the concerto (H. 190) is an original composition, conceived somewhat along the lines of Sebastian's Italian Concerto but clearly intended for clavichord or fortepiano. Unlike any of Bach's other sets, the collection closes with two contrapuntal pieces: a short canonic *solfeggio* in two parts (H. 149) and a three-part fugue in G minor (H. 101.5). Bach's keyboard fugues all date from a brief period following the death of his father in 1750. Apparently these years coincided with a surge in interest in contrapuntal forms among the Berlin musical intelligentsia, for the same period saw the publication of the *Art of Fugue* as well as Marpurg's *Abhandlung von der Fuge*, whose two volumes were dedicated to Friedemann and Emanuel, respectively. But most of Emanuel's seven authentic fugues have a certain academic quality, most noticeably the triple fugue H. 102, which, perhaps because of its use of archaic style, was designated as a work for organ. Its ambitious design recalls the great triple Contrapuncti of the *Art of Fugue*. But while the piece reveals solid contrapuntal technique, Emanuel never gained his father's facility in combining advanced fugal devices with idiomatic, musically effective keyboard writing. Thus the best fugues are those that frankly abandon self-consciously "fugal" writing over long stretches. The fugue from the *Clavierstücke* is one of these, and it brings the set to a brilliant close with a coda in octaves; this mirrors the *unisono* writing found in the opening ritornello of the concerto, the first piece in the collection.

Few of the little minuets, polonaises, and various other small keyboard pieces are of much distinction, and some appear to be workaday arrangements of pieces originally for ensemble or for mechanical instruments. Those accustomed to the polonaises of Chopin may be surprised by the prevalence of a minuet-like version of the dance among Bach's works; it was in fact a popular type of piece during the eighteenth century, but Emanuel never wrote anything like the twelve virtuoso polonaises of his brother Friedemann.[63] A few of Emanuel's minuets, such as a palindromic one in C (H. 216), employ some sort of canonic technique but beyond that are of limited musical interest.

Worthy pieces can, however, be found in Emanuel's two sets of "Short and Easy Keyboard Pieces with Varied Reprises and Fingerings for Beginners," which appeared in 1766 and 1768.[64] Each contains twelve pieces of different types; modern lists indicate only eleven, but Bach counted the two minuets in each set separately. In general, these pieces really are "easy," at least by comparison with Bach's other music. While not explicitly arranged in order of increasing difficulty, the more complex pieces tend to come toward the end of each set, and the second set is in general more advanced, even opening with two unusually contrapuntal pieces.

Variations

Despite Bach's habitual use of variation technique in every sort of keyboard music, the ten variation cycles are mostly minor works. While certain of the early Variations on a Minuet by Locatelli H. 14 possess considerable charm, even this is generally lacking in the more routine variation sets of the 1740s and 1750s. What is perhaps the most imaginative set, the Variations with Varied Reprises H. 259, is based on a work composed in 1777 as a piano trio H. 534; since the theme was in binary form, Bach was able to add varied reprises in every statement.[65]

Suites and Character Pieces

Finally, one must mention the suites and the so-called character pieces, which continue the tradition of the French *pièce de clavecin* even though dynamic markings and other details show that these were mostly conceived for clavichord or fortepiano. The character pieces all date from the mid-1750s, and were presumably written for Bach's friends and students. Some adopt traditional titles, such as *La Capricieuse* H. 113; others are perhaps portraits of the figures named in the titles, although these may merely be dedications. The titles of the often anthologized pair *La Xenophon* and *La Sybille* H. 123 might reflect their unusually "distant" keys, C-sharp minor and major, respectively, though neither wanders very far from these tonalities.[66]

Many of these pieces, such as *Les langueurs tendres* (H. 110), clearly borrow from the style of Couperin, although in this case there also seem to be reminiscences of Sebastian's F-minor Sinfonia in the many chromatic passing tones. Other pieces have little to do with Couperin; *La Boehmer* H. 81, arranged by Mozart as the third movement of the concerto K. 40, is a *murky* but is also close to the Mannheim symphonic style.

Bach's two suites follow the older tradition more closely, though hardly slavishly, for three movements of the earlier suite (H. 6)—an allemande, adagio, and echo—could have formed a sonata practically indistinguishable in style from Bach's early works in that form. The first movement of the later suite (H. 66), composed just after Sebastian's death in 1751, is an allemande skillfully modeled after that of the First French Suite. Even here, however, one recognizes that formulas familiar from Emanuel's sonatas are being used to fill out the old dance forms. As in Mozart's suite after Handel (K.399 [385i]), the style has become neo-Baroque, a conscious evocation of something already belonging to the past.

Notes

1. See, for example, Wagner 1988.
2. Burney 1775, quoted from Scholes 1959, 219, and Reichardt 1774, 1: 124.
3. Bach 1753–1762 (hereafter, *Versuch*), i.3.13. To facilitate reference to both the original and the English translation, citations to volume 1 will be by chapter, section (if any), and paragraph. Since the translator altered the numbering of sections in volume 2, there page numbers will be given for the English version.
4. There is nothing new in this; Bach's formulation is close to a passage in Mattheson's *Vollkommener Capellmeister* (Hamburg, 1739), ii.12.31, and an ultimate source has been found as far back as Horace; see Dahlhaus 1972.
5. See Schering 1938.
6. As Bach himself did, perhaps tongue in cheek, in the preface (*Vorbericht*) to the programmatic Trio Sonata in C minor H. 579. On the "H" numbers used to identify Bach's works, see the discussion below of the Helm catalogue.
7. See, for example, the second movement of the D-minor Sonata H. 38, with its persistent sarabande-like rhythm, or the almost unbroken sixteenths of the first movement of the Sonata in G minor H. 118.
8. On the technical meaning of the term, see Sheldon 1975.

9. *Versuch,* i.1.7. See also Marshall 1976.

10. Forkel-Vetter 1968, 79.

11. See *Versuch,* i.3.19–20. Both techniques are indicated by staccato dots drawn under a slur; *Bebung,* a type of vibrato, occurs on a single sustained note, while the *Tragen der Töne* is a portato usually occurring on a series of scalar notes.

12. There is a simple pedal part in the one-movement sonata or praeludium in D H. 107. Pedal parts provided by modern editors for other organ works are inauthentic and unnecessary. There is a pedal part in the organ chorale *Ich ruf zu dir, Her Jesu Christ* BWV Anh. 73, a reworking of J. S. Bach's BWV 639 (from the *Orgelbüchlein*) that bears a plausible attribution in one of its eighteenth-century sources to C. P. E. Bach. I am grateful to Russell Stinson for bringing this piece to my attention.

13. *Versuch,* i.3.29 and i.introduction.15.

14. His instruments are listed in the estate catalogue, discussed below. For further discussion of instrumentation and other performance questions, see Schulenberg 1988.

15. See, e.g., *Versuch,* i.introduction.11 and i.2.3.36.

16. For an opening crescendo, see the F-major Sonata H. 243, where the initial *piano* marking corresponds with the "wrong-key" entrance. A closing diminuendo appears as early as the Second Prussian Sonata. In both cases the gradual change in dynamic level is implied by successive dynamic markings; Bach rarely used the words *crescendo* or *diminuendo.*

17. The term "mannerist" seems first to have been applied to Bach in Rosen 1972, 105. It was later taken up in Berg 1975.

18. The line occurs occasionally in Sebastian's basses as well, e.g., in the Second Brandenburg Concerto, first movement, mm. 109–12. Godt 1979 describes its particularly intensive use in one piece.

19. *Nachhero zweimal durchaus verändert,* according to the estate catalogue (see note 26 below). The original version was H. 150, the "varied" versions H. 156 and 157.

20. *Versuch,* i.3.31. The Mitchell translation includes at this point an interesting footnote taken from the preface to the *Reprisen-Sonaten* of 1760.

21. On BWV 1038, see Schulenberg 1982.

22. The idea of varied reprises is reminiscent of but probably distinct from the *agrémens* attached to several movements in Couperin's *Premier Ordre* and imitated in Sebastian's English Suites. In these cases the ornaments appear to represent alternate versions, not varied reprises.

23. See, e.g., the corrente of Partita 6 (originally part of a violin sonata), and the prelude in D from Part 2 of the *Well-Tempered Clavier.*

24. See, for example, the sonatas H. 29 (first movement, mm. 81–96), H. 30 (third movement, mm. 104–29), and H. 173 (first movement, mm. 55–65, and second movement, mm. 22–28).

25. See the letter to J. J. Eschenburg (January 21, 1786) quoted in Plamenac 1949, 585. The convincing argument that we no longer possess the original versions of most of the early works (Horn 1988) is somewhat modified in Leisinger and Wollny 1993.

26. *Verzeichniss des musikalischen Nachlasses des verstorbenen Capellmeisters Carl Philipp Emanuel Bach* (Hamburg, 1790; facsimile ed. Wade 1981).

27. Wotquenne 1905; Helm 1989.

28. Darrell Berg, ed., *The Collected Keyboard Works for Solo Keyboard by Carl Philipp Emanuel Bach 1714–1788*, 6 vols. (Hereafter *Collected Works*.)

29. Among the most likely candidates (in addition to the early pieces mentioned below) are a suite in G preserved anonymously in the manuscript Berlin, Staatsbibliothek Preussischer Kulturbesitz Mus. ms. Bach P 368; and a suite in B-flat, listed by Helm as the doubtful work H. 370. Several movements of the G-major suite share a bass line similar to that of the Goldberg Variations. The suite includes a version of the polonaise H. 340, which elsewhere bears a dependable attribution to C. P. E. Bach. For discussion of these and other pieces see Wollny 1993, 96–98; also Leisinger and Wollny 1993, 168–70.

30. On the engraving see Butler 1986, 12–15.

31. For example, the minuet of Partita 5 BWV 829, published the preceding year. There exist similar minuets by W. F. Bach—F. 25/2, preserved in a manuscript copy by the youthful Emanuel Bach—and by the anonymous composer of the G-major suite preserved in the manuscript P 368. See note 29.

32. Georg von Dadelsen first argued for Emanuel's authorship in the *kritischer Bericht* to *J. S. Bach: Neue Ausgabe sämtlicher Werke (Neue Bach-Ausgabe)*, V/4, 87–88; see also Berg, *Collected Works*, 6:xii, and Leisinger and Wollny 1993, 143–44.

33. One of the sonatas, not listed by Wotquenne or Helm (but mentioned in Helm's entry for H.1), is printed in an appendix to *Neue Bach-Ausgabe*, V/4.

34. On the successive revisions of this work, see Schulenberg 1984, 122–24, which should be read in light of the newer research presented in Horn 1988, 81–88 and 233–40, and Berg 1988a, 139–46. The Marche BWV Anh. 127, which is in the same key and has the same opening motive as the "Solo," is one of several other anonymous pieces in the Anna Magdalena Bach manuscript that might be by Emanuel; see Leisinger and Wollny 1993, 146–51.

35. Bach sources provide considerable evidence for the performance of Italian ensemble music on keyboard instruments, as in Sebastian's transcriptions of concertos by Vivaldi and others.

36. Compare the Invention in F BWV 779.

37. Quantz 1752, xv.11ff. For cadenzas by Bach, see the sonata H. 133, the rondo H. 267, and the varied version of H. 36 (discussed below).

38. Modern editions provide an unnecessarily simple realization of the figured bass, which might well include arpeggiated chords involving both hands, like those in the Chromatic Fantasia.

39. See, for example, the last movement of Prussian Sonata 6 H. 29 or the first movement of the Sonata in F-sharp minor H. 37, discussed below. A similar (probably later) imitation of recitative occurs in Friedemann Bach's E-minor fantasia F. 21.

40. The set takes its name from its dedication to Duke Carl Eugen of Württemberg.

41. See the embellishments in Berg, ed., *The Collected Works*, 6: 161–63; Berg has edited the two versions simultaneously in *C. P. E. Bach: Klaviersonaten: Auswahl, Band 1* (Munich, 1986).

42. See the Sonata in E H. 41, which eventually appeared in an anthology published in 1762, and the Sonata in B-flat H. 51, published only in two inaccurate posthumous editions. Bach's first real symphony, H. 648, and its keyboard reduction, H. 45, both date from the 1740s as well.

43. In a letter to Forkel (February 10, 1775); see Suchalla 1985, 241–42. Suchalla identifies the works referred to as belonging to the Württemberg set.

44. Bach's autobiography was inserted into the German edition of Burney's Musical Tours (*Carl Burney's . . . Tagebuch seiner musikalischen Reisen*, vol. 3 [Hamburg, 1773]); facsimile as *Carl Philipp Emanuel Bach's Autobiography*, ed. William S. Newman (Hilversum, 1967).

45. The poet Gerstenberg, who was responsible for this version, later issued another based on Socrates' last speech in the *Apology*. For a discussion including a complete facsimile of both versions, see Benary 1989.

46. By Wolfgang Wiemer. See Wiemer 1988.

47. On Bach's tempo rubato, see *Versuch*, i.3.28 (additions for 1787 edition).

48. H. 127 and H. 158 (last movement only).

49. Berg includes all three versions in her *Auswahl* (see note 41). The slow movement lacks a double bar, but it is in ternary sonata form and the varied versions might be used for the two later sections.

50. Webster 1991, 179, with reference to Forkel 1784, 27.

51. The meaning of the title is unknown. For further discussion and analysis of this piece, see Berg 1988b, 9–12. On the various theories concerning the origin of the term *murky*, see Brusniak 1988, 171–76.

52. Since the manuscript reported to have contained Bach's explanatory note is lost, the circumstances of the piece's composition cannot be confirmed; see Berg, ed., *The Collected Works*, 5:xix. Bach evidently replaced the instrument with one by Jungcurth, who is known to have been in Hamburg from 1782; see Ottenberg 1987, 168, 263.

53. For a consideration of those questions see Schulenberg 1984, 148–53.

54. Bach gives essentially this definition in the *Versuch*, ii.41.1 (English version, p. 430).

55. *Versuch*, ii.41.3 (English version, p. 430).

56. See Lee 1988.

57. Heinrich Schenker analyzed Bach's fantasia and gave a somewhat tendentious interpretation of Bach's analysis of it in Schenker 1925.

58. Letter to Forkel (February 10, 1775), in Suchalla 1985, 243.

59. H. 536. The violin part is entirely subsidiary to the keyboard part, which is largely unaltered. Bach also added a scherzando finale similar to those in several Berlin works (e.g., H. 73, from the *Probestücke*, or the B-minor keyboard-and-violin sonata H. 512).

60. The opening Adagio has been connected with an aria in Bach's *Auferstehung* (Resurrection) cantata (H. 777) of 1774–1780; the Largo theme resembles that of the song "Andenken an den Tod" (first line: *Wer weiss, wie nah der Tod mir ist?*) H. 752/12, published in 1781. See Schleuning 1973, 263–83, and Poos 1988. Schleuning's argument is further elaborated in Wiemer 1988, and in Schleuning 1992.

61. Letter to Breitkopf of October 15, 1782.

62. Conceivably the structure of the set was suggested by the third part of J. S. Bach's *Clavierübung*, which has also been likened to an ideal recital program; see Wolff 1986.

63. F. 12. These were probably written at Berlin around 1765; see Falck 1913, 81–82.

64. *Kurze and leichte Clavierstücke mit veründerten Reprisen und beygefügter Fingersetzung für Anfänger von C. P. E. Bach.* Despite the title, only the first set is fingered throughout.

65. The theme itself is the little Andantino H. 249, written in 1775. Regarding the sources and text of the variations, see Schulenberg 1987, 111.

66. For further discussion of the titles and other aspects of these pieces, see Berg 1988b, 19 and *passim.*

Musical Editions

Bach, Carl Philipp Emanuel. *The Collected Keyboard Works for Solo Keyboard by Carl Philipp Emanuel Bach 1714–1788.* 6 vols. Ed. Darrell Berg. New York, 1985. [*Collected Works*]

———. *Klaviersonaten: Auswahl.* 3 vols. Ed. Darrell Berg. Munich, 1986. [*Auswahl*]

Literature Cited and Selected Bibliography

Note: Clark, *C. P. E. Bach Studies,* and Helm, *Thematic Catalogue* (both listed below) contain comprehensive bibliographies of writings on C. P. E. Bach to about 1987. The present list focuses on recent writings relevant to the keyboard works.

THEMATIC CATALOGS

Helm, E. Eugene. *Thematic Catalogue of the Works of Carl Philipp Emanuel Bach.* New Haven, 1989.

Wade, Rachel, ed. *The Catalog of Carl Philipp Emanuel Bach's Estate.* New York, 1981. Annotated facsimile of *Verzeichniss des musikalischen Nachlasses des verstorbenen Capellmeisters Carl Philip Emanuel Bach.* Hamburg, 1790.

Wotquenne, Alfred. *Catalogue thématique des œuvres de Charles Philippe Emmanuel* [*sic*] *Bach (1714–1788).* Leipzig, 1905. Reprint. Wiesbaden, 1964.

EXHIBITION CATALOGS

"Er ist original!" Carl Philipp Emanuel Bach: Ausstellung zum 200. Todestag des Komponisten 14. Dez. 1988 bis 11. Feb. 1988. Wiesbaden, 1988. Exhibit at Berlin.

Lohmeier, Dieter, ed. *Carl Philipp Emanuel Bach: Musik und Literatur in Norddeutschland. Ausstellung zum 200. Todestag Bachs.* Heide in Holstein, 1988. Exhibit at Hamburg and Kiel.

LIFE AND WORKS

Bach, Carl Philipp Emanuel. [Autobiography.] Published as an insert into Charles Burney, *Tagebuch seiner musikalischen Reisen,* 3: 199–211. German translation of Burney's text by C. D. Ebeling (vols. 1–2) and J. C. Bode (vol. 3). Hamburg, 1772–1773. Facsimile in one volume, ed. Richard Schaale. Kassel, 1959. Translation in William S. Newman, "Emanuel Bach's Autobiography." *Musical Quarterly* (henceforth *MQ*) 51 (1965): 363–72.

———. *The Letters of C. P. E. Bach.* Translated and edited by Stephen L. Clark. Oxford: Clarendon Press, 1997.

———. *Versuch uber die wahre Art das Clavier zu spielen.* 2 vols. Berlin, 1753–1762. Facsimile in one volume, with "Nachwort" by Lothar Hoffmann-Erbrecht and supplement containing additions from the Berlin edition of

1787–1797. Leipzig, 1981. Translated by William J. Mitchell as *Essay on the True Art of Playing Keyboard Instruments*. New York, 1949.

Benary, Peter. "Vom Als-Ob in Musik und Musikanschauung des 18. Jahrhunderts." *Basler Jahrbuch für historische Musikpraxis* 13 (1989): 99–139.

Berg, Darrell Matthews. "The Keyboard Sonatas of C. P. E. Bach: An Expression of the Mannerist Principle." Ph.D. dissertation, State University of New York at Buffalo, 1975.

—————. "Carl Philipp Emanuel Bachs Umarbeitungen seiner Claviersonaten." *Bach-Jahrbuch* (hereafter *BJ*) *1988:* 123–61. [Berg 1988a]

—————. "C. P. E. Bach's Character Pieces and His Friendship Circle." In *C. P. E. Bach Studies*, ed. Stephen L. Clark. Oxford, 1988, 1–32. [Berg 1988b]

Brusniak, Friedhelm. "Ein Murky von Carl Philipp Emanuel Bach?" In *Studien zur Instrumentalmusik: Lothar Hoffmann-Erbrecht zum 60. Geburtstag*, ed. Anke Bingmann et al. Tutzing, 1988, 167–88.

Burney, Charles. *The Present State of Music in Germany, the Netherlands and the United Provinces*. 2 vols. London, 1775.

—————. *Carl Burney's . . . Tagebuch seiner musikalischen Reisen*. Vol. 3. Hamburg, 1773.

Butler, Gregory. "The Engraving of J. S. Bach's *Six Partitas.*" *Journal of Musicological Research* 7 (1986): 3–27.

Clark, Stephen L., ed. *C. P. E. Bach Studies*. Oxford, 1988.

Dahlhaus, Carl. "Si vis me fiere . . . , *Die Musikforschung* 25 (1972): 51–52.

De clavicordio: Proceedings of the International Clavichord Symposium. Five volumes to date. Magnano: Musica antica a Magnano, 1994, 1995, 1997, 2000, and 2002. Many articles are directly relevant to C. P. E. Bach and his keyboard music.

Falck, Martin. *Wilhelm Friedemann Bach: Sein Leben und seine Werke*. Leipzig, 1913.

Forkel, Johann Nikolaus. *Musikalischer Almanach für Deutschland auf das Jahr 1784*. Leipzig, 1784. Reprint. Hildesheim, 1974.

—————. *Über Johann Sebastian Bach Leben, Kunst und Kunstwerke* (Leipzig, 1802). Ed. Walther Vetter. Kassel, 1968.

Fox, Pamela. "C. P. E. Bach's Compositional Proofreading." *Musical Times* 129 (1988): 651–55.

Godt, Irving. "C. P. E. Bach, His Mark." *College Music Symposium* 19 (1979): 154–61.

Horn, Wolfgang. *Carl Philipp Emanuel Bach: Frühe Klaviersonaten*. Hamburg, 1988.

Lee, Douglas A. "C. P. E. Bach and the Free Fantasia for Keyboard: Deutsche Staatsbibliothek Mus. Ms. Nichelmann 1N." In *C. P. E. Bach Studies*, ed. Stephen L. Clark. Oxford, 1988, 176–84.

Leisinger, Ulrich, and Peter Wollny. "'Altes Zeug von mir': C. P. E. Bachs kompositorisches Schaffen bis 1740." *BJ 1993:* 127–204.

Marshall, Robert L. "Bach the Progressive." *MQ* 62 (1976): 313–57.

Marx, Hans Joachim, ed. *Carl Philipp Emanuel Bach und die europäische Musikkultur des mittleren 18. Jahrhunderts: Bericht über das Internationale Symposium der Joachim Jungius—Gesellschaft der Wissenschaften Hamburg 29. September–2. Oktober 1988*. Göttingen, 1990.

Ottenberg, Hans-Günter. *Carl Philipp Emanuel Bach*. 2nd edition. Leipzig, 1982. Trans. Philip J. Whitmore. Oxford, 1987.

Plamenac, Dragan. "New Light on the Last Years of Carl Philipp Emanuel Bach." *MQ* 35 (1949): 565–87.

Poos, Heinrich. "Nexus vero est poeticus: Zur fis-Moll-Fantasie Carl Philipp Emanuel Bachs." In *Studien zur Instrumentalmusik: Lothar Hoffmann-Erbrecht zum 60. Geburtstag*, ed. Anke Bingmann et al. Tutzing, 1988, 189–220.

Powers, Doris Bosworth. *Carl Philipp Emanuel Bach: A Guide to Research.* New York and London: Routledge, 2002.

Quantz, Johann Joachim. *Versuch einer Anweisung die Flöte traversiere zu spielen.* Berlin, 1752. Facsimile of the 3rd edition (Berlin, 1789). Kassel, 1953. Translated by Edward J. Reilly as *On Playing the Flute.* 2nd edition. New York, 1985.

Reichardt, Johann Friedrich. *Briefe eines aufmerksamen Reisenden die Musik betreffend.* 2 vols. Frankfurt, 1774–1776. Reprint. Hildesheim, 1977.

Richards, Annette. *The Free Fantasia and the Musical Picturesque.* Cambridge: Cambridge University Press, 2001.

Rosen, Charles. "Bach and Handel." In *Keyboard Music,* ed. Denis Matthews. New York, 1972.

Schenker, Heinrich. "Die Kunst der Improvisation." *Das Meisterwerk in der Musik.* 1 (1925): 11–40. Trans. Richard Kramer as "The Art of Improvisation" in *The Masterwork in Music* 1, ed. William Drabkin. Cambridge, 1994: 2–19.

Schering, Arnold. "Carl Philipp Emanuel Bach und das 'redende Prinzip' in der Musik." *Jahrbuch der Musikbibliothek Peters* 45 (1939): 13–29.

Schleuning, Peter. *Die Freie Fantasie: Ein Beitrag zur Erforschung der klassischen Klaviermusik.* Göppingen, 1973.

————. "The Chromatic Fantasia of Johann Sebastian Bach and the Genesis of Musical 'Sturm und Drang.'" In *The Harpsichord and its Repertoire: Proceedings of the International Symposium. Utrecht 1990,* ed. Pieter Dirksen. Utrecht, 1992, 217–29.

Scholes, Percy, ed. *Dr. Burney's Musical Tours in Europe.* London, 1959.

Schulenberg, David. "Composition as Variation: Inquiries into the Compositional Procedures of the Bach Circle of Composers." *Current Musicology* 33 (1982): 57–87.

————. *The Instrumental Music of Carl Philipp Emanuel Bach.* Ann Arbor, MI, 1984.

————. Review of Berg, ed., *The Collected Works. Journal of the American Musicological Society* 40 (1987): 105–12.

————. "Performing C. P. E. Bach: Some Open Questions." *Early Music* 16 (1988): 542–51.

————. "Composition and Improvisation in the School of J. S. Bach." *Bach Perspectives* 1. 1995.

Sheldon, David A. "The Galant Style Revisited and Re-Evaluated." *Acta musicologica* 47 (1975): 240–70.

Suchalia, Ernst, ed. *Briefe von Carl Philipp Emanuel Bach an Johann Gottlob Immanuel Breitkopf und Johann Nikolaus Forkel.* Tutzing, 1985.

Wagner, Günther. "Die Entwicklung der Klaviersonate bei C. Ph. E. Bach." In *Carl Philipp Emanuel Bach und die europäische Musikkultur des mittleren 18. Jahrhunderts,* ed. Hans Joachim Marx. Göttingen, 1990, 231–43.

Webster, James. *Haydn's "Farewell" Symphony and the Idea of Classical Style: Through Composition and Cyclic Integration in His Instrumental Music.* Cambridge, 1991.

Wiemer, Wolfgang. "Carl Philipp Emanuel Bachs Fantasie in c-Moll—ein Lamento auf den Tod des Vaters?" *BJ 1988:* 163–77.

Wolff, Christoph. "Johann Sebastian Bach's Third Part of the Clavier-Übung." In *Charles Brenton Fisk, Organ Builder: Essays In His Honor,* ed. Fenner Douglass et al. Easthampton, MA, 1986. 1: 283–91.

Wollny, Peter. "Studies in the Music of Wilhelm Friedemann Bach: Sources and Style." Ph.D. dissertation, Harvard University, 1993.

CHAPTER SEVEN

Johann Christian Bach and the Early Classical Italian Masters

Daniel E. Freeman

With its qualities of simplicity, pleasantness, and "naturalness," the keyboard music of early Classical Italian masters (and the Italianate Johann Christian Bach) provided the principal stylistic alternative to the north German *empfindsamer Stil* during the mid-eighteenth century. These two styles form the most important keyboard repertories of their era and during the twentieth century have been the subject of many competing national claims for excellence and enduring influence. Each has its strengths and weaknesses, and both contributed elements that were incorporated into the works of the great Classical-era composers.

Whatever the merits of the claims that have been made for the Italian "school" of composers, however, there is no denying the sad spectacle of declining quality and loss of interest in keyboard music in Italy during the second half of the eighteenth century: the early Classical period was the last in which Italian keyboard music was widely disseminated and admired in Europe. Thereafter, keyboard composition in Italy swiftly slid into decadence, so much so that by the early 1770s Charles Burney was prompted to remark after a visit, "I have neither met with a *great* player on the harpsichord, nor an *original* composer for it throughout Italy."[1] The prestige of Italian musical traditions was such that a certain taste for its keyboard styles endured until near the end of the eighteenth century, but by that time, German composers had at last achieved a self-confidence that enabled them to assert the superiority of their music. The only significant new figure with an Italian surname to emerge after about 1770 was Muzio Clementi, a cosmopolitan composer whose talents were largely developed only after he had left Italy at the age of fourteen.

The Repertory

Although a number of Italian keyboard composers, in particular Giovanni Benedetto Platti, contributed some interesting and beautiful works to the concerto repertory, it was only the Italian solo sonata that achieved popularity throughout Europe during the early Classical period. The production of concertos was simply not great enough to exercise broad influence; moreover, a unified stylistic tradition never evolved for the concerto to the extent that it did for the Italian sonata. Much the same can be said for accompanied keyboard music, which started to appear among the Italians only as their interest in the keyboard was beginning to decline. Even then, the cultivation of this repertory was concentrated among expatriates in England, not in Italy itself, and the approach to form and style manifested in it was to a large extent merely an extension of techniques pioneered in the solo sonata. For these reasons, the central focus here will be on the development of the solo sonata for keyboard.[2]

In surveying the literature of the early Classical keyboard sonata in Italy, the first question to be addressed is a surprisingly fundamental one: What sorts of works are encompassed by this term? Confusion arises from the consistent designation "sonata" for single- or multimovement works in binary form used by modern scholars in contrast to the much looser terminology admitted during the eighteenth century. The terms "divertimento," "toccata," "lesson," "partita," "overture," or even "aria" could be equated with "sonata," depending on the whim of a composer or publisher or the country in which a work was produced; in general, however, these designations implied few, if any, special characteristics. There were, to be sure, certain common principles of organizing sonata movements, but neither the number of movements nor their arrangement by character was ever subject to rigid standardization (as long as stylistic variety and unity of key were maintained). In fact, not even two movements were necessary to define a work as a sonata: single-movement works are not at all uncommon in the sources of early Classical Italian sonatas. Nearly half of the sonatas attributed to the prolific master Baldassare Galuppi, for example, are preserved in single-movement format, and two of the most important printed collections, the Parisian publisher Venier's opp. 1 and 2 (ca. 1758 and 1760, respectively), consist exclusively of single-movement "sonatas" extracted from larger cycles. The decisive element defining a harpsichord "sonata" in the mid-eighteenth century was the presence somewhere of binary form with repeat signs, either in a single movement or at least one of several.

Social Function, Social Status

The performance of keyboard sonatas typically took place in intimate surroundings, the audience—if any—a small circle of acquaintances. Indeed, the social or recreational function of the sonata turns out to be one of the most important determinants of its style, especially as regards technical demands. Keyboard sonatas were frequently aimed toward amateur performers (usually women), and the performance of sonatas by dilettantes required a modest level of virtuosity as one of their commercial attractions. That composers were perfectly willing to observe such considerations is evident from Charles Burney's remark that J. C. Bach's keyboard compositions were "such as ladies can execute with little trouble,"[3] and it is attested as well by a collection such as Giovanni Marco Rutini's op. 7, which was explicitly tailored for the capabilities of ten-year-old girls. It is not surprising, then, that few early Classical Italian keyboard sonatas satisfy the desires of the modern professional harpsichordist or pianist for technical brilliance. Rather, these works are most profitably approached today as they were originally intended to be: as a vehicle of pleasant musical diversion in a relaxed domestic atmosphere. Their artless style is most appealing when they are simply sight-read; few of them reward painstaking analytical scrutiny. In sampling this repertory one is not likely to discover more than occasional individual movements of surpassing quality, but many works still have considerable power to charm and amuse.

Inextricably bound with the intimate character of keyboard sonata performance was the low compositional prestige of this genre—a fact that must be borne in mind when evaluating its role in the development of Classical-era music. Our view of the importance of keyboard repertories is colored by their central position in the musical culture of the nineteenth and twentieth centuries. But in the eighteenth century keyboard music occupied a much lower status. William S. Newman has noted the opinion of Johann Adolph Scheibe (in his *Critischer Musicus* of 1740) that sonatas were of much less consequence than symphonies, concertos, or overtures, and he also quoted a vow of the composer Johann Wilhelm Hässler (in his autobiography of 1786) that "mere keyboard sonatas I shall not be writing so much any more, since I am urged on all sides to [compose] more important works."[4]

In light of such attitudes, it is quite understandable that the best Italian composers sought to enhance the expressive range of their keyboard sonatas by adopting the characteristic gestures of the "more important" genres—opera, symphony, concerto—which were associated with public performance, lofty artistic goals, and greater musical virtuosity. Throughout the eighteenth century, composers recognized and exploited the suitability of harpsichord and piano as instruments of transcription. One can easily imagine the pleasure of playing parts of a symphony or concerto by and for oneself. It is still a most enjoyable occupation. At the same time, this susceptibility to stylistic influence from nonkeyboard genres (often imported, it seems, to lend a certain grandness or profundity to many works) reminds us that it was really not until the time of Beethoven that the keyboard sonata was considered fully equal to the symphony and similarly prestigious genres as a vehicle for the exploitation of sophisticated compositional techniques and the most subtle expressive communication.

The Founders of the Venetian Tradition: Marcello, Alberti

The great flowering of early Classical Italian harpsichord music began during the 1730s; before then there was little cultivation of pieces called "sonata" for stringed keyboard instruments. Except for the uncertain number of works by Benedetto Marcello and Domenico Scarlatti that may be presumed to date from the 1710s or 1720s, the term appears to have been used without consistent meaning, generally carrying a connotation of novelty when applied to harpsichord music. Important collections preserved from the late Baroque period by composers such as Bernardo Pasquini, Domenico Zipoli, Giuseppe Maria Buini, Azzolino Bernardino della Ciaja, and Pietro Giuseppe Sandoni take as their point of departure well-established genres of string chamber music,[5] testimony both to the common practice of performing violin sonatas in the form of keyboard transcriptions and the intimate association of the term "sonata" at this time with violinistic idioms. None of these composers initiated lasting traditions of keyboard sonata composition in their pioneering works, however. Rather, it was the Venetian nobleman Benedetto Marcello who established viable, fruitful models for the early classic Italian masters.

Benedetto Marcello (1686–1739)

The keyboard sonatas of Benedetto Marcello form a seminal repertory that marks a departure from the multimovement toccata as the most typical vehicle for Italian composers of harpsichord music. Their circulation throughout Europe is documented by numerous manuscripts, but only two sonatas are represented in printed collections from the eighteenth century, both in Venier's op. 1 (Paris, ca. 1758).[6] None of the sonatas (or their manuscripts) can be dated accurately, and William S. Newman's conjecture that they were written around 1710–1720 cannot be verified.

The eighteen sonatas found in the three principal manuscript sources are typically laid out in a fashion that was to be adopted or refined by many later Italian composers. The key feature is an opening slow movement followed by an indeterminate number of faster movements (usually two or three). This trait can easily be related to practices observable in the works of several contemporary composers of violin sonatas, among them Giuseppe Tartini and Giovanni Battista Somis, for whom a tempo pattern of slow-fast-fast was standard. Marcello's sonata movements betray a marked preference for binary form corresponding to that found in violin sonatas of the same period. The binary design is generally absent only in opening movements of a preludial nature that serve to introduce the sonata "proper." (The disappearance of such introductory movements was deplored by Giovanni Marco Rutini in the preface to his sonatas op. 7 published in 1770.)

The treatment of binary form by Marcello and most Italian keyboard composers of the 1720s, 1730s, and 1740s is similar to that found in contemporary violin sonatas. In particular, there is a preference for "rhyming" binary schemes where only the closing motives of the first repeated section, not its opening motives, are recapitulated in the tonic during the latter portion of the second repeated section. At the beginning of the second repeated section, the opening motives of the first section are simply transposed to the dominant or relative major. Mechanical transposition of the opening motives would remain by far the

ILLUSTRATION 7.1. Domenico Alberti: Sonata in G Minor Op. 1 no. 4. Movement 2. Printed by John Walsh (London, 1748). Note how an early owner saw fit to embellish the final cadence. Reproduced courtesy of the Music Library, University of Illinois at Urbana-Champaign.

most common way of beginning the nascent "development" section throughout the middle years of the eighteenth century. The sonata movement by Domenico Alberti reproduced in Illustration 7.1 exemplifies the structure quite well.

The influence of string chamber music in Marcello's work affected not only formal structures, but also their thematic material and character. The opening theme of Example 7.1 imitates the texture of a solo violin sonata with continuo accompaniment. Such devices as the "spiral ascent" in mm. 1 and 3 and the wide leaps are clearly much more idiomatic for violin than harpsichord.[7]

EXAMPLE 7.1. Benedetto Marcello: Sonata in A Major C 739a. Movement 2, mm. 1–4

Along with these reminders of the violin's predominance in sonata composition of the early eighteenth century, however, there are also numerous instances of the idiomatic keyboard mannerisms that would become a trademark of many Italian composers in the 1730s and 1740s, devices such as hand crossing and cadential arpeggiations familiar to most performers only from the works of Domenico Scarlatti. Another important stylistic resource for Marcello was the toccata of Alessandro Scarlatti. This influence can be observed most readily in sections consisting of improvisatory arpeggiation of block chords or featuring sixteenth-note passagework based on the elaboration of parallel thirds. Example 7.2 shows one of a number of the common figural types that endured for many decades after Marcello's time.

EXAMPLE 7.2. Benedetto Marcello: Sonata in G Major C 731. Movement 2, mm. 5–8

Domenico Alberti (ca. 1710–1740)

The next significant stage in the development of the Italian keyboard sonata is represented again in the work of a Venetian: Domenico Alberti. While the number of surviving sonatas by Alberti is small (only fourteen complete sonatas plus ten stray movements), there is no question that many more once existed, and they clearly enjoyed a much wider dissemination than did the somewhat dry sonatas of Marcello. Alberti's popularity may be gauged not only by the unusually large number of copies still available of his op. 1 sonatas (first published in London by John Walsh in 1748), but also by the existence of some fourteen manuscripts preserved in libraries throughout Europe.[8] It is thought that most of Alberti's sonatas were written in Rome, where the composer, during the last few years of his life, was a member of the household of the Marquis Molinari.

Ironically, the nearly complete lack of Alberti's sonatas in modern edition has not prevented his name from achieving universal recognition among keyboard players.[9] The reason for this, of course, is the characteristic accompanimental pattern named for him, "Alberti bass" (Ex. 7.3).

EXAMPLE 7.3.

Alberti had already been credited with its invention in the eighteenth century, and modern research has failed to turn up any consistent use of this type of figuration before him, at least when a strict definition of its form is applied.[10] Left-hand arpeggiations of various types have been a commonplace in keyboard music for centuries, but the Alberti bass is specifically a particular four-note arrangement of sixteenth- or eighth-notes outlining a triad or seventh chord, almost always in close position (a six-note pattern is the usual form in compound meters). The shape usually adopted is given in Example 7.3a: note how the first interval marks off the widest range of the pattern and how the prevailing beat determines the rate of its repetitions. Related patterns, such as those in Examples 7.3b–e, are often considered forms of Alberti bass, but were actually used infrequently, if at all, by Alberti himself. The Alberti bass proper is so much the personal achievement of this composer that its presence in anyone else's work can be taken as a clue for dating the composition no earlier than about 1740. The Alberti bass was not particularly common in Italian keyboard music until the 1750s, however, and was not overused until the 1760s.

The Alberti bass has been disparaged ever since the eighteenth century as a facile and monotonous way of filling out left-hand parts, always a ready standby for the unimaginative composer, but it could be used with great effectiveness. Alberti himself has left examples that reveal how the strategic introduction of its rhythmic busyness could signal and enhance the sense of harmonic movement accompanying the modulation to the dominant during the first repeated section of binary form (Ex. 7.4),

EXAMPLE 7.4. Domenico Alberti: Sonata in F Major op. 1 no. 2. Movement 1, mm. 1–5

and the device was especially appropriate as an unobtrusive background for vocally-oriented themes (Ex. 7.5).

EXAMPLE 7.5. Domenico Alberti: Sonata in G Major op. 1 no. 6. Movement 1, mm. 1–4

Example 7.5. (*continued*)

Some composers also took care to introduce interesting voice-leading patterns into their "Alberti" accompaniments, especially with respect to the bass line, sometimes obtaining deeply expressive results (Ex. 7.6).

Example 7.6. Johann Christian Bach: Sonata in A Major op. 17 no. 5. Movement 1, mm. 1–4

Later abuses notwithstanding, Domenico Alberti must be recognized for having developed a means for accompanying melodies that was wholly idiomatic to the keyboard at a time when most Italian composers were satisfied with far less effective accompanimental styles derived from the string chamber music repertory.

Alberti's methods of organizing the constituent movements of a sonata also proved to be influential during the early Classical period. More than anyone else, it seems to have been Alberti who popularized the two-movement sonata, a type commonly referred to as the "Italian" sonata, but its use by Alberti and others appears to have been little more than a modification of Marcello's multimovement model consisting of an opening slow movement followed by two or three quicker movements. In Alberti's sonatas, the first movement is generally slower than the second. But when lighter, more popular movements, such as minuets or variations, are present, this rule is suspended, and a quick movement of serious character often replaces the customary slow movement. Such Albertian practices governed the design of two-movement cycles for decades; but the simple principles on which they are based (a relatively slow opening movement and the reservation of minuets, variations, or—at a later time—rondos, for the end) were readily transferred to three-movement cycles as well. On the whole, the general principles governing the character of the opening and closing movements, as just described, provide a more accurate description of the "Italian" sonata at mid-century, since they encompass many more compositions than merely those belonging to the two-movement design.

Early Classical Style

Alberti's music, unlike Marcello's, exemplifies those trends of the 1730s that are generally characterized as the early Classical or *galant* style, and before proceeding further, it will be convenient to describe several of them in some detail.

Tempo

One of the most important developments of Alberti's generation was the moderation of the slower tempo markings: where Marcello might place a *Largo*, Alberti would more typically prefer an *Andante*, *Andantino*, or even *Allegro ma non troppo*. In addition, Alberti's sonatas import into keyboard music the quick 3/8 finales that were a specialty of many styles of instrumental music during the mid-eighteenth century.

Texture

Alberti's sonatas exhibit the treble-dominated style favored during the early Classical period. The melodic and rhythmic interest of bass lines tended to be neutralized beginning about 1730, and the use of the Alberti bass is in fact symptomatic of this trend. Another indication of the transferral of melodic interest away from the bass is the "drum bass" accompaniment, as shown in Example 7.4, which consists of a simple repetition of eighth-notes.

Melody

The nondescript character of many accompanimental patterns inevitably focuses attention on the upper voice, which often abounds in rhythmic complexities, above all the mixture of triplets and duplets, and fussy, small-note appoggiaturas. This is in sharp contrast to the rhythmic evenness characteristic of Marcello's melodies. A softening of downbeats by means of syncopated rhythmic patterns is also very common (see Ex. 7.7).

EXAMPLE 7.7. Domenico Alberti: Sonata in G Major op. 1 no. 1. Movement 1, mm. 1–3

An alternative style of melodic writing, a prototype of the "singing alle-gro" for which early Classical Italian keyboard music is famed, is shown in Example 7.5. The chief hallmarks of this style are stepwise contours, restricted range, an avoidance of rhythmic complications, and long, "singing" appoggiaturas. But whereas a straightforward diatonicism is favored for the "singing" style, Alberti occasionally wrote passages that are quite chromatic. The repeated emphasis on leading tones (both above and below) often creates angular melodic contours that remind players immediately of Domenico Scarlatti's sonatas. The frequent sound of "sliding" semitones in fact is one of the mannerisms of this period.

Techniques of Extension

The Alberti movement reproduced in Illustration 7.1 (p. 234) illus-trates the common tendency of early Classical composers to use simple repetition as a technique of extension (typically as a substitute for se-quential repetition). Repetitions of short motives and phrases can be found throughout this movement, but the most ubiquitous cliché of the 1730s and 1740s is the repetition of cadential formulas at the end of each of the two repeated sections of binary form. These are the forerun-ners of the immense codas found in later eighteenth-century music; but even at this time they serve the same structural purpose: to emphasize important tonal resting points. Whereas the movement reproduced in Illustration 7.1 largely typifies the Baroque ideals of continuous rhythmic motion and frequent cadential overlapping between phrases, other Alberti movements reflect a trend evident in the 1730s towards clearly separated and stylistically contrasted phrases.

Form

The Alberti sonatas exhibit an increased use of "rounded" binary designs; indeed, half of the movements of the op. 1 set are rounded. In contrast to the "rhyming" scheme, where only the latter half of the first repeated section is recapitulated in the second section, the "rounded" scheme features a full recapitulation of the motives of the first repeated section beginning roughly halfway through the second section. As the eighteenth century progressed, rounded binary schemes increasingly replaced the rhyming schemes, eventually developing into what is now recognized as "sonata" form.

Contemporaries of Marcello and Alberti: Platti, Martini, and Others

The tradition of sonata composition developed by the Venetians Marcello and Alberti provided the most important models for later generations of Italians, but there were other notable composers of Italian birth who produced keyboard sonatas during the 1730s and 1740s. Some of these issued isolated collections that reflected little or no Venetian influences; others began writing independently of Venetian trends only to adopt them in the end. Among the former was the Neapolitan Francesco Durante (1684–1755), a composer well known for his six *Sonate da cembalo divise in Studii e Divertimenti* ("harpsichord sonatas divided into studies and divertimentos"), published in Naples, circa 1732. Each follows a unique two-part plan whereby the first movement is a "study" (i.e., a contrapuntal exercise or "invention"), and the second is a "divertimento" (i.e., a short, whimsical movement, usually in compound meter). In general, the studies exhibit a rather academic contrapuntal style animated by figural passagework derived from toccata style. The compositions are remarkable at this late date for their lack of repeat signs within the binary structures and despite their fame are essentially isolated curiosities.

Lodovico Giustini (1685–1744)

Contemporary with Durante's publication is a set of twelve sonatas by Lodovico Giustini, an obscure organist from Pistoia. Giustini's collection, entitled *Sonate da cimbalo di piano e forte, detto volgarmente di martelletti* ("sonatas for the soft and loud harpsichord, popularly called the hammered harpsichord"), op. 1, published in Florence in 1732, constitutes the first known keyboard music to specify pianoforte.[11] No other composer would indicate this instrument in a keyboard collection until the 1760s. The appropriateness of Giustini's music for pianoforte, however, extends for the most part no further than to a generous sprinkling of dynamic markings. These are generally used in a simple, "terraced" fashion to enhance contrasts in tessitura and texture between phrases or to reinforce cadential flourishes; only occasionally (as in the corrente of Sonata 7) are crescendo and decrescendo effects required. The Giustini sonatas consist of four- or five-movement cycles, usually unconventional arrangements of preludial movements, dances, contrapuntal excursions, and novelties reminiscent of Francesco Maria Veracini's op. 1 violin sonatas of 1720. (Veracini was a fellow Tuscan whose works may well have provided models for Giustini.) Alongside evocations of traditional harpsichord writing derived from toccata style and French *style brisé*, many violinistic idioms appear in these sonatas, to such an extent that they frequently resemble keyboard transcriptions of violin sonatas with continuo accompaniment.

Giovanni Benedetto Platti (1690s–1763)

Of much greater intrinsic musical value than the sonatas of Durante and Giustini are those of Giovanni Benedetto Platti, a composer of Venetian origin who was undoubtedly the most talented Italian-born composer of keyboard sonatas before 1750, excepting only Domenico Scarlatti. Platti served in a variety of capacities at the archiepiscopal court of Würzburg from 1722 until his death, and his residence in Germany provided him contact with the great traditions of German keyboard music, a stylistic resource he was able to incorporate most successfully into his sonatas. In general, his compositions exhibit a pleasing mixture of Italian tunefulness with the textural and tonal richness of German keyboard styles.

Unfortunately, Platti's posthumous reputation has been inextricably associated with the attempts of the Italian musicologist Fausto Torrefranca to portray the composer as a master of the first rank, a part of his long campaign to magnify the importance of various Italian composers in the development of Classical-era music—at the particular expense of C. P. E. Bach.[12] While Torrefranca's estimation of Platti's talents was undoubtedly exaggerated, it is clear nonetheless that he was an unusually gifted composer, and his works have been highly praised in more balanced studies.[13] In particular, Platti's imaginative phrase extensions reveal him to be a most sophisticated musical artist.

Platti's contribution to the keyboard sonata literature consists of eighteen surviving works, all available in modern edition thanks to the pains of his tireless partisan Fausto Torrefranca.[14] The sonatas numbered I–VI by Torrefranca correspond to Platti's op. 1, a set of harpsichord sonatas published in 1742 by the Nuremberg music printer Johann Ulrich Haffner. These six sonatas, perhaps the most successful of Platti's keyboard works, are also the most conservative in style, and at least some of them were probably composed much earlier than their date of publication. The overall format of the op. 1 sonatas usually resembles the four-movement plan of the Italian *sonata da chiesa* (slow-fast-slow-fast). Platti's charming imitations of Italian orchestral and chamber styles, such as Vivaldian solo concerto (cf. Sonata V/3), the early symphony (cf. Sonata I/2), and the solo sonata for violin or flute (cf. Sonata I/1), are unsurpassed in this period, while the influence of German keyboard styles is reflected in such details as the organization of Sonata III, essentially a German dance suite with an opening movement of moderate tempo to replace the allemande. There are also evocations of the single-voiced style of the German toccata or fantasia, where scales and arpeggios are neatly divided between the hands (cf. Sonata IV/2), and it is worth noting the affinity of the third movement of Sonata IV with the slow movement of J. S. Bach's Italian Concerto. Not surprisingly, Torrefranca never acknowledged the influence of German keyboard music on Platti's style or the ways in which it expanded his protagonist's expressive range.

Despite the conservatism pervading the op. 1 sonatas—their frequent reliance on archaic dance styles and continuo textures—it is clear that Platti participated in the trends associated with Italian *galant* music of the 1730s and 1740s. There are numerous examples of the light two-part textures, phrase repetitions, and rhythmic complexities that are typical of this period; Platti's consistent preference for rounded binary forms in the fast movements of his op. 1 sonatas is striking indeed. This formal predilection does make Platti exceptional for the 1740s, but although Platti's binary schemes often contain themes and motives of sharply contrasting character, there is still no intimation of thematic function as practiced by later eighteenth-century composers, in other words, consistent use of motivic types corresponding to the formalized succession of "first" themes, "bridge" themes, and "second" themes recognized by modern scholars in high Classical sonata form. Moreover, there is no consistent attempt to emphasize the modulations and tonal arrivals in the dramatic manner typical of the high Classical period. In Platti's sonatas, the retransition to the tonic in the second repeated section of binary form is effected in what is essentially a Baroque idiom: there is simply a peremptory cadence on a related key (usually the mediant minor in major-key movements) followed almost immediately by the opening theme in the tonic.

A few years after the appearance of the op. 1 sonatas, Haffner brought out a second collection of Platti keyboard sonatas as the composer's op. 4.[15] The op. 4 sonatas purge many of the archaic traits found in op. 1, and certain features of the Albertian sonata style are intensified. Now only one sonata (the first of the set) is constructed on the *sonata da chiesa* plan; the others follow either the three-movement arrangement favored by German composers of the day (fast-slow-fast) or the more characteristically Italian plan beginning with a slow movement. Light, two-part textures relying on passagework in parallel thirds and sixths are much in evidence, while continuo styles, contrapuntal textures, and imitations of late Baroque string music are not nearly so prominent. Examples of Alberti bass can be found, and there are numerous instances of hand crossing. The use of sequential repetition as an expansive device is common, however, as it is in all of Platti's sonatas.

The Sonatas XIII–XVIII are known only from manuscript sources. On the basis of style, they are generally accepted to date still later than the op. 4 set; and they do manifest more modern compositional traits than the two published sets. In fact, they are more similar to the works of Platti's Italian contemporaries than any of his presumed earlier works and would be quite comfortable as late as the 1750s. The pervasive chromaticism of opp. 1 and 4 is considerably relaxed in favor of clear diatonic writing, and the strings of parallel thirds and sixths are now almost an affectation. The four-movement plan of the *sonata da chiesa* has been entirely abandoned, while Alberti bass and related accompanimental patterns are much more prominent. At the same time, the musical materials here are not nearly so interesting as in opp. 1 and 4, so that these sonatas leave the impression that they were the products of an aging composer relying on facile devices.

Giovanni Battista Martini (1706–1784)

A parallel to the two Platti prints, the first conservative, the second strongly influenced by the newer Venetian trends, can be found in two sets of keyboard sonatas by Giovanni Battista Martini, the renowned Bolognese theorist, music historian, and composer. The first, published by La Cène in Amsterdam about 1742,[16] and the second, published in Bologna by Lelio dalla Volpe in 1747,[17] are almost exactly contemporary with Platti's opp. 1 and 4. Each specifies either harpsichord or organ as the solo instrument. In addition to these published sonatas, which are by far the best known of Martini's keyboard works, some seventy-eight more keyboard sonatas are housed in the Civico Museo Bibliografico Musicale in Bologna.[18] Some of these are single-movement liturgical sonatas in the Baroque tradition; others, multimovement sonatas more suited for harpsichord. Martini also composed some miscellaneous dances for harpsichord and dozens of short organ pieces, such as *versetti*, *introduzioni*, toccatas, and fugues, that were intended for liturgical functions. Martini was indeed the only Italian composer of the early Classical period for whom a large body of sacred keyboard music survives.

The twelve sonatas of the 1742 set are surprisingly archaic in style (even for the 1730s when they were actually written)[19] and seem to take as their point of departure the Baroque multimovement toccata. Generally in five movements, they begin with a prelude and fugue, the prelude usually typifying the sixteenth-note passagework and *arpeggiando* chords found in Alessandro Scarlatti's toccatas, unfortunately in a fashion even more stilted and unimaginative than in the older composer's work. The fugues are very dry, their severe counterpoint almost never relieved by homophonic episodic material. These fugues are followed by slow movements, almost always of the profusely ornamented type found in the Scarlatti toccatas, and then lighter movements, such as dances, variations, or "arias." The inclusion of "arias" among the dances calls attention to the use of this term in Italian keyboard music. Despite the modern assumption of a connection with vocal music, this was not necessarily what was intended at all. The term "aria" derives from French Baroque theater music, where an "air" could denote either a vocal set piece or a dance number not belonging to one of the standard types. In sonatas, the light character and binary form of the "aria" movements are vestiges of these dance origins, and these qualities most characteristically define what is meant by "aria" in instrumental music. Martini's old-fashioned dances are usually similar to their original French models, most particularly in the case of the famous *Gavotta* that closes the last sonata of the set. The charm of this piece is sadly all too exceptional in Martini's keyboard compositions, which exhibit fluency and craftmanship, but few memorable musical ideas.

The 1747 set of sonatas, composed in the early 1740s as part of a proposed set of twelve, is considerably more modern than its predecessor, with *galant*-style rhythms, textures, and melodic characteristics used to a much greater degree. Fugues and older dance styles are purged, and the number of movements is reduced to two or three, usually organized according to the newer models. But although the *Gavotta* of the 1742 set finds a parallel in the lovely *Rondeau* of the fifth sonata, the 1747 set has little more to recommend it.

Only one of the remaining harpsichord sonatas can be dated reliably (a sonata in C major bearing the date 1766), but it does show that Martini continued to absorb *galant*-era trends in sonata composition, not only in his treatment of internal style, but also in his adoption of the two-movement format Allegro-Rondeau.

Mid-Century Developments: Rutini, Galuppi

By the 1750s virtually all Italian composers of keyboard sonatas followed or expanded on the stylistic precedents developed by Marcello and Alberti. It was at this time, too, that the Italian style of writing keyboard sonatas reached the zenith of its popularity, as measured by the dissemination of Italian works in print. The 1750s and 1760s saw the publication in Nuremberg (Haffner's *Raccolta musicale* in five volumes, 1756–1765) and Paris (Venier's opp. 1 and 2 of ca. 1758 and 1760, re-

ILLUSTRATION 7.2. Oil portrait of Giovanni Marco Rutini. Artist unknown. By permission of the Civico Museo Bibliografico Musicale, Bologna.

spectively) of major anthologies devoted almost solely to Italian works and also the appearance in London of numerous prints of solo and accompanied sonatas by Italian composers. There was no other nationality in Europe whose keyboard sonatas could have been marketed abroad in this way, simply by having attention drawn to the country of origin. Yet the vogue for Italian keyboard sonatas expired quickly; even by 1770 an anthology such as Haffner's would have had difficulty finding a ready audience as Italy was losing its position in keyboard composition to the more gifted Germans.

Giovanni Marco Rutini (1723–97)

In considering the musical styles current during the 1750s and 60s, it is good to start with the work of Giovanni Marco Rutini, a composer of opera and instrumental music who received his formative training in Naples (Ill. 7.2). The steady stream of Rutini sonatas that appeared in print after 1748 provides a rare chance to consider a large number of works produced within a reasonably secure chronological framework, rather than having to confront a mass of undatable manuscripts (as in Galuppi's case) or the isolated prints that survive from most other Italians.

A large portion of Rutini's keyboard sonatas were written and published outside of Italy, a reflection of his periods of activity in Prague, Berlin, Dresden, and St. Petersburg during the years 1748 to 1761. Opp. 1–3, 5, and 6 were all published by Haffner in Nuremberg during the 1750s, while the sonatas of opp. 7, 8, 9, 12, and 13 were printed in Bologna and Florence between 1770 and 1782.[20] In addition, five sonatas not found among the numbered collections appear in volumes I–V of the Haffner *Raccolta musicale,* and there are three numbered sets of accompanied sonatas (opp. 10, 11, and 14), all published in Florence between 1778 and 1786.

The sonatas published in Nuremberg exemplify many of the stylistic features typical of keyboard sonatas written during the 1750s. Compared to those of the 1730s or 1740s contrapuntal and continuo textures are now rare, typically replaced by various two-part homophonic textures, some pioneered during the generation of Alberti, some newer. A trademark of Rutini's is the use of "fragmentary" themes interrupted by many rests (as in Ex. 7.8).

EXAMPLE 7.8. Giovanni Marco Rutini: Sonata in F Major op. 6 no. 3. Movement 1, mm. 1–4

(continued)

EXAMPLE 7.8. (*continued*)

The triplet ornamental figures that often accompany these themes lend a shallow, frilly sound. On the other hand, the "singing allegro" tradition still flourishes (as in the second movement of op. 5 no. 1), as do "symphonic" themes (the first movement of op. 3 no. 4).

Although movements in minor keys were not uncommon among Italian composers of the 1730s and 1740s, they suddenly become rather rare after about 1750; and the dominant minor tended to disappear in favor of the mediant major as a choice for the modulation during the first repeated section of binary form. Indeed, there is not even one minor-key sonata, only some scattered movements, in Rutini's opp. 1 and 2. The order and number of movements in Rutini's collections up to op. 6 generally follow the well-established patterns set during the generation of Marcello and Alberti, including the use of nonbinary, improvisatory "preludes" to open some works. Considering that Rutini composed these sonatas north of the Alps, the appearance of the fast-slow-fast pattern in several works is not surprising.

Rutini's roughly equal choice of rhyming and rounded binary schemes is quite typical of his generation, as are a number of manifestations of the ongoing evolution of the internal structure of binary forms. The length of binary movements was expanding more and more, and the constituent themes became ever more contrasting in style and ever more separated by means of clearly articulated cadences. In order to insure continuity and musical momentum between motivic groups, pauses or "caesuras" on the dominant (or dominant of the dominant) were frequently introduced. This "rhetorical" device, not without precedent in earlier decades, leaves internal motivic groups open-ended and creates the expectation of significant new thematic areas to follow. It could also be used to draw attention to the modulation during the first repeated section of binary form. A passage such as that reproduced in Example 7.9 reveals these articulations to be the ancestor of the much more formalized and dramatic means of heralding "second" theme groups later in the eighteenth century.

EXAMPLE 7.9. Giovanni Marco Rutini: Sonata in C Major op. 3 no. 3. Movement 1, mm. 8–12

Although some of Rutini's movements (such as the first movement of op. 3 no. 4) already have soft, lyric "second" themes, one must be careful not to exaggerate their formal significance. At this time their presence is better understood as an experiment with thematic contrasts than as the expression of a highly developed sense of thematic function.

The style of Rutini's later sets of solo sonatas (opp. 7–9, 12, and 13) betray a deliberate attempt to render them more accessible to students and amateurs, both with respect to technical difficulty and melodic appeal. This agenda is in fact set forth by Rutini himself in the prefaces to these sets. The simple, two-movement works that make up Rutini's later collections nonetheless contain many delightful passages. Moreover, the monotony often created in earlier sets by endless successions of binary-form movements is often broken here, either by the short preludes of op. 7 or the rondo movements that now appear frequently. In addition, gestures borrowed from symphonic and operatic styles greatly enrich the later sonatas. The earlier sonatas, which are generally resistant to such influences, tend to be filled with writing that is idiomatic for the keyboard, to be sure, but seem little able to elicit an emotional response from modern performers and listeners.

Baldassare Galuppi (1706–1785)

Rutini's most important Italian contemporary was Baldassare Galuppi, a composer sometimes called "Il Buranello" after his birthplace on the island of Burano near Venice. Galuppi was renowned in his own day as a composer of opera buffa, but he is also notable for the composition of more solo keyboard sonatas (123 are attributed to him) than any other Italian of the eighteenth century except Domenico Scarlatti. Galuppi's activity was centered in Venice throughout his career, but he is known to have spent brief periods in London (1741–1743) and Russia (1765–1768) and to have visited Vienna in 1748 and Berlin en route to Russia.

It is possible that Galuppi actually participated in the establishment of the mainstream Venetian keyboard sonata style that emerged during the decades just before 1750; but unfortunately there exists a distressing confusion concerning the chronology of Galuppi's sonatas and their sources that makes this hypothesis impossible to verify. The vast majority of Galuppi's sonatas survive only in undated manuscripts; perhaps owing at least in part to his infrequent residence abroad, relatively few of Galuppi's sonatas are preserved in datable prints.[21] The most important printed works include the twelve sonatas of his opp. 1 and 2, published by John Walsh in London in 1756 and 1759, respectively, and the three sonatas published in volumes I, II, and V of the Haffner *Raccolta musicale*. The Venier opp. 1 and 2 contain eleven Galuppi movements, while a series of London publishers brought out other individual sonatas between 1765 and 1778.

Aside from the *terminus ante quem* supplied by these few prints, the chronology of the Galuppi sonatas remains highly conjectural. Earlier scholars such as Fausto Torrefranca and Felix Raabe felt that the majority of the forty-nine authentic sonatas known to them probably dated from about 1740 to 1760. Raabe even went so far as to divide all of the sonatas he knew into two groups: one dating before 1750, the other after.[22] William S. Newman rejected this chronology completely, concluding instead that most of the Galuppi sonatas were written between 1755 and 1785.[23] In weighing the merits of the competing chronological theories, one must acknowledge that Raabe's division of Galuppi sonatas is based on sensible considerations of texture, thematic types, and the presence or absence of Alberti bass; it might well hold up if an accurate chronology could ever be documented. Galuppi's works are to a large extent dominated by the sort of soft, syncopated themes that were described above in connection with Alberti and reached their height of popularity in the 1740s. In general, the Newman chronology can be accepted only on the assumption that Galuppi was stubbornly resistant to the new repertories of thematic types that entered keyboard composition during the 1760s, 1770s, and 1780s.

Most of Galuppi's best-known sonatas—that is to say those known to Torrefranca and Raabe plus the six sonatas in the *Passatempo al cembalo* set—follow the usual Albertian principles of organizing sonatas in two or three movements. But many other arrangements exist as well, including the fast-slow-fast pattern and a number of cases where the last movement is a slow movement. The most surprising revelation emerging from the most recent attempts to collate the Galuppi sources has to do with the preponderance of single-movement sonatas. Pullman's index contains no fewer than fifty-five, nearly half the total.

Although the beauties of an unidentified Galuppi sonata were enough to inspire Robert Browning's fatuous poem "A Toccata of Galuppi's,"[24] the composer's work on the whole is rather mediocre. As might well be expected, the medium in which Galuppi shows himself to best advantage is in movements of slow or moderate tempo written in imitation of ornamented vocal lines. The beginning of one of the finest is reproduced as Example 7.10.

EXAMPLE 7.10. Baldassare Galuppi: Sonata in E-flat Major P. 24/I. 24. Movement 1, mm. 1–5

The manner in which attention is drawn to the entrance of the melody, that is, by setting out the accompanimental pattern beforehand, is a device that many mid-eighteenth-century composers, including Rutini, experimented with.

Galuppi's fast movements, in contrast, repeatedly disappoint, despite some interesting experiments with chromatic harmonies and dissonances. The thematic types are ordinarily dull, for example, Galuppi's version of "fragmentary" themes that involve the sharing of motivic material between the hands without invoking counterpoint (Ex. 7.11).

EXAMPLE 7.11. Baldassare Galuppi: Sonata in C Minor P. 54/I. 38. Movement 1, mm. 1–5

Equally insipid, and even more characteristic, are extensive passages in parallel thirds and a style of arpeggiation where the left hand is given single notes or octaves on the beat while the right hand fills out the time of the beat with sixteenth-notes. Example 7.12 shows a basic form, which could be adapted to accommodate any common meter or tempo.

EXAMPLE 7.12. Baldassare Galuppi: Sonata in D Minor P. 11/I. 11. Movement 1, mm. 83–86

Galuppi's sonatas include pedestrian imitations of the usual string genres, such as opera overture (P. 59, 73, 99 / I. 63, 83, 103), French overture (P. 31, 51 / I. 31, 55), and violin sonata (P. 3, 35 / I. 3, 45), not to mention the Scarlattian toccata (P. 15 / I. 15); but certain other sonatas appear to imitate German preludial types quite successfully (P. 10 / I. 10 and P. 50 / I. 34).

Some of Galuppi's sonata movements bear traits of the fully developed Classical-era sonata form, but the composer never acquired a strongly developed sense of thematic function. As with Rutini's sonatas, the resemblances to later Classical-era sonata form here seem to derive from experimentation with various means of presenting a succession of themes while creating a sense of continuity among them. All in all, it is difficult to share William S. Newman's opinion that Galuppi's sonatas exhibit a "superior grasp of form."[25] Newman ascribed to Galuppi an "intensive" rather than "extensive" approach to his materials, meaning that he repeatedly "returns to a few ideas" instead of presenting a succession of unrelated themes. But while this approach can be observed to yield pleasing results in a small number of movements (such as the second movement of P. 24 / I. 24 and the single-movement sonata P. 3 / I. 3), it is not actually common in Galuppi's work, and even when it is followed, it hardly mitigates the lackluster effect produced by conventional thematic materials.

The Italian Keyboard Sonata Abroad

The prolific output of Rutini and Galuppi stands out among Italian composers of their generation, but many other Italians cultivated the genre. Indeed, they carried the light, playful style of Italian keyboard writing to every corner of Europe. The most important expatriates were active in London, a group to be discussed shortly, but Russia, Germany, Scandinavia, Spain, and France were also visited by itinerant Italian keyboard composers.

Galuppi's short period of activity at the court of Russia coincided with that of the violinist Vincenzo Manfredini (1737–1799), who wrote keyboard sonatas only during his employment at the imperial court in St. Petersburg and Moscow from 1758 to 1769. Manfredini is represented in the Haffner *Raccolta musicale,* but of greater interest is a set of six sonatas dedicated to Catherine the Great that appeared in 1765. Although there is nothing especially incompetent about Manfredini's sonatas, this collection was harshly criticized in 1766 by the composer Johann Adam Hiller in a review that stands as a symbol of the new self-confidence flaunted by German composers at this time and their sense that Italian keyboard music was somewhat shallow and superficial.[26]

The Italian traditions of keyboard sonata composition were upheld in Scandinavia by the opera composers Francesco Antonio Baldassare Uttini (1723–1795) and Giuseppe Sarti (1729–1802), each of whom produced one set of harpsichord sonatas during his residence in the north. Uttini's sonatas, published in Stockholm in 1756, have a tunefulness reminiscent of Platti, while Sarti's set, published in Copenhagen in 1769, is notable for the preludes that begin each sonata in the manner of Rutini's op. 7. Farther south, besides the numerous Italians represented in Haffner's *Raccolta musicale* of 1759–1765, there is an interesting set of single-movement sonatas published by Ignazio Fiorillo (1715–1787) in Braunschweig in 1750 and a set of six sonatas dedicated to the Elector of Saxony by Antonio Ferradini (1718–1779), now housed in the Sächsische Landesbibliothek in Dresden.

Better known than these obscure German collections are the *XXX ariae pro organo et cembalo* of Giuseppe Antonio Paganelli (1710– ca. 1763), published in Augsburg in 1756. Paganelli, a Paduan composer who was the apparent successor of Scarlatti as director of chamber music at the court of Spain, wrote these pieces to be used during the Elevation of the Mass, a favorite moment for instrumental music during Catholic worship. Consistent with its usual meaning in eighteenth-century instrumental music, the designation "aria" here denotes simply a binary movement of light character. Sonatas also composed in Spain by the very obscure composer Girolamo Sertori (copied in 1758) have been considered Scarlattian in a recent study.[27]

The first important set of Italian keyboard sonatas published in England during the early Classical era was composed by Giovanni Battista Pescetti (ca. 1704–1766), a Venetian organist, harpsichordist, and opera composer active in London during the late 1730s and early 1740s. Pescetti was something of a prototype of the eighteenth-century Italian composers who were originally attracted to London to write operas, but also produced keyboard sonatas as a means of cashing in on their reputations. The wealthy English middle classes provided an eager market for recreational keyboard works by expatriate Italians throughout the early Classical period (Ill. 7.3). Pescetti's set of nine sonatas, published in 1739, constitutes the composer's only significant keyboard works.[28] Pescetti's sonatas are stylistically very eclectic, but generally based on Marcello's habit of arranging quick movements after an opening slow movement. Among the styles of string music evoked in the sonatas are violin sonata, concerto grosso, and French overture, but the well-established keyboard styles of toccata, fugue, and French *style brisé* also make their appearance.

ILLUSTRATION 7.3. "Mrs. Eyre." A drawing, ca. 1750, by Paul R. A. Sandby (1725–1809). Middle-class Englishwomen provided an eager market for Italian keyboard works during the mid-eighteenth century. Reproduced by permission of the Huntington Library, San Marino, California.

After Pescetti, no Italian composer resident in England published original keyboard sonatas for some time. It is true that the Roman castrato Giuseppe Jozzi (ca. 1720–ca. 1770) published some of Alberti's sonatas as his own in 1745, precipitating a scandal that led to the publication of Alberti's posthumous op. 1 in 1748; but it was not until 1751 that Vincenzo Ciampi (1719?–1762) brought out a set of six sonatas, apparently in response to the interest in keyboard sonatas created by Alberti's works. Ciampi, resident in London from 1748 to 1756, conformed to the usual pattern of Italian opera composers who produced sonatas as a sidelight. His set exhibits great stylistic variety, in some movements evoking the sixteenth-note passagework in parallel thirds so typical of Marcello's sonatas, in other movements styles of violin passagework or Albertian textures. This was the first of the Anglo-Italian collections to follow the Albertian two-movement formats, which were to become standard in London throughout the 1750s and 1760s.

Ciampi's sonatas were followed shortly by the twelve *Sonate di gravicembalo* of Pietro Domenico Paradisi (or Paradies) (1707–1791), brought out by John Johnson in 1754 and reprinted at least six times in London and Paris during the eighteenth century. Paradisi was a failed Neapolitan composer of opera who found success as a teacher of voice and harpsichord in England. His one published set of harpsichord sonatas consists of two-movement works that are strikingly similar in style to the sonatas of Domenico Scarlatti. Example 7.13 shows just one of the innumerable Scarlattian mannerisms that appear in Paradisi's collection (Ex. 7.13).

EXAMPLE 7.13. Pietro Domenico Paradisi: Sonata X in D Major. Movement 1, mm. 38–41

The resemblance is indeed so close that some sort of connection seems all but certain, probably arising either out of their common Neapolitan background (perhaps to improvisatory traditions) or direct contact with Scarlatti's work, perhaps the *Essercizi* previously published in London. Whatever the explanation for their similarity to Scarlatti's music, the

Paradisi sonatas form a very fine set indeed, the epitome of the easy grace one encounters in the best Italian sonatas composed in London. The musical materials are rather conservative: Alberti bass and other *galant* idioms of the 1750s are generally absent. But it is Paradisi's very conservatism (something that never put one at a disadvantage in England) that contributes to the success of his sonatas. From the standpoint of the modern critic, many composers of the mid-eighteenth century had much better luck relying on tried and true techniques held over from the Baroque rather than experimenting with newer styles.

The Accompanied Sonata

Parallel to the publication of solo sonatas by Italian composers such as Ciampi, Paradisi, and Galuppi in London during the 1750s was the beginning of a vogue for accompanied sonatas. The landmark publication was a set by Felice de Giardini (1716–1796), the *Sei sonate di cembalo con violino o flauto traverso* op. 3 in 1751. During the 1760s and 1770s, the accompanied sonata was actually the more typical vehicle for Italians in London. Besides offering flexible alternatives for performance (either with or without the accompanying instrument), its popularity can also be attributed to its suitability for performance by married couples. The violin or flute part would typically be taken by the husband (male amateur musicians were usually proficient in one or the other), the keyboard part by his wife. The interaction between the two was conditioned by two concerns: on the one hand, the sonata had to offer the possibility of performance without the violin or flute part; on the other, the fundamental rule of amateur chamber composition had to be observed, namely, each participant had to have something interesting to play. The solutions to this double challenge in the Anglo-Italian collections were positively ingenious and were made possible by their publication in score format. (In contrast, most chamber music of the period composed on the continent, including accompanied sonatas, was published in parts.) Thus, in Giardini's accompanied sonatas, which include passages for solo violin with continuo accompaniment, the solo keyboardist if playing alone could simply play the violin part in the right hand and ignore the figures. Other common devices included little flourishes for the violin at phrase endings, which could easily be omitted, and the doubling of themes at the octave, third, or sixth, which allowed the violinist a chance to present them, but also gave the keyboardist the option to "transcribe" the doublings or simply omit them.

Besides Giardini, the principal Italian composers of solo or accompanied sonatas in England included Tommaso Giordani (ca. 1730–1806), resident in London and Dublin after 1735; Giusto Ferdinando

Tenducci (ca. 1735–1790), a singer active in several parts of Great Britain after 1763; Mattia Vento (ca. 1735–1776), active in London from 1763; Pietro Guglielmi (1728–1804), a popular master of opera buffa resident in London from 1768 to 1772; and Antonio Sacchini (1730–1786), another popular composer of operas active in London, ca. 1772–1782. Two other Italians, Ferdinando Pellegrini (ca. 1715–ca. 1776) and Carlo Antonio Campioni (1720–1788) may not have gotten any closer to England than Paris, but they did have many of their works published in London during the 1760s.

The greatest strength of this group of composers lay in their melodic inventiveness, rhythmic animation, and delightful evocations of string ensemble music. But their works frequently suffer from a lack of continuity between musical ideas and an absence of carefully planned musical climaxes; at their worst, many of the movements resemble a quilt of charming melodies strung together willy-nilly. Moreover, it is clear that some of the opera composers—for example Guglielmi—were not completely comfortable with keyboard composition. Nonetheless, the almost complete unavailability of their works in modern edition hardly seems deserved.

Johann Christian Bach (1735–1782)

Ironically, it was at the hands of the German-born Johann Christian Bach that the traditions of early Classical Italian keyboard composition reached their culmination (Ill. 7.4). Much like Platti, J. C. Bach was able to coordinate the best features of German and Italian keyboard styles, and he was uniquely conversant with both as a result of early study with his father, J. S. Bach, in Leipzig, with his half-brother C. P. E. Bach in Berlin between 1750 and 1754, and, most important, with Padre Martini in Bologna after his arrival in Italy in 1754. J. C. Bach had his first operatic successes in Italy in 1760, and it was on their strength that he found the opportunity to come to London in 1762. He may thus be compared to such sonata composers as Pescetti, Sacchini, and Guglielmi, who were originally drawn to London owing to their reputations as composers of Italian opera. Bach's activities were centered in England for the remainder of his life; but he did make trips to the continent in 1772–1773 and 1776, to fulfill operatic commissions for Mannheim, and in 1778–1779, to fulfill another commission from the Académie Royal de Musique in Paris. Despite his early success in London as a composer, teacher, and performer, Bach suffered severe financial reversals and a great decline in the popularity of his music during the last few years of his life.

ILLUSTRATION 7.4. Thomas Gainsborough: Oil portrait of Johann Christian Bach. By permission of the Civico Museo Bibliografico Musicale, Bologna.

Solo Sonatas

J. C. Bach's most important solo keyboard compositions are his two published sets of sonatas, op. 5 (London, 1766) and op. 17 (London, ca. 1779)—the latter published earlier (Paris, 1773 or 1774). Also of undisputed authenticity are a number of dances, two sonatas in the Civico Museo Bibliographico Musicale in Bologna (B-flat major, A-flat major), a multimovement "solo" in the Staatsbibliothek in Berlin (A minor), a binary "toccata" in B-flat minor in the Civico Museo Bibliografico in Bologna, and transcriptions of some of the composer's own overtures and symphonies.[29] The sonatas left unpublished at the time of Bach's death are presumably early works, their survival in archives in Berlin and Italy are likely indications of provenance. Despite some effective passages (such as the second movement of the A-flat major sonata, which provides evidence of early experimentation with the melodious style for which Bach's keyboard music is famed), they are of little interest.

The sonatas of opp. 5 and 17, on the other hand, represent an unprecedented standard of excellence in England. They are notable not only for their virtuosity and melodic inventiveness, but also for their exploitation of the expressive capabilities of the pianoforte. During the 1760s and 1770s J. C. Bach was indisputably a great pioneer in the composition of music specifically intended for the pianoforte. His op. 5 was indeed among the first publications to indicate the pianoforte since the appearance of Giustini's op. 1 in 1732. In contrast to the Giustini collection, the suitability of Bach's sonatas for pianoforte extends far beyond mere dynamic control to the invention of thematic types whose brilliance or tenderness is greatly enhanced by the tonal resources of the instrument.

It is clear that Bach composed the sonatas of opp. 5 and 17 with careful attention to the Italian traditions that had been cultivated successfully by so many foreigners in England. Before his arrival in England, all of J. C. Bach's multimovement keyboard works—whether solo sonatas, accompanied sonatas, or concertos—followed three-movement formats based on German keyboard traditions or the Italian *sinfonia*. Yet, as soon as he needed to market works in England, Bach wholeheartedly adopted the Albertian two-movement patterns in all of these genres, most consistently of all in the accompanied sonatas. Among the published solo sonatas, seven are cast as two-movement cycles, one adopts the fast-slow-minuet pattern of the Italian *sinfonia*, while the typically German fast-slow-fast pattern appears in only three works. One other sonata (op. 5 no. 6) seems to represent a modernization and truncation of the Martinian five-movement plan encountered in the Le Cène collection of 1742. This three-movement work opens with a prelude and fugue and closes with an Allegretto (actually a *gavotte en rondeau*) similar to the light dances that conclude Padre Martini's sonatas. The archaicism of the prelude and fugue format and its affinity with Martini's work suggest that it may have been composed while Bach was still in Italy. If so, it is of much finer quality than the other early sonatas, perhaps the only sonata composed in Italy that Bach deemed worthy of inclusion in a published set.

The presence of a concluding rondo in the sonata op. 5 no. 6 is a reflection of the great popularity of rondos that took hold during the 1760s. The rondo of this sonata is rather old-fashioned in that it consists solely of regular eight-bar phrases and simple, dance-like tunes. The rondos of op. 5 nos. 4 and 5, in contrast, make use of irregular phrase lengths, contain transitional material between the rondo themes and the episodes, and exhibit a much more varied thematic content than was common in earlier Italian rondos. There is still no trace, however, of the thematic and harmonic procedures of the sonata-rondo in these works or even in the rondos found in the accompanied sonatas of the 1770s. Oddly enough, Bach dispensed with rondo finales entirely in the op. 17 sonatas, preferring instead rollicking, compound-meter finales reminiscent of the sonatas of Alberti, Ciampi, and Paradisi.

Bach's solo sonatas are distinguished by a melodic sweetness that brought the "singing allegro" style to its greatest perfection before Mozart. Moreover, Bach combined his exceptional gift for melody with a sure sense of how to take standard, often hackneyed figural types and put them to effective use. Examples 7.14 and 7.15 show two devices in use since the generation of Alberti, generally as filler, but here incorporated with much more purpose and a more satisfying melodic profile (Exx. 7.14, 7.15).

EXAMPLE 7.14. Johann Christian Bach: Sonata in G Major op. 5 no. 3. Movement 1, mm. 30–33

EXAMPLE 7.15. Johann Christian Bach: Sonata in A Major op. 17 no. 5. Movement 2, mm. 1–9

Bach's Alberti bass patterns are also far more imaginative than those of most of his contemporaries, often possessing a pleasing contour in the bass line (see Ex. 7.6 above). Bach also knew how to use Alberti bass and related accompanimental figures to infuse new musical energy within a movement, for example at the ends of phrases.

Consistent with his historical position as an "early Classical" master, J. C. Bach betrayed no decided preference either for rounded or rhyming binary schemes in his keyboard sonatas, but his work does manifest a sense of thematic function that was an essential component in sonata form of the high Classical era. In particular, the modulation to the dominant during the first repeated section of binary form is strongly and consistently emphasized by such devices as rhythmic busywork, a *forte* dynamic, and a pause on the tonic or dominant of the new key. The resources used to articulate this modulation or "transition" are often borrowed from symphonic style, as can be seen in Illustration 7.5 mm. 9–18, which features imitations of string tremolo.

ILLUSTRATION 7.5. Johann Christian Bach: Sonata in D Major op. 5 no. 2. Movement 1, beginning. Printed by Pierre Leduc (Paris, ca. 1781). This sonata was one of the three op. 5 sonatas arranged by Mozart as piano concertos. Reproduced courtesy of the Music Library, University of Illinois at Urbana-Champaign.

As another means of intensifying a sense of thematic function, J. C. Bach's sonatas make sophisticated use of the repetition technique mentioned earlier in connection with Alberti's sonatas. By Bach's time, the simple repetition of closing cadence formulas had developed into much larger cadential structures (or "closing" themes), although still based on the principle of repetition (Ex. 7.16).

EXAMPLE 7.16. Johann Christian Bach: Sonata in A Major op. 17 no. 5. Movement 1, mm. 35–41

Bach's typical manner of constructing "first" and "second" themes also represented a refinement of earlier repetition techniques, as can be seen from a comparison of the sonata openings reproduced in Illustrations 7.1 and 7.5. Whereas the latter example is especially clear-cut, many of Bach's other themes subtly vary the phrase endings. The whole point of such repetitions in first, second, and closing themes, of course, is to make them more apparent to the listener as structural reference points and areas of relative tonal stability. Bach's development sections tend to be much longer and more complex than those in the works of most Italian composers, but they are occasionally rambling and unbalanced, as in the finale of op. 17 no. 5. Among other features, Bach's developments reflect a trend of the 1760s and 1770s to begin the second repeated section of binary form in an unpredictable way, rather than simply beginning with the first theme transposed to the dominant.

Accompanied Sonatas and Concertos

As an heir to the Anglo-Italian tradition of keyboard composition, Bach inevitably produced several sets of accompanied sonatas. Eight manuscript sonatas in the Conservatorio di Musica Giuseppe Verdi in Milan survive as examples of early experimentation, but Bach's most important collections are his opp. 2 (1764), 10 (1773), 15 (1778), 16 (1779), and 18 (1781), all published in England. Whereas the Albertian two-movement formats are used exclusively in the English collections, the fast-slow-minuet pattern of the Italian *sinfonia* can be found in the Italian sonatas. By the time of the later collections, the violin part was so integral to the musical fabric that it could not always be omitted successfully, a characteristic of many accompanied sonatas composed in the late 1770s, including Mozart's. Opp. 15 and 18, incidentally, introduce yet another type of amateur musical entertainment as the final number of each collection: a piano duet. The special characteristics associated with duets (which only started to be published frequently beginning in the 1770s) were an increased capacity to imitate orchestral effects (owing to the additional hands available) and the frequent echoing of themes and motives between the parts, yet another response to the desire of amateur chamber players each to have an interesting and important share of the musical action.

J. C. Bach's keyboard concertos form a similarly notable part of the composer's output of keyboard music, and again they offer an interesting contrast between early and mature works. The early works comprise five harpsichord concertos preserved in manuscript in the Berlin Staatsbibliothek. These works appear to be heavily influenced by C. P. E. Bach. All follow the fast-slow-fast pattern and employ the four-part string accompaniment that prevailed in most parts of Europe throughout the Classical period, especially in north Germany. Bach's six concertos op. 1, however, published in 1763 almost immediately after his arrival in England, belong to an Anglo-Italian style of chamber concerto calling for a three-part string accompaniment that was pioneered by such composers as Giuseppe Sammartini (1695–1750) and Vincenzo Ciampi. As with the accompanied sonata, flexible performance options were available to amateur musicians interested in buying such works. They could be performed either as chamber concertos for soloist, two violins, and bass or simply as keyboard solos. The latter choice was made possible by the careful transcription of the orchestral tuttis into the keyboard part. Again, this is a characteristic of English music publishing unique in Europe. The association of such works with chamber performance is also signaled by their use of Albertian two-movement formats. Even in England there was little precedent for two-movement solo concertos. Two further sets of keyboard concertos by J. C. Bach followed. The op. 7 concertos of 1770 are much like those of op. 1, except that they are somewhat longer, somewhat more suited for use with pianoforte as the solo instrument, and include *ad libitum* horn parts. The principal innovation of the op. 13 concertos of 1777 was the option of performance with oboes; but in spite of their more ambitious conception, they still belonged to the English chamber tradition and permitted performance as solos.

Influence

The keyboard music of J. C. Bach has long been of interest to Mozart specialists on account of its presumed influence on the latter's style. This claim is certainly not without merit as regards the piano sonatas.

Mozart's cordial personal contacts with Bach, begun during a visit to England in 1764–1765 and renewed in Paris in 1778, are well known; and his familiarity with J. C. Bach's solo sonatas cannot be questioned. Three sonatas from the op. 5 set (nos. 2–4) were arranged during the early 1770s by the young Mozart and his father as concertos (K.107); moreover, letters of Leopold Mozart from 1774 record the use of Bach's sonatas in the Mozart household. Finally, a letter of Wolfgang Mozart from 1778 alludes to his use of them as teaching pieces in Mannheim.[30] The similarity in melodic style is immediately recognizable to most listeners, and one wonders whether Mozart may actually have found in J. C. Bach's work specific models for some of his movements. The first movement of the Sonata in D major K.284 of 1775, for example, is in the same key as the first movement of Bach's op. 5 no. 2 (earlier arranged by Mozart as a concerto) and exhibits a remarkably similar succession of theme types.

The influence of J. C. Bach on Mozart in the genres of accompanied sonata and piano concerto is not so easy to document, although the proposition has been taken virtually as an article of faith with regard to the piano concertos. A general similarity in melodic style is certainly present; on the other hand, Mozart never cultivated the simple chamber concerto style as did J. C. Bach, nor did he follow him in matters of instrumentation, keyboard virtuosity, or the number and arrangement of movements. Bach's possible influence on Mozart's formal procedures in first-movement concerto form is a question that cannot yet be evaluated conclusively.

In this connection, a significant degree of direct stylistic influence on Mozart by any of the leading Italian composers of early classic keyboard music has yet to be demonstrated convincingly. Fausto Torrefranca's claims, never widely accepted, that Rutini was Mozart's "first teacher" have been specifically rebutted by Giorgio Pestelli (whose own efforts to suggest even a modest influence of Rutini on Mozart, Haydn, and even Beethoven on the basis of vague similarities between individual themes seems hardly more fruitful).[31] The sonatas K.309 and 330 by Mozart are perhaps closest in style to a native Italian *galant* taste, and may even represent a deliberate attempt to evoke it. But for the most part Mozart seems to have found little to emulate in the works of Rutini, Galuppi, or their contemporaries that was not already part of a common vocabulary of keyboard composition shared by composers all over Europe. The same may be said of Haydn as well, whose keyboard works of the 1760s and 1770s seem primarily influenced by the Austrian divertimento tradition and by his own experiments in chamber and orchestral composition. It is interesting to note Beethoven's use of arrangements akin to the Albertian patterns in such sonatas as op. 49 no. 1 and op. 78; but any connection with such distant stylistic impulses is obviously open to question.

With the passing of the generation of Rutini and Galuppi the importance of Italian keyboard composition faded, although it hardly ceased. After the 1770s Italian composers continued to compose sonatas and other types of keyboard works. The leading masters of the later phases of the Classical era included Giovanni Battista Grazioli (1746–ca. 1820), Ferdinando Turini (ca. 1740–ca. 1812), Luigi Cherubini (1760–1842), Giovanni Paisiello (1740–1816), Domenico Cimarosa (1749–1842), Giovanni Antonio Matielli (ca. 1733–1805), and Giacomo Gotifredo Ferrari (1763–1842). Many of these followed the pattern of earlier Italian composers who wrote keyboard music only while abroad. It is not that the sonatas of these composers are inferior to those of their predecessors; rather, the 1770s mark the point after which Italian works are no longer at the forefront of keyboard composition. Compared with the sonatas of the most talented German composers of the same period, their work is of only minimal importance in evaluating and identifying the principal stylistic trends of the day. One has only to compare the sonatas of Mozart and Haydn with those of Grazioli written in the 1780s to realize how far stylistic developments had passed the Italians by. Their sonatas are like those of their predecessors in that they provide the listener and performer with at most a pleasant succession of musical ideas, if their imaginations were even equal to that task. A striking confirmation of the new balance of national strengths can be observed in Clementi's conversion from the modest two-movement cycles he composed in England during the 1770s to the grander three-movement works he composed after traveling to Vienna in the early 1780s. In the 1750s it was the German Johann Christian Bach who was inclined to adopt Italian idioms of expression. The quick passing of their ascendancy notwithstanding, the Italian keyboard masters of the early Classical period must be recognized for a host of innovations—among them the Alberti bass, the "singing allegro," the first music explicitly for the pianoforte—but perhaps most of all for their role in establishing the sonata as the preeminent genre for composers of keyboard music in the high Classical era, thus setting into motion stylistic developments that were to culminate in the works of Beethoven.

Notes

1. See Percy A. Scholes, ed., *Dr. Burney's Musical Tours in Europe* (London, 1959), 1: 236.

2. For the reader interested in the complex stylistic traditions associated with the emergence of keyboard concertos among Italian composers, two recent studies will provide a useful introduction: Freeman 1985–1986, and Iesuè 1986.

3. Quoted in Terry 1967, 70.

4. Quoted in Newman 1983a, 37.

5. All of the earliest sets of Italian sonatas for harpsichord are described in Newman 1954. Inexplicably, William S. Newman rejected Domenico Zipoli's *Sonate d'intavolatura* (Rome, 1716) as "true" sonatas and omitted them from serious consideration. This odd remark about the *Sonate d'intavolatura* is found in Newman 1983b, 196: "... they are not of direct concern here, since 'Sonate' appears only as a generic term in the over-all title, with no further application to the individual pieces." No matter what Newman was trying to express in this passage, it is very clear that the collection does contain four *sonate da camera* for solo keyboard and is very important in helping to identify the 1710s as the key decade in Italy when the keyboard sonata began to establish itself permanently.

6. The sources of Marcello's keyboard music are described exhaustively in Selfridge-Field 1990. The numbering system supplied by this work has been adopted for use here. More detailed stylistic discussion may be found in Newman 1983b, 174–79, Newman 1957, 1959.

7. Even more striking is the opening movement of the Sonata in C minor, C712a, which features an extraordinary imitation of concerto grosso style that is most unsuitable for keyboard by reason of its constant successions of repeated sixteenth notes at *presto* tempo.

8. See Wörmann 1955 for a complete discussion of the sources of Alberti's keyboard sonatas and the probability of a large repertory that is now lost.

9. Only three of Alberti's sonatas are available in modern edition: op. 1 no. 8, in William S. Newman, ed., *Thirteen Keyboard Sonatas of the 18th and 19th Centuries* (Chapel Hill, 1947); op. 1 no. 2, in Franz Giegling, ed., *The Solo Sonata: Das Musikwerk* (Cologne, 1960); and Sonata XII of the Wörmann numbering, ed. C. Zecchi and H. Fazzari (Milan, 1971).

10. See Marco 1959 and Newman 1983a, 180–82.

11. The Giustini sonatas are available in facsimile edition as No. 49 of the series *Archivum musicum* (Florence, 1982), No. 1 of the series *Utrecht Early Music Festival Facsimiles* (Utrecht, 1985), and an unnumbered volume in the series *Clavecinistes européens du XVIIIe siècle* (Geneva, 1986). A new facsimile edition under the editorship of Gerhard Doderer is now in press from the Academia Brasileira de Música of Rio de Janeiro. Doderer's edition will contain an extensive preface detailing the fascinating new biographical information concerning Giustini that has come to light only in the last few years.

12. Torrefranca's views are principally set out in Torrefranca 1930, a collection of earlier essays.

13. See Newman 1983a, 365–73, and Hoffmann-Erbrecht 1954, 83–89.

14. All of the sonatas known to have been written by Platti, including those destroyed during World War II, are edited in Torrefranca 1963. This work also contains detailed biographical information and exhaustive stylistic commentary. A supplement to the source information found in this work is provided in Iesuè 1975.

15. These sonatas correspond to Sonatas VII–XII of Torrefranca's numbering system and are estimated by Hoffmann-Erbrecht to have appeared ca. 1746 in his article "Der Nürnberger Musikverleger Johann Ulrich Haffner," *Acta musicologica* 26 (1954): 124.

16. The sonatas of the 1742 set are available in facsimile edition (New York, 1967).

17. The sonatas of the 1747 set are available in a modern edition edited by Lothar Hoffmann-Erbrecht: *Mitteldeutsches Musikarchiv*, Series 1, vol. 5 (Leipzig, 1954).

18. See Brofsky 1963.

19. Martini's correspondence with the publisher Le Cene confirms rough dates of composition for the sonatas of both the 1742 and 1747 sets. This correspondence is summarized in Leonarda Busi, *Il padre G.B. Martini: musicista-letterato del secolo XVIII* (Bologna, 1891), 349–58.

20. The bibliographic complexities associated with Rutini's sonatas are sorted out most fully in Newman 1983a, 204–27, and Lombardi 1972.

21. The most useful catalogue of Galuppi's sonatas and appraisal of their sources is provided in Pullman 1972. The only published catalogue of Galuppi's sonatas is found in the preliminary pages of Edda Illy's edition of fifteen *Sonate per cembalo* by Galuppi (Rome, 1969).

22. See Raabe 1929.

23. See Newman 1983a, 191–92. Newman's chronology was derived partly based on the mistaken assumption that the collection of sonatas *Passatempo al cembalo* ("Pastime at the harpsichord") was written in 1785. The manuscript used as the basis of Franco Piva's edition of the *Passatempo* sonatas (Venice, 1964), however, proves that the *Passatempo* sonatas could not have been written any later than 1781. It is very difficult to understand why Galuppi would suddenly wish to cultivate the composition of the humble genre of keyboard sonata at about the age of fifty during the peak of his career as a composer of opera buffa. No obvious artistic or remunerative benefits could have accrued from the composition of keyboard sonatas during a period of waning interest in Italy. We do have the precedent of Domenico Scarlatti perhaps writing large numbers of keyboard sonatas at a comparable age, but as a part of his duties at the court of Spain, Scarlatti would have had a ready need for sonatas that Galuppi did not have.

24. Browning's poem is reprinted in full in Mary Louise Serafine's edition of six keyboard sonatas by Galuppi (New York, 1980).

25. Newman 1983a, 198.

26. This review is discussed in Newman 1983a, 776–77.

27. Giorgio Pestelli, "Sei sonate per cembalo di Girolamo Sertori (1758)," *Rivista italiana di musicologia* 2 (1967): 131–39.

28. Pescetti's keyboard works are discussed in Degrada 1966.

29. Additional copies of the sonatas in B-flat major and A-flat major and the "toccata" in B-flat minor have been identified recently in the library of the Conservatorio di Musica Giuseppe Verdi in Milan and the library of the Monumento Nazionale of Montecassino. All of J. C. Bach's keyboard compositions are now available in various volumes of *The Collected Works of Johann Christian Bach 1735–1782*, ed. Ernest Warburton (New York, 1984–99). Vol. 48 of this edition is a new *Thematic Catalogue* (New York, 1999) intended to replace the one found in Terry 1967.

30. See Emily Anderson, ed., *The Letters of Mozart and His Family*, 3rd revised edition (New York, 1985), 251–52, 482.

31. See Torrefranca 1936 and Pestelli 1978.

Literature Cited and Selected Bibliography

Bieler, Maria. *Binärer Satz, Sonate, Konzert: Johann Christian Bachs Klaviersonaten op. V in Spiegel barocker Formprinzipien und ihrer Bearbeitung durch Mozart.* Kassel and New York, 2002.

Brofsky, Howard. "The Instrumental Music of Padre Martini." Ph.D. dissertation, New York University, 1963.

Caselli, Ala Botti. "Le 'Sonate da cimbalo di piano e forte' di Lodovico Giustini— L'Opera di un prete galante agli albori della sonata per pianoforte." *Nuova rivista musicale italiana* (hereafter *NRMI*) 12 (1978): 34–66.

Degrada, Francesco. "Le sonate per cembalo e per organo di Giovanni Battista Pescetti." *Chigiana* 23 (1966): 89–108.

Freeman, Daniel E. "The Earliest Italian Keyboard Concertos." *The Journal of Musicology* 4 (1985–1986): 121–45.

Frum, Bernard. "An Early Example of Dramatic Procedures in 18th-Century Keyboard Music." *The Musical Quarterly* (hereafter MQ) 56 (1970): 230–46.

Fuller, David. "Accompanied Keyboard Music." *MQ* 60 (1974): 222–45.

Harding, Rosamond E. M. "The Earliest Pianoforte Music." *Music and Letters* 13 (1932): 194–99.

Hoffmann-Erbrecht, Lothar. *Deutsche und italienische Klaviermusik zur Bachzeit.* Leipzig, 1954.

Iesuè, Alberto. "Il concerto con cembalo solista nel XVIII secolo in Italia." *NRMI* 20 (1986): 539–63.

—————. *Giovanni Benedetto Platti.* Milan, 1997.

—————. "Note su Antonio Ferradini." *NRMI* 15 (1981): 241–46.

—————. "Le opere a stampa e manoscritto di Giovanni Benedetto Platti." *NRMI* 9 (1975): 541–51.

—————. *Le opere di Giovanni Benedetto Platti, 1697–1763: catalogo tematico.* Padua, 1999.

Kamien, Roger. "Style Change in the Mid-18th-Century Keyboard Sonata." *Journal of the American Musicological Society* 19 (1966): 37–58.

Kidd, Ronald R. "The Emergence of Chamber Music with Obligato Keyboard in England." *Acta musicologica* 44 (1972): 122–44.

Lombardi, Carlo, "A Revision of the Instrumental Catalogue and an Examination of the Form-Types of the Six Sonatas for Cembalo, Opus X, of Giovanni Marco Placido Rutini (1723–1797)." Ph.D. dissertation, New York University, 1972.

—————. *Giovanni Rutini: Father of Classical Sonata Procedures.* Oakdale, N.Y., 1997.

Marco, Guy A. "The Alberti Bass before Alberti." *The Music Review* 22 (1959): 93–103.

Mekota, Beth Anna. "The Solo and Ensemble Keyboard Works of Johann Christian Bach." Ph.D. dissertation, University of Michigan, 1969.

Newman, William S. "A Checklist of the Earliest Keyboard 'Sonatas' (1641–1738)." *Notes* 11 (1954): 201–12.

—————. "The Keyboard Sonatas of Benedetto Marcello." *Acta musicologica* 29 (1957): 28–41 and 31 (1959): 192–96.

————. *The Sonata in the Baroque Era.* 4th edition. New York, 1983. [Newman 1983b]

————. *The Sonata in the Classic Era.* 3rd edition. New York, 1983. [Newman 1983a]

Pestelli, Giorgio. "Mozart e Rutini." *Analecta musicologica* 18 (1978): 290–307.

————. "Sei sonate per cembalo di Girolamo Sertori (1758)." *Rivista italiana di musicologia* 2 (1968): 131–39.

Pixley, Zaide Elizabeth. "The Keyboard Concerto in London Society, 1760–1790." Ph.D. dissertation, University of Michigan, 1986.

Pullman, David E. "A Catalogue of the Keyboard Sonatas of Baldassare Galuppi." M.A. thesis, The American University, 1972.

Raabe, Felix. *Galuppi als Instrumentalkomponist.* Frankfurt-an-der-Oder, 1929.

Roe, Stephen. *The Keyboard Music of C. Bach: Source Problems and Stylistic Development in the Solo and Ensemble Works.* New York, 1989.

Sanders, Donald Clyde. "The Keyboard Sonatas of Giustini, Paradisi, and Rutini: Formal and Stylistic Innovation in Mid-Eighteenth-Century Italian Keyboard Music." Ph.D. dissertation, University of Kansas, 1983.

Schenk, Erich. *Giuseppe Antonio Paganelli.* Vienna, 1928.

Schmitz, Hans-Bernd. "Die Klavierkonzerte Johann Christian Bach." Ph.D. dissertation, Julius-Maximilians-Universität Würzburg, 1981.

Selfridge-Field, Eleanor. *The Music of Benedetto and Alessandro Marcello: A Thematic Catalogue with Commentary on the Composers, Repertory, and Sources.* Oxford, 1990.

Staral-Baierle, Ilse Susanne. "Die Klavierwerke von Johann Christian Bach." Ph.D. dissertation, University of Graz, 1971.

Stevens, Jane. "Concerto No. 6 in F Minor: By Johann Christian Bach?" *RMA Research Chronicle* 21 (1988): 53–56.

————. *The Bach Family and the Keyboard Concerto: The Evolution of a Genre.* Warren, Mich., 2001.

Stone, David. "The Italian Sonata for Harpsichord and Pianoforte in the Eighteenth Century." 3 vols. Ph.D. dissertation, Harvard University, 1952.

Terry, Charles Sanford. *Johann Christian Bach.* 2nd edition. London, 1967.

Torrefranca, Fausto. *Giovanni Benedetto Platti e la sonata moderna. Istituzioni e monumenti dell'arte musicale italiana,* n.s. 2. Milan, 1963.

————. *Le origine italiane del romanticismo musicale: i primitivi della sonata moderna.* Turin, 1930.

————. "Il primo Maestro di W. A. Mozart (Giovanni Maria Rutini)." *Rivista musicale italiana* 40 (1936): 239–53.

Wörmann, Wilhelm. "Die Klaviersonate Domenic Albertis." *Acta musicologica* 27 (1955): 84–112.

CHAPTER EIGHT

Haydn's Solo Keyboard Music

Elaine Sisman

In a remark to his biographer Griesinger, Haydn evoked the image of a composer who worked at the keyboard, whose fingers gave voice to his inspiration:

> Haydn always composed his works at the clavier. "I sat down, began to improvise, according to my mood, sad or happy, serious or playful. Once I had seized upon an idea, my entire effort went toward putting it into effect and sustaining it according to the rules of art." (Gotwals, 61)

To Dies he made the keyboard even more intimate:

> If it's an Allegro that persecutes me then my pulse beats harder and harder, I can't sleep. If it's an Adagio then I notice that my pulse beats slowly. My imagination (*Phantasie*) plays on me as if I were a keyboard. . . . I am really just a living keyboard. (Gotwals, 141)

The keyboard, then, was so much the source of Haydn's ideas that he experienced composition viscerally as though he were being played himself. Only after finding his principal ideas, "according to [his] mood," did he continue the piece in writing. In a sense, the keyboard represented for Haydn the purest form of inspiration, the translation of affect to music, unmediated by considerations of genre; it allowed him to speak in a direct rhetorical voice.

Yet if the keyboard helped Haydn to compose freely, he was not entirely unconstrained in composing his music *for* keyboard: tempered by the graceful amateur pianism of his dedicatees, students, and imagined public, and circumscribed by his publishers' requests ("to suit your taste, I have newly written the third Sonata with variations," he wrote to his publisher Artaria in 1789).[1] Because compositions that make only moderate technical demands are today typically judged less valuable than those combining virtuosity with musical substance, Haydn's sonatas before the London period have been tainted by this association with dilettantism and the market. This judgment, however, was not universally held by Haydn's contemporaries; an astute observer of the musical scene in Vienna and Prague in the 1790s praised Haydn's keyboard pieces precisely because they were pleasing and usually easy to play, and thus more useful than the excessive difficulties with which other composers belabored students (Schönfeld 21). Haydn's modest claims for his own keyboard ability ("I was not a wizard at any instrument . . . ; I was not a bad clavier player"), which have also helped to create the impression that his writing for the keyboard was peripheral to his career, ought not to distract attention from the ways in which his sonatas, variations, and capriccios reveal a flair for keyboard sonorities as well as his deepest compositional concerns.

Haydn's keyboard works emerge as significant both on their own terms and as the point of entry for new ideas which he then transferred to other genres, notably symphonies. Sonatas and symphonies were the only instrumental genres which he composed virtually without interruption throughout his career; of the many genres he abandoned after the late 1760s or early 1770s, he returned only to the piano trio (1784) and string quartet (1781). At times participating in the Viennese keyboard styles of Wagenseil and Steffan (Štěpán), and at others clearly drawing on C. P. E. Bach's highly individual textures and figures, Haydn forged an approach by turns playful and expressive, brilliant and improvisatory. Moreover, his extraordinary piano trios, still not well known (despite Charles Rosen's eloquent defense in 1971 and subsequent scholarly attention), fill out the picture of Haydn as a keyboard composer of genius. The reader interested in the trios is encouraged to consult Charles Rosen, *The Classical Style* (Rosen 1971), the comprehensive book by A. Peter Brown on all of Haydn's keyboard music (including chamber music and concerti: *Joseph Haydn's Keyboard Music*) (Brown 1986), as well as the articles by Katalin Komlós and W. Dean Sutcliffe listed in the bibliography. The following discussion will deal with the solo keyboard music: fifty-four extant sonatas and six *Klavierstücke* as published in the complete critical edition,[2] in roughly chronological groupings.

The Early Works

The unknowable chronology of Haydn's early sonatas—about eighteen works written before 1765—has caused an enormous disparity between the two excellent critical editions currently in use. In the Henle edition, based on the Haydn complete works (*Joseph Haydn Werke*), George Feder has produced an eminently reasonable and convincing organization: instead of attempting a speculative chronology, he has distinguished between larger and smaller works that were probably intended for students at different levels of technical proficiency, thus avoiding the reductionist idea that smaller is always earlier or more "primitive" stylistically.[3] He uses the numbering system of the Hoboken catalogue, which will be retained here as well.[4] Christa Landon's edition for Universal, in attempting a comprehensive chronological renumbering, is more problematic in this respect (its ordering is based on size, and it also includes the lost sonatas in the numbering system), although textually it is very fine.[5] The many problems of authenticity that plague these sonatas, solved somewhat differently by these editors, cannot be taken up here.[6]

The early sonatas, virtually all of them written before Haydn joined the Esterházy musical establishment as Vice-Kapellmeister in 1761, are full of midcentury Viennese clichés, especially the stereotyped combinations of triplets and trills in opening themes and cadence patterns. Every one of them has a minuet and trio, sometimes as part of a fast-slow-minuet cycle, sometimes as the middle movement in a fast-minuet-finale cycle. Because the terminology for instrumental genres was not fixed, these pieces were called "Partita" or "Divertimento," the latter a generic designation for music for soloists; Haydn began to use the title "Sonata" in the early 1770s. In technical difficulty, they are roughly comparable to the sets of sonatas published by Wagenseil in the early 1750s. Standouts among Haydn's sonatas from the 1750s and early 1760s are the G-major sonata XVI:6, with its unusual four-movement format,[7] operatic figuration and cadenzas in the slow movement, and ambitiously dissonant trio, and the B-flat-major sonata XVI:2, with a similarly poignant slow movement in G minor. These embellished cantilenas over a chordal bass appear not only in the sonatas and keyboard trios of this period but also in the string quartets of op. 1 and op. 2; they resemble slow movements of Haydn's concertos as well.

Beginning in 1765, Haydn embarked on a series of keyboard works that manifested both a deepening of expressive resources and a certain quirky individualism, at the same time expanding the formal and textural possibilities of the genre. Among the earliest of these was the G-major Capriccio, Hob. XVII:1, based on the coarse and repetitious folksong "Acht Sauschneider müssen seyn" ("It takes eight men to castrate a boar"). Described by David Wyn Jones as Haydn's "most ambitious early work for keyboard,"[8] and by A. Peter Brown as "one of the watersheds in the history of keyboard music,"[9] the Capriccio employs imaginative restatements of the theme in different keys, punctuated by returns in the tonic, in a way that eerily resembles C. P. E. Bach's rondos, none of which had yet been published.[10] Its format is a study in circularities, emanating from the four tonic statements of the theme; each tonic statement gives rise to a cycle of returns in related keys linked by sequential passages (see Table 8.1). The first such cycle spins off into

TABLE 8.1
Capriccio in G Major, Hob. XVII:1, Formal and Tonal Organization.

I. mm. 1–132	A	A	A	A	A
	G	D	Am	Em	C
	aba app.a	*aba app.b*—seqs.	*aba*—seqs.	*ab*—seqs.	*a*—seqs.
	m. 1 14	24 40	62	85	114

II. mm. 133–264	A	A	A	A	
	G	Bm	C	F	
	ab app.a	*ab*—long prog.	*aba app.c*	*aba* seqs.	
	133	157	190 202	233	

III. mm. 265–368	A	A	A	A	
	G Gm	Bb	[G]	G	
	ab ab—seqs.	*aba app.c*	*app.a*—seqs.	*ab a/coda*	
	265	296 309	317	341	

progressively liquidating statements in D major, A minor, E minor, and C major: after the *aba* structure of the tonic theme is reiterated in the dominant (each with a different appendix passage), the next three statements yield to sequences after a shorter and shorter span: during the last *a* section in A minor, during the *b* section in E minor, and during the first *a* section in C major. The second cycle beginning with G major reconstitutes the theme gradually (the first two entries missing only the final *a*, the second two complete) but adds another type of development, the fantasia-like arpeggiated chord progression between the B-minor and C-major segments. Finally, the last cycle expands from the center, when the return of *a* is in G minor instead of major and gives rise to a B-flat-major statement before returning to the tonic. Thus, the entire piece may be seen as a series of cycles decreasing both in number of thematic units and in size.

The aspect of varied repetition and circularity represented by the Capriccio is sometimes palpable in the sonatas of the late 1760s and early 1770s, bringing up the vexing question of C. P. E. Bach's "influence" on Haydn's sonatas. Haydn certainly studied Bach's widely circulated treatise *Essay on the True Art of Playing Keyboard Instruments,* as he told his biographers, and many of Bach's sonatas were available in Vienna, especially the 1760 set with varied reprises (Sisman 1990a, 158–59). North German critics lambasted Haydn for "parodying" Bach's style.[11] Brown argues that Bach's works became known to Haydn at a later stage than is usually credited, the 1760s instead of the 1750s; other scholars prefer to place Haydn's sonatas up to the early 1770s among Austrian contemporaries.[12] Three elements of resemblance between Haydn and Bach immediately strike the ear: the varied repetitions of phrases and periods, a tendency to exploit the lower registers of the keyboard, especially in two-part texture and especially at cadences, and the striking use of rhetorical pauses. One imagines these two composers developing their ideas at the keyboard with the same delight in the sonorous surface of the instruments available to them, especially the different registral timbres of the clavichord and fortepiano.

The Late 1760s and Early 1770s

Of the fifteen sonatas datable to the late 1760s and early 1770s, nearly half are lost (Hob. XVI:2a-e, 2g-h) and one is in fragmentary form (Hob. XVI:5).[13] Based on dynamic indications, it is possible that the latest sonatas in this group were Haydn's first to be written for a touch-sensitive instrument.[14] The loss of pieces in D minor, E minor, and B major (nos. 2a, 2e, and 2c, respectively) is especially unfortunate in light of the significance generally accorded to Haydn's prominent use of minor and other uncommon keys in this period. Although the choice of key makes no inherent claim on the level of expressivity, drama, or expansiveness of a composition, it serves as a convenient if misleading indicator of the stylistic shift now known as the *Sturm und Drang*. With only one minor-key sonata extant from this period, the C-minor Hob. XVI:20, (1771, but not published until 1780), and only one unusual key, the D-flat-major slow movement of the A-flat-major sonata Hob. XVI:46, it has thus been harder to assess the participation of Haydn's keyboard sonatas in that style. If Haydn's symphonic style changed in response to his duties as composer of theatrical music and his sensitivity to the dramatic rhetoric of the theatre, then certainly a heightened sense of drama and play might suffuse the rest of his music from this period.[15] But the special features of these sonatas have little in common with the contemporaneous symphonies and quartets and seem instead more alive to registral oppositions and expressive embellishments. Indeed, Haydn's keyboard sonatas through the 1780s seem to underscore the distinction made by contemporary writers between a "symphony style" of broad gestures and sweeping contrasts, and a "sonata style" of expressive nuance and more tightly-constructed phrases and periods (Broyles 1983).

The most striking sonatas of the later 1760s and early 1770s are those in D major (XVI:19), A-flat major (XVI:46), G minor (XVI:44), and C minor (XVI:20). This group was probably inaugurated by the E-minor sonata XVI:47, Haydn's only sonata to begin with an Adagio. Each movement pointed in an important new direction. The opening Adagio, a limpid *siciliana,* employs an immediate registral contrast in its first theme; the Allegro contains two themes in the tonic; and the phrase construction of the Tempo di Menuet depends upon repetitions and varied repetitions. The implications of these ideas are apparent in Sonata 19, a beautiful application to the keyboard of Haydn's longstanding interest in *concertante* instrumentation, the highlighting of individual instruments in an ensemble texture, often by means of register and figuration in addition to timbre. Its slow movement is laid out registrally like a concerto, with an upper-register ritornello, a tenor-range "solo," and a cadenza at the end (Ex. 8.1).[16]

EXAMPLE 8.1. Sonata in D Major Hob. XVI: 19/ii

(continued)

EXAMPLE 8.1. (*continued*)

And the finale, Haydn's first rondo-variation movement, with two varied returns of the theme interspersed with episodes in related keys, as well as a final "redundant" return (ABA$_1$CA$_2$A$_3$), similarly distinguishes between an upper-register theme and its variations, and the lower-register episodes. Only in the last variation, a "rescored" reprise, are the registers united. The first movement's irregular phrase lengths (3 + 5) are made almost symmetrical by judicious use of varied repetitions, a technique that from this point on becomes more and more essential to Haydn's style. Its exposition is in three sections, with a lengthy middle section modulating to the dominant. The idea of repetition, elaborated in the opening measures, is maintained in each of the sections and serves to give coherence to the movement despite surface contrast of rhythmic patterns. For example, interior pedal tones in the theme (the repeated pitch A in the right hand) become outright repeated notes after the first group together with the repetition of scale patterns, while the development section reworks those middle-section repetitions into intense passages combining stasis and motion (Ex. 8.2).

EXAMPLE 8.2. Sonata in D Major Hob. XVI: 19/i. Repetition in exposition and development

(*continued*)

EXAMPLE 8.2. (*continued*)

The A-flat-major sonata XVI:46, after an interestingly unbalanced parsing of its opening eight measures (3 + 2½ + 2½) becomes by turn brilliant and delicately filigreed, changing rhythmic and textural character frequently and offering many chances for the performer to add and revise ornaments. Its exposition seems to make palpable an improvisatory thought process by returning twice to the rhythm and texture of its main theme as a kind of interruption of momentum, a mental swerve from the inevitable cadence set in motion each time by a II$_6$–V progression in the dominant (mm. 22–23 and 30). The development section similarly uses F minor as the occasion for lengthy elaboration; indeed, a sequential restatement of the main theme in F minor gives rise first to an invention-like development of the second group, then a long chord progression of triplets broken between the hands that moves through B-flat and E-flat minors before returning to F minor. The racy Presto finale offers a light counterpart to these textures.

At the heart of the sonata, and surely one of Haydn's most poetic movements in any genre, is the D-flat-major Adagio (Ex. 8.3). Suggesting at first a passacaglia built on repetitions of a four-measure unit, the austere two-part texture in a middle register then expands upward into three-part and then outward into four-part counterpoint. Although the resemblance to passacaglia ends after the third statement, the four-measure pattern holds sway for the rest of the twenty-eight-measure exposition (only mm. 13–20 naturally group themselves into an eight-measure sentence).

EXAMPLE 8.3. Sonata in A-flat Major Hob. XVI: 46/ii. Exposition

Yet for all its evocations of a continuous older style, the exposition falls into a modern three-part division of material: the first group with modulating transition (mm. 1–12); the second group (mm. 13–20); closing group (mm. 21–28), all neatly demarcated by pauses. After the double bar, however, the second section of the piece becomes a study in expansions, contractions, and reconstitutings of the four-measure unit. First, the main theme, in its three-part version, is expanded through elision into a nine-measure passage modulating from A-flat (V) through E-flat minor (ii) to B-flat minor (vi), and is itself elided to a high-register revision of that theme that moves sequentially back to the tonic. Recapitulatory feeling is denied, however, when the main theme returns in two-measures "bits," descending chromatically from tonic to dominant, and preparing the true moment of return: the second group, recast in its entirety in the tonic, at m. 52. The masterstroke of the movement is the harmonic expansion of the closing group: with extraordinary chromaticism (ultimately moving through D-flat minor to B-double-flat major!) and an air of improvisatory excess, it anticipates the exceptional coda of the F-minor piano variations written nearly twenty-five years later.

With the B-flat major and G-minor sonatas, Hob. XVI:18 and 44, we see the first of the large-scale two-movement sonatas that Haydn wrote throughout his career.[17] In both cases, the second movements are Tempo di Menuets in all but name (marked "Moderato" and "Allegretto," respectively). The dynamic indications of Sonata 18 seem to place it at about the same time as the C-minor sonata XVI:20, which has an autograph fragment dated 1771. If Sonata 44 has affinities with no. 18, then it too might belong in the early 1770s, as Georg Feder has argued.[18] The G-minor, like the A-flat-major one of Haydn's most frequently performed and recorded earlier sonatas, is filled with expressive details. Its principal vehicles of motivic unity are the triplet upbeat and "sighing" appoggiaturas of the first group, both used to good effect in subsequent sections of the movement (Ex. 8.4).

EXAMPLE 8.4. Sonata in G Minor Hob. XVI: 44/i. Main theme and climax of development section

(continued)

EXAMPLE 8.4. (*continued*)

In fact, the triplet upbeat generates a true climax of the development section (mm. 46–51). The rapid-fire alternation of left and right hands at the ends of the exposition and recapitulation is not purely for harmonic purposes, as it was in XVI:46/i, but is part of a varied restatement of the closing theme.

The finale of the G-minor sonata adumbrates Haydn's later alternating-variation series, here in the guise of the minuet returning in varied form after a related trio in the opposite mode. But the idea of alternation is not yet fully played out. The openended *maggiore* "trio" that follows the minor theme is almost a variation of it, with identical rhythmic and motivic patterns and similar structures (Ex. 8.5).

EXAMPLE 8.5. Sonata in G Minor Hob. XVI: 44/ii. Beginning of *minore* and *maggiore* ("Minuet" and "Trio")

A varied return to the minor theme puts the segments out of order, and the final appearance of the *maggiore* is partial and coda-like:

$$\text{A} \quad \text{(G minor): } \|: a_v :\|: b \ a_I :\|$$

$$\text{B} \quad \text{(G major): } c_I \mid d \text{ retrans.}$$

$$\text{A}_1 \quad \text{(G minor): } a_v \ a_I{}^1 \mid b^1 \ a_I{}^2$$

$$\text{B}_1 \quad \text{(G major): } c_I \text{ appendix}$$

The brooding C-minor sonata XVI:20 was actually the first of all the sonatas of this period to be published, when Haydn chose to include it in the set dedicated to the Auenbrugger sisters in 1780; at that time he described it as the "longest and most difficult in the set," and he saved it for last.[19] The opening Allegro Moderato movement achieves a pensive tone like that of the G-minor sonata, something Haydn rarely sought in other sonatas, whatever their mode; among the minor-key works, the later E-minor sonata (XVI:34) aims for a disjunctive energy, while the

B-minor and C-sharp-minor sonatas (XVI:32 and 36) maintain a balance between assertive and inward modes of expression. The ability of the C-minor to lose itself in reverie is exemplified not so much by its many dynamic markings and frequent changes in rhythmic activity and texture, but in particular by its composed-out cadenza in both exposition and recapitulation that culminates in a few dreamy Adagio bars (mm. 24–26, to a poignant V_9) before the shock of a forte chord in the bass (Ex. 8.6).

EXAMPLE 8.6. Sonata in C Minor Hob. XVI: 20/i.

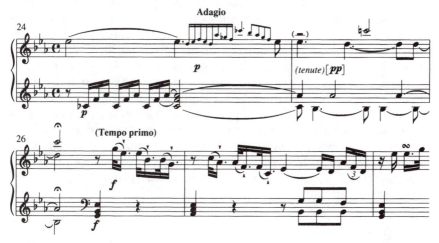

One can almost hear the hand of the composer in the unusually long development section, forcibly stopping the forward motion in order to change harmonic direction (mm. 51–53). Similar to the D-flat Adagio of Sonata 46 in its continuous motion and ornamentation of repeated tones, the Andante con moto of No. 20 creates a special aura with its circular themes and langorous syncopated passages.

The introspective qualities of the first two movements are somewhat mitigated by the faster tempo, sharply pointed articulations, and greater virtuosity (including hand-crossings) of the finale. But the main interest of the Allegro is its curiously redundant sonata-form structure: an ornamented theme reprise after a retransition—what ought to be the recapitulation—leads into an extended passage of harmonic development followed by a second attempt at return, this one ultimately successful. That the impetus for this dual return may be the antecedent-consequent structure of the first theme, as well as the rather jumpy and ungrounded character of the rest of the exposition, suggests a kind of spatial plotting of material. Haydn uses the first six-measure phrase for the "first recapitulation"—after which the digressive material also ends on the dominant—and its second phrase as a "second recapitulation," matching even the lower register of that statement.

The two variation sets that virtually delimit this period—XVII:2 from about 1765 and XVII:3 from sometime between 1770 (when the theme, a minuet in the quartet op. 9/2 was written) and 1774—mark a striking change in Haydn's approach to the form.[20] The A-major set, XVII:2, is of the constant-harmony type of variation, whereby the harmonies and period structure of the theme is maintained in each of the variations, but the theme's melody is only occasionally present in a version either unadorned or decorated; here it appears but once (var. 9, in a middle voice). Presenting many imaginative ways to recast an essentially trivial theme, Haydn also aimed at a comprehensive survey of keyboard technique, with hand-crossings (var. 3), consecutive practice in right-hand and left-hand runs (var. 5, 6), repeated notes (var. 8), octaves (var. 20), and many other kinds of dexterity yoking together compositional and pedagogic interest. The E-flat-major set, by contrast, is primarily a set of melodic-outline variations, in which the main notes of the theme's melody are recognizable, especially at the beginning; only variations 5, 6, and 8 significantly depart from it. Possibly the use of a preexistent theme inspired Haydn to maintain greater similarity to it than in the earlier movement. The cantabile style of several of the variations, in which decorative additions give shading and even poignance to the melodic line (var. 1, 2), contrasts with those in which a given rhythmic figure is pervasive (var. 6, 8).

Three Sets of Six, 1773–1780

In 1773, Haydn departed markedly from his earlier practice of composing sonatas for students and for other private uses, and dedicated six newly composed sonatas to his patron, Prince Nikolaus Esterházy (Hob. XVI:21–26). Six was the canonical number of pieces to be published as a set, and these duly appeared from Kurzböck in Vienna in 1774, marking Haydn's first Viennese publication; they subsequently became well known through Hummel's Berlin edition as op. 13. Despite his respect for his prince, and his desire for a worthy publication—indeed, the first overseen by himself—there are signs of haste in the last sonata of the set (A major, XVI:26). After an ambitious first movement, Haydn simply borrowed the minuet *al rovescio* of Symphony 47 (1772), a learned device in which the second reprises of both minuet and trio consist of the first reprise played backwards. Yet he did not include any of the witty dynamics and slurs that in the symphony had emphasized the strangeness of the retrograde. And the unusually short finale—twenty-six measures—seems more appropriate as the theme of a rondo rather than an entire movement.[21] The autograph manuscript has two significant omissions: neither the middle movement nor Haydn's typical concluding "Laus Deo" at the end of the finale is present.

These six sonatas have been criticized as conservative and conventional, partly because they contain no minor-key work, yet they continue some of the more original features of those just discussed, and add some of their own. Formally speaking, they mark a different kind of exposition, in which the first theme in the dominant articulates a second group (21/i, 24/i), as well as a new external shape for a variation movement (22/iii, 24/iii). The finale of Sonata 22 takes up again the idea of mode alternation together with variation introduced in Sonata 44; this time the alternation is expanded in a second trio and second and third minuet varying the first (ABA₁B₁A₂). The variations on the two returns of the E-major minuet are always presented as varied repeats, but the movement is otherwise unadventurous; when Haydn next turned to alternating variations, in symphonic slow movements of the late 1770s (e.g., Symphonies 63 and 70), his approach was much more imaginative. Yet the brief, open-ended *minore* of Sonata 22 returns with its parts inverted, a contrapuntal ploy perhaps stemming from the invertible counterpoint of the slow variation movement of Symphony 47 (the piece also plundered by Haydn in Sonata 26, as we have just seen). The canonic minuet of Sonata 25 also suggests that the contrapuntal works of 1772, including the op. 20 quartets, were fresh in his mind. And the Presto finale of the D-major sonata XVI:24, with its single variation, actually reverts to a much older stereotype, the dance movement plus *double*, characteristic of the Baroque suite, but with a twist: a da capo (m. 81) that turns into a coda of repetitions and deceptive cadences.

The three minor-mode slow movements in the set (22, 23, 24) show a particularly lovely melodic curve in their opening themes, each of which engages expressively with a high pitch (Ex. 8.7a).

EXAMPLE 8.7a. Slow movements of Sonatas Hob. XVI: 22, 23, 24

XVI: 22/ii

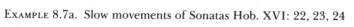

XVI: 23/ii

XVI: 24/ii

That curve in the F-major sonata, XVI:23, resonates with the minor episode in the second group of the first movement (Ex. 8.7b, mm. 29ff), one of its most memorable moments, and which is strategically omitted from the recapitulation. Like the first movement of Sonata 19, the F major employs a variation principle to organize its sonata-form elements, from the varied repetition of the opening phrase, to the enduring principle of progressive diminution of note values in consecutive functional areas of the exposition (first group—eighths and dotted sixteenths; varied repeat—eighths and thirty-second-notes; bridge—sixteenths in both hands; second group—thirty-seconds). In fact it is the decorated repetition of the first four measures that provides figural shapes for the rest of the movement, from the oscillating thirty-second-note upbeat, to the descending arpeggios, to the descending chains of thirds. In this scheme, only the minor passage of the second group has no previous counterpart, and serves instead as a kind of unsuspected anticipation of the Adagio.

EXAMPLE 8.7b. Sonata in F Major Hob. XVI: 23/i. Progressive diminution and minor passage in exposition

The rest of the sonatas of the 1770s were also produced in "sets": the six sonatas, Hob. XVI:27–32, "Anno 1776"—as Haydn identified them in his own catalogue, known as the *Entwurf-Katalog* (Larsen 1979)— which were distributed in manuscript by Viennese copyists and published by Hummel in Berlin as op. 14 (1778), and the six dedicated to the Auenbrugger sisters in 1780, Hob. XVI:35–39, 20, Haydn's first print by the fledgling Viennese house of Artaria. The 1776 set runs two gamuts: the first, of historical style, goes from the austere Baroque counterpoint and walking bass of the Allegretto middle movement of Sonata 31 to the trivially *galant* first movement of the G-major sonata (27), with its Alberti bass pattern, while the second, a gamut of expressive power, ranges from the restrained E-flat-major sonata (28) with its neutral minuet to the powerful B-minor sonata (32) with its ethereal minuet and furiously climactic finale.[22] The last three sonatas are more serious than the first three; Somfai even suggests that the set is arranged in order of increasing technical difficulty, a kind of *Gradus ad Parnassum* of keyboard proficiency (Somfai 1980, 100). Moreover, the variation principle, which had begun to assert itself in the Esterházy set, comes to the fore here: fully five of the six conclude with some type of strophic variation movement, and four of these feature a single variation in the minor mode. Because Haydn's variation movements after 1776 never have more than four variations, a *minore* has the power to reorganize the whole set whether perceived as an episode or as a variation. Rarely decorative, Haydn's *minores* normally do not retain the harmonic structure of the theme, tending instead toward a simple first period moving to the relative major, and then a more complex second period; each is handled somewhat differently. The most interesting of these finales is that of the E-major sonata (31) because the *minore*, which bears no melodic resemblance to the theme, intensifies a move away from the theme already begun in the altered harmonies of the previous (second) variation. In Sonatas 27 and 28, the frequent reprises of the theme melody suggest a rondo-like recycling of the theme, while the *minore* in Sonata 29 is actually an *alla zoppa* trio (unlabeled) to the Tempo di Menuetto with its two variations (ABA_1A_2).

More interesting from the perspective both of movement organization and relationship to earlier movements in the cycle is the sonata in A major, XVI:30, whose Tempo di Menuet finale with six easy variations might easily be (and has been) dismissed as quotidian and unserious. Yet it concludes a sonata in which not a single previous movement came to a final cadence, the first and only such fully linked cycle in Haydn's *oeuvre;*[23] indeed, the theme provides the first structural final cadence in the sonata. That the theme is then followed by six such final cadences in the variations drives home the point emphatically: the finale acts as a kind of reiterated cadential pattern for the sonata as a whole.

Haydn's longest strophic set among the sonatas (six variations, his limit in a variation movement) is punctuated by melodic returns of the theme, varied by means of additions best described by the rhetorical figure *pleonasm*, or superfluous ornamental additions to the original material. Here, pleonastic additions take the form of new contrapuntal lines (as in the second variation) or by additions to the melodic line itself (first variation).[24] The contrasting nature of the first two pleonastic variations reorganizes the set. The first variation (A_1) is closely linked to the theme in bass line and melodic direction, while the contrapuntal second varia-tion (A_2) inaugurates a series of contrapuntal, invention-like variations (Ex. 8.8): A_3 in two parts, A_4 in three parts, a partial disintegration in the arpeggiated flourishes of A_5, a final doubly varied A_6 with both per-iphrasis (see n. 24) and pleonasm.

EXAMPLE 8.8. Sonata in A Major Hob. XVI: 30/iii. Pleonastic variations in invention style

But each of the variations between the first and the last has a kind of dual identity. A_2 is a melodic reprise in the same register as A_6 and so acts as a link between the theme and the end, while A_4, despite its coun-terpoint, returns to the initial melodic pitches and contour of the theme in its original register.

An important consideration in Sonata 30 is the way the finale recalls and perhaps resolves elements of the first two movements, and thus jus-tifies the run-on construction. In the opening Allegro, the eight-measure theme closes in the tonic, only to be followed immediately by another melody in a lower register; the second of these melodies closes with a hunting-fanfare passage that recurs at the end of the exposition. It is this fanfare that is denied with a declamatory flourish at the point of transition into a slow movement. In the finale, not only does A_2 bring back the theme in a lower register, but the final variation, A_6, unites a first reprise in a lower and its varied repeat in a higher register, at the same "heights" as the themes of the Allegro. Secondly, during the Ada-gio—which sustains two-part texture nearly throughout—the left hand has a series of arpeggiations of the same type that appear in the varied repeats of A_6. Since the passages in question in A_6 also recall the eighth-note counterpoints in A_2 and A_4, the reemergence of the slow-movement version at the close of the sonata suggests that those contrapuntal variations were a reclothing of the "archaic" style of the Adagio. Thus, the finale synthesizes the *galant* aspect of the Allegro with the through-composed and *empfindsam* Adagio by means of a kind of *galant* counterpoint. This sonata deserves better than its contemporary reception suggests.[25]

Finally, the B-minor sonata immediately sets the stage for paradoxical effects by its disjunct ascent of an octave and a half over two measures and its simultaneous reversal in expression from aggressively pointed to cantabile.[26] Every element of this theme gives rise to later continuations and development: the bass pattern (elaborated in m. 17ff. and 34ff.), dotted rhythm (extended in m. 10ff. and 39ff.), deceptive cadence (m. 26). The minuet is an oasis after this turbulence, and even has a dreamy dominant ninth like that of the C-minor sonata (mm. 17–20). The trio, on the other hand, plays with darker forces, forecasting the perpetuum mobile of the finale with its incessant turning figures (present in the finale's second group, m. 39ff.). The finale itself is playfully witty yet stark in texture, creating both melodic figures and imitative counterpoints out of accompaniment patterns; even the dotted-rhythm passage in mm. 28–37 contributes to the constant eighth-note pulsation.

The sisters Katharina and Marianna Auenbrugger received the dedication of Haydn's 1780 set of sonatas, Hob. XVI:35–39 and the older C-minor sonata no. 20. Beginning with a C-major sonata still often assigned to beginning pianists, the set reflects Haydn's growing preoccupation with pleasing a wider public. Even the dedication suggests that the set is safe for amateurs. Like the six string quartets, op. 33, "written in a new and special way," published by Artaria the following year, the finales (with the exception of the older C-minor) are mostly in sectional forms: two rondos (35 and 37), one minuet (36), one short Allegro in da capo form (38); only the delightful Prestissimo finale of No. 39 is in sonata form. In addition, the middle movement of Sonata 36 and the first movement of Sonata 39 are easy-to-take rondo-variation types on nearly identical themes, which caused Haydn to fret about the sale and reception of the set (Sisman 1981). Yet a public destination need not imply a necessary weakening in quality, as the addition of Sonata no. 20 ought to make clear. And the first movement of the G-major sonata (39) anticipates the more famous first movement of the G-major piano trio, XV:25 (1795), and even some elements of its concluding "Gypsy Rondo." The best of the remaining pieces include the well-known D major, with its brilliant opening movement and brief Largo, a sarabande of considerable stateliness and pathos, and the Adagio of Sonata 38, a *siciliana* with varied reprises on the C. P. E. Bach model, with Haydn's characteristic omission of the varied repetition of the second section.

Both the C-sharp-minor (36) and E-flat-major (38) have first movements that feature the peculiar digressive style that gives to so much of Haydn's piano music the quality of informal speech. The slightly varied repetition of the opening theme of the E-flat-major finds the means of continuation in the repetition of small rhythmic patterns (repeated notes turning into dotted rhythms turning into turning figures in mm. 8–9), as does the restatement of the main theme in the dominant in m. 13 (using repeated notes to go in a different direction); that the development surprisingly begins with the first of these repeated-note continuations attests to the importance of a seemingly innocuous pattern. Yet the slightly meandering quality of the first group and transition becomes positively dilatory in the second group (mm. 19ff), filled with rests, repetitions, and fermatas, as well as a cadenza-like concluding passage, complete with double trill cadence and punctuating "tutti" chords. In no. 36, both the second group and the development section begin with a variant of the main theme in the relative major (E), which similarly lends an air of developmental circularity related to the variation principle.

The 1780s

Three sonatas published in 1784, but originating at different times and not intended as a set, are XVI:43, 33, and 34; Sonata 33 must have been composed before its dated copies of 1778 and so predates the Auenbrugger set. Sonata 43 has passages in common with the earlier A-flat sonata, XVI:46, as well as the recycling of the opening theme in the dominant just discussed in Sonata 36, while its finale is a rondo-variation with somewhat more playful decoration than that found in Sonata 19. Similarly, Sonata 33 recalls the G-minor sonata 44 with sighing passages in sixteenth-notes instead of eighths, as well as some of the concerto-figures of the 1773 sonatas (arpeggios leading to trill cadences, for example; cf. Sonata 24). Its finale is a more fully developed alternating rondo-variation than the minuet finale of Sonata 22 in that the *minores* are variations of the *maggiore*.

A better example of this kind of movement is the finale of the brilliant and frequently performed E-minor sonata (34). Neither the first variation on the minor theme nor the first on the major theme maintains its structure, so that the overall shape of the movement is varied. With its inexorable momentum and, as in the B-minor, continuously changing expression, the entire first movement goes toward "sustaining [the idea] according to the rules of art," in Haydn's words, involving it in a continuous skein of development, varying first the upbeat (into sixteenth notes), then the downbeat (into an appoggiatura), then combining left and right hands into the new texture of the second theme, and inverting the hands for the retransition.

Haydn's remaining sonatas are the 1784 set of three, nos. 40–42, for Princess Marie Esterházy, the new wife of Prince Nikolaus's grandson Nikolaus (and the dedicatee of his six late masses), two single works of 1789 (XVI:48), written for Breitkopf, and 1790 (XVI:49), written with Marianne von Genzinger in mind, and the three late sonatas, two of which were written for the London pianist Theresa Jansen Bartolozzi. Each of the three of 1784 is in two movements, and again the variation principle dominates, as it did in the 1776 set: both movements of Sonata 40, the finale of Sonata 41 (an ABA variation), and the first movement of Sonata 42 are in some kind of variation form. In fact, beginning with the trio, Hob. XV:5 (1784), nearly every piano trio from this point on also has significant variation, whether in ABA movements or actual variation movements on one or two themes.

The G-major sonata (40) is paradigmatic of the attractive, light, amateur style in sonatas of the period, as evidenced by its "Allegretto e innocente" heading and the swaying 6/8 meter, rarely used either in first movements or in variations (only 47/i and 34/iii, respectively). Yet an examination of the relationship between the major and minor themes reveals a progressive framework (Ex. 8.9).

EXAMPLE 8.9. Sonata in G Major Hob. XVI: 40/i. Relationship of themes

In addition to the swaying pattern of the opening measures, the A theme is characterized by repeated notes, both in its off-downbeat cadences, and in the waiting passage on the dominant in the second reprise (first right hand, then left hand), mm. 12–13. The B theme is clearly derived from the latter passage, but a new motive, the affective half-steps of the third and fourth measures, offers a corrective to the innocence of the A theme. When A₁ returns, the half-steps find their way into the figured accompaniment, now less intense in expressive orientation. In B₁, the half-step becomes an appoggiatura decorating even the opening repeated notes, and the accented half-step passage now turns into an improvisatory outburst, the first such unrestrained activity in the piece. The final two repeated notes, mid-measure, are a subdued final recognition of relationship with the *maggiore*. In the last variation, A₂, the half-steps are again neutralized, and the repeated notes are fully drawn out, intensifying rhythmically and expanding structurally in the second half. The original relationship between themes, their shared repeated notes, is now convincingly emphasized. It is left to the A theme only to take on the improvisatory chord-and-scale outburst of B, but now as a stabilizing cadential force. The theme of the finale may even be read as an intensified variation of both A and B, moving from a compression of the A theme opening together with the repeated notes found throughout the first movement, but particularly in A₂.

The first movement of the D-major Sonata XVI:42 has a highly ornate surface, yet its rests are among its most significant features: they make the theme seem to be caught in the act of its own invention, as befits one of only two movements in the sonatas to be marked "con espressione" (the other being the first movement of Hob. XVI:48).²⁷ After a simple pleonastic variation, the *minore* creates an extraordinary fantasy in overture or preludial style: the contrapuntal, suspension-laden opening actually generates an astonishing climax at the moment the opening passage should return (m. 53), its first three measures compressed in the bass together with powerful figuration (Ex. 8.10).

EXAMPLE 8.10. Sonata in D Major Hob. XVI: 42/i. Theme and *minore*

(*continued*)

EXAMPLE 8.10. (*continued*)

Yet the figures during this last *maggiore* turn to a more virtuosic version of self-creation, in effect uniting the rhetorical modes of both theme and *minore*. How can Haydn follow up such a movement? With a restless Vivace assai that establishes no clear tonic at the onset—indeed, moving immediately to the dominant—and remains harmonically in motion (Ex. 8.11).

EXAMPLE 8.11. Sonata in D Major Hob. XVI: 42/ii.

(*continued*)

EXAMPLE 8.11. (*continued*)

As a two-reprise form, the piece must surely be the most unbalanced ever written: its proportions are ‖ :8: ‖ :93: ‖ ! The first tonic cadence, in measure 45, is deceptive instead, and no other cadence replaces it until measure 87, fourteen measures before the end of the piece. Normal recapitulatory maneuvers are avoided, and every quasi-restatement of the opening bars after the beginnings of the two reprises (mm. 26, 46, 56, 83) leads in a different direction. Beghin views the unusual proportion of the finale as necessary to the sonata understood as "a complete oration" (Beghin 1997).

Like the first movement of Sonata 42, an improvisatory quality pervades the first movement of the C-major Sonata XVI:48 (1789), also Andante con espressione. An unusual five-part construction in which the B-sections are different parallel-minor variants of A, the movement alternates in mode yet is not an alternating variation per se. Rather, it explores the ramifications of its idea in different registers, directions, and modes. Each successive segment takes as its starting point some aspect of the most recent version of A. In the first *minore,* the opening recasts the opening of A in the minor, but, to distance it from the minor phrase after the double bar in A (mm. 11–17), now features imitative entries, and a varied reprise. The returning *maggiore* (A₁) has two varied reprises, and its simplest melodic outline; Brown calls this the "pure form" of the theme (Brown 1986, 340–44). The next *minore* (B₂) continues with the outline, develops the rhythm of its second measure, and instead of a varied reprise a return to the original format of the theme in A-flat major. A bit of A₂ returns to round off the movement.

Works that invent themselves as they go along, as do Sonatas 42 and 48, seem literally to exemplify the stories of Haydn composing at the keyboard (Gotwals, 61, 142; Schafer 1987). His delight in keeping the main idea of Sonata 48 going can be seen in the constant reworkings of the opening two-bar unit, as well as the manifold performance indications. Many of the dynamic inflections seem counterintuitive—for example, the soft closing chords in mm. 9–10, especially the *pp* on the fullest sonority in the theme—and probably were a palpable part of its creation. It is conceivable that the rhetorical approach to performance style, especially the ever-varied presentation of small cells, represents Haydn's conscious attempt to please a north-German audience, hitherto very critical of his works: this sonata was commissioned by Breitkopf in Leipzig, and may represent his first commission for Germany (Landon

Unlike that of Sonata 42, however, the finale of Sonata 48 is a smoothly controlled "textbook example" of a musical form—in this case, sonata-rondo—with witty figures and rhythms similar to the finale of Haydn's Symphony 88 in G major, probably completed in 1787. It is one of Haydn's very few labelled rondos of any sort. While the recapitulatory parts of Haydn's sonata rondos are often extensively recomposed, here the material originally heard in the dominant returns on schedule in the tonic, and since the "second theme" is virtually identical to the main theme, the rondo element is brought even more strongly to the fore, as Table 8.2 makes clear. The table perhaps too schematically represents the first return of the rondo refrain in the tonic (m. 93) as having no counterpart in sonata form; in fact, it might be heard as an incipient repeat of the exposition.

TABLE 8.2
Sonata in C Major, Hob. XVI:48/ii, Rondo: Presto.

Rondo	*Sonata*	
A	[EXP]	Theme 1 ‖ :12: ‖ :18: ‖
B		Bridge, m. 31: closing reiterated; modulates to V; passage on V pedal
		Theme 2, m. 54: Theme 1 in V
		Closing, m. 64: figuration, plus rhythm of A
retrans		m. 88
A	. . .	m. 93, no repeats
C	[DEV]	m. 122: C minor; then modulates and develops motives from A
retrans		m. 166
A	[RECAP]	Theme 1, m. 174, no repeats, truncated second section, conflated with beginning of
B		Bridge, m. 194
(A)		Theme 2 in I, m. 222
		Closing, m. 232
codetta		m. 256

The other work of 1789 for solo piano is the maverick Fantasia in C major Hob. XVII:4, completed in the same month as the C-major sonata; Brown suggests that it might be "successfully combined" with the sonata (Brown 1986, 236). Immediately published by Artaria, its composition was inspired by Haydn's decision to publish his much older Capriccio in G major. The new Fantasia (which he also referred to as a Capriccio in his correspondence) was also based on a folk song (Brown 1986, 226), but possesses a demonic energy and extraordinary keyboard effects not found in the earlier piece. Indeed, as a kind of free, developmental rondo whose first move is to the dominant, but whose shocking dynamic surprises, remote key juxtapositions, disorienting chromaticisms, and breakneck speed completely subvert any sense of traditional order, the Fantasia seems to be the reverse side—the tangled threads and rough edges—of the smooth cloth worn by the rondo finale of Sonata 48; the metaphor seems apt in the context of eighteenth-century descriptions of form which often used the term *Einkleidung* for the formal guise of a movement. Yet the form itself is not that wild (Table 8.3): an exposition with a contrasting theme in the dominant, a beautiful horn-fifths passage sounding from afar; the sudden forte arpeggios in B-flat major are a reminder of the genre of the piece but not an indicator of chaos; a truncated refrain introduces a lengthy development, after which a truncated refrain heralds a recapitulation with some secondar·· development (a term coined by Rosen 1988, 106).

TABLE 8.3
Fantasia in C Major, Hob. XVII:4.

Rondo	Sonata	
A	[EXP]	8 + 8; trans.
B		m. 29 Bridge on A; contrapuntal; V pedal
		m. 70 Second theme, V, horn fifths and neighbor motif
		m. 88 B♭ major "shock" (arpeggios)
A	. . .	m. 124 (first phrase)
C	[DEV]	m. 132 on themes and textures from exposition
		m. 132 imitation on A (cf. Bridge)
		m. 156 on second theme motive
		m. 164 harmonic development of A, to dying bass
		m. 195 on second theme, B♭ major and trans.
		m. 222 on A
A	[RECAP]	m. 255 (first phrase)
dev		m. 263 secondary development on A, C minoɪ- E♭ major/minor-B major, to dying bass
B		m. 305 second theme, I
		m. 324 A⁷-Dm "shock" (arpeggios)
		m. 356 Bridge on A (contrapuntal; developmentally extended; V pedal)
A	[CODA]	m. 453 (codetta)

In simplified terms, which do not deal with the quality and effect of the material, the piece's formal outline is no more than a sonata rondo with secondary development and a fantasia-like "intrusion" into the exposition and recapitulation (the forte arpeggio "shocks"). But Haydn's unprecedented attention to keyboard sonority exacerbates every one of the unusual harmonies and sudden digressions. Especially effective is the bass octave that the performer is enjoined to "let die away" before continuing, in part because the recurrence of the horn-fifth theme at that point reinforces its spatially distant quality (Ex. 8.12).

EXAMPLE 8.12. Fantasia (Capriccio) in C Major Hob. XVII: 4. "Dying" piano sonority, second theme heard from afar

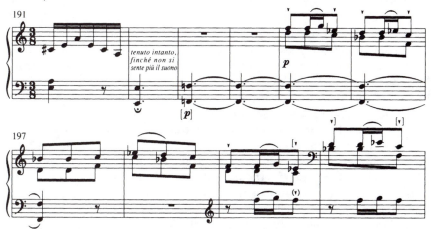

The year 1790 saw the completion of two works for solo piano: the "Genzinger" sonata in E-flat major Hob. XVI:49, begun in 1789, and the little variations in C major on an Andante theme Hob. XVII:5, published by Artaria as "agréables et faciles." That theme is among the most melodically detailed Haydn ever provided for variations, and he adheres very closely to it, even when changing to a march topic (var. 3) or a *minore* (var. 5). Sonata 49 opens with a perfectly proportioned sonata form, one whose concern for detail is already evident in the opening theme: broken thirds in the right hand accompanied by simultaneous thirds in the left, followed by a triadic upbeat in a new rhythm (labeled a, a_1, and b in Ex. 8.13).

EXAMPLE 8.13. Sonata in E-flat Major Hob. XVI: 49/i. Motives of main theme, retransition

(continued)

EXAMPLE 8.13. (*continued*)

Both the second group and the closing group begin with first theme material, a and b respectively; moreover, the closing continues with a_1, then states the anacrustic b motive with repeated thirds, in a passage famously similar to Beethoven's Fifth Symphony. The other crucial element of the exposition is the invention-like texture of the modulatory passage (c), that recurs (together with thirds) in the closing groups; this will become a full-fledged contrapuntal invention at the beginning of the development section, and recalls the E-minor Allegretto of Sonata 31/ii. A combination of these elements, both motive and invention, animates an unusually long coda at the end of the movement. And some of the three-note upbeats found in the transitions of the Tempo di Menuet finale seem to recall the b motive of the first movement.

The slow movement of Sonata 49 affords an interesting view of Haydn's late techniques of varied repetition. In a letter to Marianne von Genzinger of 20 June 1790, Haydn described the Adagio as "quite new . . . [and] contains many things which I shall analyze for Your Grace when the time comes; it is rather difficult but full of feeling. It's a pity, however, that Your Grace has not one of Schantz's fortepianos, for Your Grace could then produce twice the effect" (Landon 1976–1980, 2:744). An ABA form in which the turn to minor in the second period of A increases the density of minor mode even before the contrasting B section (as in 48), Sonata 49/ii is as "decorative" as Sonata 48 in its elaborations of the opening phrase, but every aspect of the melodic contour is smoother and more controlled. And its B-section, far from intensifying the varying of A, is a completely new *Gestalt:* in fact, its subject is a variant of the principal two-bar unit of Sonata 48/i! What the A sections of Sonata 49 have, and what Sonata 48 lacks, is a sense of the roundedness of each melodic particle, one of the conventions of late eighteenth-century phrase- and period-structure that enabled passages to cohere and conclude.

The Last Works

Of Haydn's last three sonatas, the justly celebrated "Grand Sonata" in E-flat major, Hob. XVI:52, was written for the virtuoso pianist—surely the most accomplished of his lady dedicatees—Therese Jansen

Bartolozzi in 1794, as the autograph attests.[28] Powerfully evoking the sound of the larger English piano that was later to inspire Beethoven, this is a grand work indeed that announces itself as such from its first sonorities, the densely spaced opening chords. The C-major (no. 50) was also linked to Bartolozzi in its first edition, but the D-major (no. 51) has no such documentary trail and may have been written for another lady.[29] Indeed, the D-major sonata does not apparently "belong" with the other two in that it is a two-movement work that recalls the D-major sonata of the previous decade (no. 42), in its Andante-fast binary movement combination; it was not published until 1805. The circularities of the Andante, a sonata movement without repeat signs that flirts with sonata-rondo in its return to the main theme before the development, distract one from the uneasy juxtaposition of assertive, "noise-killer" opening theme, and Schubertian cantabile sequel;[30] it is the latter style that predominates in the movement but the former that calls forth Haydn's characteristic varied restatements.

In Sonata 50, the variation principle embodied in the opening theme comes to dominate the movement, and calls for a dazzling array of pianistic effects, including the pianissimo open pedal in the development section that is later elaborated in the recapitulation; the modern grand piano cannot do justice to this sound. In fact, the idea of variation permeates all three movements, in what might be called thematic, ornamental, and motivic concepts, respectively. In the opening Allegro, varying the main theme in different functional areas of the sonata form becomes an intellectual puzzle solved by means of different textures and sequels (Ex. 8.14a).

EXAMPLE 8.14. Sonata in C Major Hob. XVI: 50. Types of variation in (a) first movement and (b) third movement

a. XVI: 50:1

(*continued*)

EXAMPLE 8.14. (*continued*)

b. XVI: iii. Second period

(*continued*)

EXAMPLE 8.14. (*continued*)

In the Adagio, variation serves as the rhapsodic sweep of new figurations, draped ever more luxuriantly as the movement progresses; and in the Finale, the main idea varies itself as it tries to generate enough of a consequent for a convincing cadence, yet keeps going hilariously wrong (Ex. 8.14b). This last movement is uncannily like the minuet of the B-minor string quartet, op. 64 no. 2, written in 1790, which uses the same rhythmic motives (𝅘𝅥 | 𝅘𝅥 𝅘𝅥 𝅘𝅥 | 𝅘𝅥𝅮 𝅘𝅥𝅮𝅘𝅥𝅮) to exciting contrapuntal and dissonant effect.

The big E-flat-major sonata XVI:52 occupies a category of its own in Haydn's keyboard oeuvre both because it is so frequently performed and recorded, and because its virtuosity and sweeping sonorities seem the wave of the future; it is the only one of Haydn's sonatas to seem "Beethovenian," in the sense usually reserved for invidious comparisons of the two composers. (The opening harmonic gesture of XVI:52 is the same as that of Beethoven's E-flat-major piano trio, op. 1/1, written at about the same time: I-V^7/IV-IV in the key of E-flat. This, however, does not reflect the scope of "Beethovenian.") Schenker analyzed it; Tovey graced it with an extended essay; and Leonard Ratner made it the subject of an entire chapter, a treatment he otherwise accorded only to Mozart's *Don Giovanni*.[31] Ratner's analysis is based on the magisterial resources of the rest of his work on topics, the individual stylistic codes that made the Classical musical language intelligible to its audience, and suggests that the character of the first movement emerges from a rapid-fire exchange of such topics, from the French overture style of the opening dotted rhythms and its *stile legato* sequel (mm. 6–8), to music box effects in horn fifths (second group, m. 27 and development), "brilliant" style (thirty-second-note passages), *Empfindsamkeit* (the sensitive shading of m. 3), a brief evocation of the supernatural in the operatic *ombra* (mm. 37, 111), and the familiar Turkish style (m. 29, m. 101). Topical analysis offers important perspectives for performers.

One of the most striking aspects of the first movement is its *spatial* quality, brought about by a dazzling manipulation of register, dynamics, and sonority. For example, the registral opposition between the massive opening chords and their delicate echo in m. 3 is not brought into balance and allowed to achieve closure until m. 10: first the echo generates a run in thirds that ushers in the sequel phrase (Ratner's *stile legato,* m. 6) with a deceptive cadence, another cadential elision with a return to the opening flourish an octave higher, and only then a sweeping gesture that unites the elements, "an impulsive run down nearly four octaves of scale," in Tovey's words. That each of these particles creates some kind of linkage with the next idea is significant in creating a tissue of development throughout the movement—even the closure in m. 10 is immediately countered by a return to the sequel in a higher register with its parts inverted so that what had previously been accompaniment is now a plaintive series of appoggiaturas in the right hand. The first "unlinked" passage is thus the second theme, a combination of horn fifths and music-box sonority (m. 27), now marked as a new point of departure. Moreover, by virtue of its soft dynamics, high register, and especially the horn fifths, this theme is heard as though from afar (as was the second theme of the C-major Fantasia). These aspects of the second theme are precisely the ones exploited by Haydn in the development section, in which it functions as a frame. Both the C-major/F-major entry in m. 46 and the notorious E-major/A-major entry in m. 68 are set off by a G-major chord preparing C minor, grounded in a low register and dying away with a fermata; thus they sound far in the distance as well as far from the expected key or mode.

Much has been made of the preparation for the key of the slow movement, E major, by the appearance of the "music-box" theme in that key already in the first movement.[32] This works out nicely on paper but it is fair to say that only the *fact* of being tonally shocked really prepares the listener to expect subsequent shocks, not the esoteric reinterpretive possibility of a particular key. A similarly celebrated moment is the restoration of E-flat at the beginning of the finale by a theme that repeats an unharmonized third degree, G, a moment that contradicts the E-major final cadence of the slow movement with a kind of grotesque good humour, given emphasis by the jabbing and apparently anacrustic repeated notes. Was this effect "prepared" by the middle section of the Adagio in G major, or the righthand repeated notes that accompanied a lefthand restatement of the theme in that movement? Or is the joke that the theme is immediately repeated on the supertonic, with the repeated notes now A-flats, the no-longer-recognizable G-sharp of the Adagio? Such long-range harmonic "clues" again seem farfetched. More important is the central role the repeated notes take on in the course of the movement: like the finale of Sonata 48, all the principal themes here employ variants of that same eighth-note rhythm in repeated notes, the second theme (m. 44) and closing theme (m. 78) adding jolting sforzatos on the upbeats. The hammering quality is particularly effective in light of the contrasting fleet-fingered toccata passages of mm. 65–77, 146–170, and 267–281. The identical chords end the first and third movements.

The most intensely moving of Haydn's keyboard works, indeed one of his greatest works in any genre, is the famous Andante in F minor for piano Hob. XVII:6, written between the two London visits in 1793. Its lengthy and finely etched minor theme sounds more like a character piece than a variation theme from the first plaintive dotted rhythms, which dominate the melancholy proceedings. The major theme, in contrast, is more playful and pastoral, more delicately figured and thinner in texture than the *minore*. Every variation employs a more or less standard type of figuration (e.g., scales, turning figures), but the syncopation of A_1 with accented offbeat appoggiaturas increases the theme's evocative qualities. Sources of scholarly controversy about the piece are the linked questions of its titles and the versions embodied in the autograph. Some authentic sources including the autograph call it "Sonate," while an authentic copy dedicated to the former Mozart pupil Barbara Ployer is headed "un piccolo divertimento," perhaps reflecting Haydn's sometimes excessive modesty, documented by visitors throughout his life. Moreover, the work underwent several revisions that affected its structure and level of expression (Sisman 1993, 193–94; Plantinga and Johnson [1994]). The original format was an alternating strophic-variation set $(ABA_1B_1A_2B_2)$ in six parts, at which point Haydn may well have intended to write more movements to make a sonata; first-movement precedents to that time for alternating strophic variations include the C-minor Piano Trio Hob. XV: 13, and the F-minor String Quartet op. 55 no. 2; models with a five-part alternation include Sonatas 40 and 48. In all the authentic sources, the original five-measure ending in F major after the last B-variation was never crossed out, and appears before the theme reprise and coda; it has been published in the Hoboken catalogue (1:791) and in the *Wiener Urtext Edition* by Franz Eibner (1975). But the addition of a theme reprise and coda did more than simply create a unique seven-part alternating set. Instead, these additions, especially the coda, at first match and then surpass the minor theme in intensity. Arising as an emotion-filled interruption of the reprise, the coda gains in power until it propels itself into a cadenza-like outburst, and yields to the close of the reprise, now transfigured (Ex. 8.15). Its insistence upon diminished-seventh chords and intervals associate it unmistakably with the so-called pathetic style.[33]

EXAMPLE 8.15. Variations in F Minor Hob XVII: 6. Coda

[End of theme reprise]

(continued)

EXAMPLE 8.15. (*continued*)

What makes the coda special, beyond its obvious and unprecedented chromaticism, is that it concentrates only on the dotted motive
of the theme, the single most rhetorically powerful gesture of the piece.
Part of the tension in the relationship between minor and major themes
is that the tolling tonic pitch of A is disregarded by B for nearly its entirety. Yet at the same time, the B theme appropriates other elements of
A: the successive thirds of B are a closely written variation of the *minore's*
lefthand accompaniment, and B shares a similarly strong directional
opening evolving into more complicated figures. B is necessary as a
digression from A, however, not as its antithesis. The meaning of B is
made clear in the five-measure codetta in major after B₂ that Haydn
never actually canceled: to reiterate the cadence flourish of A₂ and thus
temporarily to bring those themes onto common ground, before safely
abandoning B entirely. In thus yoking together the more expressive with
the more formally conventional modes of the Classical style, Haydn
achieved his most intimate voice in variations and, at the same time, at
the keyboard.

Notes

1. Letter of 29 March 1789, concerning the piano trio in C minor,
Hob.XV:13; *Joseph Haydn: Gesammelte Briefe und Aufzeichnungen*, ed. Dénes Bar-

tha (Kassel, 1965), 202; translation differs slightly from H. C. Robbins Landon, *The Collected Correspondence and London Notebooks of Joseph Haydn* (London, 1959), 82.

2. *Joseph Haydn Werke XVIII: Klaviersonaten,* ed. Georg Feder, 3 vols. (Munich, 1966–1970), also issued as a Henle Urtext Edition (Joseph Haydn, *Sämtliche Klaviersonaten* [Munich, 1972]).

3. Feder also distinguishes between genres that are more serious or less serious, sometimes based on intended recipient. See "Probleme einer Neuordnung der Klaviersonaten Haydns," in *Festschrift Friedrich Blume zum 70. Geburtstag,* ed. Anna Amalie Abert and Wilhelm Pfannkuch (Kassel, 1963), 92–103, and "Die beiden Pole im Instrumentalschaffen des jungen Haydn," in *Der junge Haydn,* ed. Vera Schwarz (Graz, 1972), 192–201.

4. Anthony van Hoboken, *Joseph Haydn: Thematisch-bibliographisches Werkverzeichnis,* 3 vols. (Mainz, 1957–1971), 1: 733–81.

5. Christa Landon, ed., *Haydns Klaviersonaten* (Vienna, 1966).

6. See Georg Feder's worklist in James Webster and Georg Feder, *The New Grove Haydn* (London and New York); the critical reports to both the C. Landon and Feder editions; Brown 1986, chap. 3, "Authenticity"; and the Round Table on the Raigern sonatas in *Haydn Studies,* ed. Jens Peter Larsen, Howard Serwer, and James Webster (New York, 1981), 107–20.

7. Haydn's autograph manuscript, the only extant autograph of an early sonata, lacks the fourth movement. Hob. XVI:8 also has four movements.

8. Landon and Jones 1988, 70. All the musical chapters in this book are by the latter, while Landon's chapters abridge the documentary material in his *Haydn: Chronicle and Works* (Bloomington, IN, 1976–1980).

9. Brown 1986, 14. He gives the text of the folksong.

10. Brown suggests that its key scheme corresponds to Bach's remarks on the free fantasia in his *Versuch über die wahre Art das Clavier zu spielen;* see Brown 1986, 221–26.

11. The relevant documents are set out in Brown 1986, 203–205.

12. See Brown 1986, chap. 7; *idem,* "Joseph Haydn and C. P. E. Bach: The Question of Influence," in *Haydn Studies,* 158–64; and for the latter view, for example, Bettina Wackernagel, *Joseph Haydns frühe Klaviersonaten* (Tutzing, 1975).

13. In all matters of chronology, this essay follows Georg Feder's worklist in the revised *New Grove Dictionary* (London, 2001), 11: 204–63. Reprinted in *The New Grove Haydn* (London and New York, 2002).

14. A. Peter Brown collects all the available evidence of instruments in Haydn's milieu as well as his terminology and the internal evidence of the sonatas in Brown 1986, chap. 5, "The Question of Keyboard Idiom."

15. See Elaine R. Sisman, "Haydn's Theater Symphonies," *Journal of the American Musicological Society* 43 (1990): 292–352.

16. Based on the "solo" range and on Haydn's increasing involvement with compositions for baryton between 1766 and 1769, I have suggested the similarity of this movement to a baryton concerto, in "Haydn's Baryton Pieces and his Serious Genres," *Internationaler Joseph Haydn Kongress Wien 1982,* ed. Eva Badura-Skoda (Munich, 1986), 429–30.

17. László Somfai refers to these two-movement works as "Ladies' Sonatas (*Damensonaten*); see Somfai 1995, 174, 178–79.

18. A. Peter Brown summarizes scholarly suggestions in Brown 1986, 120.

19. Letter to Artaria of 31 January 1780; *Haydn Briefe,* 89. The other sonatas were published in the late 1780s.

20. For more on Haydn's variations, see Sisman 1993. On the different versions and textual variants of XVII:2, which exist in a G-major and A-major version with either twelve or twenty variations, see Brown 1986, 88–92.

21. See Somfai 1980, 9In. I disagree with Somfai's opinion (p. 99) that the two-movement format of the E♭-major sonata, no. 25, is another sign of haste, given the complex canonic aspect of the Tempo di Menuet as well as the precedents in Sonatas 18 and 44.

22. The E-major piano trio Hob. XV:28 (1795) also has a Baroque-style walking-bass middle movement in E minor.

23. Other sonatas have slow movements that lead directly to their finales; of interest is the fact that 24, 30, 31, and 33 have concluding variation movements. A study that deals with the issues raised by linked cycles is James Webster, *Haydn's "Farewell" Symphony and the Idea of Classical Style: Through-Composition and Cyclic Integration in his Instrumental Music* (Cambridge, 1991).

24. When the original notes are replaced rather than augmented by new figures, we may use the rhetorical term *periphrasis* to describe it; in the periphrastic parts of this movement, the shape of the figuration has been altered. For a rhetorical interpretation of this movement, see Sisman 1993, chap. 2, "The Rhetoric of Variation."

25. Outside of its run-on nature, Brown calls the sonata "conservative" and "commonplace." Brown 1986, 308, 312.

26. This sonata has been characterized as "masculine" by Eva Badura-Skoda ("Haydn, Mozart, and Their Contemporaries," in *Keyboard Music,* ed. Denis Matthews [New York, 1972], 133), and as "not for the fair sex" by David Wyn Jones (in Landon and Jones 1988, 167).

27. Haydn used this marking very rarely in instrumental music (a flute trio, Hob. IV: 10/i, with similar rests in the melodic line, and the overture to *Philemon und Baucis,* Hob. XXIXb Nr. 2), but rather more often in vocal music: 31 Scottish songs (Hob. XXXIa); 8 Welsh songs (Hob. XXXIb); and the celebrated Lied with piano "She never told her love," Largo assai e con espressione.

28. See Strunk 1934. She was still Theresa Jansen at the time, not marrying Bartolozzi until 1795.

29. Jerald C. Graue convincingly separated the E-fiat from the other two on documentary grounds. See Graue 1981. Brown suggests that no. 51 might have been composed any time during the London years. See Brown 1986, 54–55.

30. Somfai proposes the term "noise-killer" for opening chords of some of Haydn's London string quartets, in "The London Revision of Haydn's Style," *Proceedings of the Royal Musical Association* 100 (1974): 159–74. Graue suggests that "Dussekian" is as valid as the commonly used "Schubertian"; see Graue 1981, 429.

31. Heinrich Schenker, "Haydn: Sonate Es Dur," *Der Tonwille* 1 (1922): 3–21; Donald Francis Tovey, "Haydn, Pianoforte Sonata in E-fiat, No. 1" (1900), in *Essays in Musical Analysis: Chamber Music* (Oxford, 1972; first pub. 1944), 93–105; Leonard Ratner, *Classic Music,* 412–21. See also Lawrence K. Moss, "Haydn's Sonata Hob XVI:52 (ChL. 62) in E-fiat Major: An Analysis of the First Movement," in *HS,* 496–501.

32. Among the writers who comment are Rosen, *The Classical Style*, 115 and 441; Tovey, "Haydn Sonata in E-flat," 100, 102–3; Ratner, *Classic Music*, 416; Moss, "Haydn's Sonata Hob. XVI:52," 500–501; Brown, *Haydn's Keyboard Music*, 361.

33. See Elaine R. Sisman, "Pathos and the *Pathétique:* Rhetorical Stance in Beethoven's C-minor Piano Sonata, op. 13," *Beethoven Forum* 3 (1994), 81–105.

Literature Cited and Selected Bibliography

Note: An extensive bibliography is included in Brown 1986.

Agawu, V. Kofi. "Haydn's Tonal Models: The first movement of the piano sonata in E-flat major, Hob. XVI:52." In *Convention in Eighteenth- and Nineteenth-Century Music. Essays in Honor of Leonard G. Ratner*, ed. Wye J. Allanbrook et al., pp. 3–22. Stuyvesant, NY, 1992.

Badura-Skoda, Eva. "Haydn, Mozart, and Their Contemporaries." Trans. Margaret Bent. In *Keyboard Studies*, ed. Denis Matthews, pp. 108–65. New York, 1978. (First published 1972).

Beghin, Tom. "Haydn as Orator: A Rhetorical Analysis of His Keyboard Sonata in D Major, Hob. XVI:42." In *Haydn and His World*, ed. Elaine Sisman, pp. 204–54. Princeton, 1997.

Brown, A. Peter. *Joseph Haydn's Keyboard Music: Sources and Style*. Bloomington, IN, 1986.

————. "Critical Years for Haydn's Instrumental Music." *The Musical Quarterly* (hereafter *MQ*) 62 (1976): 374–94.

————. "The Structure of the Exposition in Haydn's Keyboard Sonatas." *Music Review* (hereafter *MR*) 36 (1975): 102–29.

————. "Joseph Haydn and C. P. E. Bach: The Question of Influence." In *Haydn Studies* (hereafter *HS*), ed. Jens Peter Larsen, Howard Serwer, and James Webster, pp. 158–64. New York, 1981.

Broyles, Michael. "The Two Instrumental Styles of Classicism." *Journal of the American Musicological Society* (hereafter *JAMS*) 36 (1983): 210–42.

Feder, Georg. "Probleme einer Neuordnung der Klaviersonaten Haydns." In *Festschrift Friedrich Blume zum 70. Geburtstag*, ed. Anna Amalie Abert and Wilhelm Pfannkuch, 92–103. Kassel, 1963.

————. "A Comparison of Haydn's and Mozart's Keyboard Music." *HS*, 414–15.

————. "Haydns frühe Klaviertrios: Eine Untersuchung zur Echtheit und Chronologie." *Haydn-Studien* (hereafter *HSt*) 2 (1969–1970): 289–316.

Fillion, Michelle. "Sonata-Exposition Procedures in Haydn's Keyboard Sonatas." *HS*, 475–81.

————. "Scoring and Genre in Haydn's Divertimenti Hob. XIV." *Internationaler Joseph Haydn Kongress Wien 1983 (hereafter JHK)*, ed. Eva Badura-Skoda, pp. 435–44. Munich, 1986.

Gotwals, Vernon. *Haydn: Two Contemporary Portraits*. Madison, WI, 1968. Contains translations of Georg August Griesinger, *Biographische Notizen über Joseph Haydn* (Leipzig, 1810), and Albert Christoph Dies, *Biographische Nachrichten über Joseph Haydn* (Vienna, 1810).

Graue, Jerald C. "Haydn and the London Pianoforte School." *HS*, 422–31.

Kleindienst, Sigrid. "Haydns Clavier-Werke. Kriterien der Instrumentenwahl." *JHK,* 53–64.

Komlós, Katalin. "Haydn's Keyboard Trios Hob. XV: 5–17: Interaction between Texture and Form." *Studia Musicologica* 26 (1987): 351–400.

————. "The Viennese Keyboard Trio in the 1780s: Sociological Background and Contemporary Reception." *Music and Letters* (hereafter *ML)* 68 (1987): 222–34.

Landon, H. C. Robbins. *Haydn: Chronicle and Works.* 5 vols. Bloomington, IN, 1976–1980.

————, and David Wyn Jones. *Haydn: His Life and Music.* Bloomington, IN, 1988.

Larsen, Jens Peter. "Sonata-Form Problems." In *Essays on the Handel, Haydn, and the Viennese Classical Style,* trans. Ulrich Kramer, 269–79. Ann Arbor, MI, 1988.

————. *The New Grove Haydn.* Worklist by Georg Feder. New York, 1983.

————. *Three Haydn Catalogues.* 2nd ed. New York, 1979.

LaRue, Jan. "Multistage Variance: Haydn's Legacy to *Beethoven.*" *Journal of Musicology* (hereafter *JM)* 1 (1982): 265–74.

Loesser, Arthur. *Men, Women, and Pianos: A Social History.* New York, 1954.

Moss, Lawrence K. "Haydn's Sonata Hob. XVI:52 (ChL. 62) in E-flat Major: An Analysis of the First Movement." *HS,* 496–501.

Neubacher, Jürgen. "'Idee' und 'Ausführung.' Zum Kompositionsprozess bei Joseph Haydn." *Archiv für Musikwissenschaft* 41 (1984): 187–207.

Newman, William S. *The Sonata in the Classic Era.* 3rd edition. New York, 1985.

————. "Haydn as Ingenious Exploiter of the Keyboard." *JHK,* 43–53.

Petty, Wayne C. "Cyclic Integration in Hayden's Eb Piano Sonata Hob. XVI:38." *Theory and Practice* 19 (1994): 31–55.

Plantinga, Leon, and Glenn Pierr Johnson. "Haydn's *Andante con variazioni:* Compositional Process, Text, and Genre." In *The Creative Process,* Studies in the History of Music 3. New York, 1992, 129–67.

Radice, Mark A. "Haydn and his Publishers: A Brief Survey of the Composer's Publishing Activities." *MR* 44 (1983): 87–94.

Ratner, Leonard. *Classical Music: Expression, Form, and Style.* New York, 1980.

Ripin, Edwin M. "Haydn and the Keyboard Instruments of his Time," *HS,* 302–308.

Roscoe, Christopher. "Haydn and London in the 1780s." *ML* 49 (1968): 203–12.

Rosen, Charles. *The Classical Style.* New York, 1971.

————. *Sonata Forms.* Revised edition. New York, 1988.

Schafer, Hollace. "'A Wisely-Ordered Phantasie': Joseph Haydn's Creative Process from the Sketches and Drafts for Instrumental Music." Ph.D. dissertation, Brandeis University, 1987.

Schönfeld, Johann Ferdinand. *Jahrbuch der Tonkuust von Wien und Prag.* Vienna, 1796. Facsimile, ed. Otto Biba. Munich-Salzburg, 1976.

Schwarz, Vera. "Missverständnisse in der Haydn-Interpretation, Dargestellt an Beispielen aus seiner Klaviermusik." *Österreichische Musikzeitschrift* 31 (1976): 25–35.

Shamgar, Beth. "Rhythmic Interplay in the Retransitions of Haydn's Piano Sonatas." *JM* 3 (1984): 55–68.

Sisman, Elaine R. *Haydn and the Classical Variation.* Cambridge, MA, 1993.

————. "Tradition and Transformation in the Alternating Variations of Haydn and Beethoven." *Acta Musicologica* 62 (1990): 152–82.

————. "Haydn's Hybrid Variations." *HS*, 509–15.

Somfai, László. "Opus-Planung und Neuerung bei Haydn." *Studia Musicologica* 22 (1980): 87–110.

————. *The Keyboard Sonatas of Joseph Haydn: Instruments and Performance Practice, Genres and Styles.* Trans. by the author and Charlotte Greenspan. Chicago, 1995.

Strunk, Oliver. "Notes on a Haydn Autograph." *MQ* 20 (1934): 192–205.

Sutcliffe, W. Dean. "Haydn's Piano Trio Textures." *Music Analysis* 6 (1987): 319–32.

————. "The Haydn Piano Trio: Textual Facts and Textual Principles." In *Haydn Studies*, ed. W. Dean Sutcliffe, pp. 246–90. Cambridge, 1998.

Tovey, Donald Francis. "Haydn's Pianoforte Sonata in E Flat, No. 1 (1790)." *Essays in Musical Analysis: Chamber Music.* London, 1951.

Walter, Horst. "Haydns Klaviere." *HSt* 2 (1970): 256–88.

————. "Haydn's Keyboard Instruments." *HS*, 213–16.

Webster, James. "The Triumph of Variability: Haydn's Articulation Markings in the Autograph of Sonata No. 49 in E flat." In *Haydn, Mozart, & Beethoven. Studies in Music of the Classical Period. Essays in Honour of Alan Tyson*, ed. Sieghard Brandenburg, pp. 33–64. Oxford, 1998.

CHAPTER NINE

Mozart's Solo Keyboard Music

Robert D. Levin

Mozart's first surviving compositions, written when he was five, were for solo keyboard. Although an accomplished violinist and violist, he was renowned first and foremost as a keyboard virtuoso, continuing to write concertos for his favorite instrument until the year of his death.

Mozart's legacy as a keyboard composer reflects the social and commercial uses made of keyboard music. A favorite instrument for amateurs, the keyboard (harpsichord, clavichord, fortepiano) was the center of music-making in the home, and demand for solo works (later, for chamber music with keyboard) was brisk. Thus, whereas Mozart's concertos were primarily conceived for his own use in his subscription concerts, his sonatas and shorter pieces were for the most part written with the public in mind.

Mozart's solo keyboard repertoire consists of twenty piano sonatas, a number of sonata fragments, three rondos, fourteen[1] sets of variations (primarily on themes by other composers), several fantasias, numerous fugues and fugue fragments, a large body of short pieces (including his earliest compositions and the London sketchbook K.15a–15tt), and dances transcribed from original versions for orchestra.[2]

Compositional Fundamentals: Improvisation and Variation

In evaluating this legacy it is essential to bear in mind the primacy of keyboard improvisation in Mozart's career. Clues to his style of improvisation are to be found in virtually every keyboard genre he cultivated. The first movement of the C-major Sonata K.279, is a typical example of spontaneously created music preserved in polished form. In it, structural rigor yields to constantly shifting textures and melodic ideas; its evident appetite for variety and impulsiveness reflects the aesthetic of improvisation. The fantasies in D minor K.397 (unfinished),[3] in C major (actually a praeludium) with fugue K.394, and in C minor K.475, reveal an evolution from a keyboard style closely related to that of C. P. E. Bach[4] to a less impulsive, more structurally coherent succession of sections.[5]

The most fascinating glimpse into the world of Mozart's improvisation is provided by the modulating preludes he composed in 1777 at the instigation of his sister, Nannerl.[6] These highly whimsical fragments, mostly without meter, reveal a side of Mozart's temperament not found in any other music by him, including the cadenzas to the piano concertos (Ex. 9.1).

EXAMPLE 9.1. Mozart: Modulating Prelude K.deest + 624/626a, Part II, I: Anhang C 15.11. Opening section

Mozart's letters refer to more preludes than have come down to us. Altogether we have five:

A. Four preludes K.284a, formerly known as the Capriccio in C K.395/300g (October 1777):

1. C major to B-flat major (a modulation specifically requested by Nannerl in her letter of 28 September 1777 to Wolfgang)
2. B-flat major to E-flat major (actually starting on a dominant seventh in E-flat)
3. E-flat major to C minor (actually starting on a D-flat major sixth chord)
4. C major labeled *Capriccio* and containing flashy passage work[7]

All four preludes end with incomplete measures: a quarter-note chord with fermata and a double bar. This shows that the former practice of playing the four together as a single work, rather than as connective tissue linking other pieces in the prescribed keys, was incorrect.

B. A modulating prelude, ca. 1776–1777, from F major through E minor to C major (Ex. 9.1). The first leaf of the manuscript, notated on one side and containing the passage from F major to E minor, became separated from the rest of the prelude. This had two consequences: (1) the first part is not mentioned in any edition of the Köchel catalogue, whereas the second part was once catalogued among the piano concerto cadenzas (K.624/626a Anh. I), then mistakenly catalogued as "spurious/dubious" in the 6th edition (K[6] Anh. C 15.11); (2) the two parts are published separately in the only published edition, that of the NMA.[8]

The elaborate surface of these preludes is constructed on harmonic progressions easily denoted as a figured bass. This Baroque procedure is described in detail by C. P. E. Bach in the last chapter of his famous treatise, devoted to the free fantasy. Indeed, Nannerl's attempts at sketching such figured bass progressions is documented on the last page of the prelude just described.[9]

The influence of improvisation is also evident in the keyboard variations. Mozart's first sets of variations (K.24, K.25) date from his first European tour (1766). These, like many of his subsequent sets, display the conventional approach to variations: the tune is given a succession of increasingly active accompaniments or melodic guises, punctuated by various textural devices (syncopation, imitation, dotted rhythms, crossed hands); a *minore* variation and a slow, highly decorated one are likewise standard features. This casual, rather superficial approach may approximate the way Mozart improvised variations on given themes in his public appearances. There is an obvious brilliance and *Affekt* to these works, some of which (e.g., the "Fischer" variations K.179/189a) Mozart often performed as display pieces. Only later did he develop an interest in the variations genre as a vessel for serious expression and compositional imagination—especially within sonatas, quartets, and concertos, where the decision to use variation form is voluntary. Nonetheless, a number of the sets of variations are more than mere display pieces. Among the more distinguished are those on "Je suis Lindor" K. 354/299a (spring or summer 1778), "Lison dormait" K.264/315d (late summer or autumn 1778); "Les Hommes pieusement" ("Unser dummer Pöbel meint") K.455 (August 1784);[10] "Ein Weib ist das herrlichste Ding" K.613 (March 1791); and the perfectly shaped Andante with five variations for piano duet in G major K.501 (4 November 1786).[11]

Early Keyboard Compositions

In the 1760s, when Mozart began composing his first pieces, dance movements in binary form, inherited from the Baroque era, provided the primary structural mold. After the first tentative short pieces (K.1a–1d) we see a succession of minuets and binary miniatures of similar shape (K.1/1e, 2–3, 5a, 5b; the piece in F major K.33B is likewise binary). Almost immediately, however, Mozart began composing sonatas. These, too, contained movements in binary form; a *rondeau* finale with its couplets (episodes) constitutes an occasional exception. Reflecting the taste of the time, Mozart's first such efforts were keyboard sonatas with violin accompaniment (K.6–9 and K.26–31) and sonatas with *ad libitum* violin or flute and cello (K.10–15). These early works can be performed as solo pieces without qualms: the *ad libitum* lines are not superfluous, but scarcely indispensable.

Like much of the keyboard music of the time, the left hand in these compositions is almost unrelievedly dependent on the Alberti bass. They would seem to have been corrected and revised by his father, for they display none of the frequent voice leading anomalies and gaucheries found among the solo keyboard pieces and *particella* versions of orchestral music contained in the London sketchbook (K.15a–15tt). Leopold's role as advisor, editor, and teacher is also reflected in the presence of a minuet from his Serenade in D in Wolfgang's Piano and Violin Sonata K.6,[12] and in Wolfgang's piano concerto arrangements, K.37, 39–41, and 107. (See chapter 10.)

Even allowing for Leopold's guidance and revisions, the sixteen sonatas K.6–9, 10–15, and 26–31, are more conventional reflections of contemporary norms than significant contributions to the genre. Most of them are performed, when at all, because of the identity of their composer rather than for their inherent worth. Nonetheless, they attest to the child's seemingly effortless and unfathomable ability to grasp all of the stylistic conventions and compositional devices that mature musicians around him were employing. In addition to the standard fast outer movements and cantabile middle movements and minuets, there are the occasional character pieces (the "carillon" trio, for example, in the Sonata for Piano and Violin/Flute in C K.14).[13]

Munich, 1775: Six Sonatas K.279–284

Mozart's first abiding contribution to the piano sonata repertoire is the set of six works K.279–284 (K⁶189d-e-f-g-h, 205b), now dated to Munich, 1775.[14] The grouping of six and the deliberate tonal layout of descending, then ascending fifths from C major through F, B-flat and E-flat, then G and D, reflect Baroque tradition. Their variety of texture, rhythm, character, and structure reveals not a precocious nineteen-year-old, but a mature, thoroughly secure composer. The phrases unfold in succession in a skillful way; interruptions and elisions avoid the monotony of constant 4 + 4 period structure. While Mozart's strides as a keyboard composer are divulged in the sets of variations that separate K.31 from K.279/189d, it is the very nature of variation form that the prevailing rhythmic pattern of each variation be relatively consistent. Variety is achieved over the larger structure.

The six sonatas thus constitute a true watershed: in them Mozart's freedom and variety of rhythm emerge in full flower, both in the spontaneity of melodic flow and in the choice of textures. The earlier dependence on the traditional Alberti bass has disappeared, supplanted by the ingenious development of a set of permutations of the Alberti figure and a variety of alternative accompaniment patterns. Most important of all, the sonatas reflect Mozart's evolution from a purely instrumental to a vocal composer: for the rest of his life, the primary impulse informing virtually all his music, regardless of genre and medium, will be vocal and dramatic. Henceforth, the balanced fusion of instrumental and vocal elements is to be an essential attribute of his style. It is difficult to exaggerate the achievement represented by this synthesis. It contributes in no small way to Mozart's universality and distinguishes his music from that of his contemporaries, whose primary status as either vocal or instrumental composers is generally evident in their musical rhetoric. Mozart's ability to construct a line of constant inflection, of untrammeled flow, is manifested by a melodic surface that typically links a few longer rhythmic values—often appoggiaturas—with a flexible succession of faster-moving connective pitches. The more rapid patterns serve to highlight the longer tones and impart a sense of organic growth.[15] Indeed, the synthesis of the two makes it possible for Mozart to use a tone repeatedly within a phrase without eliciting a feeling of redundancy (Ex. 9.2; the arrows denoting the repeated E-flats).

EXAMPLE 9.2. Mozart: Trio in E-flat for Piano, Clarinet and Viola K.498. Beginning of Movement 3

While Mozart's melodies respect period structure (typically, but not unvaryingly, in the 4 + 4 mold), it is the bass line whose arrival in the fourth measure is explicitly punctuated by a rest; the upper voice frequently flows on into the next phrase (Ex. 9.3).[16]

EXAMPLE 9.3a. Mozart: Sonata in D Major K.576. Beginning of Movement 2

EXAMPLE 9.3b. J. Haydn: Sonata in E-flat Hob. XVI: 49. Beginning of Movement 2

It is doubtful that these qualities would be so evident had Mozart composed the K.279–284 sonatas for the harpsichord. The vocal quality of their melodies relies on an instrument sensitive not just to articulation but to dynamic shading as well. In any case, the detailed dynamic indications of the manuscript leave no doubt that they were conceived for fortepiano.

The first of the set, in C major, gives the impression of an improvisation subsequently set down on paper: it is the most explicitly pianistic of the six. This is to say that the work's surface is openly fashioned from stock keyboard figuration, rather than to imply that Mozart's keyboard music is at times not idiomatic.[17] The whimsical qualities of K.279's finale (cf. the boisterousness of its cross-register exchanges) reappear in the second sonata (F major), whose first movement shares with K.279 a distinct rhetorical ease. It is the second movement of K.280/189e that strikes out in a more expressive vein, with a *siciliano* in F minor whose wrenching intensity (note the contradictory tonal shifts after the double bar) exceeds the bounds of a mere set piece.

In the third sonata (B-flat) K.281/189f, the interruptions and backtracking of the first movement evoke the wit of Haydn. The poised elegance of the middle movement might imply Mozart's retreat behind a suave mask but for the tempo indication, *Andante amoroso*, which surely challenges the performer to fill the vessel with personal persuasion. The finale is Mozart's first surviving full-blown keyboard sonata rondo, with its characteristic contrasting episodes in the relative minor and subdominant replacing the so-called development. The inclusion of a writtenout "lead-in"[18] and a pause that could occasion a second one (m. 70) suggests a flamboyance that reaches full flower in the work's sister sonata in B-flat K.333, written eight years later.

The E-flat Sonata K.282/189g harks back to the *sonata da chiesa* in its slow opening movement. Mozart employs a binary design that encapsulates sonata form: the second theme appears at m. 9. After the double bar the first theme is used for the development; Mozart therefore skips it at the return, saving its appearance in the tonic key for the coda after the second double bar. This practice was soon to serve him in several sonata allegros.[19] Another interesting feature of the E-flat Sonata is the use of the dominant key (B-flat) for the second movement minuet. Minuets are most commonly heard in the tonic in works with four or more mcvements (quartets, symphonies, divertimentos, and serenades) or as finale (tempo di menuetto). The choice of the dominant may have been a consequence of two factors: the use of a slow tempo in the first movement and the composer's desire for tonal variety within the overall structure.[20]

With the G-major Sonata K.283/189h, Mozart turns the circle of fifths radiating from C major in the other direction. There are certain superficial similarities between the first movement of this work and that of K.280/189e. On the other hand, Mozart's tendency to associated specific characters with specific keys may account for the appearance of the flourish-like figure of mm. 16ff. of K.283/189h in the cadenza to the first movement of the G-major Piano Concerto K.453 (1784). Similarly, the motives of K.283's slow movement—themselves related to the first movement of K.282—will be encountered anew in the finale of the C-major Sonata K.330 (1783). A comparison of the finales of K.280/189e and 283/189h reveals Mozart's progressive formal ambition: the brilliance and impulsiveness of the former is preserved within a richer and more extended structure in the latter. The delight in practical jokes is confirmed by the labeled coda—which consists of nothing but two chords, dominant and tonic.

The last of the six sonatas, in D major K.284/205b, begins with a synthesis of keyboard and symphonic rhetoric. This strategy seems to have required some focusing: the manuscript preserves a discarded version of the first movement in which the orchestral element is less distinct. The scope and content of the second movement are far grander than in any of the previous sonatas. It is not merely because of the form (*Rondeau en Polonaise*), which interpolates the expected interludes in relative minor and subdominant: we encounter a plethora of dynamics, striking melodic passages in octaves, and notably, a series of decorations of the main idea whose imagination and whimsy provide one of Mozart's many demonstrations of the art of embellishment.

Mozart seems to have regarded this sonata highly, for he chose to have it published in 1784 by Toricella in Vienna, together with the (then) recently completed sonatas in B-flat, K.333, and K.454 (the latter with violin). At that time he substantially enriched the dynamics and provided a more elaborate version of the already embroidered Adagio variation in the last movement. As mentioned earlier, Mozart's variations deserve special attention when his use of the form was voluntary—here, because he had already employed rondo form for the middle movement. The independence of the hands invites attention (Var. II, III, IV, IX); and the ornamentation of the slow variation—in which the repeats are written out—are another lesson in how to embellish those passages that, for practical reasons, do not survive with ornamentation.[21]

Mannheim and Paris, 1777–1778: Three Sonatas K.309–311

Mozart's next three keyboard sonatas (K.309–311) originated during his 1777–1778 voyage. According to the latest datings, the sonatas in C major K.309/284b, and in D major K.311/284c, were composed in Mannheim during October–November 1777, whereas the Sonata in A minor K.310/300d is dated Paris 1778 and was probably written during the summer. All three were published for the first time circa 1781 by Heina in Paris.[22] Both Mozart's father and sister observed that K.309/284b bears obvious traits of the Mannheim style. It certainly displays an orchestral bluster that takes farther the discourse of K.284/205b, and there is a showy willfulness that pits successions of melodic fragments against one another in a manner that contrasts with the more polished rhetoric of K.279–284. This is especially noticeable in the Rondeau, whose stagey coyness (Ex. 9.4) and garrulousness create a movement of unprecedented length.[23]

EXAMPLE 9.4. Mozart: Sonata in C Major K.309/284b. Movement 3, mm. 58–76

(*continued*)

EXAMPLE 9.4. (*continued*)

The slow movement of K.309/284b is equally unusual, moving by fits and starts punctuated with *fp*s and constant dynamic contrasts. According to Mozart himself, it is a "portrait" of Rose Cannabich, daughter of the composer Christian Cannabich, for whom Mozart wrote the sonata during his sojourn in Mannheim.[24] Its written-out elaborations of both main theme and middle subject deserve to be aligned over one another to reveal to the student of improvised embellishments the essence of Mozart's rhetorical language.[25]

The first movement of K.311/284c represents a recasting of K.284/205b in the Mannheim style: the symphonic traits are thrust to the fore (cf. the tremolo passage at m. 48ff.), and brilliance rather than intimacy of scale prevails. Even the cross-hand passages—long a stock device in variations—have a symphonic flavor (a characteristic motive is often passed from "violins" to "basses"). The most notable structural feature of the movement is the quotation of the flourish on the dominant (mm. 13–16) as the development swings back to the tonic key (mm. 75–78). In sweeping forward to the second theme, Mozart then follows the order of the exposition; but having circumvented the first theme, he had to find a suitable spot for it to recur—which proves to be after all but the final flourish of the second group has been heard. Such a reversal of theme groups in the recapitulation has been described as a Mannheim trait. It is revealing that the same device appears in another brilliant sonata in the same key from the same period: the piano and violin sonata K.306/300l.[26] These two sonatas share many other features as well: like K.306/300l, the rondeau finale of K.311/284c is a flashy display in $\frac{6}{8}$ meter in which the abrupt contrasts of K.309/284b again abound.[27] (There is a written-out lead-in before the recapitulation as opposed to the full-length cadenza in the duo sonata.) Both works employ not only a symphonic, but a concertante element, featuring tutti/solo contrasts. The metric structure of K.311/284c's third movement resembles that of a gavotte, in which the first stressed downbeat is the second measure after the upbeat, not the first. To balance the furor of the outer movements Mozart composed a second movement cantilena whose overt vocality and luminous serenity are without peer in the earlier sonatas. The coda

includes one of the few passages in which the use of pedal can be sur-
mised with some certainty (Ex. 9.5).

EXAMPLE 9.5. Mozart: Sonata in D Major K.311/284c. Movement 2, mm.
86–90

The A-minor Sonata K.310/300d is an altogether different achievement. It may well be one of Mozart's few surviving autobiographical
works. Little imagination is required to picture Mozart in Paris, crushed
by the calamity of his mother's death, the mercilessness of his professional failure, and the impending grief and wrath of his father, pounding the lefthand chords of the first movement of K.310 with his fist in
the fury and frustration of his situation—much as he is known to have
done as a nine-year-old boy during an examination conducted in London by Daines Barrington.[28] Such characterization would have little le-
gitimacy in today's de-Romanticized approach to biography, were the
content and expression of this sonata not diametrically opposed to those
exhibited by all the other works Mozart is known to have composed in
and for Paris.[29]

Lightness, brilliance, overt symmetry, and a penchant for attractive
melody are all eschewed. Instead we encounter violence of rhetoric, extremes of dynamic contrast (never again did Mozart repeatedly oppose
fortissimo and *pianissimo,* as in the first movement development), and of
figuration (the diabolically unidiomatic but breathtakingly spectacular
leaps in the eighth-note figuration of the last movement)—a paroxysm
not to be found even in such works as the D-minor and C-minor concertos. The chatter of sixteenth-notes in lieu of a second subject (first
movement, mm. 23–48) have a manic quality not unrelated to certain
moments in Poe or Dostoevsky; and the cataclysmic explosion at mm.
126–127 evinces an articulateness in the face of despair that knows only
Shakespeare as its peer.

The second movement's *fps,* ornate rhythmic surface, and rich dynamics might seem to recall the Mannheim sonatas, but they are used to
a different end here, having neither entertainment nor portraiture as
their purpose—unless the turbulence of the development is meant as

self-depiction. The passage beginning at m. 43 is particularly striking (Ex. 9.6).

EXAMPLE 9.6. Mozart: Sonata in A Minor K.310/300d. Movement 2, mm. 43–51

The leaps within the sixteenth triplets are largely responsible for the intensity of the discourse. However, the decision to give the bass rhythmic and melodic profile (rather than simply outlining the notes necessary for the progression) strengthens the characterization. What is remarkable is that this passage is taken from a movement of a piano sonata by Johann Schobert that Mozart had used eleven years earlier in one of his four pasticcio concerto transcriptions (K.39, second movement, Ex. 9.7).

EXAMPLE 9.7. Mozart: Piano Concerto in B-flat K.39. Movement 2, mm. 62–67 (=Johann Schobert: Sonata in F Major op. 17/2, Movement 1)

Mozart's phenomenal ability to recall and embroider at will a work that struck him many years before can be documented repeatedly by careful study of the *oeuvre*. Mozart drew again upon Schobert's movement in 1785—eighteen years after he had learned it—for the middle movement of the Piano Concerto in C major K.467 (chapter 10).

The Middle Period, 1783–1784: Five Sonatas K.330–333, 457, and the Fantasia K.475

Mozart's next four piano sonatas are now known to have been composed in 1783. The three sonatas K.330–332 were conceived as a cycle, entitled *Sonata I–II–III* in the autographs and published in 1784 by Artaria in Vienna as such.[30] Now that a chronological distance of six to seven years between these works and K.309–311 has been established, it is all too easy to recognize the greater maturity and mastery of the later set. There is no longer any reliance on conventional accompaniment figures: the standard Alberti bass has all but disappeared.

A virtually limitless variety characterizes the C-major sonata K.330. The permutations of the accompaniment—moving from two to three levels of sixteenth-notes, with and without sixteenth-rest punctuation, to chordal eighths (or longer values), single eighths, and triplet sixteenths—show an imagination that is often overlooked in evaluating the quality of Mozart's sonatas. It may be true that the posture of many of them lacks the earnestness or ambition associated with Beethoven's; but it is pointless to denigrate works for not being what they do not seek to be.[31] The disposition of the first movement of K.330 is defined by its beginning in the upper register, to which it repeatedly returns. The lightness, the conversational ease of the movement is stunning, with impulsive changes of surface shape and energy at every turn, an abundance of ideas (after the opening theme there are the motives at mm. 16, 19, 26–27, 35ff., 42ff., and 54ff.!), and an ability to weave into an elegant stream the formerly abrupt dynamic segments of the Mannheim sonatas.

The evolution in the form of the second movement is quite instructive. The autograph reveals the first concept to have been a simple A-B-A structure, with F-major and F-minor binary subsections; the da capo of the first section was not written out but rather indicated by a verbal direction. Mozart then appended the four-measure postlude to the F-minor section, with its soaring dissonance in m. 39, as an afterthought (Ex. 9.8).

EXAMPLE 9.8. Mozart: Sonata in C Major K.330/300h. Movement 2, mm. 36b–40a

Just prior to publication he seems to have added the epilogue (mm. 61–64), which is missing from the autograph—a touching, more personal ending that provides a satisfying structural balance with the earlier insert.

The finale is in many ways a recasting of the first movement in more formal terms, in which a flavor of solo (mm. 1–8, 21ff.) and tutti (mm. 9–20) emerges. Of great importance for the flexibility of the surface is the now regular alternation between sixteenths and sixteenth triplets. The final theme, for its part, displays a subtlety of articulation in its two appearances that is rare even for Mozart. (Cf. Ex. 9.9, and note the appearance of one of Mozart's characteristic dynamics: *mfp*.) In the second appearance at the end of the movement we encounter a detail that is the essence of Mozart's delectable childlike spirit: he overextends the coda idea like a child that wants just one more candy, just one more bedtime story, and manipulates its parents (and Mozart his audience) with superb skill until things go just a bit too far, with the cuteness of the deceptive cadence (m. 169). Enough! bellows the parent, enough! bellows the audience, but we are beside ourselves with sheer delight (Ex. 9.9).

EXAMPLE 9.9. Mozart: Sonata in C Major. K.330/300h. Movement 3, mm. 160–71.

The A-major Sonata K.331, with its celebrated variations and even more celebrated Turkish Rondo, is one of the most frequently performed. We see again that when Mozart chooses to write a set of variations within a sonata structure, he bestows his full store of expressive resources upon the form. Once more we observe compositional virtuosity in the variety of textures. Each variation has an entirely personal character, for example, the use of octaves for the melody in Variation III, or thirds in the cross-hand variation (IV). As in the E-flat Sonata K.282, Mozart begins with a slow movement and continues with a minuet, but here he continues in the tonic key, not the dominant, so that all three movements are in A.[32] Whereas K.282's minuet could easily be transcribed for strings, that of K.331 is utterly a keyboard piece, encompassing the decorative and the poignant. The trio takes up the translucent color of the cross-hand variation; in its second half, as in the minuet proper, an unexpected earnestness and harmonic stress emerge. The *Alla Turca* surely requires no *explication de texte;* but perhaps a plea should be uttered on its behalf, and on behalf of all such pieces whose popularity has reduced to hackneyed familiarity the imaginative traits that elevated it to such fame in the first place.

Whereas the intimacy of K.330 and K.331 (*Alla Turca* notwithstanding) makes them more suitable for the smaller circle or the salon than the concert hall, the F-major Sonata K.332 has a theatricality that sets it apart: above all, in the first movement's unexpectedly stormy transition (mm. 23ff.), and especially in the uproarious temperament of the last movement, with its peals of laughter petering out in discombobulating dead-ends. The second movement, like the finale to K.284/205b, was greatly elaborated in the first edition (Ex. 9.10).

EXAMPLE 9.10. Mozart: Sonata in F major K.332/300k. Movement 2, mm. 21–26. First Edition and Autograph Versions

(*continued*)

EXAMPLE 9.10. (*continued*)

What would today's critics and conservative musicians say if a performer dared to add to the slow movement of one of the other sonatas a sweeping run of the kind Mozart unhesitatingly supplied at the return?

Mozart's next sonata, in B-flat major K.333, was composed in Linz at the end of 1783.[33] Of all Mozart's works in the genre, perhaps none melds expressive grace, humor, *Affekt,* and structural integrity with such poise.[34] The texture at the opening of the first movement is an indication of the virtuosity of rhythmic deployment. The right hand's melody is based on a symmetrical idea, whose decorations and melodic direction provide dextrous variety. The down beat eighth-rests in the left hand propel the piece forward for four bars. Then the accompaniment changes to broken thirds without the rest; and a sudden pause in m. 6 sends the right hand into a flurry of activity, which begins the preparation of the cadential flourish (Ex. 9.11).

EXAMPLE 9.11. Mozart: Sonata in B-flat K.333/315c. Beginning of Movement 1

(*continued*)

EXAMPLE 9.11. (*continued*)

The bridge passage (mm. 11–22) culminating in the half-cadence before the second theme is full of teasing flirtatiousness; indeed, the whole movement displays an impulsive vivacity and an inclination to arrive at expected cadences through harmonically coloristic routes (m. 25, m. 35, mm. 46–50, and especially their extension in the recapitulation at mm. 142–152)—a device that Schubert was to exploit with such wizardry. After the onset of the development section the sudden substitution of F minor for F major (m. 71) causes the piece to "take off"; rarely do we encounter a passage in Mozart that seems so liberated. Instead of the typical presentation of modulating sequences or goal-oriented harmonic progressions, the piece revels in its freedom, from the leap to the very top of the keyboard in m. 73 to the imaginary land of C major (m.75)— quickly corrected to minor but followed within three beats by E-flat minor, and three bars later by a first inversion D dominant seventh chord— oil and water alternations whose potency ought not be attenuated one iota by the rationalization of harmonic analysis. Like the development, the sixteenth-note passages toward the end of exposition and recapitulation hint at a performance virtuosity that proceeds hand in glove with compositional flair. Mozart's deftness in following the grand concluding passage of mm. 152–161 with an intimate five-measure epilogue is not merely disarming: it shows how easily he could reconcile—or at least link—his public and private personae.

The second movement of K.333 begins with a decidedly vocal theme—one he had already used in the second movement of the Piano Concerto in D K.175—and carries the synthesis of operatic and instrumental elements even further, savoring danger (m. 19, where the right hand's f-sharp threatens to be a g-flat) and audacity (the first sonority at m. 32, just after the double-bar). Here, as in the first movement, the development constitutes a stream-of-consciousness improvisation, in which A-flat major (mm. 40–43) seems an inspired rescuer. The appalling sound of D-flat minor in m. 47 has alas become commonplace through familiarity; the modern use of equal temperament certainly does not help.

The finale is an unabashed hybrid, as if it were Mozart's answer to Bach's Italian Concerto. For the most part it would be a simple matter to turn the movement into the concerto finale it mirrors. In fact, it is a pendant to the first movement in character, but with more flamboyance. Mozart's standard tonal strategy for the central episode of his sonata rondos (relative minor followed by subdominant) had never been executed with such impulsive frivolity. In the middle of the G-minor section (m. 72) he glances away, changes gears, and—off he goes in E-flat, leaving the relative minor unrequited and unremembered. The cadenza, prepared by a ritornello of typically orchestral substance, reveals many of the ingenious transformations Mozart's concerto cadenzas work upon the material of the main movement. The conclusion is a model of insouciance, with a grand ending followed by the virtually expected intimate postlude, then the sudden triumphant pounce on the tonic as the audience was already thinking about the next work.[35]

The C-minor Fantasia and Sonata K.475/457 are often considered Mozart's greatest solo keyboard composition. The fantasia is dated 20 May 1785 in Mozart's autograph catalogue of his own works; the Sonata is dated 14 October 1784. That they belong together despite the disparity of dates, and the fact that the sonata antedates the fantasia, is supported both by their publication together in Vienna in 1785 (advertised for the first time on 7 December 1785) and their survival as a double autograph. It is difficult to imagine that the decision to publish them together was made by anyone other than Mozart.[36] They exemplify the emotional world that the key of C minor represents for Mozart—one in which anger, brooding, and solemn severity have central places, not the demonic spirit of D minor or the despair and tirades of G minor. Interestingly, the themes of Mozart's C-minor works share a common shape, in which the tonic triad and the interval of a diminished seventh (A-flat–B-natural or E-flat–F-sharp) are combined.[37]

For Mozart to have chosen such a key for a piece dedicated to his student [Maria] Theresia von Trattner is utterly remarkable. There is scarcely another solo work by Mozart that gazes so unflinchingly into the abyss as does the opening section of the fantasia with its eerie moves from D-flat major to B major, from a dominant seventh on A to an F-minor sixth chord, from E-flat minor back to B major (though this is technically quite a close enharmonic relation): the languages of Schubert and Wagner are suddenly at hand. What is uncanny in Mozart's visionary modulations is that often the most astonishing moment is the simplest move, not the most daring—such as the sudden stop of the bass on a G-major chord at m. 18 (Ex. 9.12).

EXAMPLE 9.12. Mozart: Fantasia in C Minor K.475, mm. 10–18

The most striking passages in the fantasia are those in which the momentum pulls the work out of conventional poses and lurches toward
crisis: mm. 56–82 (61–87),[38] for example, when, after the whirlwind of
the sequence the arrival on the dominant of B-flat is stunning. At the
opposite end of the spectrum, after the frenzy of thirty-seconds from
mm. 125 (130) on, we arrive exhausted but relieved at the equivocal calm
of A-flat in m. 138 (143), only to see Mozart turn almost casually to F
minor, setting in motion the events that ineluctably bring us back to the
tonic. This passage culminates in a figure that Beethoven evidently emulated in the *Appassionata* Sonata op. 57, first movement (Ex. 9.13).

EXAMPLE 9.13a. Mozart: Fantasia in C Minor K.475, mm. 157–60

EXAMPLE 9.13b. Beethoven: Sonata in F minor (*Appassionata*) op. 57.
Movement 1, mm. 12–16

The rhythmic angularity of the sonata's first movement theme is set in relief by its contrast to the opening of the fantasia. The sonata is an obvious model for Beethoven's "*Pathétique*" op. 13: the crossed-hand second theme, and in particular, the middle theme of the second movement, m. 24, which Beethoven used for the principal idea of his middle movement. The first movement—particularly the storminess of its development section and its unnerving cutoff at m. 94—must have impressed him deeply, even if he was unwilling to adopt Mozart's *pianissimo* ending. The embellished reprises of the second movement comprise another lesson from the master in the art of elaboration—a lesson that is more detailed now that the double autograph of fantasia and sonata has been rediscovered and is available in a handsome facsimile edition.[39] The appearance of metrically free sweeps of small notes not in a cadenza but within the course of the movement (mm. 29ff., 51) is a novelty that anticipates Chopin. The last movement is notated after the first movement and before the second in the autograph; its theme also displays the characteristic blend of tonic triad and diminished seventh. Particularly revealing are the appearances of performance directions that become common only in the nineteenth century—*agitato*, entered by Mozart into the dedication copy[40]—and *a piacere* (mm. 228–229). The incisive rhetoric of the first movement is even more prominent in the finale (mm. 24, 38, 102, 128, 141, 144, 156). There are alternative readings for the two crossed-hand passages (mm. 92–99; 291–297, and 304–308) in manuscript and first edition.[41] The version of the autograph is extravagant, with four-octave crossings. In the final passage Mozart began with the simplified version found in the first edition, then placed the bass notes in mm. 304–308 an octave lower. Perhaps the simplification came at the instigation of the publisher; with today's wider keyboards, the original version is slightly more difficult than it was then. Even the simplified version has an unrepentant, adamant quality to it that appears again in the last measures of the C-minor Concerto K.491.

The Threshold to the Late Period: Three Rondos K.485, 494, 511

Mozart's next solo works were individual rondos—in D major K.485 (10 January 1786), in F major K.494 (10 June 1786), and in A minor K.511 (11 March 1787). These works are distinct in character and substance. It has been speculated that K.485 was written for an amateur pianist from the nobility;[42] the work certainly remains within circumscribed technical and emotional confines. It is actually a sonata movement in which first and second groups use the same theme (as is often the case in Haydn). While displaying Mozart's customary suavity, K.485's temporal proximity to the A-major Concerto K.488 reveals a gaping disparity in expressive intensity. However, its lightness and modesty were hardly a miscalculation; to this day it serves admirably the modest purpose for which it was composed.

The F-major Rondo K.494 seems at first glance to be a similar composition but it quickly emerges that this time Mozart is far more interested in his material. While technical prowess is largely reined in, there is masterful elaboration of the theme (culminating in the triumphant sweep of mm. 126–131) and imaginative use of the registers—beginning in the soprano range and finishing at the very bottom of the instrument. We do not know the original inspiration for its composition; but Mozart's high regard for the work is implied by his decision to incorporate it into one of his most extraordinary sonatas, K.533 (see below, pp. 332–34).

With the Rondo K.511 we enter an intimate realm, equally distant from Mozart's public virtuosity and his private tutelage. The A minor of this rondo differs from the harrowing fulmination of the Sonata K.310/

300d. More than any other solo work it seems forlorn, dejected; its fundamental bleakness drags against the articulateness of the ornamentation, which struggles with increasing intensity against a manifestly hopeless fate. The F-major and A-major episodes provide welcome foils, but both are ultimately undone by an insidious chromaticism that betrays the affected repose in the first episode and slithers back to the return from both episodes (mm. 71–74 and 118–122). The effect of these passages is all the more disorienting for the rational music that surrounds them. They are a harbinger of Mozart's late style, whose traits begin to emerge early in 1787.

Many of K.511's details hint at the more idiosyncratic language displayed by the music of Mozart's last four years. Expression is intensified by means of increasingly daring chromaticism and dissonance—for example, at the work's conclusion, where the arresting B-flat amid the threatening growl of the lefthand triplets transports the listener from Mozart's to Chopin's expressive habitat (Ex. 9.14).[43]

EXAMPLE 9.14. Mozart: Rondo in A Minor K.511. Conclusion

Another characteristic of Mozart's later music is his deepening interest in polyphony. He inclines increasingly toward a lean two-part contrapuntal texture, often inverting the voices in the manner of a Bach invention. The resultant astringency—note the contrast in *Affekt* between the opening of K.511 and the coda (mm. 163ff.)—denotes a withdrawal from the easy attractiveness of melody and accompaniment (Ex. 9.15).

EXAMPLE 9.15a. Mozart: Rondo in A Minor K.511. Beginning

EXAMPLE 9.15b. Mozart: Rondo in A Minor K.511, mm. 163–73

Mozart's growing fascination with counterpoint as an expressive and rhetorical vehicle is reflected in his articulation patterns. In the above excerpt we observe Mozart's "contrapuntal" use of slurs: only occasionally do the two voices share an articulation after the bar line (mm. 165,

167, 168, 172). This contrasts with the consistent declamation of the earlier music, in which articulation stems from conventional patterns more than individual characterization.

The Late Piano Compositions: Four Sonatas K.533, 545, 570, 576, and the Adagio K.540

The new currents in Mozart's language were to coalesce quickly. Less than a year later—on 3 January 1788—Mozart entered into his thematic catalogue an Allegro and Andante to a Piano Sonata in F that was to be completed by the incorporation of the Rondo K.494 as finale. The first two movements bear the Köchel number 533, but as we shall see, it would be advisable to dispense with the traditional double number 533/494 in referring to this sonata and to use 533 to represent the entire work.

The first movement announces the new stylistic direction at once (Ex. 9.16).

EXAMPLE 9.16. Mozart: Sonata in F Major K.533. Beginning of Movement 1

For one thing, Mozart takes up the two-voice invertible texture introduced in the coda to K.511. For another, the opening is a departure from Mozart's previous keyboard music. Hitherto, the opening idea might have been impulsive (K.279, 281), but it was always clearly etched.

Normally, the first theme had a settled character that often assumed the same public stance as a quartet or symphony. Here we have the impression of watching a sculptor mold the clay: Mozart seems to pause in mid-air right away (m. 2), ponders (thus the half-note upbeat rather than the original quarter), apparently finds his original idea satisfactory after all, and only then does the left hand enter to confirm that the decision has been made. Over the accompaniment the right hand reaches a closed arrival on the tonic (m. 8)—an articulation on the dominant is nowhere to be found.[44] There is no antecedent-consequent period structure here: instead we reach a dead end and must start all over. Of course, Mozart's rhetorical conceit is a perfect mold for the two-part contrapuntal texture he has adopted.

The unfolding of the entire exposition not only conveys a sense of freedom—improvisation is no stranger to Mozart's rhetoric—but hints at an exploration of the expressive potential of a speculative approach. Elements are repeated and considered, sometimes to be rejected, sometimes to be followed. The use of repetition as an intensification device—usually in conjunction with harmonic evolution (mm. 37ff.) or polarization (mm. 82, 84, 86) had never been more pervasive. The second group (mm. 41ff.) pursues the double counterpoint set up by the opening. There follows a remarkable gambit at m. 66, in which, so late in the exposition, a second major half-cadence on the dominant is reached and a sort of alternate second theme—grounds for further "speculation"—is presented on a dominant pedal in C. That Mozart allows the music to "stumble" into D minor and forces a rescue shows how self-confident he has become as a composer.

This is no longer music that caters to *Kenner*, let alone *Liebhaber:* Mozart follows his inclination and challenges the audience to follow him, if it can. The flourish that ends the exposition—a chain of C-major arpeggios—shows a reduction to essentials that on this scale is as foreign to Mozart's earlier music as it is idiomatic to Beethoven's. The drama and energy generated by the systematic working out of all three ideas—the superimposition of first theme and coda flourish plus the second theme in double counterpoint and stretto—attest to a rigor surpassing that displayed in the chronologically intermediate work composed in this style: the A-major Piano and Violin Sonata, K.526. Likewise, the "stream-of-consciousness" extension at mm. 215ff. of the sequence from the exposition (mm. 80ff.) expands the techniques explored in K.511 with a harmonic vocabulary of cross relations that again looks well ahead into the nineteenth century.

The crown of K.533, however, is the slow movement. Its riveting harmonic audacity (mm. 19ff., 28ff.) and the relentless grating of the parallel thirds in the development—that catapults the piece over the precipice in a moment of breathtaking awe—have no parallel in any other Mozart solo keyboard work (Ex. 9.17).

EXAMPLE 9.17. Mozart: Sonata in F Major K.533. Movement 2, mm. 59–72

Here, too, a preoccupation with double counterpoint creates many of the movement's most striking passages and balances the more homophonic opening. The parallel sixths and thirds in mm. 5ff. are representative of Mozart's new style. A peculiar feature of that style is the complete lack of dynamics—a circumstance that has led to some disparity of interpretation (e.g., playing the bars just before the recapitulation with a *diminuendo* to *pianissimo*). This quite perplexing situation—Mozart's abandonment of performance prescriptions at a time when his music turns away from conventions to become more individual—is not a momentary quirk. It will be encountered again in the slow movements to the Sonatas in C K.545, in B-flat K.570, in D K.576, and in nonkeyboard works as well.[45]

In adapting the Rondo K.494 to its new venue Mozart made a number of striking changes. He altered the tempo from Andante to Allegretto,[46] revised the articulation,[47] and interpolated a striking twenty-seven-measure expansion between measures 142 and 143—whose centerpiece is a stretto on the main theme constructed on a tonic six-four (mm. 152ff.). The movement has thus become a different composition in significant ways and could be considered a component of K.533 without qualms.

Two-and-a-half months later (19 March 1788) Mozart entered into his catalogue an Adagio in B minor (K.540), whose despondency recalls the mood of the A-minor Rondo. Here the sighs are overt, the turmoil underscored with a plethora of dynamic contrasts, cross-hand registers, and a further pursuit of harmonic and registral coloration that recall the C-minor Fantasy, K.475 (Ex. 9.18).

EXAMPLE 9.18. Mozart: Adagio in B Minor K.540, mm. 26–34

A further distinction of K.540 is its major-key coda: the tonality of B major is not otherwise to be encountered in Mozart's solo keyboard music.[48] Furthermore, he displaces the beat in the coda from the beginning of the measure to the third beat and never restores the metrical accent to the first beat of the measure.[49]

Mozart's next keyboard work is the Sonata in C major K.545, dated Vienna, 26 June 1788. It is one of the most familiar works in the literature. Mozart called it "A small piano Sonata for beginners"; the subtitle, "*Sonata facile*," has accompanied it since the first edition (1805).[50] Its pedagogical function has been richly mined in the intervening two centuries, and its content can hardly be recognized beneath the endless playings that professionals and laypersons have endured. It is curious that this sonata is the only one with a subdominant recapitulation, just as it is unremarkable that Mozart uses the ploy of the open-ended "bi-focal" half-cadence to continue either in the dominant (in the exposition) or in the tonic (in the recapitulation) without the need for composing or modifying a bridge passage. (This shortens the movement, keeping it within a length well suited to students—73 measures, compared with 239 for K.533, 185 for K.457, or 165 for K.333.)

That the Andante is a measure longer and contains repeats of mm. 1–16 and 17–32 suggests that Mozart did not consider the repeats in the first movement to be optional.[51] The written-out embellishment of the main theme appears three times—five, if one counts the repeats. Because the autograph has disappeared, we cannot ascertain how much of this music may have been indicated by "da capo 8 measures" (as found in the autograph notation of the main theme to the second movement of K.457); nor can we determine whether Mozart might have provided varied reprises, had the work (again as in the case of K.457) been published during his lifetime. As things stand, the ornamentation is not varied and is remarkably undifferentiated rhythmically, being essentially a chain of sixteenth-notes. Furthermore, the texture in mm. 9–10 underscores implied parallel fifths between the upper and lower voices. It is an altogether curious situation for such a central work, but Mozart may have meant it as a trifle for immediate teaching purposes and might have been astonished at its celebrity.

The Rondo is anything but a piece for beginners; the arpeggios in the A-minor episode and the double thirds at the end have inspired groans around the globe for a long time. The fact that the movement begins on an upbeat and adheres to this metric frame for most of its length is often overlooked in student performances. Mozart's care in such matters is documented by his corrective rebarring of passages in order for them to end on the downbeat.[52] In the end K.545, like its sister sonata for piano and violin in F K.547, and the D-major Rondo K.485, may not contain Mozart's most distinctive or personal utterances, but considering their purpose, they communicate the norms of a language without any concession to ease in matters of phrasing or texture. Their very success at achieving their pedagogical goal is surely their most significant epitaph.

Mozart's last piano sonatas were composed in 1789—the B-flat-major sonata K.570 in February and the D-major K.576 in July. Until quite recently K.570 was neglected by pianists. The work had been published in 1796 by Artaria with an accompanimental violin part; this resulted in its inclusion among the piano-violin sonatas and its exclusion from the solo sonatas until well into the twentieth century. Mozart refers to the sonata in his catalogue of works as a sonata for solo piano, and a portion of his autograph—which contains no violin part—survives. There is no evidence to support his authorship of the subservient violin part. Compared with the sonatas K.457 or K.533, K.570 makes only moderate technical demands on the performer.[53] The first movement is motivically terse, adopting Haydn's practice of reusing the main theme at the head of the second group. Similarly, the entire development reproduces prior material, with modulating sequences supplanting the tonally stable presentation of the exposition. Double counterpoint is decidedly less salient, though exchanges of voices do occur (mm. 49ff./57ff.: mm. 111ff./ 117ff./125ff.).

The second movement is a rondo whose tonal organization and content (e.g., the first episode at m. 13) betray a marked kinship with the middle movement of the Piano Concerto in C minor K.491. The lack of any embellishment of the main theme, which occurs four times (six, if one counts the repeats), is surely due to the fact that the work was not published in Mozart's lifetime. His likely intentions are to be gleaned not from the unornamented sources, but from those for K.457 (*q.v.*). The finale shares the light texture of the first movement: its form is a succession of binary ideas, with and without linking transitions. The contrapuntal treatment of the second part of the E-flat episode and the ensuing retransition create the only challenge (quoted at mm. 79ff.) in what is otherwise a recreational work par excellence. The seamless synthesis of all the episodes on the last page reveals that Mozart nonetheless did not abandon his intellectual standards.

Between the composition of K.570 and 576 Mozart was to undertake a journey that brought him to the Prussian court at Potsdam— where he curried favor with the court music master and cellist Jean Pierre Duport by writing a set of variations on a theme by him (K.573)— and to Leipzig where, for the only time in his life, he was to hear choral music by J. S. Bach. His inscription in the autograph book of Karl Immanuel Engel, the Saxon court organist, seems to honor not Bach, but Handel: the little mischievous Gigue in G K.574, full of quirky simultaneous appoggiaturas and a devilishly explosive coda, appears to pay homage to the gigue from Handel's Eighth Suite in F minor from the 1722 collection.[54]

The Sonata in D major K.576, completed after Mozart's return to Vienna, is his last surviving sonata. Its first movement carries the compositional techniques of K.533 yet further, its counterpoint being both more virtuosic (note the canon at the temporal distance of an eighth-note at mm. 28–33 and 138–143) and more playful (cf. the interpolated interlude shortly after the recapitulation begins). The development, with its startling modulations (B-flat major and B minor are but ten bars apart) shows the cogency Mozart's counterpoint brings to a style of musical rhetoric he had used previously in the finale to the F-major sonata K.332. The synthesis of boisterous, serious, and ebullient elements is remarkable, as is the reshuffling of ideas in the recapitulation, capped by the crash of the diminished seventh chord at m. 152 and Mozart's nonchalantly dusting off his pants, smiling ingenuously, and continuing straight on into the coda.

The slow movement displays a dazzling rhythmic fluidity and a reliance on color as a central expressive device (compare the motion of the first beat of m. 2 to E, of m. 6 to E-sharp, and of m. 14 to G). The middle episode in F-sharp minor, one of Mozart's rarest keys,[55] reveals Mozart's ability to concentrate the poignant language of the A-minor Rondo and the B-minor Adagio into the shortest possible theme (seven measures). His ability to shock the audience with the intense coloration of m. 22 and to surpass this at the return of the passage (m. 37, where the A-sharp is surely meant to be interpreted at first as a B-flat) belies the miniaturization of the structural scaling (Ex. 9.19).

EXAMPLE 9.19a. Mozart: Sonata in D Major K.576. Movement 2, mm. 21–24

EXAMPLE 9.19b. Mozart: Sonata in D Major K.576. Movement 2, mm. 36–39

The return to the main theme seems to reattain radiant daylight after the harrowing torment of the middle section; the overt formalism of K.570's finale could not be more distant.

There is scarcely a more dashing, more flamboyant movement by Mozart for solo piano than K.576's finale. In it harmonic process is rendered as linear as possible, with an absolute minimum number of passages with vertically conceived accompaniment. The storm ensuing from the substitution of D minor for D major at m. 82 is spellbinding, all the more so in that the fiery temperament of the passage is achieved almost exclusively in two-part counterpoint.

Mozart's ability to organize a section of this relentless length (mm. 80–116) had long been a hallmark of his operas, where the focusing of dramatic tension is central to great comedy and tragedy alike. On the other hand, his keyboard sonatas had followed a different aesthetic, in which dapper banter predominated, using a flexible, flowing rhythmic surface that contrasted, for example, with Haydn's sturdier and more cellular rhythmic language. The operatic element had been present, but as rhetorical color rather than structural determinant. In K.457 Mozart drew upon the style of the great serenade for wind octet K.388/384a (likewise in C minor) to create a work of irascible angularity; in K.533 the contrapuntal process was not merely the vehicle for eloquence but seemed itself an expressive goal. In K.576 all of the threads of his prior styles reached a synthesis.

The Duo-Piano Works

Mozart's works for piano four hands and two pianos owe their existence to his performances with his sister, Maria Anna ("Nannerl") Mozart, prior to 1781, and to his talented pupils in the Vienna years. The first of the four-hand sonatas, in C major K.19d, is not free of doubts concerning its authenticity. To be sure, it has the naiveté one would expect of a nine-year-old, but it is unclear why a work presumed to have been composed in London in 1765 would be published in France in 1787 and at whose instigation. The manuscript has not survived, and a London edition seems to be based on the French one. However, Mozart was known to have performed four-hand music with Nannerl in London, and K.19d may have been written for that purpose.

The four-hand sonatas in D major and B-flat major, K.381/123a and K.358/186c, have been redated by Wolfgang Plath to the end of 1773 or the beginning of 1774 (Plath 1976/1977, 151). The D-major sonata, one of the staples of the repertoire, is an Italian symphony conceived for the keyboard. The fanfares and infectious merriment of its boisterous outer movements receive a perfect foil in the ingenuous charm of the middle movement cantilena. The presence of alternating solo passages for each player achieves the needed reconciliation between rhetoric and medium. The B-flat sonata uses the same textural devices while displaying increased formal invention—the structuring of the music around the first movement's repeats and the full-fledged development in the finale. The imitative passage at the end of the first movement exposition and recapitulation, in which stealth creates a delightful anticipation, may be another indication that this is the later of the sonatas.

Mozart wrote no further duo-piano solo works in Salzburg, but the Concerto for Two Pianos in E-flat K.365/316a (1779) and the version for two pianos of the Concerto for Three Pianos in F major K.242 were written for joint performance with Nannerl. Shortly after his arrival in Vienna in 1781, Mozart began to teach Josepha Auernhammer. Mozart's letters to his father are merciless about the lovestruck young woman who "is a nightmare! but plays enchantingly. . . ." He retrieved the two-piano concerto from Salzburg to play with her, and in November 1781 wrote one of his most dazzling keyboard masterpieces, the Sonata for Two Pianos in D major K.448/375a, for performance with her. Its breathtaking virtuosity is matched only by its impeccable poise, and to the present day performances of it do not fail to bring the audience to its feet. It is a remarkable tribute to Fräulein Auernhammer's abilities. At approximately the same time Mozart began a Larghetto and Allegro in E-flat major for performance with her but broke the work off at the end of the exposition, having already started to write out a separate performance part for her. The fragment has been completed a number of times, from Maximilian Stadler in the 1790s to Paul Badura-Skoda, Franz Beyer, and the author in recent years.

Shortly thereafter Mozart composed a fugue in C minor for two pianos: K.426. He changed the date on the manuscript from 29 December 1782 to 1783; thus the work might owe its existence to his performances with Fräulein Auernhammer, but its inspiration was undoubtedly the confrontation with Handel and J. S. Bach, born of the soirées at Baron van Swieten's. The rigorous, relentless counterpoint of K.426 is in every way the antithesis of the two-piano sonata: taut and almost claustrophobic rather than airy and untrammeled. Yet the message is crucial: with this work Mozart came to terms with the contrapuntal heritage of the Baroque and was henceforth to employ it for expressive purposes, not for intellectual show.

After a hiatus of over a decade Mozart returned to the four-hand idiom with a series of masterpieces, beginning with the Sonata in F major K.497 (1 August 1786)—the most ambitious of his works for the medium and one whose aspirations and achievements satisfy the highest Mozartean standards. The language reflects the formal maturity of the great piano concertos and the dialogues of the two piano quartets. The turbulence of the Adagio introduction to the first movement returns in the superb development; in the second movement the duet between soprano and tenor registers is a veritable operatic *scena*. The finale encompasses an unprecedentedly broad expressive range—cheerful, uproarious, fiery, tender, jubilant. Had the work been composed for another medium, it would be one of Mozart's most celebrated, but its demands upon the players and the rarity of four-hand recitals have relegated it to relative obscurity. (The fact that Mozart's four-hand works have yet to be published in score has made serious study of them difficult.)

Shortly after K.497 Mozart composed perhaps his most perfect four-hand work, the Andante with Five Variations in G major K.501 (4 November 1786). For sheer elegance of voice leading and chord spacing the work is not to be surpassed. The music-box enchantment of the third variation draws on one of the sources of Mozart's expressive power and reminds us that his maturing never caused him to forget the wonderment of the child.

The last of Mozart's four-hand sonatas, in C major K.521 (29 May 1787), was written for his pupil Franziska von Jacquin, who also premiered the "Kegelstatt' Trio in E-flat major K.498 (with clarinetist Anton Stadler and Mozart playing viola). The first movement bears the scoring "Cembalo I" and "Cembalo II." (Mozart used the term *forte-piano* only once in a score: for the "Coronation" Concerto in D major K.537.) But the work is performable at a single keyboard. It has more of the regular alternation between players of the earlier duos and less of the splendor found in K.497, being an ideal piece of *Hausmusik* rather than a public utterance. However, the fire of the second movement's middle section reminds us that even for domestic enjoyment Mozart was no longer willing to be a purveyor of mere entertainment.

The remainder of the works encountered in collections of Mozart's four-hand works are fragments and transcriptions. The Fugue in G minor K.401/375e (1772—a fragment completed by Maximilian Stadler) is for organ; and the two great fantasias in F minor K.594 and 608 (1790–1791) were composed for mechanical clock organs. The Handelian grandeur of K.594's central section, and the wrenching pathos of the outer sections, are perhaps outshone by K.608's audacious, even terrifying, chromaticism and the virtuosity of its fugal writing. The so-called Sonata in G major K.357 is in fact a pair of completions, probably by Johann Anton André, of two separate fragments from 1787 and 1791. It is a great pity that Mozart did not complete the first of these, whose exposition has an exotic modulating passage that slides effortlessly in and out of distant keys in a manner that Mozart became increasingly fond of in his later music.

Impact

That K.576 was fated to be not just Mozart's first solo sonata in a consummately masterful idiom, but his very last, is particularly tragic. However, its lessons were not lost on Haydn (cf. the first movement of the Sonata in C major Hob. XVI:50) or Beethoven, for whom a two-part texture was a common feature, and whose compositions based loosely or strictly on Mozartean prototypes take in a considerable portion of his oeuvre. Most of Schubert's solo works reflect new aesthetic values, though the early ones owe something of their melodic grace to Mozart. Ultimately Haydn and especially Beethoven seem to have been a more lasting influence on Schubert, whose formal sense was far less hierarchical than Mozart's. (But then, this could be said of all of Mozart's contemporaries and successors.)

Mozart's harmonic style was not widely imitated, though Hummel's music often displays a convincing grasp of some of Mozart's characteristic progressions; the stylistic road from Mozart through Hummel and Moscheles to Mendelssohn then intersects the path from Haydn and Beethoven to Schumann. With Beethoven, however, the sonata as a vehicle for amateurs and a source of income for composers had begun to yield to a more ambitious genre destined for first-rank performers, transforming it into a peer of the quartet and the symphony. At the same time its formal evolution all but ceased, and sonata form by recipe became the norm; even development sections largely lost their freedom and became large-scale sequential structures.[56] Thus, all of the characteristics of Mozart's piano music—its structural variety, rhetorical whimsy, and its willingness (until the very last works) to engage rather than confront his audience—were to disappear from the scene within a generation. The character pieces that formed the basis of salon music may be its social heirs, but hardly its spiritual brethren.

Epilogue: Practical Issues

Performance Style

It is clear from the texture and articulation of the solo works that Mozart favored a clear, translucent sound with sparse use of pedal, and a singing melody ("It must flow like oil," he repeatedly affirmed) that he inflected with a plethora of articulate detail. A musician who perhaps more than any other defined the values that were to be central to Romanticism remained nonetheless one directly indebted to Baroque performance tradition. Mozart complained that one of his best pupils, Josepha Auernhammer, "chopped up" everything. That Beethoven characterized Mozart's own playing as choppy shows the direction that musical aesthetics were to follow for a century—a direction visually delineated by Beethoven's longer slurs and Chopin's even longer ones. By the time Mozart's music was published in the *Gesamtausgabe* of Breitkopf & Härtel starting in 1881 virtually every passage in sixteenth-notes was labeled "legato"—a direction Mozart did not use—because a lively surface as opposed to a smooth one was inconceivable to musicians by and of that time. For the performer it is far easier to play an endless smooth line than to provide the balletic poise that Mozart's music prescribes. The corrective reinstatement of his values has been one of the more rewarding fruits of the historical performance movement.

Editions

There have been a number of so-called *Urtext* editions of Mozart's sonatas and piano pieces, starting with Ernst Rudorff's at the end of the nineteenth century, republished by Kalmus/Belwin Mills. Since the end of World War II many such editions have appeared—among them those published by Presser, Henle, the *Wiener Urtext Edition* (WUE), and Bärenreiter.

It is both enlightening and sobering that these editions have striking divergencies, suggesting that the term *Urtext* (i.e., original text) is chimerical. In fact, one of the reasons for the disparities lies in the changing source situation. By far the largest collection of Mozart manuscripts belonged to the Prussian State Library in Berlin (the former Royal Library, now the Staatsbibliothek zu Berlin, Preußischer Kulturebesitz). During World War II the library's holding were evacuated for safekeeping, and many manuscripts vanished at the end of the war—until it was officially announced in 1980 that they were in Cracow at the Jagiellonian Library, where they are housed to the present day. Editions made before the mid-1980s had to make do with secondary sources. The Henle and WUE editions date from this period, but revisions have been introduced into recent printings. The Bärenreiter edition is an offprint of the NMA (1986) and thus claims the highest authority.

In evaluating these editions, several factors have to be weighted: the Bärenreiter edition, being a reproduction of a critical edition, contains no fingerings. While some users might consider this to be a disadvantage, the opposite is true: the fingerings given even in *Urtext* editions often vitiate the painstakingly restored articulations by prescribing a technical solution that undermines them.

Henle has made the decision to render Mozart's wedges (strokes) as dots, so that the distinction found in other editions between the former (a heavier articulation, related to an accent and found at times on note values as long as a whole note or over the first note of a slur) and the latter (a short, light articulation) is obliterated.[57]

A disadvantage of the Bärenreiter/NMA edition is that its readings occasionally reflect the personal taste of the editors rather than the state of the sources; by objective criteria some of these readings are questionable.[58] Underlying this problem is the central dilemma of a critical edition: to select an authoritative reading among occasionally conflicting sources while attempting to correct the composer's occasional errors or supplement his incomplete notation. The scholarly, theoretical, and practical musical sophistication required for such a task is formidable, and at times the readings presented even by the finest editions might seem to overlook one or another compositional detail. Furthermore, modern editors have a disturbing tendency to prefer consistency of dynamics and articulation in allegedly parallel passages when faced with differences in the sources. To a performer, it is hardly a disadvantage for similar sounding music to be performed in a contrasting way! Indeed, the observance of repeats challenges the performer to find a different, stylistically appropriate inflection. A divergency of readings would be helpful, not deleterious.

The experienced musician learns to live with such problems, but a student will be unaware of them and accept the editor's decisions without question. At a time when music education is increasingly sketchy, performers are confronted with many decisions—choices of edition, of instruments (historic *vs.* modern), proper execution of ornaments, use of embellishment or improvisation—for which they are scarcely prepared. While answers to some of these questions are to be found in treatises and recent monographs and articles,[59] there can be no substitute for immersion in a style, its conventions, and the personal languages of its greatest practitioners.

Notes

1. This figure does not include fragmentary and doubtful works.

2. An exception is the set of six German dances K.509, which Mozart seems to have written in the piano version first. Cf. Marius Flothuis, "Neue Erkenntnisse in bezug auf Mozarts Tanzmusik. Ein Arbeitsbericht." *Mitteilungen der Internationalen Stiftung Mozarteum* 28 (1980), 12–15.

3. The standard version of the work incorporates a completion (mm. 98–107) that is probably the work of August Eberhard Müller; cf. the *Neue Mozart-Ausgabe* (NMA) Vol. IX/27, Band 2.

4. Mozart's knowledge of the north German style is shown by a curious piano piece in his handwriting entitled *Adagio variée* (*sic*) in a foreign hand, K^3 206a/K^6 Anh. A 65. The work, a binary piece with exceedingly florid ornamentation, may be Mozart's embellishment of a work by another composer, or a copy of such a work. From its paper and handwriting it would seem to date from his seventeenth year.

5. The autograph of K.475 documents Mozart's decision to delete its opening key signature while working on it. This suggests his awareness of the psychological effect upon the performer: the instability of the work is surely heightened by the missing visual corroboration of the tonal center.

6. The latest chronology of Mozart's works is the product of the pioneering work of Wolfgang Plath (Mozart's handwriting) and Alan Tyson (the paper types of the manuscripts). See Plath 1976/77 and Tyson 1987.

7. The virtuoso middle section of the first prelude is also labeled *Capriccio*.

8. Cf. NMA IX/27, *Klavierstücke*, Band 2: *Einzelstücke*, 4–5, 148–151.

9. Cf. the facsimile in NMA IX/27, Band 2, XXXIX.

10. The work is dated 25 August 1784 in Mozart's autograph catalogue, but Daniel N. Leeson and David Whitwell have shown that the first ten entries of the catalogue (K.449–458) were back-dated, and that Mozart was seriously ill on the day he later claimed to have completed K.455. "Mozart's Thematic Catalogue," *Musical Times* 114 (1973): 782.

11. This work seems to be a pendant to the twelve variations on an Allegretto in B-flat K.500 (12 September 1786), which immediately preceded it. In K.500 the theme is as economical as could be imagined: binary form with four measures in each half. In K.501 this is expanded to 8 and 10—the second half featuring a two-measure insert whose expansional effect far transcends its duration.

12. Wolfgang transposed the minuet from G major to F major. It also appears in a version for solo piano in Nannerl's Notebook; cf. NMA IX/27, Band 1, 76.

13. Printed in the NMA as a piano trio with cello.

14. These are not the first solo piano sonatas Mozart composed. Four sonatas in G, B-flat, C, and F, K.33d-e-f-g, have been lost (cf. NMA IX/25, Band 1, Foreword, X–XI). On the other hand, two compositions occasionally considered part of the corpus of piano sonatas (K.46d-e) are in fact for two string instruments or string instrument and continuo (*ibid.*, NMA VIII/21, Foreword, VII).

15. This technique, clearly vocal in inspiration, contrasts with the instrumental procedure of constructing phrases out of a smaller motive that is repeated or developed. The latter practice is characteristic of Haydn and was taken over by Beethoven, who turned such an economical—even obsessive—use of cellular rhythms into an outstanding feature of his personal style.

16. The appearance of Mozart's vocal style in Haydn's later music is important evidence of the younger composer's influence. A comparison of the slow movements of Mozart's Sonata in D K.576 (July 1789) and Haydn's Sonata in E-flat, Hob. XVI:49 (1789–1790) shows Haydn's adoption of a more purled surface. Note, for example, the melodic connection over the half-cadence in mm. 4–5 of both examples. Nonetheless, there is more punctuation in the Haydn (mm. 2, 6). It must be emphasized that this is not at all a question of virtue *vs.* fault: Haydn's interruptions have a beguiling quality of casual humor. Such comparisons cannot answer the question as to whether Haydn's rhetoric differs here because he sought to set general limits on the use of Mozart's approach or because the character he desired set the limits for him. (It would be foolish to claim that he was unable to adopt Mozart's device at this point in his development.)

17. Despite Mozart's challenges to the most advanced performers—and the more advanced the player, the more challenging Mozart often seems—he always tailors his vocal and instrumental music perfectly, not just to the medium but usually to the individual performer. One of the few exceptions to this phenomenon is the A-minor sonata K.310, *q.v.*

18. A short cadenza preceding the primary theme, frequently beginning on the dominant (as opposed to a true cadenza, which is prompted by the cadential six-four).

19. See, e.g., the Sonata in D K.311/284c, and the Sonata for Piano and Violin in D K.306/300l.

20. It is perhaps not entirely coincidental that the "Kegelstatt" Trio for piano, clarinet, and viola K.498—in the same key—uses the same sequence of movements (with a minuet in the dominant in the middle).

21. Two factors seem to have determined the presence or absence of written-out embellishment: (1) whether the work was intended for Mozart's own use—in which case it was usually left in a semi-finished state upon which he could improvise *ad libitum*, e.g., most of the piano concertos—or for students, who required a polished surface, e.g., the C-minor sonata K.457, as preserved in the dedication copy for Maria Theresia von Trattner; and (2) the work's publication history: published sonatas were provided with explicit dynamics and ornamentation, as these were required by amateurs (K.284/205a, K.332 in F major), whereas unpublished ones were not (K.570 in B-flat major).

22. For the dating of the first edition see Gertraut Haberkamp, *Die Erstdrucke der Werke von Wolfgang Amadeus Mozart* (Tutzing, 1986), 128.

23. 252 measures in *Allegretto grazioso* tempo or ten pages in a typical modern edition, as opposed to the nearest competitor, 277 measures of 3/8 Presto, on five pages. (The theme with twelve variations of K.284/205b is of equal if not greater length, but does not bear the weight of a structural arch.)

24. Regarding the identification of K.309 as the sonata for Rose Cannabich, cf. NMA IX/26, Band 1, Foreword, XIII–XIV.

25. This procedure is carried out with the A-minor Rondo K.511 in Levin 1992.

26. Cf. n. 19.

27. The finale of K.306/300l is predominantly in 6/8, though the first theme is an allegretto 2/4—a device borrowed from the Violin Concerto in D major K.218.

28. As part of his examination Barrington requested that Mozart improvise a *Song of Rage*, and reported that "in the middle of it, [Mozart] had worked himself up to such a pitch, that he beat his harpsichord like a person possessed, rising sometimes in his chair." Barrington's account is quoted in Otto Erich Deutsch, *Mozart, Die Dokumente seines Lebens* (= NMA X/34) (Kassel, 1961), 89.

29. The Sonata for Piano and Violin in E minor K.304/300c, written shortly before, suggests that Mozart did not purge himself of these explosive feelings easily.

30. Cf. Haberkamp, *op. cit.,* 136. The earlier speculative datings by Köchel—Salzburg, 1779, and Einstein (in the third edition of the Köchel catalogue)—Paris, 1778; have been overturned by Plath's and Tyson's research, which dates the sonatas in 1783 without being certain of the venue (Vienna or Salzburg): cf. Plath 1976/77, 171, and NMA IX/25, Band 2, Foreword, IX; Tyson, "Mozart's use of 10-Stave and 12-Stave Paper," *Festschrift Albi Rosenthal,* ed. Rudolf Elvers (Tutzing, 1984), 285–87, reprinted in Tyson 1987, 229–32. The K^6 numbers for these sonatas (300h-i-k), and for the Sonata in B-flat major, K.333 (315c), therefore have little chronological value.

31. When Mozart sought to write an ambitious sonata with a public profile, he had no trouble doing so; cf. the C-minor sonata K.457!

32. Of course, the *Rondo alla Turca* begins in A minor, but it has substantial sections in the *maggiore* and ends in major.

33. See Tyson, "The Date of Mozart's Piano Sonata in B-flat, K.333 (315c): the 'Linz' Sonata?" *Musik, Edition, Interpretation. Gedenkschrift Günter Henle,* ed. Martin Bente (Munich, 1980), 447–54, reprinted in Tyson 1987, 73–81.

34. Only one more sonata—the C minor K.457—belongs to what one could justifiably describe as Mozart's "middle" period, which culminates in 1786 with the works numbered in the K.490s. Thereafter, the language becomes more idiosyncratic: the sonata K.533 is wilfull in a way that K.333 is not, and no one would confuse the String Quartet in F K.590, with one from the set dedicated to Haydn.

35. In a master class, Konrad Wolff once related an anecdote about Schnabel playing loudly and slowly a series of six numbing dissonances as Wolff entered Schnabel's studio one day. "Incredible, isn't it?" remarked Schnabel. Wolff could only mumble baffled agreement until Schnabel played the passage surrounding mm. 216–218 of K.333's finale (11th, 11th, 9th, 9th, 7th, 7th) at tempo. See Konrad Wolff, *Schnabel's Interpretation of Piano Music,* 2nd ed. (New York, 1972), 45–46.

36. Indeed, the foreword to Wolfgang Plath's and Wolfgang Rehm's NMA edition suggests that Mozart composed the fantasia with an eye toward the double publication with the sonata; cf. NMA IX/25, Band 2, XIII. At the very least, performance and evaluation as a totality respects their historical tradition.

37. Cf. the Serenade for Eight Winds K.388/384a (also transcribed for string quintet, K.406/516b); the Piano Concerto K.491; and the C-minor interlude from *Thamos, König in Ägypten* K.345/336a.

38. The numbers in parentheses apply to those editions that print a second

time the second half of the D-major episode (mm. 26ff.) rather than using repeat signs.

39. Wolfgang Amadeus Mozart, *Fantasie und Sonate c-Moll für Klavier KV 475 & 457*. Facsimile edition (Salzburg/Kassel, 1991). The autograph is more useful for what it reveals of Mozart's compositional process—the original notation of the fantasia with the C minor key signature of three flats, quickly deleted, and the two different ornamentations of the recurring subject of the middle movement—than as a source for the definitive text. Again we see the importance of publication history: Mozart evidently undertook considerable elaboration and correction of his work prior to its publication.

40. Now in the Jewish National & University Library, Jerusalem.

41. The autograph shows that Mozart originally conceived a shorter ending, with quarter-note Cs on the first beat of m. 301, followed by the two chords at the present end of the movement.

42. Cf. NMA IX/27, Band 2, Foreword (Wolfgang Plath), XVI–XVII.

43. That K.511 was composed in 1787, some fifty years before Chopin's maturity, suggests how profoundly the evolution of musical style might have been altered had Mozart lived as long as Beethoven (i.e., to 1813), or as long as Haydn (1833!). The stylistic congruence between Mozart and Chopin reminds us of Chopin's reverence for Mozart, who, along with Bach and the bel canto school, was the primary influence on his work.

44. To be sure, Mozart had earlier experimented with alternatives to period structure. e.g., in K.333/i, where the opening is built out of the classic I-IV-V-I progression, and where an emphasis on the tonic provides, with extension, a unitary construction of the opening (mm. 1–10). But there the rhetoric, while both conversational and self-possessed, does not exhibit the speculative tone of K.533.

45. For example, the second movement of the Divertimento in E-flat for string trio K.563.

46. This surely does not imply that Mozart found these terms interchangeable, but that in transforming an independent work to a part of a greater whole he chose to alter its pacing to suit its new context. Charles Rosen made this very point in an exchange with Eva Badura-Skoda. See *Haydn Studies,* ed. Jens Peter Larsen, Howard Serwer, and James Webster (New York and London, 1981), 218.

47. The revised version does not survive in Mozart's hand; its only source is the first edition—Hoffmeister, Vienna, 1788, according to Haberkamp's dating (*op. cit.,* 300). Nonetheless, the changes compared with the autograph of K.494 are substantive and unlikely to have been made by a Viennese publisher with whom Mozart had close relations unless he had sanctioned them.

48. Mozart never chose as principal key a tonality with more than four sharps or flats; in fact, the only time such keys appear are in major/minor exchanges (such as in the variations), or in modulatory passages.

49. Had Mozart wished to adhere to the meter he could have begun the first ending a half-measure earlier, keeping the second ending where it is. This would move the bar lines and bring the phrasing back to the first beat.

There are other cases of metric displacement in Mozart—notably the slow movement to the "Hunt" Quartet in B-flat K.458. Normally Mozart ultimately inserts a half-bar to recapture the notated meter.

50. Cf. NMA IX/25, Band 2, Foreword, XVII–XVIII.

51. In fact, there is no evidence to suggest that repeats were not to be taken wherever indicated, and much evidence to support their strict observance, even in da capos of minuets. However, we should acknowledge that what may have been done two hundred years ago, when most pieces were heard for the first time, may not necessarily be obligatory today, when the standard repertoire is performed before an audience with dozens, even hundreds, of performances of the work within its experience.

52. Cf. the duet *"Bei Männern, welche Liebe fühlen"* from *Die Zauberflöte* and the slow movement of the Piano Concerto in F K.459.

53. Although K.570 antedates Mozart's voyage to Potsdam and Berlin, one might wonder if it—not the D-major sonata K.576—was one of the six easy sonatas for Princess Friederika of Prussia mentioned in Mozart's letter of 12 July 1789 to Michael Puchberg. This would explain its lack of virtuosity. K.576 cannot be considered easy by any criterion.

54. Cf. NMA IX/27, Band 2, Foreword, XVII–XVIII.

55. The only movement he was ever to write in that key is the middle movement to the Piano Concerto in A K.488.

56. Cf. in particular Schumann's piano sonatas, chamber works, and symphonies.

57. Indeed, the Henle edition occasionally deletes Mozart's wedges altogether when their use—for instance on long notes—contradicts the conventional *staccato* meaning of dots.

58. It should be emphasized that all editorial additions in Bärenreiter/the NMA are visually apparent—added accidentals are printed in smaller type, added slurs are dotted, etc. Still, it is easy for the user to overlook this or assume that these additions must be based upon sound judgment rather than subjective preference.

59. Cf., for example, Levin 1992; also Levin 1989, Badura-Skoda 1962, and Neumann 1986.

Selected Bibliography

Abert, Hermann. *W. A. Mozart. Neubearbeitete und erweiterte Ausgabe von Otto Jahns "Mozart."* 2 vols. 7th edition. Leipzig, 1955. Index by Erich Kapst. Leipzig, 1966.

Anderson, Emily. *The Letters of Mozart & His Family.* Chronologically arranged, translated, and edited with an introduction, notes, and indexes. 3rd edition. London, 1985.

Badura-Skoda, Eva, and Paul Badura-Skoda. *Interpreting Mozart on the Keyboard.* Trans. Leo Black. London and New York, 1962.

Bilson, Malcolm. "Some General Thoughts on Ornamentation in Mozart's Keyboard Works." *The Piano Quarterly* 24 (1976): 26–28.

Dennerlein, Hanns. *Der unbekannte Mozart: Die Welt seiner Klavierwerke.* Leipzig, 1951.

Einstein, Alfred. *Mozart. His Character, His Work.* Trans. Arthur Mendel and Nathan Broder. New York, 1945.

Freeman, Daniel E. "Josef Mysliveček and Mozart's Piano Sonatas K. 309 (284b) and 311 (284c)." In *Mozart-Jahrbuch 1995,* 195–209.

Levin, Robert D. "Instrumental Ornamentation, Improvisation and Cadenzas." In *Performance Practice. The Grove Handbooks in Music,* ed. Howard Mayer Brown and Stanley Sadie. London, 1989, 267–91.

———. "Improvised embellishments in Mozart's keyboard music." *Early Music* 20 (1992): 221–33.

Mercado, Mario R. *The Evolution of Mozart's Pianistic Style.* Carbondale, IL, 1992.

Neumann, Frederick. *Ornamentation and Improvisation in Mozart.* Princeton, 1986.

Plath, Wolfgang. "Beiträge zur Mozart-Autographie I. Die Handschrift Leopold Mozarts." *Mozart-Jahrbuch 1960/61:* 82–117.

———. "Beiträge zur Mozart-Autographie II. Schriftchronologie 1770–1780." *Mozart-Jahrbuch 1976/77:* 131–73.

Ratner, Leonard G. "Topical Content in Mozart's Keyboard Sonatas." *Early Music* 19 (1991): 615–19.

Rosen, Charles. *The Classical Style: Haydn, Mozart, Beethoven.* New York, 1971.

———. *Sonata Forms.* Revised edition. New York, 1988.

Tovey, Donald Francis. *Essays in Musical Analysis.* 6 vols. London, 1935–1939.

Tyson, Alan. *Mozart: Studies of the Autograph Scores.* Cambridge, MA, 1987.

Van Reijen, Paul Willem. *Vergleichende Studien zur Klaviervariationstechnik von Mozart und seinen Zeitgenossen.* Buren, 1988.

Wyzewa, Théodore de, and Georges de Saint-Foix. *Wolfgang Amadée Mozart. Sa vie musicale et son oeuvre. Essai de biographie critique.* 5 vols. Paris, 1912–1946.

CHAPTER TEN

Mozart's Keyboard Concertos

Robert D. Levin

The Concerto Principle: Formal and Aesthetic Premises

By the time Mozart had composed the first of his original keyboard concertos in December 1773, he had many aesthetic and stylistic sources on which to draw. His natural gift for character portrayal had deepened as a result of his considerable experience as an opera and aria composer. He now proceeded to carry this ability over to the concerto genre: indeed, each of Mozart's concertos possesses a distinct persona. In his concertante vocal and instrumental works Mozart successfully reconciled virtuosity with the needs of dramatic expression, deploying a fluid rhythmic language and an increasingly voluptuous orchestral fabric.

The influence of Mozart's vocal music on his instrumental concertos is apparent in many rhetorical details imported from the former sphere to the latter—for example, the recitative-like passages in the slow movements of many piano concertos (K.451, 466, 467, 537, 595; cf. Ex. 10.6 below).[1] The variety of accompaniment patterns in the orchestra—as many as three within a single phrase—and the vivacity with which the ensemble responds to and provokes the soloist parallel the practice cultivated in arias and accompanied recitatives, in which the orchestra effectively functions as alter ego of the soloist.

Many of these devices owe much to the *galant* style of J. C. Bach. Bach's keyboard writing epitomizes an Italianate elegance of phrasing and an equally Italian natural, *cantabile* idiom that likewise informs Mozart's concerto rhetoric. Mozart's harmonic language effects a telling synthesis of Italian ebullience, the richer German vocabulary, and an interest in sophisticated compositional procedures that reflects the influence of Joseph and Michael Haydn. If the structure of Mozart's concertos owes much to its forerunners (J. C. Bach in particular), it is nevertheless altogether his own. Mozart was to make few changes in his concerto archetype: from his first surviving original concerto through his last, he retained the formal structure he had borrowed from his arias.[2] This structure is not only common to all of Mozart's concertos,[3] it distinguishes them from those of all other composers. Even Beethoven, who in many ways sought to emulate Mozart, did not chose to duplicate his concerto prototype—perhaps because of its great thematic complexity. As is generally acknowledged, Beethoven's motivic construction and usage reflects Haydn's practice; to Beethoven Mozart's plethora of melodic ideas may well have seemed profligate.

Arthur Hutchings has described the thematic richness of Mozart's concertos by likening it to pieces in a jigsaw puzzle,[4] although such an analysis denies the specific purposes for which the various themes were designed. Whereas some have similar functions, a flourish, for instance, is not interchangeable with a main theme. Mozart's ordering of material reflects specific structural concerns. Consider the ritornellos of the first movement of the B-flat-major concerto K.456. Reflecting Mozart's habit, the middle tutti (mm. 173ff.) and the one to the cadenza (mm. 337ff.) begin with the first energetic motive from the opening ritornello (mm. 18ff.); similarly, the tutti after the cadenza begins with the first energetic closing idea (mm. 51ff.) from the opening ritornello. Thus, the eight different thematic ideas in the movement (seven in the opening ritornello plus an additional theme for the soloist at m. 102ff.) are not ordered randomly.

The hierarchical organization of Mozart's concertos enabled him to construct movements of elaborate and varied content without sacrificing cogency. He thereby avoided two common pitfalls: mechanical formalism and lack of structural tautness. Many concertos by his contemporaries offer chains of musical ideas of similar character in loose, episodic discourse.[5] Evidently, not even the finest concerto composers of the time—Viotti and Haydn—were able to achieve Mozart's symbiosis of rhetoric and form. Within the exposition or recapitulation of a Mozart concerto no two adjacent sections have the same structural or expressive function, but a work such as Haydn's 'Cello Concerto in D (Hob. VIIb:2) (1783) contains several such repeated presentations of material (mm. 41ff., 65ff.), during which the discourse loses focus. Unlike the consistent dimensions and proportions of Mozart's concerto form, the individual concertos of Haydn and Viotti vary considerably in length, content, and proportion.

The Early Period, 1767–1779

Concerto Transcriptions

When one considers that Mozart began to perform in public at the age of six, then it seems singular that his earliest surviving original keyboard concerto—the Concerto in D major K.175—dates from December 1773, when he was almost eighteen.[6] The absence of original concertos from Mozart's early period is particularly striking in light of the large number of arias he composed from the age of nine. These compositions reveal that Mozart was conversant with the conventions of concerted vocal music for many years before he turned his hand to an instrumental concerto.

Although Mozart's initial neglect of the instrumental concerto remains unexplained, the Viennese concert tour he was to undertake in 1768 seems to have provided the motivation for the preparation, during the preceding year, of four keyboard concertos: the concertos in F major K.37 (April 1767), in B-flat major K.39 (June 1767), in D major K.40 (July 1767), and in G major K.41 (July 1767).

For some time these concertos were considered original compositions. They were numbered 1 to 4 in the *Gesamtausgabe* of Breitkopf & Härtel (hereafter B & H), so that the standard numbering beyond that from 5 to 27—still prevalent in concert programs and the literature—gives a false impression of Mozart's output, which consists of twenty-one solo concertos and two concertos (B & H nos. 7 and 10) for multiple keyboards. At the beginning of this century Théodore de Wyzewa and Georges de Saint-Foix established that K.37, 39–41 were *pasticci*—that is, a potpourri of solo keyboard pieces by various composers—mostly extracted from sonatas and fitted with orchestral accompaniments to transform them into concertos. Apart from minor revisions, the solo keyboard parts are not by Mozart but by Carl Philipp Emanuel Bach, Johann Gottfried Eckard, Leontzi Honauer, Hermann Friedrich Raupach, and Johann Schobert.[7] With the exception of C. P. E. Bach all were German expatriates living in Paris at the time of Mozart's first visit to the French capital in 1763–1764.

Mozart's procedure for transcribing solo pieces in binary form into concerto movements was quite straightforward:

1. An introductory ritornello in the tonic key is inserted at the very beginning of the movement.
2. The first half of the original solo movement then appears, supplemented by a free orchestral accompaniment. (Sometimes the soloist is allowed to play without orchestral support.)
3. After the original double bar at the midpoint of the movement a second ritornello is interpolated to underscore the arrival in the dominant key, or to provide a preparation in the dominant for the second half, analogous to the introductory ritornello.
4. The second half of the binary solo movement ensues, accompanied as in section 2.
5. A pair of ritornellos in the tonic is added at the end of the movement to prepare and follow the soloist's cadenza.

In 1772 or soon before, Mozart prepared similar transcriptions of three solo sonatas by Johann Christian Bach.[8] The autograph manuscript for these concertos bears the title *Tre Sonate del Sgr. Giovanni Bach ridotte in Concerti dal Sgr. Amadeo Wolfgango Mozart.* Unlike K.37/39–41, these were not included in B & H and remained unpublished until 1932.

Both sets of concerto transcriptions represent the collective effort of Leopold and Wolfgang, as documented by the presence of both handwritings throughout the manuscripts. As Wolfgang Plath has shown, Leopold not only carried out some of the mechanical copying (including the figuration of the bass in the tutti passages) for the earlier set, but also corrected his son's work.[9] Scholars have hinted at the importance of Leopold's compositional tutelage in Mozart's first published works (the sonatas K.6–9 and the sonatas/trios K.10–15), and it appears also to have continued in Mozart's early teens.

Two questions arise at this juncture: Why did Mozart initially transcribe other works into concertos rather than write his own, and why, with his own abilities as both pianist and violinist, did it take him so long to finally start composing concertos? One possible explanation may be that the keyboard concerto had yet to be widely cultivated. After J. S. Bach's pioneering efforts, the composition of keyboard concertos was at first primarily a north German phenomenon, with remarkable contributions to the genre by C. P. E. Bach.[10] During the 1770s, however, keyboard concertos became increasingly popular.

Concerto in D K.175 (B & H 5)

Mozart's first surviving original keyboard concerto bears the date December 1773 in its (now missing) autograph. It has a scoring unique among all the concertos: 2 oboes, [bassoon ad libitum,][11] 2 horns, 2 trumpets, timpani, and strings.[12] Given that the upper range of the solo part is limited to d^3, Mozart may have had a particular instrument—perhaps the organ—in mind.[13]

The outer movements of K.175 are typical of Mozart's brilliant Italianate style, with repetitions of local subphrases for rhetorical vivacity. The lefthand writing shows Mozart's efforts at freeing himself from the unrelieved Alberti bass that deadens so many movements of the *pasticci* concertos and his own earlier sonatas for piano and violin:[14] a number of different sixteenth-note patterns coexist with the standard one. Nonetheless, it is clear that something of a *horror vacui* is operating. When the sixteenths pause in the left hand, they are immediately taken up by the right; there are only three bars in the solo exposition (repeated in the recapitulation) in which the sixteenths abate. The same practice is to be found in the finale (with *alla breve* eighth-notes). If this relentless motion does not grate on the ear it is because Mozart gives every phrase a direction and purpose. By integrating the motoric rhythm into a larger character and structure, he enables the listener to hear beyond the local chatter. We shall see how far these abilities were to take the master when we consider the finale of the E-flat concerto K.271.

As Marius Flothuis has noted, there are striking similarities between the motivic content of K.175's second movement and that of the *scena* (recitative and aria) *"Alcandro, lo confesso"/"Non sò d'onde viene"* K.294, written in Mannheim for Aloysia Weber contemporaneously with Mozart's Mannheim performance of K.175.[15] It is telling that the moments of most intense expression in this movement rely on stock formulas that Mozart had taken over from J. C. Bach (Ex. 10.1).

EXAMPLE 10.1. Piano Concerto in D Major K.175. Movement 2, mm. 61–65 (orchestra omitted)

The effect of such formulas is limited, however, because of their localized treatment. The pattern cited above is used in K.175 to open a new section directly after the middle tutti, and it stops after four bars on the dominant, leaving the orchestra to repeat it with an enriched harmonization and texture. Thus, there is no growth to or from the progression. Mozart did not abandon such formulas in his later years, but he integrated them into the larger discourse with greater skill: a sequence like this one would appear as the culmination of a long phrase and was often succeeded by further motion before coming to a stable cadence. The following excerpt, from the middle movement of the E-flat concerto K.449, is typical (Ex. 10.2).

EXAMPLE 10.2. Piano Concerto in E-flat Major K.449. Movement 2, mm. 103–107

Mozart performed K.175 in Vienna on 3 March and 23 March 1782. In a letter to his father dated 23 March Mozart announced that he was sending along a new finale to the work—the Rondo K.382.[16] The revised version with the new rondo proved to be a tremendous success—indeed, the rondo had to be repeated. Given the unabashed brilliance of the writing, with its dependence on the flourish-like trilling figure of the descending theme, this is scarcely surprising.

Despite Mozart's use of the title *Rondo*, K.382 would more properly be described as a theme with variations. The rondo designation may have been prompted by the orchestra's interpolation of the first half of the theme after the first and third variations and at the beginning of the final section in 3/8 meter (mm. 33–40, 73–80, 137–152).

Why did Mozart replace the Salzburg finale? Marius Flothuis has observed that all of Mozart's concerto finales except for K.175 and the nearly contemporaneous Violin Concerto in B-flat K.207 are cast as rondos and variations. The finales of both K.175 and K.207 are in sonata form, and in both cases Mozart replaced them.[17] It is enlightening that he could supplant music of great intrinsic worth owing to the imperatives of high-level structural considerations.

Concerto in B-flat K.238 (B & H 6)

The autograph of Mozart's next keyboard concerto, K.238, is dated January 1776. Compared with K.175, K.238 more successfully breaks the relentless sixteenth-note motion by introducing alternative textures (lefthand eighth-notes in thirds, m. 47ff.; imitative syncopation, m. 69ff., the later taken from the first "tutti"). The delicate coloration of the second movement, underscored by the presence of flutes instead of oboes, is marked by a number of passages of great timbral beauty, notably the chain of descending trills and the ensuing sextuplet decorations (mm. 34ff. and 71ff.). The finale shows the influence of the violin concertos composed the previous year in several respects: the movement begins with the solo instrument (unlike either K.175/3 or K.382); it includes lead-ins (short cadenzas) for the soloist after the exposition (m. 99) and features the mediant key in the rondo's central episode (mm. 141–168). In a further parallel, the first and last orchestral ritornellos feature quiet conclusions.

Concerto for Three Pianos in F K.242 (B & H 7)

In February 1776, a month after completing K.238, Mozart composed his one concerto for three pianos K.242. It was written for performance by Countess Antonia Lodron and her two daughters, Aloisia and Josepha. The concerto is a model of rococo elegance, its *galanterie* beguiling throughout. The middle movement's songful charm exploits the sonic possibilities of the trio of keyboards, particularly when heard on period instruments. Toward the end of the finale Mozart sets up a delightful hoax: after apparently ending the movement he interjects a casual melodic rejoinder that airily leads to a final statement of the main theme.

The third piano part of the concerto is significantly less demanding than the first and second, reflecting the abilities of the younger Lodron daughter. Subsequently, Mozart transcribed the concerto's solo parts for two instruments, most likely for performance with his sister, Nannerl.[18] (They are known to have played the two-piano version in Salzburg on 3 September 1780.)

Concerto in C K.246 (B & H No. 8)

In April 1776 Mozart wrote a concerto for Countess Antonia Lützow. If the work makes relatively modest demands on the performer, this surely reflects the Countess's abilities. The technical accessibility of the concerto led Mozart to use it frequently as a teaching piece. It is perhaps for this reason too that three sets of cadenzas survive. Some of these are quite short and bear a relation to vocal cadenzas, which according to a general eighteenth-century criterion were to be singable in one breath. Unique to the "Lützow" concerto is a surviving autograph continuo part. Earlier contentions that it documented Mozart's intended realization of the *col Basso* direction in his concertos have been disproved convincingly by Linda Faye Ferguson, who has shown that it was designed for two-piano performance without orchestra and thus is unrelated to Mozart's continuo playing.[19]

It is noteworthy that this concerto, Mozart's first in C major, contains materials that he was to return to in later concertos in the same key. Compare the second themes of the first movements to K.246, 415/387b, and 503 (Ex. 10.3):

EXAMPLE 10.3. Second themes from the first movements of three Piano Concertos in C Major (orchestra omitted)

a. K.246

b. K.415/387b

c. K.503

Concerto in E-flat K.271 (B & H 9)

Mozart's next keyboard concerto, K.271, is universally recognized as a watershed in his artistic development. It was written for a French virtuosa, referred to by the Mozarts as Mlle Jeunehomme, who came through Salzburg in January 1777—the date of the concerto—and whom Mozart was to encounter during his stay in Paris in 1778.[20] Judging from the concerto, her technical abilities must have been prodigious. The work uses the standard scoring of 2 oboes, [bassoon ad libitum,] 2 horns, and strings that Mozart employed for most of his 1773–1778 concertos, but nothing else about the work is routine. For the first and only time in his concerto output Mozart has the solo instrument interrupt the orchestra's opening motive with a cockiness that is to characterize both of the work's outer movements. Indeed, there is a quality of hubris about the soloist's constant interjections within the orchestral ritornellos, and the sparkle of the passagework, punctuated in the development by daunting cross-hand writing, creates an exuberance that is new to Mozart's rhetoric. One suspects an element of flirtation in the delight of the barely twenty-one-year-old master, setting the young woman an intimidating challenge while displaying his compositional prowess. The finale, a dazzling virtuosic showpiece, breaks its pace but once—with the astonishing interpolation of a serene minuet in A-flat major.[21] All the more remarkable, then, that Mozart should have decided to eschew a charming slow movement for one of wrenching poignancy, whose operatic character extends beyond the open use of recitative in both orchestra and solo.

Concerto for Two Pianos in E-flat K.365/316a (B & H 10)

In early 1779 Mozart composed a double concerto for joint performance with Nannerl. The work undoubtedly reflects the influence of the *symphonies concertantes* that were the latest rage during Mozart's visit to Paris in 1778. Apart from effective antiphonal banter between the players, K.365/316a features rapid passages in parallel thirds, tremolo flourishes, and octave doublings to exploit the full sonic potential of the two players, thereby anticipating the equally brilliant two-piano sonata K.448/375a composed two years later.

The slow movement is a serenade that beguiles the listener despite the fact that there is not a single structural modulation to be found: a brief interlude at measure 46 starts in E-flat major and reaches C minor at m. 50 to regain B-flat major at m. 54—eight measures out of a total of 105!

The Three Concertos of 1782–1783

A season after he had settled in Vienna, Mozart composed a series of three piano concertos for his subscription concerts. These concertos,

K.414–413–415/385p–387a–387b, his first works in the idiom after his move to the imperial capital, were among the few published within his lifetime. Initially distributed in manuscript copies (1783), they appeared in print shortly thereafter (1784–1785). In an oft-cited letter to his father dated 28 December 1782, Mozart described them as follows:

> These concertos are a happy medium between what is too easy and too difficult; they are very brilliant, pleasing to the ear, and natural, without being vapid. There are passages here and there from which connoisseurs alone can derive satisfaction; but these passages are written in such a way that the less learned cannot fail to be pleased, though without knowing why.[22]

Mozart wrote the concertos with *ad libitum* wind parts and conceived the string texture so that *a quattro* performance (with single strings) was possible.[23] It might seem that no particular compositional effort would be required to insure an effective performance with single strings, but this is not so: the symphonic writing of the later Vienna concertos would sound scrappy in many of the *forte* sections if played by single strings, whereas these three concertos display a notable care in the counterpoint and texture of the string writing that makes chamber performance successful.[24]

Concerto in A K.414/385p (B & H 12)

Documentary evidence reveals that the A-major concerto K.414/386a/385p was the first of the three to be composed. The relationship between K.414 and the Rondo in A K.386, whose autograph is dated 19 October 1782, has been the subject of debate. Some scholars have suggested that K.386 is a replacement finale for K.414; others contend that K.414's finale replaced K.386. An important clue to their relationship is that K.386 contains a part for obbligato 'cello, making *a quattro* performance impossible. K.414 and K.386 have virtually the same scoring: 2 oboes, [bassoon ad libitum,] 2 horns, and strings (to which K.386 adds obbligato 'cello).

Mozart was noticeably conservative about his choice of keys—although emphatically not about modulations within those keys. This conservatism is linked to a specific sense of character and coloration that he seems to have associated with each of the keys between four sharps and four flats to which (with the exception of *minore* variations) he limited himself. While the most normative keys—D major and C major—display, respectively, a brilliance and majesty that are typical of many composers of the period, the decidedly more individual personality of other keys is readily apparent. Mozart's A major is a tonality of radiance and serenity—qualities that are evident in later works, notably the piano concerto K.488 and the quintet and concerto for clarinet (K.581, K.622).

The first movement of K.414 glows with the same lyrical ardor that suffuses Belmonte's and Pedrillo's love music in *Die Entführung aus dem Serail,* which was composed at the same time. Indeed, one of K.414's themes contains a cadential figure found in the second act of the opera (Ex. 10.4).

The development of the first movement is arresting in its sweep. It moves quickly to F-sharp minor and stays there until mere seconds before the recapitulation—this is virtually Mozart's only concerto development with a single structural axis. (The norm is a two-part development, in which the first part leads to a crisis on the dominant of one key—often the relative minor—precipitating a second half whose climax is the act of returning to the tonic.)

The second movement's main theme is closely related to Johann Christian Bach's Overture to Baldassare Galuppi's opera *La Calamità dei Cuori* (1763).[25] The "London" Bach was a good friend of Mozart and it has been suggested that this quotation was a homage to the master, who had died in London on 1 January 1782. This andante achieves a perfect synthesis of aria and instrumental concerto, to which Mozart had aspired since the composition of K.175. It is remarkable that he is able to maintain the melodic flow despite the regularity of the phrase lengths: in the solo exposition the only phrase not four bars long is the last one (2 + 4 = 6). The roving dialogue between soloist and orchestra in the movement's development is the antecedent for the miracle of K.453 only two years later.

The rondo adroitly treads a line between the flirtatious and the ingenuous. The moments of tension are deliberately stagey; indeed, the most dramatic passage (mm. 190–197) was inserted subsequent to the completion of the movement, which originally ended the cadenza at the *tempo primo* in m. 197. Comparison with K.386 is enlightening. The character of the latter rondo is quite similar to the opening movement of the concerto. While K.386 is in a distinctly more lyrical vein than K.414/3, its passagework is flashier than anything in K.414.[26]

Concerto in F K.413/387a (B & H 11)

The second of the 1782–1783 concertos is the only one by Mozart whose outer movements are both in triple meter ($\frac{3}{4}$). Indeed, there are only two other piano concertos—in E-flat major K.449, and in C minor K.491—whose first movements are in triple meter. This fact is not merely of statistical interest: in Mozart, moderate to fast movements in three beats are felt in a single beat. This has two principal consequences. First, the nature of harmonic rhythm in triple meter often causes the sense of forward motion to be more palpable than is the case in $\frac{4}{4}$ meter. Second, the number of measures in a phrase has metrical significance (cf. the passage from mm. 145–164). Mozart's choice of $\frac{4}{4}$ for the spa-

EXAMPLE 10.4a. Piano Concerto in A Major K.414/385p. Movement 1, mm. 50–54

EXAMPLE 10.4b. *Die Entführung aus dem Serail* K.384. Act 2, no. 16. Quartet, mm. 209–212

cious second movement—a meter he used only one other time for the middle movement of a piano concerto (K.242)—may be due to these factors.

In the finale the solo/tutti distinction is underplayed throughout, creating a continuous chamber music discourse that masks the structural articulations—a rarity for a composer who normally strives for maximum architectural clarity.

Concerto in C K.415/387b (B & H 13)

The last of the three subscription concertos originally had the same scoring as K.414 and 413: 2 oboes, 2 horns, and strings. The autograph shows that Mozart added parts for 2 bassoons, 2 trumpets, and timpani later.[27] K.415 thus has the richest set of performing options of the three concertos: full orchestra, string orchestra with oboes and horns, string orchestra without winds, *a quattro*. Nonetheless, it is clear from the string writing that Mozart was turning from the intimacy of K.413 back to symphonic sonorities. It is not the imitative opening that manifests this, but rather the *forte* that follows, driven by the tremolos of the inner strings and culminating in the imitative passage between bass and viola under syncopated double stops in both violins. The magnificence of sonority is mirrored in the virtuoso solo writing in the coda sections of the first movement's exposition and recapitulation, passagework that surpasses anything in K.414 or K.413. The rhetoric is also more arch, encompassing all the lyrical and flirtatious elements of K.414 but profiting from the greater energy to add pranks as well as drama.

A crossed-out sketch reveals that Mozart had originally planned a slow movement in C minor, but then chose to write the most operatic middle movement since that of K.271. Nonetheless, he did not abandon his original plan to introduce unexpected pathos in the midst of high-spirited music to confound his audience: he merely raised the stakes. The finale, a rollicking $\frac{6}{8}$ set piece of a kind Mozart continued to write later in his career, begins with the solo instrument and is propelled by a lengthy tutti displaying both festive and gentle elements. The scoring of the big tune at m. 31, with the violins in octaves and the violas woven between and below the melody, hearkens back to one of Mozart's favored Salzburg textures. Arriving on a grandiose cadence on the dominant, we expect a solo entry of appropriate flamboyance. Instead, Mozart interposes an adagio in C minor, whose poignance draws upon all the favored operative devices—leaps of diminished seventh and octave, sighing appoggiaturas, the augmented sixth chord. Having arrived at a second half-cadence, what does he do? He frolics without a trace of contrition into the reprise of the $\frac{6}{8}$ theme. Given Mozart's decision to emphasize theatricality, it is revealing that he eschews the obvious boisterous ending and chooses instead a coyly elongated decrescendo to *pianissimo.*

The Twelve Great Concertos (1): 1784

The year 1784 was to prove to be Mozart's *annus mirabilis* in the composition of keyboard concertos. Within ten months he composed no fewer than six concertos—three commissioned, three for himself—and transformed the genre from one of courtly entertainment to a vessel of the highest aspirations, on an equal footing with the symphony and his most cherished domain, opera.

Concerto in E-flat K.449 (B & H 14)

Despite the symphonic ambitions of K.415, Mozart continued to be interested in the advantages (commercial and artistic) of the *a quattro* style. Contemporaneously with the composition of the three subscription concertos he began another piano concerto, in E-flat major. However, it was not until early 1784 that he had a practical reason to finish the work—a commission to compose a concerto for his gifted student Barbara (Babette) Ployer. The quality of this work suggests that she was not just a fine pianist but a sensitive musician.

The finished concerto is the first composition Mozart entered into the thematic catalogue of his works he kept until his death. It is dated 9 February 1784 in the manuscript and in the catalogue. The scoring reflects the *a quattro* norm: 2 oboes, [bassoon ad libitum,] 2 horns (the winds *ad libitum*), and strings.

K.449 constitutes one of Mozart's most sophisticated achievements. In it the composer adopts an experimental approach to his materials. This is especially noticeable in his drawing out of phrase endings, for instance in mm. 11–16 of the first movement's opening ritornello. The first movement, one of only three in $\frac{3}{4}$ time, contains Mozart's only opening ritornello that unequivocally modulates—first to C minor, then to the dominant, where it remains for an appreciable length of time. This exception to the otherwise carefully preserved distinction between non-modulating ritornello and modulating solo exposition should be understood within the work's overall speculative character. During the course of the movement we repeatedly encounter a readiness to "float" rather than to "shape," suggesting a passive hedonism that assigns the soloist an altogether different persona. At the very end of the recapitulation, the soloist's trill is made to collide with the orchestra's willful modulation to C minor, taken from the exposition (Ex. 10.5).

EXAMPLE 10.5. Piano Concerto in E-flat Major K.449. Movement 1, mm. 316–320

As the result of an early error these two events became detached from each other, placing the orchestra a measure after the soloist's trill. The only printed edition that reproduces the text correctly is that of Marius Flothuis for the NMA.

The experimental tone of the first movement also characterizes the second, whose most arresting feature is its tonal design. After the second theme appears in the dominant key of F, there is a modulation to A-flat major, and the movement begins again, as if we were at the recapitulation. But A-flat major lies outside the orbit of the movement's tonic, B-flat—even though it is the subdominant of the concerto's principal key of E-flat. What follows is uncharacteristic in every way: Mozart reproduces without alteration the events of the solo exposition (he normally introduces both rhetorical and structural modifications), reaching E-flat major for the second theme. The network of connections is bewildering: from the modulation by fifth we might think we were back in the tonic key, but we are in E-flat—subdominant of the middle movement and tonic of the outer ones. At the point where Mozart reaches the modulating passage that took him from F to A-flat in the exposition, he modulates enharmonically from B-flat minor to B minor, moves toward G minor, and in a second miraculous enharmonic transformation, floats back down to the original tonic, B-flat. We then get a "second recapitulation," this time with material not heard since the orchestral opening. The second theme, in B-flat at last, leads seamlessly to the passage quoted above in Example 10.2.

After two audacious movements, the finale returns to Mozart's familiar language. The precedent of K.271 is palpable (for example, in the cross-hand antics), but the character is self-assured rather than headlong. The narrative ease of the keyboard's motion to the dominant, the adroitness of the imitative writing, and the use of broken octaves are harbingers of the great concertos to come. At the end of the movement Mozart adapts a convention taken from his variation technique: he concludes in compound meter.[28] The movement ends much as K.271, with a drawn-out set of ever-softer good-byes interrupted by the *forte* whoop at the end.

Concerto in B-flat K.450 (B & H 15)

In his correspondence Mozart drew a clear distinction between K.449 and the concertos he wrote later in 1784. The latter were "*grosse Concerte*" ("grand concertos"), which he did not wish to have compared with K.449. Indeed, it is with the Concerto in B-flat K.450, dated 15 March 1784 in his catalogue, that the celebrated succession of "great concertos" begins. This is not to say that K.449 is in any way inferior to them, but that with K.450 Mozart's concertos became symphonic in scale and texture.

In fact, it is Mozart's concertos (and operas), not his symphonies, that effected the evolution in his orchestral writing during the Vienna years. The emancipation of the winds, central to the stylistic development of his piano concertos, is symbolized by the first movement of K.450—his first orchestral composition to open with obbligato winds. From this point on Mozart elevates the wind band to a privileged entity within the orchestra: in the concertos K.482 and K.491 they occasionally displace the strings. This transformation of the orchestral texture does not manifest itself in the symphonies until the "Prague" K.504 (1786), composed in 1786.

Speaking of the work and its sister concerto, K.451, Mozart remarked, "I really cannot choose between the two of the them, but I regard them both as concertos which are bound to make the performer perspire."[29] K.450 may well be the most technically demanding of the entire series. Its cross-hand writing in the finale is particularly devilish. The parallels between concerto and aria now become even more explicit: the soloist's flourish that interrupts the conclusion of the first ritornello (mm. 59–70) runs up to a fermata that recalls the standard vocal device known as the *fermata sospesa*—an entrance with an imperiously held note cows the orchestra into submission, permitting fioritura while the accompaniment pauses.[30] The solo sections of the movement show fully formed the formal and textural techniques that characterize the rest of the series: the rhetorical ease of the solo part, effortlessly leading but occasionally just as happy to surrender the reins to the orchestra, in order to accompany with passagework or provide a sixteenth-note gloss on the orchestra's principal material.

The middle movement is a reflective theme with variations. Best known is the finale, a hunting rondo with a brash theme that is the starting point for breathless and oft-breathtaking virtuosity. It is astounding that so little time separates K.450 from K.415; the sweep and acrobatics reach a level that knows no contemporary peers. At the end of the development (mm. 198ff.) Mozart precipitates the recapitulation with a harmonic sleight of hand that becomes a trademark in future works: he reaches a cadence on a chord (here V of the mediant key, or A major) that seems hopelessly remote from the tonic (B-flat), then proceeds to traverse the vast distance in seconds through an uncannily smooth succession of voice leadings.[31] The movement's conclusion, in which horn fanfares rise above a string tattoo from *pp* to a jubilant flourish, is as clearly designed to win the public by storm as K.415's to triumph through charm.

Piano Concerto in D K.451 (B & H 16)

On 22 March 1784, just a week after he entered K.450 into his thematic catalogue, Mozart added K.451 to the list. While he is known to have completed the "Linz" Symphony K.425 within four days, he may have worked simultaneously on K.450 and K.451, finishing one a week before the other.

K.451 is the first of four consecutive piano concertos that begin with the march rhythm of ♩ ♫♩♩ ♩ . Nonetheless, the character of each is altogether individual. D major is the standard trumpet-and-drum key of both Baroque and Classical eras, and K.451's opening movement exploits the courtly splendor of its scoring: flute, 2 oboes, 2 bassoons, 2 horns, 2 trumpets, timpani, and strings. The symphonic grandeur of its rhetoric leads to a significant expansion of its scale over Mozart's earlier D-major concerto K.175. (The total movement length of K.175/1 is 238 measures; K.451/1, 325.) What makes this enlargement convincing is that the proportions among the constituent sections—that is, the observance of a compelling hierarchy from the smallest phrase to the largest structural section—has been preserved. This apt deployment of orchestral brilliance and expanded scale set the path for Mozart's subsequent concertos and symphonies.[32]

Nor is this mere grandiose posturing. The character at once defined by the orchestra is so strongly expressed that the thematic course of the first ritornello shapes the solo exposition and recapitulation more pervasively than was the case with K.450. While K.451 shares the technical ambitions of K.450, much of K.451's first movement passagework is a flamboyant accompaniment of the orchestra, not the bravado of a protagonist.

The middle movement is a rondo in the operatic style. In it Mozart first deploys what we may call a "piano recitative" (cf. the beginning of this chapter and Ex. 10.6 below). This distinctive device recalls the conversational rhetoric of vocal recitative without its stylized cadential formulas and repeated melodic notes based on prosodic necessity. The piano recitative contains short melodic phrases in the right hand, usually two or four measures long, with a string accompaniment of repeated chords. In such passages Mozart notated the general outline of the melodic contour but apparently fleshed it out with extensive embellishment in performance. His sister, Nannerl, realized this immediately upon receipt of the score to K.451.[33] Example 10.6 gives the embellishment Mozart is presumed to have supplied to her in response to her query, together with the version of the autograph. (The former is found in a set of manuscript parts preserved in St. Peter's, Salzburg.)

EXAMPLE 10.6. Piano Concerto in D Major K.451. Movement 2, mm. 56–63. Keyboard part with embellished version (orchestra omitted)

The decorated version should be used as a guide to the embellishment of the piano recitatives in the other concertos.

The third movement, a dashing rondeau[34] in $\frac{2}{4}$ time with a $\frac{3}{8}$ conclusion, contains passagework that rivals that of K.450 in its difficulty. The flirtatiousness of the movement compounds these demands, requiring mercurial shifts of inflection and effortless lightness of touch. The manuscript shows that Mozart simplified a number of passages that were even more fiendish.[35] This implies that despite his abilities at the keyboard, he often composed abstractly, later finding that the prescribed figuration eluded even *his* fingers under the pressure of immediate performance.[36]

Concerto in G K.453 (B & H 17)

The date of Mozart's next concerto, the G major, cannot be ascertained, since the sources offer conflicting testimony: 10 April 1784 (Mozart's letter of the same date to his father) *vs.* 12 April 1784 (his thematic catalogue). It is scored for flute, 2 oboes, 2 bassoons, 2 horns, and strings—a combination first encountered in the finale to K.450 and henceforth a standard instrumentation.[37] Like K.449, it was composed for Barbara Ployer.

Although Mozart's letter of 26 May 1784 groups K.453 with K.450 and K.451 as "*grosse Concerte*"—in explicit contradistinction to K.449—its character sets it apart from the rest of the series. Its iridescence may owe something to the key, but the transparency of the textures and the leading role of the winds throughout the work contribute to a delicacy and intimacy of coloration that is enhanced by the daring of the work's harmonic language. The deceptive cadence to the lowered sixth degree (E-flat) that appears in the opening ritornello of the first movement (m. 49) becomes a central element; but its overt theatricality finds a pendant in the suggestive harmony of the orchestral coda (mm. 58–59) and, particularly, in the slithering chromatic progressions of the development, which weave distant tonalities together in a passage of gossamer mystery (e.g., the modulation from B major to C minor in four measures). All this happens within a dramatic frame that allows the keyboard to be the central character in the discourse, but without the overtly energetic soloistic profile heretofore observed.

The middle movement is the most masterful of the 1784 concertos. It begins with a five-measure phrase, whose pause on the dominant under a *fermata* asks a question whose answer occupies the rest of the orchestral ritornello (Ex. 10.7).

EXAMPLE 10.7. Piano Concerto in G Major K.453. Beginning of Movement 2

The soloist, in turn, poses the question in exposition and recapitulation, but finds only wrenching operative pathos—first in G minor, later in E-flat major and C minor—as riposte. It is not until after the cadenza, bolstered by the harmonic resolution that comes with its final trill, that a satisfactory answer is found (Ex. 10.8).

EXAMPLE 10.8. Piano Concerto in G Major K.453. Movement 2, mm. 123–130

(*continued*)

EXAMPLE 10.8. (*continued*)

As we see above, the release is due not to the revelation of the soloist, but to the fortuitous turn to the subdominant in the winds.

The development establishes a dialogue between solo and orchestra in order to move relentlessly up the circle of fifths from the dominant key of G major through D minor, A minor, E minor, B minor, and F-sharp minor to the dominant of C-sharp minor: G-sharp major. The audacity of this design may be less apparent aurally in performances on modern instruments using equal temperament, but even then the contrast between the length of the journey from G major to G-sharp major (mm. 64–86) and that of the dénouement (mm. 86–90) is breathtaking.

The third movement uses variation form—one of only three such cases in Mozart's concertos.[38] As is Mozart's custom, the theme is binary; he prescribes repeats for the theme and first variation, but thereafter uses solo-tutti alternation instead of repeats—a technique also found in K.491. After five variations that range from the cheerful through the lyrical and pathetic to the boisterous, Mozart sets up an elaborate half-cadence calling for the soloist to provide a lead-in to the Presto "finale."[39] That Mozart labels not the entire last movement but rather this 176-measure headlong romp (mm. 171–346) as the finale evokes the milieu of the opera buffa. The heckling between keyboard and winds and the characteristic repetition of cadential phrases and larger subsections are standard operatic devices used to propel the work to an exuberant conclusion.

Piano Concerto in B-flat Major K.456 (B & H 18)

Mozart wrote this concerto for the blind pianist Maria Theresia Paradis. His thematic catalogue dates it to 30 September 1784, but it may have been completed well before this.[40] K.456 shares K.453's scoring, translucency of sonority and coloristic harmonic inflections. Whereas K.453 casts its final movement as a theme and variations, K.456 adopts the form for the middle movement, which is in G minor. The third of the four concertos to begin with the ♩ ♫♩ ♩ march rhythm, K.456 speeds up the pace from Allegro to Allegro vivace[41] and restores the bustle and energy that were relatively restrained in the previous concerto.

The opening ritornello encompasses a particularly wide variety of characters, concluding with material drawn from the comic opera repertory. The soloist's version of these ideas unfolds much as does K.453: the lightness of touch required for the two works could well be a reflection of the fact that Mozart wished to tailor his music to the personalities of the two women for whom he composed them[42]—a supposition that would explain the delicate shadings and lyric resignation of the middle movement's lament.

The finale is a blustery $\frac{6}{8}$ rondo. Its salient event occurs in the middle section, where Mozart again uses chromatic voice leadings to slide between two distantly related keys. However, instead of returning to the tonic key from a foreign tonality (as in K.451 and K.453, second movement) or going from one foreign tonality to another (K.453, first movement), Mozart moves from the B-flat tonic to the remote key of B minor, where he remains for a time. He sets the modulation into even sharper relief by introducing alternating changes of meter from $\frac{6}{8}$ to $\frac{2}{4}$ and back in the winds and keyboard.[43]

Concerto in F Major K.459 (B & H 19)

Mozart entered the last of his six piano concertos of 1784 into his thematic catalogue on 11 December. The architectural premise underlying it is unique and supremely successful. Mozart reverses the normal aesthetic relationship between the outer movements. The demeanor of the first movement is deliberately restrained, while the finale bears the greatest compositional weight. The dotted march rhythm is now in *alla breve* meter; unlike K.451, 453, and 456 its presence is felt throughout the movement. The faster tempo limits the passagework to triplet eighths rather than sixteenths, giving the whole movement a gentler flow. The many floating sequences produce a lightness of sonority redolent of K.453 and K.456. Mozart's cadenza is one of his most sophisticated, inverting the harmonization of the main theme (V—I instead of I—V).

The swaying allegretto is likewise of gentler character, the chromatic tinge of its orchestral introduction another carryover from the earlier concertos. The canon on the main theme, presented in the exposition in two four-bar units (flute and bassoon, mm. 44–47; piano descant and bass, mm. 48–51) becomes an enchanting eight-measure *pas de quatre* in the recapitulation (piano descant, bassoon, oboe, piano bass, mm. 103–110). In the coda, the end of the canon and the opening of the theme are deftly interwoven to create a fairy-tale ending.

But all is dwarfed by the fireworks of the finale. It begins with a cheeky tune in *buffo* style traded back and forth between piano and winds.[44] The entrance of the strings lays claim to a new realm with a vigorous fugato whose good humor cannot entirely mask the intensity of invention that underlies it. Not until m. 120 will the soloist again come to the fore. Once its untrammeled bravura is unleashed, it surges until it finally encompasses the fugato subject at the end of the exposition before drawing up abruptly for a lead-in and the return. This veers suddenly to the relative minor, where the fugato returns—this time in double counterpoint with the principal theme—in a display of contrapuntal dexterity as stunning as it is surprising within the comic frame of the movement. After the cadenza, one of Mozart's most brilliant, comes a coda in which the use of lefthand triplets substitutes for the $\frac{3}{8}$ transformation seen in earlier finales.

The Twelve Great Concertos (2): 1785

The three keyboard concertos Mozart composed in 1785 show him at the height of his creative powers. Symphonic in rhetoric, they range from the demonic (K.466) to the serenely regal (K.482), more than compensating for Mozart's neglect of the symphony from 1783 to 1786.

Concerto in D Minor, K.466 (B & H 20)

The D-minor concerto, entered by Mozart into his catalogue on 10 February 1785, was one of his few concertos that quickly became popular; it has remained so without interruption to the present day. One of Mozart's two concertos in minor keys, it epitomizes the demonic character this key represented for him—an association whose origin may lie as far back in time as the plainchant to the *Dies irae.*

The opening movement derives its power by harnessing symphonic might, operatic gesture, keyboard eloquence, and virtuosity to the pith of Mozart's formal design. These elements are more palpable in performance with historical instruments; there, the spindly vulnerability of the soloist—and even the gentler moments in the instruments—can be diabolically crushed by the dark mass of the orchestra.

The construction of the opening solo passage is a masterful balance of expressive and narrative detail (Ex. 10.9).

EXAMPLE 10.9. Piano Concerto in D Minor K.466. Movement 1, mm. 77–91 (orchestra omitted)

Terse two-measure phrases portray resignation and despair, typified by the descending appoggiaturas (mm. 77–81); the phrase length is then doubled through the use of syncopation (mm. 81–85) and then yet further expanded (mm. 85–91).[45] These four phrases are woven into an organic whole by the fluidity of the melodic ornamentation, whose ineluctable intensification is underscored by the dynamic role of the left hand.

The superbly constructed development moves from F major through G minor to E-flat major in its first half (mm. 192–230), then through sequential modulation using arpeggiations that span the entirety of the five-octave keyboard (from E-flat major to F minor, G minor, and A major, the dominant of D minor, mm. 230–242). The arrival on the dominant affords no room for conventional elegance: the timorous *piano* upbeats of mm. 252–253 are crushed by the savage nonlegato *forte* eighths that bring on the return.[46] This audacity of expression has a counterpart in the keyboard writing: compared with the 1784 concertos K.466 uses more jagged shapes—broken octaves, sixths, and thirds— than previous works.

At the recapitulation the drive to the final cadence—dramatic as it was the first time around in F major—reaches a cataclysmic fury in the minor. Mozart's use of a D-major chord at m. 346 is a masterstroke of feverish disorientation: though technically caused by the descending chromatic scale in the top voice of the progression, it creates a frenzy further intensified by the contradictory B-flat-major chord that follows it. The Neapolitan at m. 348 provides the final impetus to the six-four, upon which Mozart bestows an eerie coloration: the winds motionless on the second-inversion minor chord while the keyboard slides higher and higher to the final paroxysm.

We know from Mozart's correspondence that he wrote cadenzas to this concerto and to the Concerto in C major K.467; but they do not survive. Beethoven composed a remarkable set for K.466 ten years later; even if they do not observe Mozart's unbroken rule of keeping cadenzas within the tonic key, they maintain the concerto's relentless structural and expressive integrity. Characteristically, Mozart declined to end the first movement with fire and brimstone, but in fact the distant thunder of the quiet ending was prefigured in the opening tutti.

The second movement is entitled *Romance*. Its outer sections comprise a tender vocal *scena*, in which a predilection for short phrases and melodic cells is responsible for a tone of unaffected ingenuousness. Without this construction the effect of the middle section would scarcely be so explosive. Its texture was lifted from the development of the first movement of K.459. The earnestness of the coda melody (mm. 146ff.), exquisitely colored in the soloist's iteration by the sustained tonic pedal in three string registers, has an idealistic aspiration that is closer to Beethoven's aesthetic than many of the Mozart melodies that Beethoven borrowed directly.

No other Mozart concerto has a finale that opens with such breathtaking sweep. The held diminished seventh chord in the second full measure can barely contain the dizzying surge of motion. The orchestra's ritornello is Mozart's most powerful, using contradictions between rhythmic propulsion and interruption, surges in the harmonic rhythm, and huge leaps in the first violin to propel the music forward.

It is the interruptive effect of the diminished seventh that will be used as the key element in the transition from minor to relative major; by setting up F major with F minor Mozart subtly prepares for the recapitulation, when minor is not a foil but the work's destiny. After the grim build-up to the deceptive cadence, after the cadenza, Mozart starts the work again. But here—as in *Don Giovanni*—he provides the listener with succor and offers us the coda theme in its comfortable major-key form, ending with the jubilation of relief. This is a stance understood and appreciated in the Romantic era.

Piano Concerto in C Major K.467 (B & H 21)

Whereas the autograph of K.467 is dated February 1785, it is dated 9 March 1785 in Mozart's thematic catalogue. This concerto, one of the most popular in the canon, is written on a grand scale that prefigures the concerto K.503 and the "Jupiter" symphony, both likewise in C. After the majesty of the first ritornello the solo instrument enters in a disarmingly informal way—a device that will recur in K.503. Only after the winds have issued three invitations to the keyboard does the soloist emerge, building fragmentary outlines of the dominant triad and seventh to arrive at a fermata that calls for a lead-in.

The sonority of the concerto is pervaded by dissonances, created by melodic ornaments, pedal tones, and a rich counterpoint. (See, for example, mm. 331–39.) The move to the dominant minor underscores the seriousness of the discourse—a plan also adopted by the first movement of the next concerto, K.482. The piano doffs its usual operative persona to take up a distinctly symphonic mantle. Mozart thereby secures the gains in substance and grandeur newly achieved in K.466, and once again the development is the crown of the movement. Beginning at m. 223 in E minor—the relative minor of the dominant key—it moves down the circle of fifths to A minor, D minor, G minor, and C minor to F minor (m. 253); the latter then becomes the subdominant of C minor, and the circle of fifths continues with the tonic minor in what is surely one of the most glorious moments in the series (mm. 253–259). The augmented sixth chord at m. 265 is the only bow to operatic convention. After the half-cadence at m. 266 Mozart stretches a dominant pedal to the luxurious length of eight measures to let the tension gently unravel.

As mentioned in the previous chapter, the middle movement of K.467 can be understood as a transfiguration of the first movement of Johann Schobert's Sonata in F, op. XVII no. 2—which Mozart had used as the second movement of his *pasticcio* concerto in B-flat K.39, and alluded to again in the second movement development of the A minor piano sonata K.310. Schobert's bass line pattern and inner-voice triplets are preserved; superimposed on them is the ineffable melody whose familiarity may hide the unconventionality of its phrase lengths: (1,) 3, 3, 2, 2, 5, 3, 3. The sonorities produced by multiple suspensions in the five-measure sequence beginning in m. 12 must have been almost unbearably wrenching at the time of their composition (Ex. 10.10; cf. especially m. 15).

EXAMPLE 10.10. Piano Concerto in C Major K.467. Movement 2, mm. 11–17

As in the middle movement of K.466, the melody alternates canta-bile passages with piano recitative. The music flows continuously from first measure to last: the one- to two-measure transitions in the orchestra discreetly shepherd the colloquy past every cadential arrival but one—the big half-cadence at m. 71. There, only the piano's eighth-notes flow forward to the next bar, where the music does not return to the tonic, but moves audaciously to the distant key of A-flat major (the relative major of the parallel minor). After a few seconds suspended in reverie, Mozart plunges us into the anguish of B-flat minor and F minor; but the orchestra, responsive yet inscrutable, weaves its seamless connections to the five-measure sequence and the coda, where the triplets find their final vessel in the winds.

The uproarious finale is in $\frac{2}{4}$ time, like K.451, and begins with a catchy binary theme. The first half of the theme is repeated, but the second half does not provide the expected balance. Instead, Mozart seizes and expands on a device from the first movement, where the winds coaxed the soloist to enter. Here the buffoonery precipitates the orchestra into a peremptory unison sweep to the dominant; the soloist must improvise a lead-in before playing a single obbligato note. Thence-forth a daredevil spirit of cocky flippancy carries the day.

K.467 is the first concerto, but not the last, to contain passages in the solo part that are not fully notated. We have already seen that ad-ditional embellishment is necessary in piano recitatives and in recurrent themes, especially in rondos; here the bald passages are for the most part mechanical, requiring little more than arpeggios or the breaking of oc-taves to provide the fleshing out that Mozart presumably intended. Had he published these concertos, he surely would have provided the same kind of elaborated text he supplied for his published sonatas. As it is, the performer must devise appropriate solutions for the first movement, m. 380; second movement, mm. 58–59; third movement, mm. 302 and 304–306, where the righthand octaves should probably be broken.

Concerto in E-flat Major K.482 (B & H 22)

Mozart entered this concerto into his catalogue on 16 December 1785, but the date of its first performance is unknown. It is the first concerto whose original scoring includes clarinets, and one of only two (the other is K.488) that has no oboes. Mozart responds to the presence of clarinets by writing more spacious, less pungent music than he does in the concertos with oboes. As in K.466 and K.467, the keyboard's first entry delays rather than presents the first theme. The soloist's second theme, different from that presented by the orchestra, is more an im-provisation on the dominant than a settled musical idea. The contrast between the two themes is manifest at the recapitulation, where the re-pose of the former can be supplanted by the instability of the latter as preparation for the orchestra's drive to the cadenza.[47]

The middle movement of K.482, a dirge with variations, has both reflective and plaintive facets. The role of the winds is preeminent: in a decision of great refinement, Mozart allows two of the five variations (the second and fourth) to be in major keys (E-flat and C), with the piano silent in both. The first is a seven-voice wind serenade, the second a tender dialogue between flute and first bassoon with string accompaniment. The silky texture of the passage from mm. 201–209 is rendered more ghostly by a C-major triad that represents an unattainable peace. The slithery chromatic scales up to the *pianissimo* minor-key ending epitomize Mozart's coloristic imagination. It is a tribute to the refinement of the Viennese public that Mozart had to repeat the movement at the premiere.

The hunting horn finale melds the rhythmic frame of K.450 and the key and structure of K.271. After the pomp of the orchestra's ritornello the slyness of the solo entry shows that Mozart continues to develop dramatic–rhetorical ideas from concerto to concerto. The clever displacement of the melodic highpoint at mm. 125 and 317 baffles with an apparent 7/8 measure (Ex. 10.11).

EXAMPLE 10.11. Piano Concerto in E-flat Major K.482. Movement 3, mm. 122–128 (orchestra omitted)

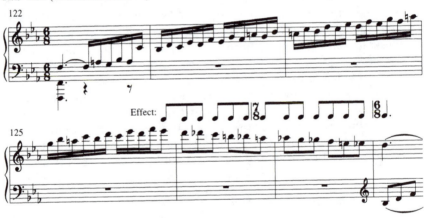

Once again, as in K.271, a minuet in the subdominant key of A-flat interrupts the rollicking progress of the movement. At the end, Mozart's prank of stealing back onstage for a final flirtation after the work has ostensibly ended—only to be hustled out by the orchestra almost at once—reminds us how rare it is for such seriousness and childlike zest to coexist without compromising each other.

No original cadenzas for K.482 survive, nor are they mentioned in the correspondence. The number of sketched solo passages is greater than in K.467: second movement, mm. 181–182, 3rd movement, 164–172, 346–347, 353–356.[48]

The Twelve Great Concertos (3): 1786

There is a striking parallel in the emotional qualities of the three 1786 concertos—K.488 (A major), K.491 (C minor), and K.503 (C major)—and the last three symphonies—K.543 (E-flat major), K.550 (G minor), and K.551 (C major); K.503 is equally deserving of K.551's "Jupiter" sobriquet. This parallel hints at the nature of the relationship between Mozart's production of keyboard concertos and symphonies. Only after finishing the last of his great series of twelve concertos (K.503) did Mozart return to symphonic production (the "Prague" K.504), and the great symphonic trilogy of 1788 just mentioned came into being only after Mozart's concerto production had ceased.

Piano Concerto in A Major, K.488 (B & H 23)

Although Mozart's thematic catalogue dates this concerto to 2 March 1786, it was in fact begun in 1783–1784 or 1784–1785 and called for oboes rather than clarinets.[49] It is scored for flute, 2 clarinets, 2 bassoons, 2 horns, and strings; despite the more opulent wind scoring, K.488's lineage with K.414 is unmistakable. The structure of solo exposition and recapitulation follows that of the orchestra's ritornello more exactly than does any other Mozart concerto. Thus, there is no motivic material reserved for the soloist apart from the arpeggios before the second theme and the coda passagework. This intensifies the quality of intimacy created by the scoring—clarinets without trumpets and drums—and further reflected in the grace of the solo figuration.

Altogether new is the introduction of a previously unheard theme in the orchestra's middle ritornello, embroidered by the soloist and taken up again toward the end of the recapitulation. Exceptionally, the first-movement cadenza is notated in the score;[50] apart from the passagework at the beginning, it is a free fantasy unrelated to the motives of the rest of the movement. But for this one case, we would not know that Mozart had an alternative procedure to the taut motivic construction he seems to have preferred in his written cadenzas.

The second movement, the only piece Mozart ever wrote in F-sharp minor, bespeaks an elegiac grief equally distant from the warmth of the first movement and the dash of the finale. The dolorous figures in the winds (mm. 12ff.) plumb the depths of despair within an astonishing economy of space (eight measures). The helpless pleading of the solo instrument against the winds' unbending lament, initially in the flute, then with added clarinet, and finally with flute, clarinet, and bassoon, is undoubtedly the most despondent moment in the cycle. We possess a highly embellished version of the keyboard part to this movement in the hand of Barbara Ployer—perhaps the most valuable source of ornamentation in Mozart's mature concertos to have come down to us.[51]

The finale—an allegro assai in ¢ time—is Mozart's most extended concerto finale. Its prodigality is reflected in the fleeting appearance of a winsome tune in D major (mm. 262ff.) that disappears after a single hearing. Undoubtedly the most characteristic passage in the movement is the coda theme, a cheeky idea backed by a pedal in the horns and pizzicato strings (mm. 176–187). Mozart must have been proud of the passage, a sure crowd-pleaser, for he uses it not twice but three times.

Piano Concerto in C Minor K.491 (B & H 24)

The turbulence of the C-minor concerto is reflected in the autograph manuscript, which reveals that the sections in the first movement's opening tutti were originally in another order.[52] As a rule, Mozart notated the draft of a work directly into the manuscript in fair copy, sketching where necessary on separate leaves in a hasty, private script. The orchestral parts in the autograph of K.491 are in his normal clean hand, but for considerable stretches the piano part is in private shorthand: the outer notes of passagework and a few of the inner details are represented, in barely legible handwriting (cf. Ill. 10.1, p. 382).[53]

Mozart's thematic catalogue dates the concerto 24 March 1786; he allegedly premiered it on 7 April 1786. It is scored for flute, 2 oboes, 2 clarinets, 2 bassoons, 2 horns, 2 trumpets, timpani, and strings. The richness of wind sonority, due to the inclusion of oboes *and* clarinets, is the central timbral characteristic of K.491: time and again in all three movements the winds push the strings completely to the side.

K.491 has a more complicated character than that of K.466. The temperament of the D-minor concerto reflects a consistent persona. While its moods range from restless to demonic, its phrase structure and harmonic rhetoric are consistent and clear. In the C-minor concerto the harmonic language is troubled and ambiguous. The phrase structure at the onset is opaque: it is not immediately evident if the third or fourth measure is meant to be stressed. The chain of diminished sevenths (mm. 4ff.) implies a descending circle of fifths, starting with the dominant of G minor (m. 4) and descending through C minor, F minor, and B-flat minor toward E-flat minor. This slide into an harmonic abyss at the very beginning of a movement, before the tonality has been defined, is one of Mozart's most disturbing and visionary passages. Just at the moment when the dominant of E-flat minor is reached, Mozart adjusts the orientation through the subtle intervention of the oboes. By entering at this moment with the pitches b^1 and a-flat^2, they tilt the dominant function of E-flat into that of C minor through the enharmonic substitution of B for C-flat. Nor does the ambiguity end there: two measures later (m. 10) Mozart suggests the dominant of D-flat major, deflected through another enharmonic substitution (G-flat/F-sharp), leading finally to a clear cadence in C minor at m. 13.

The irregularity of phrasing and harmony of this opening remains at the core of the work's expression. The richness of orchestral textures and moods never obscures the primary role of the main motive—particularly the rhythm ♪|♩ ♩ ♩|♩ ♩ .

In the solo exposition Mozart again takes up the open-ended potential of his main theme, giving it to the flute with piano accompaniment in E-flat major. This time he does not impede the downward spiral, and in a moment we find ourselves in F-sharp major—a key as remote from the C-minor tonic as the tonal system allows. The audacity, the sheer adventure of this passage, places the movement at the pinnacle of Mozart's inspiration.

The effect of such a section is strengthened by the variety of other types of music within the movement. The restful passages in E-flat are significantly more extended than the F-major episodes in the D-minor concerto. And while both works have their fiery moments, the direct confrontation between soloist and orchestra in the development of K.491 (mm. 330ff.) is the closest Mozart's rhetoric ever comes to the Romantic ideal of the concerto as confrontation between individual and society.

Mozart left no cadenza for K.491. The coda, in which the ghostly keyboard figuration over a tonic pedal amplifies the *danse macabre* of the winds' imitation, acts as an emotional pendant to the disquiet of the movement's opening. (The precedent of K.466 is palpable.)

The second movement is a rondo in E-flat with two couplets, both of which are introduced by the winds alone. Only once—when the orchestra takes up the soloist's initial theme—do the first violins have an independent melody, and then only for two bars (mm. 5 and 7), being twice interrupted by the winds. Symmetrical four-measure phrases are unusually dominant; interest derives from the diversity of character of the ideas, and rests upon subtle rhythmic and harmonic inflections at each of their appearances.[54]

In choosing variation form for the finale to K.491 Mozart crystallizes the difference between this work and K.466. Instead of the violent frenzy of the earlier work, the closed-in binary form of the variations traps soloist and listener alike; the escape offered by K.466's struggle and ultimate major-key ending is denied. Mozart had evident difficulties with the surface of the keyboard part. In the second variation the corrections in the keyboard part mount many staves toward the center of the score, and even the standard version has been crossed out in favor of an incomplete revision, written with a thin quill, that—even in its fragmentary state—clashes with the accompaniment and therefore is in part unworkable. (See Ill. 10.1.)

ILLUSTRATION 10.1. Mozart: Autograph Score of the Piano Concerto in C
Minor K.491. Movement 3, mm. 37–48. RCM MS 402, F. 26r. By permission of
the Director, Royal College of Music, London.

Here the traditional goal of a critical edition—the composer's definitive
version—is unattainable.

There are two relief variations, in A-flat major and C major, again
introduced by the winds. These are separated by a chromatic variation
of polyphonic intricacy, whose lefthand sixteenths are denoted for the
most part by shorthand; their specific identity cannot be determined and
interpreters have made divergent choices in pitches and rhythmic speed
(e.g., mm. 145, 157, 163). After the sunny ease of C major, the return
to the tonic minor leads swiftly to a stormy crisis, a lead-in for the soloist,
and a ⁶⁄₈ finale in which the following enharmonic phrase encapsulates
the gap between hope and despair with utmost terseness (Ex. 10.12):

EXAMPLE 10.12. Piano Concerto in C Minor K.491. Movement 3, mm. 229–240

(*continued*)

EXAMPLE 10.12. (*continued*)

While attending a performance of K.491—quite possibly at this very passage—Beethoven cried out to Johann Baptist Cramer, "My dear Cramer, we shall never be able to do anything like this!" The unmistakable borrowings of K.491 in Beethoven's Piano Trio op. 1/3 and the Third Piano Concerto, both in C minor, attest to Beethoven's preoccupation with K.491.

Piano Concerto in C Major K.503 (B & H 25)

The series of twelve great Viennese concertos comes to an end with K.503, dated 4 December 1786. It is the grandest work in the series (first movement: 432 bars; rondo, 382 bars). The first movement's reliance on a single dominating motive— ♩ ♫♩ ♩ —and the majesty of the symphonic writing create a certain aloofness against which the soloist effects a range of attitudes. At first, despite the formal magnificence of the first tutti, the soloist must be coaxed in (cf. K.467). Once at the helm, the soloist tends to seek out exotic keys (E-flat major in the exposition, B major in the return). Emblematic of the movement is the solemn march heard in the opening ritornello. Omitted from the solo exposition, it is the sole material in the development, and its appearance toward the end of the recapitulation prefigures the final triumph. Both the exposition and recapitulation end with an intriguing figure in $\frac{7}{8}$ time that Mozart sketched out before incorporating it into the concerto. No original cadenzas survive.

The second movement is a serene cantilena whose notated melody is extraordinarily elaborate at some points (mm. 97–101) but quite sketchy at others (mm. 59–62). The loveliest moment is doubtless the drawn-out pedal on the dominant (mm. 63ff.), in which the keyboard's righthand filigree enriches the retransition in the winds.

As often noted, the rondo theme is drawn from the ballet music to *Idomeneo* K.367. While the keyboard part always presents an unadorned version of the tune at each return, the orchestra has a more intricate version, perhaps suggesting the text the soloist should perform just before. Once again, the soloist repeatedly challenges the formal grandeur of the structure with teasing antics (mm. 70–75) that make of the second theme one of Mozart's most casual and conversational.

Both returns of the main theme, from the exposition and from the central episode, are spectacular: the first through its web of coloristic dissonance, the second through the efflorescing drama in a retransition of vast scope (mm. 197–229). The single appearance of the radiant F-major theme at m. 163—a case parallel to the finale of K.488—is merely the apogee of the work that rings down the period of Mozart's great keyboard concertos.

The Final Concertos

The decline in Mozart's concerto production after 1786 mirrors his fortunes as a freelance virtuoso and concert entrepreneur in Vienna. As extraordinary as the total number of Mozart's keyboard concertos may seem, it would undoubtedly have been still greater had the Viennese public been less fickle.

Concerto in D K.537 (B & H 26)

This concerto seems to have been begun early in 1787 (soon after the performance of K.503) but was put aside for a time, perhaps because of the composition of *Don Giovanni,* or owing to his father's death.[55] That Mozart was in fact setting his sights somewhat lower in K.537 is confirmed by the instrumental writing. While the scoring is hardly more modest than that of its immediate predecessors, the winds, brass, and timpani are *ad libitum,* so that the work is something of a throwback to the concertos of 1782–1783. While Mozart entered the work into the catalogue of his works on 24 February 1788, we have no record of a performance before he performed it in Dresden on 14 April 1789. It owes its popular subtitle ("Coronation") to its having been performed by Mozart during the time of Leopold II's coronation in Frankfurt am Main on 15 October 1790. No authentic cadenzas survive.

The most remarkable thing about K.537 is that the left hand of large portions of the outer movements, and of the entirety of the second movement, is missing from the autograph. Only when there is a dialogue between the two hands or when the texture becomes polyphonic does Mozart notate both staves. The standard text of the left hand, which is not beyond stylistic reproach, originates with the first edition and may be the work of publisher Johann André.

The "Coronation" concerto became immediately popular in the nineteenth century, and only in the last generation have other concertos tended to eclipse it in the public's esteem. While K.537 is undoubtedly an elegant and attractive work, it has a somewhat stylized air to it. The only innovation is in the first movement—the free passage for the first violins that connects the cadence on the dominant halfway through the first ritornello with the second theme. A similar passage, only two measures long, appears at mm. 57–58. In the development an altogether uninhibited free fantasy oscillates widely in both the sharp and flat directions.

The middle movement is a miniaturization of the romances found in K. 466 and 491. The melodious A-major theme, preserved on a 1787 sketch leaf, has only a "piano recitative," likewise in A, to set it off. The rondo has a good deal of operatic swagger (the passage at mm. 19ff. suggests buffo stage business) and numerous showy passages. The surprises come toward the end of the exposition—when the harmony suddenly turns from A major to G major and F-sharp minor before swirling back to the dominant—and in the astonishing enharmonic move at mm. 185ff. from F-sharp major (the dominant of the relative minor) to B-flat major. The smoothness of the ensuing motion through B-flat minor and B minor to the firm ground of G major (the subdominant) recalls the légerdemain of the 1784 concertos.

Concerto in B-flat Major K.595 (B & H 27)

This work, the last keyboard concerto Mozart was to write, seems to have been begun some considerable time before the composer completed it. He entered it into his thematic catalogue on 5 January 1791 and premiered it on 4 March 1791. At this point in his fortunes he could not afford to sponsor himself in a concert, appearing instead as a guest in a program given by his clarinetist colleague Joseph Beer.

K.595 has an intimate, serene quality that sets it apart from its predecessors. The passagework is always decorous, but not vigorous: virtuosity is pushed to the side in favor of delicacy of expression. By eschewing a flamboyant stance Mozart is able to deepen the intensity of coloration. The development presents one of his most audacious harmonic passages, in which E-flat minor is linked to G minor by a chain of dominant seventh chords whose elliptical syntax is not far removed from Debussy (Ex. 10.13).

EXAMPLE 10.13. Piano Concerto in B-flat Major K.595. Movement 1, mm. 207–212

The Larghetto, calm and rapturous, is identical in form to K.537. Unlike the latter, its extended "piano recitative" in the middle section lacks a lead-in prior to the return, circumscribing ostentation. The winds rise to the dominant in the next-to-last measure but are silent at the close, making this the first slow movement without wind instruments in the final measure since K.451.

In choosing to write a rondo in $\frac{6}{8}$ time Mozart opts for the shell but not the ebullience of a hunting finale. A certain naïveté inhabits the opening theme. (It is thus not surprising to encounter it in Mozart's next work, a children's song entitled *Sehnsucht nach dem Frühlinge*, "Longing for Spring," K.596.) There is spirit and wit, but here as in the first movement the sixteenth-notes generally serve coloristic and sensuous rather than virtuoso ends. In fact, it is not until the cadenza that Mozart liberates his untapped reserves of energy. This may explain the cadenza's unusual length (by m. 30 of the cadenza we expect the end, but Mozart carries on quite a bit longer). An unusual feature of the movement is the complete recapitulation of the rondo theme plus a coda after the cadenza: formally speaking mm. 323–341 are an interpolation.

There are several noteworthy textual problems in K.595. In the first movement seven measures (mm. 47–53 of the NMA edition) are missing from all other modern editions, although they are present in earlier prints and copies. A lead-in for the third movement at m. 130, excluded from the NMA on grounds of dubious pedigree, has been proved authentic with the rediscovery of its autograph.

*   *   *

As recent researches have shown, the bitter struggles that marked Mozart's existence in the period from 1788–1790 were on the wane in 1791; indeed, there were many hopeful signs that at last the tide was turning in his favor. His premature death on 5 December has caused commentators to view K.595 as valedictory. Had his health not given out there might have been an even more remarkable series of piano concertos, and our evaluation of the B-flat concerto could have represented a moment of sublime repose separating two peaks of creative fervor.

Notes

1. Cf. also the vocal recitative in the slow movement of K.271, perhaps inspired by Joseph Haydn or Ignaz von Beecke. Indeed, Mozart's cadenza to an unidentified keyboard concerto by Beecke contains a recitative; cf. the *Neue Mozart-Ausgabe* (NMA), vol. X/28, *Abteilung* 2, 227–228.

2. For detailed discussion of Mozart's formal archetype in his concerto first movements, see Leeson-Levin 1976/1977, Levin 1980, and Küster 1991.

3. Contentions by Denis Forman that Mozart's concertos employ a variety of structural archetypes (cf. Forman 1971) are based on distinctions of character rather than structure; neither the similarities nor the differences in content of individual concertos are adequately explained by his models.

4. Hutchings 1948, 7.

5. This is especially true of Mozart's French contemporaries, e.g., Bréval, Cambini, and Devienne.

6. According to recent research K.175 is not Mozart's first essay in the concerto genre: he had composed the Violin Concerto in B-flat K.207 some eight months earlier, on 14 April 1773 (not 14 April 1775). Cf. NMA V/14/1, XI.

7. See NMA X/28, *Abteilung 2* (*Bearbeitungen: Klavierkonzerte und Kadenzen*), ed. Eduard Reeser (K.37, 39–41) and Walter Gerstenberg (K.107), Foreword, X–XI.

8. The three sonatas are from Bach's op. 5, no. 2 in D major, no. 3 in G major, and no. 4 in E-flat major. The set was published in 1768. Regarding the dating of Mozart's arrangements, Plath gives 1772, Tyson up to 1772. (Cf. Plath 1960/1961, 96; Plath 1976/1977, 141, 154; and Tyson 1987, 333–334).

9. Cf. Plath 1960–1961, 82–117.

10. Mozart's forerunners and contemporaries in the domain of the keyboard concerto have been given frequent attention, e.g., in Forman 1971, 27–46; Girdlestone 1948/1964, 19–23; Landon 1956/1969, 236ff; and Whitmore, 77–118.

11. The possibility of using bassoon(s) to double the bass line, even when not called for in the score, reflects Classical-period performance practice, and is included in brackets elsewhere in the listing of instruments when obbligato bassoon is not prescribed.

12. Mozart's other trumpet-and-drum concertos always have a flute and two bassoons.

13. Like all of Mozart's surviving piano concerto cadenzas except for those to the A-major concerto K.488, those to K.175 are written on separate sheets of paper. The first movement cadenza goes up to f^3—showing that it was undoubtedly written not at the time of the concerto, but for later use on a five-octave instrument.

14. Cf. the previous chapter, p. 311.

15. Cf. NMA V/15, Band 1, Foreword, VIII.

16. This rondo adds a flute to the scoring of K. 175. The editors of the NMA have assumed that Mozart composed it in February, in order for it to have been ready for the March 3 performance. Given that the original finale has two different versions of the oboe and first horn parts—as does the rest of the concerto—the chronology might be a bit different. Perhaps Mozart revised the oboe parts of the Salzburg version for the March 3 performance, composing K.382 for the concert on March 23.

17. The finale of K.207 was replaced by the Rondo K.269 (261a).

18. The NMA tentatively dates the transcription 1779.

19. Ferguson 1983, 13–14, 25–26.

20. Cliff Eisen has turned up a clue in the search for her identity: Parisian newspaper announcements on 26 December 1785 and 10 April 1786 refer to performances at the *Concert spirituel* of a concerto of "Mozard" by "Mlle Wil-

liaume"/"Mlle Villieaume." As Eisen observes, the Mozarts were fond of playing jokes with names, and could have changed her name from "old man" ("Vieil-homme") to "young man" ("Jeunehomme"). See Eisen's sleeve notes to the author's recording of the concertos K.271 and 414/385p with Christopher Hogwood and the Academy of Ancient Music (Decca Oiseau-Lyre).

21. Mozart would reuse this device in the finale of another E-flat concerto—K.482.

22. Anderson 1985, letter 476, 1242.

23. Alfred Einstein has suggested that Mozart's allowance for chamber performance was due to the influence of Samuel Schroeter's six piano concertos op. 3 (1774), which Mozart is known to have admired. (Indeed, he wrote cadenzas for three of them.)

24. Cf. Christoph Wolff, foreword to NMA V/15, Band 3, VII.

25. Cf. Christoph Wolff, foreword to NMA V/15, Band 3, IX, n. 18.

26. K.386 has not survived in its entirety. Its ending disappeared at the time Mozart's estate was inventoried and did not turn up until recently. Meanwhile, the rest of the manuscript had been dismembered and dispersed in the nineteenth century; much of it remains missing. However, Cipriani Potter made a solo piano arrangement of the work before dismemberment took place and composed an ending—a fact that was realized only when Alan Tyson discovered Mozart's version in 1980. (Cf. Tyson 1987, 262–289.)

27. The autograph of the first movement displays some important revisions of the passagework; these could have been an integral part of the compositional process, or they may have been undertaken before Mozart began to circulate the concertos.

28. He had used this technique in the Rondo K.382, which, given that it is really a set of variations, is precisely to the point.

29. Anderson, *op. cit.*, Letter 514 (26 May 1784), 1308.

30. This device is used in K.467 as well.

31. For other examples of this device, see K.451, third movement, mm. 206ff., K.453, first movement, mm. 207ff., and second movement, mm. 86ff. Perhaps the most famous example is in the last movement of the Symphony in C ("Jupiter") K.551, mm. 219ff.

32. For an example of orchestral texture borrowed from concerto to symphony, compare mm. 57–60 of K.451's first movement with mm. 294–96 of the same movement from the "Prague" Symphony K.504.

33. Cf. Mozart's letter to his father of 9–12 June 1784, Anderson, *op. cit.*, Letter 515, 1311–1312.

34. The Salzburg copy of the solo piano part is thus labeled; the autograph bears only the tempo marking, Allegro di molto. Cf. NMA V/15, Band 4, 213n.

35. However, they are not unplayable; the author has restored them in his performances of the work.

36. Another such case is the first movement of K.467, m. 183, where Mozart originally notated the melodic inversion of m. 174, then replaced it with the easier standard version.

37. It is used in K.453, K.456, K.459, and K.595; and with the addition of trumpets and drums, in K.466, K.467, K.503, and K.537 (where, however,

the winds are *ad libitum*). K.488 and K.482 are related cases, with and without the trumpets and drums, respectively, except that clarinets replace oboes. The unique work is the C-minor concerto K.491, which contains both oboes and clarinets.

38. The others are K.382 and K.491.

39. There is a g¹ in the right hand of the piano part in the first measure of the Presto in the autograph score, which shows that the lead-in is to connect to the first beat of the Presto, rather than stopping at the cadence before, as most pianists have tended to do.

40. Cf. Daniel N. Leeson and David Whitwell, "Mozart's Thematic Catalogue," *Musical Times* 114 (1973): 781–83.

41. This is the reading in the autograph; Mozart's thematic catalogue gives Allegro.

42. There is nothing sexist about such a suggestion, unless it would be sexist to suggest that Mozart wrote his arias for female characters with different nuances and characters from those for male characters.

43. Mozart had previously used this technique in the finale to the Oboe Quartet in F major K.370/368b (1781).

44. The strings, before Mozart the indispensable backbone of the orchestra, do not enter until m. 32.

45. The autograph's reading of the left hand in mm. 88–90 has provoked controversy. There are three stages of notation: quarter-notes alternating d and A; quarter-notes alternating D and A_1; and chords alternating d^1-f^1-a^1 and a-c♯¹-e¹-g¹. The chords cannot be played together with the low bass notes, but it has been suggested that Mozart conceived the passage for pedal piano. (See also chapter 2.) Leopold Mozart's letter of 12 March 1785 mentions that Wolfgang possessed such an instrument (Anderson 1985, Letter 525, 1325). Nonetheless, it is implausible for Mozart to have conceived a work exclusively for his own performance on a pedal piano, yet call for it in only 2½ measures.

46. The tendency of many performers to eviscerate the fierceness of this passage by underplaying the *forte* and smoothing out the eighth-notes attests to the survival of the nineteenth-century view of Mozart's music, according to which beauty of sound, not dramatic intensity, is paramount, and the slightest angularity is taboo.

47. As an afterthought, Mozart interpolated after m. 281 of the recapitulation mm. 19–20 of the orchestral ritornello, which he had at first omitted. Due to the restoration of these measures the NMA edition is two measures longer than all other editions.

48. Regarding the filling in of mm. 164–172, cf. Levin 1989.

49. Cf. Tyson 1987, 152–53. This explains why the clarinets are notated at the outset in A rather than transposing, in C.

50. Mozart normally notated his cadenzas on separate sheets. K.488 and the Concertone K.190 [166b, 186E], are the only deviations from this practice, and the latter cadenzas include the participation of orchestral instruments.

51. It is reproduced in the *Kritischer Bericht* (Critical Commentary) of the NMA.

52. The original ordering is mm. 1–43, 63–90, 44–62, and 91 onward. This may not be quite as sensational as it appears. Mozart may simply have decided

to insert material to give the ritornello more breadth, rather than reordering per se.

53. For examples of such passages cf. first movement, mm. 261–262, 467–470; third movement, mm. 142–145, 155–156, 159–162.

54. One of these, at m. 40, superimposes two conflicting harmonizations of the principal theme—one in the winds, the other in the keyboard. The handwriting documents that Mozart notated different voices of K.491 at different times; this is surely a case in which he overlooked the carefully composed wind variant when writing down the piano part.

55. Cf. Tyson 1991, viii.

Selected Bibliography

Bilson, Malcolm. "The Mozart Piano Concertos Rediscovered." *Mozart-Jahrbuch 1986:* 58–61.

Ferguson, Linda Faye. *COL BASSO and GENERALBASS in Mozart's Keyboard Concertos: Notation, Performance Theory, and Practice.* Ph.D. dissertation, Princeton University 1983 (Ann Arbor, MI: UMI Press).

Ferguson, Faye. "Mozart's Keyboard Concertos: Tutti Notations and Performance Models." *Mozart-Jahrbuch 1984/85:* 32–39.

Forman, Denis. *Mozart's Concerto Form. The first movements of the Piano Concertos.* New York, 1971.

Girdlestone, Cuthbert M. *Mozart and His Piano Concertos.* London, 1948/New York, 1964.

Hutchings, Arthur. *A Companion to Mozart's Piano Concertos.* London, 1948.

Kerman, Joseph. "Mozart's Piano Concertos and Their Audience." *Write All These Down* (Collected Essays). Berkeley, CA, 1994, 322–34.

Küster, Konrad. *Formale Aspekte des ersten Allegros in Mozarts Konzerten* (Bärenreiter Hochschulschriften). Kassel, 1991.

Landon, H. C. Robbins. "The Concertos (2): Their Musical Origin and Development." *The Mozart Companion.* London, 1956/New York, 1969, 234–82.

Leeson, Daniel N., and Robert D. Levin "On the Authenticity of K. Anh. C 14.01 (297b), a Symphonia [*recte:* Symphonie] Concertante for Four Winds and Orchestra." *Mozart-Jahrbuch 1976/77:* 70–96.

Levin, Robert D. "Improvisation and Musical Structure in Mozart's Piano Concertos." In *L'interpretation de la Musique Classique de Haydn à Schubert. Colloque international, Evry, 13–15 octobre 1977.* Geneva, 1980, 45–50.

Mishkin, Henry G. "Incomplete Notation in Mozart's Piano Concertos." *Musical Quarterly* 61 (1975): 345–59.

Simon, Edwin J. "Sonata into Concerto. A Study of Mozart's First Seven Concertos." *Acta Musicologica* 31 (1959): 170–85.

Tischler, Hans. *A Structural Analysis of Mozart's Piano Concertos.* Institute of Medieval Music (Musicological Studies, 10). Brooklyn, 1966.

[Tyson, Alan.] *Wolfgang Amadeus Mozart. Piano Concerto No. 26 in D Major ("Coronation"), K.537. The Autograph Score.* With an introduction by Alan Tyson, Senior Research Fellow, All Souls College, Oxford. New York, 1991.

Whitmore, Philip. *Unpremeditated Art. The Cadenza in the Classical Keyboard Concerto.* Oxford, 1991.

Wolff, Christoph. "Cadenzas and Styles of Improvisation in Mozart's Piano Concertos." In *Perspectives on Mozart Performance,* ed. R. Larry Todd and Peter Williams (Cambridge Studies in Performance Practice). Cambridge, 1991, 228–38.

Zaslaw, Neal, ed. *Mozart's Piano Concertos: Text, Context, Interpretation.* Ann Arbor, MI, 1996.

See also bibliography to chapter 9.

CHAPTER ELEVEN

Early Beethoven

William Drabkin

Virtually all of Beethoven's early music was written for the piano, alone or with other instruments. Upon arriving in Vienna in 1792 he devoted himself largely to genres that would show off his capabilities as a performing artist: piano sonatas, concertos, and variation sets, trios, and sonatas with an obbligato cello or violin part (works we now call "cello sonatas" and "violin sonatas").

One could also say that Beethoven's creativity as a composer was a creativity nurtured at the keyboard. It is generally agreed that, among his early works, those for piano solo are the most original, pointing the way to new means of expression to be developed more broadly after 1800.[1] This may help to explain why the search for antecedents of Beethoven's keyboard style has generally been unsuccessful. The best-known models for some of the early works have always been Mozart's chamber music, specifically his Divertimento for String Trio K.563, the Quintet for Piano and Winds K.452, and the String Quartet in K.464, which helped to shape Beethoven's op. 3, op. 16, and op. 18 no. 5, respectively. The ease with which we can identify such models is a measure of Beethoven's need to link his own production to works that (for him) were unquestionably masterpieces in these genres.

By contrast, there is no comparable work for piano that can be shown to have served as a model for one of Beethoven's early piano compositions (the concertos excluded). Indeed, the keyboard works most concretely associated with Beethoven's musical upbringing—the *Well-Tempered Clavier*—are far removed from the sonata tradition that dominates the early music: it is not until the "Moonlight" Sonata that we get anything resembling a keyboard prelude reminiscent of Bach. Not that it is difficult to identify Beethoven's early music with a tradition—say, that of Viennese Classicism, or the so-called "London pianoforte school"[2]—but that the stylistic features that appear to be most vital to

Beethoven's piano works are better explained from within the works themselves.

Sources

Beethoven regularly found a publisher for his piano works soon after completing them, and it is from these editions that his early piano music largely survives. There are no extant piano sonata autographs before 1801 (op. 26); only two autographs of early variation sets survive, plus those of a handful of shorter piano pieces (including some that were unpublished).

Moreover, the mistakes and inconsistencies in first editions lead us to suspect that the young Beethoven was not much troubled about the faithful reproduction of his compositional intentions, a concern later to become a notorious feature of his negotiations with publishers. As a consequence, some modern editors have ventured on occasion to suggest emendations to the text based on musical common sense rather than concrete evidence.[3]

From about 1800 onward, Beethoven customarily had his autographs professionally copied before they were sent to a publisher. One copy of an early sonata (op. 22), signed by Beethoven, survives, but it lacks the corrections or compositional refinements (usually dynamics and phrasing) that he normally made at the last minute. Since the actual musical text was left untouched, the textual value of this source is diminished.[4]

It is difficult to assess, from the surviving sketchbooks and leaves devoted to the early piano music, how much written compositional activity took place prior to the preparation of the scores of Beethoven's solo piano music. For some works we have at most a few brief jottings, for others an entire draft of a movement. Pieces drafted many times over are scarce; the situation changes radically for the later piano music. As a consequence, the study of "compositional process" with reference to an early piano piece is comparatively rare in the Beethoven literature.[5]

The reasons for the paucity of sketches are not difficult to imagine. Most of the sketches made before 1800 are on loose leaves of paper, and could thus have been easily misplaced, lost, or discarded. With the onset of deafness, however, Beethoven began to work more methodically in professionally made sketchbooks, which were available in Viennese music shops. Second, we can be reasonably safe in assuming that the young Beethoven, who was well known for his improvisations at private gatherings, spent considerable time trying over ideas for piano music at the keyboard before working them out with pen and paper. Finally, it was a general feature of Beethoven's compositional methods to use sketches more to project the shape of pieces, and autograph scores to work out problems of texture. Given the absence of "score sketches" before the late period,[6] and the fact that few autograph scores survive, the manuscript sources that have come down to us shed more light on form than on texture. Yet what distinguishes the early piano music of Beethoven from that of his predecessors is in great part its use of texture as a shaping force, rather than an unorthodox approach to sonata or variation form. So it would appear that for the early music, we are compelled to come to terms with the finished products and to disregard whatever can be deduced from the sources about their compositional origins.

Texture in the Early Piano Music

What makes Beethoven's early piano music sound full of vitality, and different from that of his contemporaries, is the degree to which he exploits a large range of textures. To be sure, there are basic keyboard patterns and techniques that operate in his music, and from which one can easily recognize his debt to the previous generation of Viennese composers: the Alberti bass accompaniment; the reinforcement of the bass, or the melodic line, in octaves; accompaniments in parallel thirds and sixths, or a mixture of the two; and various deployments of homophony (traditional four-part chorale harmony).

One special feature of Beethoven's keyboard textures is the continual variation and combination to which these basic patterns are subjected. For example, the second subject of the Sonata in E-flat op. 7 begins with chorale-like part-writing but continues with the melody in octaves (Ex. 11.1).

EXAMPLE 11.1. Sonata in E-Flat Major op. 7. Movement 1, mm. 60–67

In the consequent phrase eighth-note diminutions are introduced, in response to the last bar of the antecedent; when these are transferred to the left hand, the melody is again stated in octaves, this time supported by a lower third. Now it is the turn of the eighths to be presented in octaves, supported by thirds in the middle voices to yield a descending string of $^6_3$-chords over a dominant pedal in alternating octaves. At the climax of this passage Beethoven has arrived at a seven-note diminished seventh chord in a low register (Ex. 11.2).

EXAMPLE 11.2. Sonata in E-flat Major op. 7. Movement 1, mm. 68–81

Another technique, which Beethoven may have picked up from Mozart, is hand crossing. Conventionally, this is used to allow the melody and bass to respond to one another against a continuous accompaniment in a middle register, as we find in the second subject of the "Pathétique" Sonata (op. 13), first movement.[7] But in the slow movement of op. 2 no. 3 he is able to give an extra dimension to the counterpoint of making the crossing hand reach over by different amounts each time. In the space of only a few bars, the accented appoggiaturas are heard just above the thirty-second-note figure, far above them, and even *inside* them (m. 21) (Ex. 11.3).

EXAMPLE 11.3. Sonata in C Major op. 2 no. 3. Movement 2, mm. 19–24

(*continued*)

Example 11.3. *(continued)*

Perhaps Beethoven's most significant early contribution to piano texture was the appropriation of textures associated with other genres (chamber music and symphony) even before he had written quartets or symphonies himself. Textures of this sort frequently emerge as focal points in the main sections of minuet and scherzo movements, providing an "intellectual" foil for a pianistically virtuosic trio section (Ill. 11.1).

Illustration 11.1. Beethoven: Sonata in E-flat Major Op. 7. Scherzo: End of the Allegro and beginning of the Minore (Trio). Original edition published by Artaria. (Vienna, 1797).

But they may also be integrated with other, more pianistic textures without calling attention to themselves as examples of a learned or archaic style. In the finale of the same sonata, a dialogue between "cello" and "first violin" accompanied by "inner string parts" edges toward a straightforward righthand line with lefthand accompaniment (Ex. 11.4).

EXAMPLE 11.4. Sonata in E-flat Major op. 7. Movement 4, mm. 21–31

In the last measures of the Scherzo of op. 2 no. 3 it is not difficult to imagine a dialogue between unison strings and woodwind chords, providing a springboard for forty measures of dazzling arpeggiations in the trio (Ex. 11.5).

EXAMPLE 11.5. Sonata in C Major op. 2 no. 3. Movement 3, mm. 56–68

The key to understanding Beethoven's use of texture is the variety with which he uses it, as a means of clarifying structure. In writing sonatas on a much larger scale than either Haydn or Mozart, he recognized that the subtle inflections of texture in the older masters would not be sufficient, and that a much wider range of expression was needed. It is in Beethoven's piano music of the 1790s that, for the first time, one cannot be mistaken that the Viennese Classical style is in irreversible decline.

Genres

Beethoven's early solo piano works fall broadly into two categories: sonatas and variation sets. In concentrating on these forms, he did not write a truly different kind of keyboard music from that of his immediate predecessors. It may be surprising, given his experience in playing *ex tempore,* that he did not cultivate a freer form in his written work, as both Haydn and Mozart did on occasion and to good effect; the first, and only, fantasia dates from as late as 1809. Yet in certain parts of pieces—notably final variations and the codas of rondo movements—a more spontaneous approach to harmony and phrase structure is evident.

Beethoven's marked preference for the piano sonata as a serious genre during the early period is revealed by the fact that from the time he arrived in Vienna in late 1792, he assigned opus numbers to his published sonatas but left the variation sets unnumbered. A set of three sonatas (composed between 1793 and 1795) was published as op. 2 in 1796. These were quickly followed, over the next three years, by a sonata published singly as op. 7, a further set of three published as op. 10, and three further sonatas published as op. 13 and op. 14. The works with opus numbers from this period also include an insubstantial sonata for piano duet op. 6, and two sonatinas from the 1790s that, initially withheld from publication, were issued with an opus number (49) when they appeared in 1805.

By contrast, none of the twelve variation sets dating from the 1790s was published with an opus number. This is not to say that Beethoven thought less of these early efforts in the genre, but rather that the form itself had a lower status with publishers and the musical world at large. Among the early variation sets, the 1790 set based on the Italian arietta "Venni amore" by Vincenzo Righini was especially close to his heart, as is seen from an anecdote about his performance of them (recalled by Wegeler) and by the fact that he authorized a second edition of the work twelve years after its composition.[8] A change of attitude is in evidence by 1803, when the op. 34 set (the first on an original theme) and the so-called "Eroica" (or "Prometheus") Variations op. 35 appeared in print; this may be traced back to the composition of the Sonata op. 26 (1800), the only sonata to begin with a theme-and-variations movement.

Beethoven also composed a few "independent" pieces, but these are either very short and of little significance, or are comparable in scope to sonata movements. Some of the longer ones were rejected movements of early sonatas and thus belong to the same category of composition as the popular *Andante favori* (WoO 57) of 1803, originally conceived as the slow movement of the "Waldstein" Sonata. Beethoven kept a portfolio of short works, which he published in cycles of bagatelles (op. 33, op. 119) or used in revised form in another context (e.g., the Allemande WoO 81, which was incorporated into the second movement of the String Quartet op. 132).

The Piano Sonata

The thirty-two piano sonatas are universally reckoned as seminal works in the keyboard repertory, and are among the most frequently analyzed pieces in the literature on music. Whole books have been devoted to them, including Tovey's celebrated *Companion* (1931) and Riemann's prodigious compendium of analyses (1918–1919).[9]

Upon his arrival in Vienna, the young Beethoven began to cultivate a certain type of piano sonata that extended its utility beyond the confines of the drawing room and put it on the time-scale of the symphony, thus preparing the genre ultimately for the concert hall. The *grande sonate*, as this type was frequently designated by publishers, is a long, technically demanding work. It is in four movements, its center dominated by a substantial slow movement (usually marked *Largo* or *Adagio*), its final movement normally taking the form of a spacious rondo or sonata-rondo. The three sonatas of op. 2 belong to this category (though the outer movements of the first, in F minor, are more compact than those of the other sonatas); so does the next sonata, op. 7 in E-flat.

Toward the end of the decade Beethoven continued to develop the *grande sonate* (op. 10 no. 3, op. 22), but also wrote sonatas of a more modest scope. The first of these was op. 10 no. 2 in F major, a work whose movements are all in a fast tempo and have the character of a scherzo. The two sonatas of op. 14 have more internal contrast, but again the absence of a true slow movement diminishes their overall size.

The difference between the *grande sonate* and the more modest, three-movement sonata is nicely illustrated by the compositional history of the first of the op. 10 set, in C minor. Most commentators have been struck by the extreme brevity of the final *Prestissimo*—122 *alla breve* bars after a substantial opening movement and the weighty *Adagio molto*. When it was conceived, in 1795–1796, Beethoven intended to include a scherzo as one of the middle movements; but he was satisfied with neither of these pieces and eventually gave up making the sonata a four-movement work.[10]

That op. 10 no. 1 might have turned out to be a long affair is also seen from the genesis of the finale. Two drafts for the development section preserved in the "Fischhof Manuscript" (a collection of early sketchleaves) greatly exceed the length of the final version by building up to a quotation of the second subject.[11] Had Beethoven worked out the movement according to one of these plans, its length would have been augmented by about twenty to thirty-five bars, or about 30 percent of the movement; in its final form, the development section sounds insubstantial and fails in its traditional role to put a reasonable amount of space between the exposition and recapitulation.

Given the background of the *grande sonate*, we may ask: What could have prompted Beethoven thus to abbreviate op. 10 no. 1? It may have been that the material in the last movement could not sustain such extended treatment of the second subject (which returns again in the coda), and that shortening the sonata as a whole—by removing the scherzo—would be easier than inventing a completely new finale to cap a work written on a larger scale in all other respects. Shortly after the completion of op. 10 no. 1 (but before the publication of op. 10), ideas were emerging for a new C-minor sonata conceived with a seriousness that was to earn it the title *Grande sonate pathétique*. Though the "Pathétique" also lacks a scherzo, the first movement compensates with a *Grave* that is more than merely a slow introduction; it is integrated into the work, both thematically and in terms of musical form, in a manner unprecedented in the Classical sonata. The recasting of op. 10 no. 1 as a sonata of moderate dimensions, then, enabled the "Pathétique" to emerge in Beethoven's output not just as a bigger work, but as a different kind of C-minor sonata.

Among the earliest surviving compositions by Beethoven is a set of three piano sonatas, probably written at the age of twelve and published in 1783 with a dedication to his first patron, the Elector Maximilian Friedrich. Though these juvenile works are rarely played, they demonstrate Beethoven's skill at handling forms of moderate length. From the later years in Bonn come two fragmentary sonatinas, WoO 50 and 51, written for his childhood friends Franz Gerhard Wegeler and Eleonore von Breuning (who subsequently married each other). Of greater interest are the two well-known two-movement works, written independently in the mid-1790s but published together in 1805 as *sonates faciles* (op. 49).

First-movement Sonata Form

Until op. 26 and the two sonatas "quasi una fantasia" op. 27, the designs of individual sonata movements do not throw up many surprises. Sonata form as it is conventionally understood today was as much a reality for Beethoven as it is for us: his private analytical terminology has terms for second subject ("m.g." = *Mittel-Gedanke*), to develop (*ausführen, durchführen*), and recapitulation ("d.c." = da capo);[12] and the majority of his first movements lend themselves so well to the standard description of sonata form that one could easily be forgiven for thinking that the form was a precompositional element of these sonatas. If there are exceptions to the design, the reasons are usually easy to grasp.

One device found in the early sonatas is the division of the development section into two parts, the first ending with a "dominant preparation," which introduces an important theme in a distant key (usually the flattened submediant). The sketches for the finale of op. 10 no. 1 (discussed above) show Beethoven rejecting this technique, which results in a drastic shortening of the development section. Where it is used, the development section sometimes approaches the length of the entire exposition:

Sonata, home key	Development: key of arrival
op. 2 no. 2, A major	122–160 + 161–223: F major
op. 2 no. 3, C major	91–108 + 109–138: D major
op. 14 no. 2, G major	64–98 + 99–124: Eb major

The first movement of op. 10 no. 2 illustrates how this device is used unconventionally to restore a balance between the first and second groups that had been upset already in the exposition. Recall that the exposition had begun with a sprightly theme in F, whose restatement led to an imperfect cadence in A; Beethoven, however, continued with a theme in C major that resulted in a second group (mm. 19–66) almost four times the length of the first. At the end of the development, the first subject returns in D major, in the manner of a Haydnesque *fausse reprise*. But instead of "correcting" his mistake fully, he quotes only part of the first subject in F before moving directly to the second subject. In this way, a theme associated earlier with the secondary tonality has been moved into the first group, and the passage of what is sometimes referred to as a "secondary development section"[13] leads on to a subsequent theme in the second group (Ex. 11.6).

EXAMPLE 11.6. Sonata in F Major op. 10 no. 2. Movement 1, mm. 137–73

(continued)

EXAMPLE 11.6. (*continued*)

Now the two subject-groups (mm. 137–169, 170–202) are comparable in size.

One of the early sonatas, op. 2 no. 3, is noteworthy for features borrowed from the piano concerto. The recapitulation ends with an interrupted cadence that initiates a cadenza-like passage of harmonic instability (six diminished seventh-chords in the space of eight measures), leading to an unmeasured embellishment of a $^6_4$-chord (m. 232) and further development of the main theme before the reprise of the closing subject at m. 252. More significantly, the scope of the exposition (and recapitulation) is increased by the use of a special theme, such as we find in first movements of Mozart's concertos, to assist in the transition from the tonic to the dominant.[14]

Slow Movements

Only one of Beethoven's early sonata slow movements is cast as a typically Mozartian "sonata without development": op. 10 no. 1. The *Adagio cantabile* of the "Pathétique" is unusually a rondo with little formal sophistication. In the other slow movements there is a trend away from relatively simple ternary forms, toward sonata structure.

Simple ternary form would normally forecast a movement of modest proportions, but Beethoven achieves a larger design by attention given to any of three points. First, the A-section, which presents the principal theme of the movement, is typically a ternary shape itself, which may be broadened by an antecedent-consequent pair of phrases at the outset or by a codetta at the end. Second, the middle section may have a long lead-in to the reprise, in the manner of a dominant preparation. Third, the reprise of the A-section is often interrupted near the end, allowing for an expansive coda to emerge: in op. 2 no. 3 this is a standard interrupted cadence (m. 53: see Ex. 11.11 and discussion on pp. 413–14), in op. 2 no. 2 a surprise turn to the tonic minor (m. 58).

Of the two slow movements in sonata form, that of op. 10 no. 3, the famous *Largo e mesto*, is noteworthy for its plunge to the flatted seventh as a secondary tonality (forecasting a still more radical use of this key relation in the Scherzo of the Ninth Symphony and elsewhere), and by an explosive coda that returns the music to the climax of the development section, for further work on a thirty-second-note figure introduced there (Ex. 11.7).

EXAMPLE 11.7. Sonata in D Major op. 10 no. 3. Movement 2

a. mm. 36–40

(*continued*)

EXAMPLE 11.7. (*continued*)

b. mm. 72–75

Minuet-and-Trio Movements

All the early sonatas have a minuet or scherzo with trio except for the two C-minor works, discussed earlier, and op. 14 no. 2, whose middle movement is a set of variations. As explained above, Beethoven places far greater emphasis on the difference in character between the two sections than do earlier composers, doing so chiefly by changes in texture: the imitation of symphonic or string quartet sonorities in the main section contrasts with a more monolithic trio section, featuring broken chords, hand crossing, and other pianistic devices. A fully developed sonata-form main section, as one finds in op. 2 no. 3 and op. 7, makes the contrast seem complete.

Finales

More than half of these are rondos, and most of them are so entitled. They range widely in speed, from *poco allegretto* to *presto*, and in length, from 113 to 312 measures.

Two are specifically marked *grazioso* (op. 2 no. 2 and op. 7); these, together with the finale of op. 22, form a close-knit group by their clear structure, secure phrasing, and obvious contrasts, as well as by one other important trait: the tendency for the main theme to undergo textural and rhythmic variation from one statement to the next. The way this is achieved is perhaps best illustrated by the theme of op. 2 no. 2 in its five appearances during the movement (Ex. 11.8).

EXAMPLE 11.8. Sonata in A Major op. 2 no. 2. Movement 4

a. mm. 1–4

b. mm. 41–44

(continued)

EXAMPLE 11.8. (*continued*)

c. mm. 100–3

d. mm. 135–38

e. mm. 173–76

Though the *rondo grazioso* described here may be taken to be an archetype of the early Beethoven finale, the faster movements share many of its features, including thematic variation.

Another characteristic of Beethoven's sonata finales—and not only the rondos—is the swerving to a remote key shortly before the end, as a way of upsetting the listener's expectation that the piece is almost over; this is also a prominent feature of the early variation sets. Sometimes Beethoven is able to end the movement quickly after this interruption (op. 2 no. 3), but he is more likely to use it as an opportunity to introduce a coda (op. 7), or to bring the principal theme in once more (op. 2 no. 2).

Connections between Movements

It is natural to look at "early Beethoven" for hints of things to come later. Marveling at the tightly controlled structures of the last three sonatas and at the gigantic conception of the "Hammerklavier," we often ask ourselves: Does Beethoven anticipate these characteristics in his earlier sonatas?

It is dangerous to hunt for obscure relations, thematic or otherwise, merely to claim unity for a multimovement work. Sonatas seem to hold together more by the contrasts between the movements than by common features, and attempts to demonstrate complex webs of motivic connections operating in Beethoven's sonatas have met with increasing disfavor.[15] In one or two early examples, however, thematic relationships between the outer movements are too transparent to avoid noticing. The finale of op. 10 no. 3 takes as its principal motif a melodic pattern prominent at the beginning of the first movement (minor second plus major third ascending); in its "search" for a perfect cadence, it reaches the original pitch-level of the pattern (C♯-D-F♯) by sequence in bars 5–6 (Ex. 11.9).

EXAMPLE 11.9. Sonata in D Major op. 10 no. 3

a. Movement 1, mm. 1–4

(continued)

EXAMPLE 11.9. (*continued*)

b. Movement 4, mm. 5–7

A similar example—more obvious, but with less interesting consequences—is found in the opening notes of the outer movements of op. 14 no. 1, both spanning the fourth from b¹ to e².

The first two movements of op. 2 no. 3, in C major and E major respectively, would appear at first glance to have little in common with each other. Their main themes are only indirectly related, by the application of a turn figure to a pair of two-note stepwise descents: in the first-movement theme the note pairs outline the double neighbor-note progression 3-2-4-3 (Ex. 11.10a), whereas in the slow movement they traverse the descending fourth 3-2-1-7 (Ex. 11.10b), so one perceives at best a weak thematic link between them. But when the full force of an interrupted cadence is brought to bear on the slow movement, at m. 53, the main theme not only returns in the same key as that of first movement, and in the same register, but it is also transformed into the 3-2-4-3 shape (Ex. 11.10c):

EXAMPLE 11.10. Sonata in C Major op. 2 no. 3

a. Movement 1, mm. 1–4

Allegro con brio

b. Movement 2, mm. 1–2

Adagio

(*continued*)

EXAMPLE 11.10. (*continued*)

c. Movement 2, mm. 53–54

In this way the only movement not in the tonic—and here, in 1795, in a key far removed from the tonic—is pulled unmistakably into the central tonal orbit of the sonata.

The Variation Set

As Joseph Kerman has suggested, the variation set was an ideal medium for composer-performers, allowing ample scope not only for brilliant and expressive playing but also for imagination and careful working out of compositional details. But in the career of a genius, one might well expect compositional ideals to begin to outweigh the need for music as a vehicle for performance, and thus for the variation set gradually to cohere as a single composition, rather than as a string of miniatures. Mozart's example is instructive in this respect. The piano variations, which appear mainly in the earlier part of his career, tend to have greater internal contrast, moving easily and frequently between the virtuosic and the graceful. By contrast, the later examples, which are found more in his chamber music, work toward a single dynamic curve, enabling the variation set to be perceived with the same feeling of wholeness as a movement in sonata form.

Such a plan must start with a theme of moderate animation (*andante* or *allegretto*) in a bipartite form, that is, with two repeatable halves. The first few variations gradually increase the amount of decoration of the theme by using successively shorter note values (e.g., eighths, sixteenths, triplet sixteenths), creating the impression of a faster tempo. There follows a slow variation (e.g., an *adagio*), with elaborate decorations not confined to a single rhythmic figure, and a final variation in which the tempo is faster (e.g., *allegro*), the meter is changed (e.g., from $\frac{2}{4}$ to $\frac{6}{8}$, or from common time to *alla breve*), and the music is extended beyond the confines of the binary structure of the theme. This scheme of tempo changes is complemented by a tonal plan in which contrast is provided by having one of the central variations in the parallel minor (or major). Thus what in theory is merely an undifferentiated succession of equal-sized units becomes a highly integrated form, a kind of microcosm of cyclic form. A typical plan may be illustrated as follows:

Theme Var. 1 Var. 2 Var. 3 Var. 4 Var. 5 Var. 6 + coda

andante ♪ ♫ ♬♬ adagio allegro

tonic major —————————————— minor major ——————————

Beethoven wrote piano variations approximating this model on three occasions: in the sets based on a theme by Peter Winter WoO 75 (1799) and on "God Save the King" WoO 78 (1803), and in the second movement of the sonata op. 111 (1822). But most of his variation sets differ greatly with regard to the character of the theme, the number of variations and degree of contrast between them, and the overall shape of the set.

Themes

To begin with, the themes he chooses are diverse in length and structure, ranging from an eleven-measure "Swiss song" to the forty-nine-measure tune by Winter. Most of the early sets are based on popular songs from contemporary operas and *singspiels,* and are thus relatable to the bipartite form of Mozart's typical choice of theme. But some dispense with this altogether, for example, the theme by Count Waldstein used for the variations for piano duet WoO 67 (c. 1792), which has an extremely unorthodox phrase structure:

mm. 1–6	mm. 7–10	mm. 11–14
perfect cadence in C major	imperfect cadence in C minor	perfect cadence in C major

At times, the rhetorical phrase structure of the original song, undoubtedly motivated by the words it sets, leads to a highly repetitious theme that creates problems in variations that are intended to display continuous inventiveness. For instance, the theme of WoO 66, a tune from a *singspiel* by Dittersdorf, contains the following middle strain (Ex. 11.11).

EXAMPLE 11.11. Variations on the Ariette "Es war einmal ein alter Mann" by Dittersdorf, WoO 66. Theme, mm. 9–23

(continued)

EXAMPLE 11.11. (*continued*)

Beethoven is able to do little more than change register from one two-measure phrase to the next (e.g., variations 1–2, 5, 7–8, 10–11, 13), or to alternate between two similar diminutions (3–4, 9). Only once is he able to devise a different figure for each two-measure phrase, in bars 13ff. (Ex. 11.12).

EXAMPLE 11.12. WoO 66, Variation 12, mm. 13–25

(This variation also illustrates nicely Beethoven's use of register to humorous effect, namely, the low E after the fermata.)

Variation Techniques

Beethoven's principal methods of generating variations are little different from those of his predecessors: melodic diminution, application of a characteristic rhythmic figure, registral interplay, change of tempo, and the change to the minor mode. The only novelty is the change of meter and tempo within a variation (Ex. 11.13).

EXAMPLE 11.13. Variations on the Ariette "Venni Amore" by Righini, WoO 65. Variation 14, mm. 1–8 (and similarly for mm. 9–32)

But this technique was dropped after two trials (WoO 65 and 66) and does not reappear until the "Diabelli" set (variation 21).

Another rarely used technique is the harmonic reinterpretation of a pitch-collection. In variation 21 of the "Righini" set, the opening melody is heard over a dominant pedal of B minor (Ex. 11.14)

EXAMPLE 11.14. WoO 65, Variation 21, mm. 1–8

anticipating the more famous use of this harmonic ploy in the slow movement of the Quartet op. 18 no. 5.

Beethoven's melodic diminutions are based on scales and arpeggiations, passing notes and neighbor notes, and appoggiaturas and related accented dissonances, and are easy to relate to their thematic models. The most interesting examples combine one or more of these features, or juxtapose them in quick succession (Ex. 11.15).

EXAMPLE 11.15. Variations on a Russian Dance by Wranitzky, WoO 71.
Variation 1, mm. 11– 19

Most sets have a variation in which registral contrasts are exploited. This may take the form of a figure alternating between soprano and bass (Ex. 11.16)

EXAMPLE 11.16. Variations on the Menuet "à la Viganò" by Haibel, WoO 68. Variation 10

   a. mm. 1–2

   b. mm. 9–12

or passing through various registers (Ex. 11.17).

EXAMPLE 11.17. Variations, WoO 71. Variation 9, mm. 11–19

Beethoven always includes a variation in the minor mode; in the longer sets there are two (WoO 65 and 68) or even three (WoO 71), but only in the "Righini" set are these placed next to one another, in an effort to make a cumulative effect of their more poignant harmonies; in fact, none of these minor variations really strikes a genuinely serious pose.[16]

In WoO 76, one of the four sets dating from 1799, Beethoven composes three of the central variations in different keys, creating the large-scale harmonic progression I-VI-IV(-V)-I in variations 4–7, thus anticipating the op. 34 set of 1802, in which the theme and six variations—each in a different key—outline the progression I-VI$^{\sharp 3}$-IV-II$^{\sharp 3}$-♭VII-V$^{b-\sharp}$-I.

It is in the final variations of these early sets that Beethoven is usually at his most inventive and interesting. Most of these spill over the structural boundary determined by the theme; but instead of merely rounding off the movement with a short flurry of cadence-phrases (as we find in Mozart), they usually explore a wide range of harmonies and textures, quoting the theme successively in several remote keys. Some of these "codas," as Beethoven frequently inscribed them, extend to well over 100 measures in length, and run together several ideas for variations. Other novel ideas for endings include a *Marcia vivace* (WoO 66), a brief *Adagio* (WoO 68 and 76) and—anticipating the "Diabelli" set—a *Tempo di menuetto* (WoO 69).

Most of the extended finales, including that of the seminal "Righini" Variations (1791), start with a full-length variation—in the faster tempo—followed by further phrases emphasizing the ending; thus, the harmonic pilgrimage comes as something of a surprise—sufficient time must be allowed for the final return to the home key. The final variation of WoO 76 (1799) is exceptional, the structure of the theme being discarded from the outset; its free form and fugal opening anticipate the Finale of the "Eroica" Variations of three years later and, by extension, the "Diabelli" set of the late period.

Toward the Middle Period

The years from 1801 to early 1803 have traditionally been regarded as "transitional" in Beethoven's career as a composer. In them he is supposed to have made up his mind to "have struck out a new path," the first results of which were to be two sets of variations "worked out in an entirely new manner": opp. 34 and 35. The first of these expressions appears in an anecdote probably dating from 1802 and recounted by the piano teacher and composer Carl Czerny;[17] the second, of which much has been made by historians, is found in a letter of October 1802 from Beethoven to his publisher, Gottfried Christoph Härtel.[18] The personal background to these changes is, of course, the deafness crisis, which found an early outlet in letters written to close friends in the summer of 1801 and whose central document is the "Heiligenstadt Testament" of October 1802 in which the composer pulls himself from the brink of suicide and vows to "seize Fate by the throat."

But the gigantic scale of the principal works of 1803–1804, the *Eroica* Symphony and the "Kreutzer" and "Waldstein" sonatas, cannot easily be explained as a consequence of the music of the years immediately before; during that time, Beethoven either experiments with new approaches to multimovement planning (op. 26 and op. 27 nos. 1 and 2) or pursues the traditional three- and four-movement sonatas (op. 28, op. 31 nos 1–3). In the latter group, op. 28 is a *grande sonate* in the conventional sense, and the subtitle "sonata pastorale" sometimes associated with it (devised by Hamburg publisher Cranz) has no programmatic connotations; so also is op. 31 no. 3, though its character is more akin to that of op. 10 no. 2 and op. 14 no. 1 since none of its four movements is a slow movement. Op. 31 no. 1 is sometimes compared to the "Waldstein" because of the same harmonic plan in the first movement exposition: a modulation from the tonic to the mediant major. But the humor of its outer movements owes more to Haydn, and its centerpiece, a 119-measure *Adagio grazioso* in compound triple-time, strikes a purely early Beethoven pose.

It is only in the first movement of the so-called "Tempest" (or "Re-citative") Sonata, op. 31 no. 2, that this group strongly anticipates the future. Here Beethoven creates a sonata form in which the functions of slow introduction and first subject are inextricably linked. The *Largo-allegro* theme in mm. 1–20 functions as an introduction: it is syntactically a large-scale upbeat to the D-minor tonic in m. 21 and materially a fore-boding of things to come. But when this theme returns after the end of the development section, it can no longer sustain the suspense it held for the listener the first time; moreover, the modifications to its har-monic shape (in mm. 155–158) prepare the "secondary development section," not a solid return to D minor. In other words, what had origi-nally functioned in every respect—structurally and expressively—as an introduction to the first group actually takes over the role of first subject in the recapitulation. In this respect, the "Tempest" points the way to the Ninth Symphony and the late quartets.

If we turn our attention to the group of three sonatas of 1800–1801, we see a more conscious, sustained effort at new directions in piano mu-sic. Op. 26 is special for its beginning with a theme and variations. It is not that such first movements are unprecedented—they abound in Haydn, and Mozart's K.331 in A major is an all too familiar example—but that variation form has been redesigned for the purpose of this sonata; there are no changes in tempo, and rather than ending the movement with an extension of the final variation (i.e., with thirty-second-note diminutions), Beethoven instead introduces a new theme, somewhat more resigned than the one on which the movement is based (Ex. 11.18).

EXAMPLE 11.18. Sonata in A-flat Major op. 26. Movement 1, mm. 205–12

The work does not have the weight that would normally accrue to it from its first movement being in sonata form. As a consequence, the next two movements enjoy more a life of their own rather than as internal elements in a predetermined scheme. Thus the *Marcia funebre,* in third place, has a more significantly programmatic role to play in this work than other sonata slow movements that might have equal, or greater, pathos (e.g., the *Largo e mesto* of op. 10 no. 3).

The "Moonlight" Sonata continues this trend. Here the slow movement is in first position, and so the center of gravity is placed again at the head of the work. Now Beethoven pays considerable attention to the way one movement is followed by the next—the instruction *attacca* appears for the first time—not simply the balance between them. The minuet appears to be set free by the final chords of the *Adagio sostenuto,* starting with a first-inversion chord whose lowest note is higher than the highest note at the end of the previous movement (Ex. 11.19).

EXAMPLE 11.19. Sonata "quasi una fantasia" in C-sharp Minor op. 27 no. 2. Movement 1, mm. 66–69 and Movement 2, mm. 1–4

The transition from the minuet to the final *Presto agitato* is achieved by dynamics rather than by register; the surprise *sforzandi* at the end of mm. 2, 4, and 6 anticipate the crescendo from *piano* to *forte* that governs the first phrase and, in effect, the movement as a whole.

In the other *Sonata "quasi una fantasia"* (op. 27 no. 1) Beethoven experiments with the interweaving of movements (the *Adagio con espressione* and the final *Allegro vivace*), and with the juxtaposition of fragments to create larger musical units (the opening *Andante-Allegro-Andante*). The movements are linked both by the *attacca* marking, and by a neat form of harmonic dovetailing; the central section of the first movement anticipates the tonality of the second, and so on:

I	II	III	IV
Eb-C major-Eb	C minor-Ab-C minor	Ab-Eb-Ab	Eb

Although the idea of a sonata made up of small forms alloyed to each other or based on the interlocking of movements was anathema to Beethoven in the ensuing "heroic" period, it was to play an increasingly important part in his later years. Another group of three sonatas, dating from 1815–1816—two for piano and cello (op. 102), one for piano solo (op. 101)—demonstrates the vitality of these techniques. So do the last three piano sonatas, in which frequent changes of tempo within a movement (in op. 109), the amalgamation of slow movement and finale (in op. 110), and the shrewd use of *attacca* (in all three sonatas) radically changed the shape of the piano sonata. That Beethoven was still capable of writing a *grande sonate* is shown by the magnificent example of the "Hammerklavier," a work whose scope the composer underrated when he allegedly said that it "would keep pianists busy for the next quarter-century." But the trend in his late sonatas and quartets is toward the demise of the forms he had so imaginatively explored during his first decade in Vienna.

Notes

1. It is perhaps not surprising, in this connection, that the regular use of sketchbooks begins at the time of work on op. 18, on the first major nonkeyboard composition project.

2. The term was coined by Alexander Ringer in Ringer 1970. Reservations about this study are aptly expressed in Joseph Kerman and Alan Tyson, *The New Grove Beethoven* (London, 1983):

> Too much can be made, however, of similar themes and pianistic textures in Beethoven and Clementi, Dussek and other such composers. From the start, and even at his most discursive, Beethoven had a commitment to the total structure that makes Clementi seem very lax. (p. 97)

3. For a discussion of representative textual problems, see Drabkin 1985.

4. In particular, there are no dynamic markings for the trio section of the third movement; most editors suggest a *forte* dynamic throughout.

5. There has been only one recent study of the collected sketches for an early sonata movement: Schachter 1982. By contrast, Schenker's pioneering work on the late sonatas (especially opp. 109 and 111) has been regularly updated in monographs and doctoral theses; to this one may add the first full-length study of the sketches for a variation set, *Beethoven's Diabelli Variations* by William Kinderman (Oxford, 1987).

6. The pioneering work on score sketches, particularly with reference to the late quartets, has been undertaken by Robert Winter. See in particular his *Compositional Origins of Beethoven's Opus 131* (Ann Arbor, MI, 1982), chapter 4; and Douglas Johnson, Alan Tyson, and Robert Winter, *The Beethoven Sketchbooks: History, Reconstruction, Inventory* (Berkeley, CA, 1985), part IV.

7. It is possible that Beethoven was thinking here of Mozart's Sonata in C minor K.457, in which the right hand crosses over the left in analogous circumstances.

8. See Franz Gerhard Wegeler and Ferdinand Ries, *Remembering Beethoven* (London, 1988), 22–23. Unfortunately, no copy of the first edition of the Variations survives, and the nature and extent of Beethoven's 1802 revisions can only be conjectured.

9. Tovey 1931 is the most substantial body of "précis-analysis," a method of analysis derived from the teachings of Hubert Parry. Hugo Riemann's three-volume *Analyse von Beethoven's Klaviersonaten* (Berlin, 1918–1919), which includes analyses also of six "juvenile sonatas" (two of which are in fact spurious), is likewise a prodigious compendium of that theorist's special approach to phrase structure and harmonic analysis.

10. The earlier (and shorter) of these two works was preserved in the portfolio of bagatelles; the other, too, survived in autograph score. Both were published for the first time in the 1888 supplement to the Beethoven *Gesamtausgabe,* and catalogued by Kinsky-Halm, respectively, as Bagatelle WoO 52 (WoO = Werk ohne Opuszahl, "work without opus number"), and Allegretto WoO 53.

Another C-minor movement, originally intended for the finale to op. 10 no. 1, survives. It was published as an independent piece by Willy Hess in his *Beethoven: Supplement zur Gesamtausgabe,* vol. 9 (Wiesbaden, 1980), 19–22.

11. These sketches are transcribed in Johnson 1980, 2:32–33.

12. For a brief discussion of the composer's sonata-form "vocabulary," see Drabkin, "Beethoven's Understanding of 'Sonata Form': The Evidence of the Sketchbooks," in *Beethoven's Compositional Process,* ed. William Kinderman (Lincoln, 1991), 14–19.

13. See, for example, Charles Rosen, *Sonata Forms* 1980, 104 (revised se   d edition, 1988, 106).

14. In the soloist's exposition in several of Mozart's later piano concerto first movements, a theme in the flattened mediant or the minor dominant represents a midpoint in the harmonic progression from tonic to dominant. It is possible that Beethoven had the first movement of K.467 in mind when he designed this progression: in both pieces the path from the first group in C major to the second group in G major takes place via a distinctive theme in G minor.

15. A typical example from a previous generation of scholars is Rudolph Réti's exhaustive analysis of motif and cell in the "Pathétique" Sonata in Réti 1967. An equally typical response to it from today's generation is Nicholas Cook's critique of Réti in general, and his analysis of the "Pathétique" in particular, in *A Guide to Musical Analysis* (London, 1987), 89–115.

16. Apart from the juvenile "Dressler" Variations WoO 63 (1782) and the passacaglia-like 32 Variations WoO 80, all of Beethoven's variations for piano are based on major-mode themes, so a change of mode in the middle of the set would mean a change to the minor.

In the four-hand set WoO 67, the quirky harmonic plan of Waldstein's theme creates problems for the eighth variation, which begins in C minor. For this variation, Beethoven decides to abandon this plan altogether by extending each phrase and juxtaposing the two that end with perfect cadences:

mm. 1–6	mm. 7–14	mm. 15–23:
perfect cadence	perfect cadence	"Capriccio"
in C minor	in C minor	modulation from
		D♭ to A♭, end-
		ing on dominant
		of C

Since the original middle phrase was already in minor, Beethoven is obliged to change its key in order to make its harmonies different from those of the theme. He chooses the "Neapolitan" D♭, already much in evidence in mm. 1–14, and duly modulates to its dominant, A♭; this leads naturally to an augmented sixth chord on A♭ that resolves to the dominant of C and thus prepares the final variation, a freely structured *Allegro* in compound time interspersed with *adagio* reminiscences of the theme.

17. Carl Czerny, *On the Proper Performance of All Beethoven's Works for the Piano* (Reprint Vienna, 1970), 13. For an interesting discussion of the significance of this remark, see Carl Dahlhaus, *Ludwig van Beethoven: Approaches to his Music* (Cambridge, 1991), chap. 9.

18. Christopher Reynolds has claimed that Beethoven's creative procedures in op. 35 are evidence of a "new manner" of composition; see Reynolds 1982, especially pp. 72–74. But Hans-Werner Küthen has persuasively demonstrated that Beethoven's notion of a "wirklich ganz neue Manier" should be read alongside his hostile reaction to Antoine Reicha's recently composed Thirty-six Fugues "composés d'apreès un nouveau système," as expressed in a letter to Breitkopf & Härtel six weeks later, and that his "new manner" may be little more than sales talk for the new variation sets.

Selected Bibliography

Barth, George. *The Pianist as Orator: Beethoven and the Transformation of Keyboard Style*. Ithaca, NY, 1992.

Cooper, Barry. *Beethoven and the Creative Process*. Chapter 12: "First Conceptions: Piano Sonata in D minor, Op. 31, No. 2." Oxford, 1990.

Dahlhaus, Carl. *Ludwig van Beethoven: Approaches to his Music*. Trans. Mary Whittall. Oxford, 1991.

Drabkin, William. "Building a Music Library: I—The Beethoven Piano Sonatas." *The Musical Times* 126 (1985): 216–20.

Johnson, Douglas P. *"Beethoven's Early Sketches in the Fischhof Miscellany": Berlin Autograph 28*. Ann Arbor, MI, 1980.

Jones, Timothy. *Beethoven: the "Moonlight" and Other Sonatas, Op. 27 and Op. 31.* Cambridge, 1999.

Lockwood, Lewis. "Music for and with Piano." In *The Music and Life of Beethoven.* New York, 2003, 124–46.

Riemann, Hugo. *Analyse von Beethovens Klaviersonaten.* 3 vols. Berlin, 1918–1919.

Ratz, Erwin. *Einführung in die rausikalische Formenlehre.* Chapter 5: "Einige charakteristische Beispiele aus den Klavierwerken Beethovens." Vienna, 1951.

Réti, Rudolph. *Thematic Patterns in Sonatas of Beethoven.* London, 1967.

Reynolds, Christopher. "Beethoven's Sketches for the Variations in E-flat, Op. 35." In *Beethoven Studies* 3, ed. Alan Tyson. Cambridge, 1982, 47–74.

Ringer, Alexander. "Beethoven and the London Pianoforte School." *The Musical Quarterly* 56 (1970): 742–58.

Rosen, Charles. *Sonata Forms.* Revised edition. New York, 1988.

Schachter, Carl. "Beethoven's Sketches for the First Movement of Op. 14, No. 1: A Study in Design." *Journal of Music Theory* 26 (1982): 1–21.

Schenker, Heinrich. "Beethoven: Sonata Op. 2 Nr. 1." *Der Tonwille* 2 (1922): 25–48. Trans. Joseph Dubiel in *Der Tonwille: Pamphlets in Witness of the Immutable Laws of Music, Offered to a New Generation of Youth,* vol. 1, ed. William Drabkin. New York, forthcoming.

————. "Vom Organischen der Sonatenform." *Das Meisterwerk in der Music* 2 (1926), 43–54. Trans. William Drabkin in *The Masterwork in Music* 2, ed. William Drabkin. Cambridge, 1996, 23–30.

Sisman, Elaine. "Pathos and the Pathétique: Rhetorical Stance in Beethoven's C-minor Sonata, Op. 13." *Beethoven Forum* 3 (1994): 81–105.

Stanley, Glenn. "The 'wirklich gantz neue manier' and the Path to it: Beethoven's Variations for Piano, 1793–1802." *Beethoven Forum* 3 (1994): 53–79.

Tovey, Donald F. *Companion to Beethoven Pianoforte Sonatas.* London, 1931.

————. "Some Aspects of Beethoven's Art Forms." *Music and Letters* 8 (1927): 133–55. Reprinted in *Essays and Lectures on Music,* ed. Hubert Foss. London, 1949, 271–97.

————. *The Classics of Music: Talks, Essays, and Other Writings Previously Uncollected,* ed. Michael Tilmouth, David Kimbell, and Roger Savage. Oxford, 2001.

Index

Note: Page references for musical examples and facsimile reproductions are printed in boldface; references for extended discussions are in italics.